PROFILES IN TERROR

PROFILES IN TERROR

The Guide to Middle East Terrorist Organizations

AARON MANNES

PUBLISHED IN COOPERATION WITH JINSA PRESS

ROWMAN & LITTLEFIELD PUBLISHERS, INC.
Lanham • Boulder • New York • Toronto • Oxford

ROWMAN & LITTLEFIELD PUBLISHERS, INC.

Published in the United States of America
by Rowman & Littlefield Publishers, Inc.
A wholly owned subsidary of The Rowman & Littlefield Publishing Group, Inc.
4501 Forbes Boulevard, Suite 200, Lanham, Maryland 20706
www.rowmanlittlefield.com

PO Box 317, Oxford, OX2 9RU, UK

Distributed by National Book Network

Copyright © 2004 by Rowman & Littlefield Publishers, Inc.

Published in cooperation with JINSA Press as a JINSA book.

JINSA Press is an imprint of the Jewish Institute for National Security Affairs (JINSA).
JINSA is incorporated in the District of Columbia as a tax-exempt organization under
section 501(c)(3) of the United States Internal Revenue Code.

The opinions expressed in this book are solely those of the author and do not necessarily
express the views of JINSA Press or the Jewish Institute for National Security Affairs.

British Library Cataloguing in Publication Information Available

Library of Congress Cataloging-in-Publication Data

Mannes, Aaron, 1970–
    Profiles in terror : the guide to Middle East terrorist organizations / Aaron Mannes.
        p. cm.
    Includes bibliographical references and index.
    ISBN 0-7425-3525-8 (cloth : alk. paper)
    1. Terrorists—Middle East. 2. National liberation movements—Middle East. I. Title.
HV6433.M5M35 2004
303.6'25'0956—dc22   2004014124

Printed in the United States of America

⊖™ The paper used in this publication meets the minimum requirements of American
National Standard for Information Sciences—Permanence of Paper for Printed Library
Materials, ANSI/NISO Z39.48-1992.

To the late Claire Sterling, her groundbreaking work investigating terrorism and organized crime set the standard for everyone researching these threats to freedom.

Table of Contents

Abbreviation Key

AIS	Armee Islamique du Salut (Islamic Salvation Army)
ALF	Arab Liberation Front
AMIA	Argentine Israeli Mutual Association
ANO	Abu Nidal Organization (Fatah Revolutionary Council)
APF	Alliance of Palestinian Forces
ARGK	Arteshen Rizgariya Gelli Kurdistan (Kurdistan People's Liberation Army)
AUB	American University in Beirut
BNP	Bangladeshi National Party
CAIR	Council on American-Islamic Relations
CIA	Central Intelligence Agency (United States)
DFLP	Democratic Front for the Liberation of Palestine
DHPK-C	Dev Sol
ERNK	Rizgariya Netewa Kurdistan (National Liberation Front of Kurdistan)
ETA	Euskadi Ta Askatasuna (Basque Homeland and Freedom)
EU	European Union
FIDA	Palestinian Democratic Union
FIS	Front Islamique du Salut (Islamic Salvation Front)
FLN	Front de Liberation Nationale (National Liberation Front -- Algeria)
GIA	Groupe Islamique Armé (Armed Islamic Group)
GIS	General Intelligence Service
GSPC	Groupe Salafiste pour la Predication et le Combat (Salafist Group for Preaching and Combat)
HLF	Holy Land Foundation
IAA	Islamic Army of Aden
IAP	Islamic Association for Palestine
ICP	Islamic Committee for Palestine
IDF	Israel Defense Forces
IG	Islamic Group (al-Gama'a al-Islamiyya)
IIRO	International Islamic Relief Organization
IMU	Islamic Movement of Uzbekistan
IRA	Irish Republican Army
ISI	Interservices Intelligence Agency (Pakistan)
JeI	Jamaat-e-Islaami
JI	Jemaah Islamiyah
JuI	Jamaat-e-Ulema Islam
Kadek	Kurdistan Freedom and Democracy Congress
KLA	Kosovo Liberation Army
LeJ	Lashkar-e-Jhangvi
LTTE	Liberation Tigers of Tamil Eelam

MAK	Makhtab al-Khidmat
MAN	Movement of Arab Nationalists
MB	Muslim Brotherhood
MILF	Moro Islamic Liberation Front
NATO	North Atlantic Treaty Organization
NGO	Non-governmental organization
NSF	National Security Force
PA	Palestinian Authority
PFLP	Popular Front for the Liberation of Palestine
PFLP-GC	Popular Front for the Liberation of Palestine-General Command
PIJ	Palestinian Islamic Jihad
PKK	Partiya Karkeren Kurdistan (Kurdistan Workers' Party)
PLA	Palestine Liberation Army
PLC	Palestine Legislative Council
PLF	Palestine Liberation Front
PLO	Palestine Liberation Organization
PNA	Palestinian National Authority
PNC	Palestine National Council
PSF	Preventive Security Force
RPG	Rocket-propelled grenade
RUF	Revolutionary United Front
SeS	Sipah-e-Sahaba
SLA	South Lebanon Army
SSA	Special Security Apparatus
TIKKO	Turkish Communist Party/Marxist-Leninist-Partisan TIKKO (TKP/ML-Partisan-TIKKO)
TWRA	Third World Relief Agency
UASR	United Association for Studies and Research
UN	United Nations
UNHCR	United Nations High Commissioner for Refugees
UNIFIL	United Nations Interim Force in Lebanon
UNRWA	United Nations Relief and Works Agency
USF	University of South Florida
WAMY	World Assembly of Muslim Youth
WISE	World Islamic Studies Enterprise

Foreword

I n this volume Aaron Mannes has produced an invaluable reference for everyone interested in the terrorist organizations of the Middle East.

Many who write and speak on this complex subject are given to anecdotes, to bold generalities, and occasionally to digging in to defend positions they have taken in the past – the latter particularly illustrating John Maynard Keynes's point: that many people learn little after they are in their twenties, so the ideas of policymakers are often not the newest. In the field of terrorism my least favorite group within the haven't-learned-anything-in-years cohort is composed of those who heard somewhere years ago that in this part of the world the secular (e.g. the Ba'athists) will never work with the religious extremists (e.g. al Qaeda), and that the latter will never work with the extremists of another sect (e.g. Shi'ite Islamsits). Mannes does not tackle this or any other *idée fixe* frontally. Instead, by his systematic and careful scholarship, objective description of relationships and interactions, and precise chronologies for each group he lets the evidence speak for itself.

Like Freedom House's careful annual categorization of the degree of liberty (and lack thereof) in each of the world's governments, Freedom in the World, Mannes's work will likely soon become the standard reference on Middle East terrorist groups, the one to which all serious students will continually refer. JINSA should be congratulated for providing such a volume. It has been needed for some time and you, reading this, are lucky to have a copy.

-Hon. R. James Woolsey
Director of Central Intelligence
1993-1995

Preface

A central principle of all civilized societies is that violence is an unacceptable means of resolving disputes and that force is reserved for self-defense. Terrorism, which attempts to achieve political ends through violence against non-combatants, attacks this principle and is therefore not only an assault on civilized societies, but on the very concept of civilization. While terrorism had been a growing threat throughout the last half of the 20th Century, on Tuesday, September 11, 2001 the ability of a small group of fanatics to create mass carnage and to paralyze a great nation became evident.

Terrorist attacks are not random – although the victims may be – they are acts of war. Throughout the 1990s and before, there had been unheeded warnings that terrorists had declared war against the United States and the world's free societies. In the wake of the terrible events of 9/11, the United States has finally girded itself for a protracted war.

A primary dictum in war is to know the enemy. This volume, a modest contribution to these efforts, attempts to shed light on the intentions, histories, and methods of the major terrorist organizations of the Middle East. It should serve as a useful reference to the specialist, a comprehensive guide to the general public, and a gateway to further research for the student. Based on this survey, a few general observations about terrorism may be useful to the reader:

- Terrorist attacks are carefully planned operations supported by infrastructures that conduct reconnaissance, recruit and train members, assemble equipment, and transport operatives. Terrorist operations must be carried out with secrecy, so that local authorities are not alerted. Terrorism requires a high level of organization and coordination to be effective.

- Terrorist organizations may have conventional military wings, political and propaganda arms, and even social welfare divisions. These activities support terrorism by recruiting, indoctrinating, and training potential members of the clandestine wings that undertake operations.

- The clandestine units are usually organized in some variation of the cell or cluster structure. These organizational structures are designed to control the flow of information in order to limit the possible damage caused by the capture of an operative. A cell usually has between two and fifteen operatives, although there have been cells with several dozen operatives. Communication between cell members is carefully controlled, and sometimes is only through the cell leader. The cell leader is responsible for communications with the organization's leadership.

- In order to undertake anonymous violence, terrorists must be taught to dehumanize potential victims. To achieve this level of amorality, ideological training for terrorists is often accompanied by systematic brutality and groups of recruits are frequently required to carry out crimes in order to bind them together.

- Suicide attacks are a highly effective tactic because of the greater guarantee of striking a target, the increased flexibility in carrying out operations, and the elimination of the need for an escape plan. But they require even more in-depth indoctrination because they violate man's most basic instinct-- that of self-preservation.

- Without state support, terrorist groups can be neutralized fairly quickly. A state sponsor provides a haven for terrorists between operations, a secure logistical base for training and planning, and financial support. Terrorism is a relatively low cost endeavor – the estimated cost of 9/11 was only $500,000 – so that even an impoverished state is in a position to bring substantial resources to a terrorist organization. State institutions mentor terrorist clients, training them in organizational and military skills.

Most of the terrorist organizations profiled here are inspired by extremist interpretations of Islam. Their ideologies are not uniform and represent a range of interpretations of Islam. This important issue is beyond the scope of this work and consequently, for the reader's convenience, terrorists inspired by Islam are referred to as Islamists and their beliefs are referred to as Islamism.

Within this work there are innumerable transliterations from several languages. Rather than adhering to a standard form of transliteration, every effort was made to use generally recognizable transliterations and to keep them internally consistent.

This book was completed in February 2003. As it was being proofed the totalitarian Baathist regime in Iraq, one of the world's leading terrorism sponsors, was removed by an international coalition. This operation, along with the continuing international campaign against terrorism has brought daily revelations and developments about international terrorist networks. This book could not encompass this flood of new information, but should serve as a reference to place this new information into context.

Finally, many people helped make this book a reality with advice, research, and proofing. However, any errors within are the responsibility of the author alone.

Aaron Mannes
June 2004

Acknowledgments

C oming to the end of a challenging project, this author's first book-length endeavor, the opportunity to acknowledge some of the many people who made this volume possible is an unexpected pleasure. First, the Jewish Institute for National Security Affairs, JINSA, has underwritten this project, and it is my sincerest hope that it furthers their objectives of defending freedom and democracy in the United States, Israel, and throughout the world. Everyone at JINSA was very helpful, but I particularly wish to thank my two friends, JINSA's Director of Communications Jim Colbert and Research & Communications Manager Dan Smith, who oversaw my work and were helpful and devoted throughout this project despite their many other pressing responsibilities. JINSA also provided me with a diligent and resourceful research assistant, Jessica Altschul.

Many friends helped me with my work, and I cannot hope to acknowledge all of them. Josh Pollack, who each of the many times I asked him – as a favor – to research something, always came back with the answer and more. Towards the end Roy Kaufmann stepped up to the plate and provided some critical research support; I am truly grateful. I frequently thank, and occasionally curse, my good friends David and Meyrav Wurmser who got me into this business to begin with. Yigal Carmon of the Middle East Media Research Institute, gave me an unparalleled and informal education on terrorism and the Middle East.

Finally, I wish to thank my family – but I haven't the words to even begin.

Al-Qaeda & Its Affiliates

Al-Qaeda

Algerian Affiliates

I n Algeria, both French and Arabic are common languages. In French
the GIA or Armed Islamic Group is the Groupe Islamique Armé
and in Arabic is the al-Gama'a al-Islamiyya. The Salafist Group for
Preaching and Combat (GSPC), a splinter faction of the GIA which
has become Algeria's most dangerous terrorist organization, is known
in French as Groupe Salafiste pour la Predication et le Combat and in
Arabic as the al-Gama'a al-Salafiyya lil Dawa wal-Qital.

Ideology and Objectives

Both the Armed Islamic Group (GIA) and the Salafist Group for
Preaching and Combat (GSPC) adhere to the Salafist branch of Islam.
Salafists, from the word *salaf* or companions, believe that the only true
version of Islam is that revealed by Mohammed and his companions.
Turning Algeria into a Muslim state is the first priority of both the GIA
and the GSPC. Any recognition of the Algerian government, such as
participating in elections, is impossible. Additionally, democracy itself
is forbidden because only divine power can decree law. Ultimately,
both the GIA and the GSPC seek to expand their struggle to Europe,
particularly France, as well as to the United States and Israel.

The GIA views itself as being at war with all infidels, defined as
non-Muslims and Muslims who do not adhere to the Salafist doctrine.
This group has sought to use Islamic law to justify its massacres of
Muslims, as well as rape and pillaging.

History
Origins

Popular discontent in Algeria with the rule of the secular socialist
Front de Liberation Nationale (FLN), which had ruled Algeria as a
one party state since its independence, had become widespread by the

end of the 1980s. There had been Islamist uprisings as well as public unrest. In the late 1980s, Algerian veterans of the war in Afghanistan joined local Islamist organizations, injecting a more militant Islamist element into Algerian politics.

In 1989, the Front Islamique du Salut (FIS or Islamic Salvation Front) was founded in Algiers to spearhead opposition to the FLN as Algeria began to take steps toward democracy. In June 1990, the FIS won 54% of the vote in municipal elections while the FLN only took 28%. In December 1991, the FIS won 188 of the 231 contested seats in Parliament in the first round of elections. The FIS would have obtained an absolute majority in Parliament in the second round but, in January 1992, the Algerian military cancelled the second round of elections. In February 1992, the FIS began orchestrating riots, strikes, and attacks on the government. Algeria slid into a long, brutal civil war in which civilians were the primary target.

The Founding of the GIA

The Islamic Salvation Front's (FIS) electoral success in 1989 occurred in great part, because it represented the opposition to the unpopular Front de Liberation Nationale (FLN). While Islamist, the FIS claimed that it would build an Islamist state through elections and democracy. The FIS also accepted support from the non-Islamist majority, which identified with the FIS because it was an alternative to the FLN.

With the nullification of the elections and the FIS launching violent protests, Algerian security forces cracked down, imprisoning tens of thousands of FIS activists. The FIS began to fall into disarray. Hard-line Islamists, many of whom had fought in Afghanistan, were skeptical of democracy and began forming splinter groups that launched terror attacks. A September 1992 attempt to unite them as the armed wing of the FIS collapsed when Algerian security forces attacked the meeting, killing several leaders.

In October 1992, several Islamist militias based in the center of the country merged to form the Groupe Islamique Armé – GIA (Armed Islamic Group). The GIA brought a new level of violence to the Algerian civil war, expanding its targets from security personnel to government officials, foreigners, journalists, intellectuals, and leaders of opposition to the GIA. Since 1995, the GIA's primary targets have been Algerian civilians. A common GIA tactic is attacking villages at night and slitting the villagers' throats.

The Multi-Sided War

While the Armed Islamic Group (GIA) insisted that it was independent from the Islamic Salvation Front (FIS), there was a relationship between the two organizations. FIS figures sat on the GIA advisory council. But ultimately, they split because the FIS sought to reinstate the democratic process while the GIA's goal was to destroy the Algerian state and establish strict Islamic law. The government's continued repression made the GIA an attractive alternative and its ranks continued to swell in the early 1990s.

In May 1994, the Islamic State Movement, another armed Islamist organization, along with elements of the FIS merged with the GIA. They issued a communiqué that the GIA was the only legitimate jihad organization, effectively declaring war on other Islamist organizations. The GIA was attempting to marginalize the FIS militarily and politically. Continued GIA violence undermined FIS attempts to negotiate ceasefires with the Algerian government.

The FIS, which had also operated armed units, although on a smaller scale, responded by formally establishing the Islamic Salvation Army (Armée Islamique du Salut – AIS). The AIS, although smaller than the GIA, had between 5,000 and 10,000 fighters. Its operations were primarily in the eastern and western parts of the country, avoiding the center part where the GIA was established. The AIS sought to distinguish itself from the GIA by avoiding attacks on citizens. and focusing on fighting the security forces. The AIS claimed that its jihad was the just one, since it did not target civilians. The AIS also argued that jihad was not an end in itself, but a means to force the government to reinstate the electoral process.

The GIA responded by targeting FIS leaders and AIS fighters. In May 1995 the GIA delivered an ultimatum calling on the FIS to join them. The FIS refused and a month later the GIA expelled the FIS leaders sitting on the GIA's advisory council and decreed a death penalty on them. The GIA began murdering Islamist leaders who did not join the GIA. An FIS founder was killed in a Paris mosque in July 1995 and over 100 members of minor Algerian Islamist groups were killed.

Over the next several years the AIS and GIA fought each other, the Algerian military, and citizen militias founded by the Algerian military. While all parties committed violence against civilians, the GIA's systematic massacres became notorious. The GIA also instituted

Islamic law in areas it controlled, banning French-language newspapers, beauty salons, satellite dishes, cigarettes, and music festivals.

The GIA also attacked France because of its support for the Algerian government. In December 1994, the GIA hijacked an Air France jet bound for Algiers and killed three passengers. French commandos stormed the plane, killing all four hijackers. The hijackers had been planning to fly the plane into the Eiffel Tower. Within 24 hours, the GIA responded by murdering four Catholic priests in Algeria.

In the summer of 1995, the GIA conducted a series of bombings in France. The eight bombs killed 12 and injured nearly 200. Three of the eight attacks were on the Paris Metro; one was against a Jewish school in Lyon.

Between November 1996 and July 2001, the GIA carried out 76 massacres in addition to bombings and assassinations. During the mid-1990s over 1,000 people on average were killed per month in Algeria's civil war. The total deaths during the decade of fighting are estimated between 75,000 and 150,000 killed. Throughout this period there were persistent rumors that Algerian security forces perpetrated some massacres in order to reduce popular support for the Islamist insurgency.

Salafist Group for Preaching and Combat is Formed and Islamic Salvation Army Disbands

The scale of Armed Islamic Group (GIA) massacres shocked other radical Islamist groups and they distanced themselves from the GIA. In mid-1996, groups associated with al-Qaeda stated that the GIA had deviated from Islam. On September 8, 1997, the GIA issued a declaration justifying the massacres it had committed because the Algerian people had deviated from Islam and were not supporting the GIA. The statement also justified forcible "temporary marriages" which allowed GIA operatives to rape captured women.

In May 1998, a GIA commander and head of the GIA's European network, Hassan Hattab, disgusted with the GIA violence against civilians, split from the GIA and established the Salafist Group for Preaching and Combat (GSPC). He received substantial support from al-Qaeda, and worked with al-Qaeda to take control of the GIA's overseas network and encourage Algeria-based operatives to defect to the GSPC. By 2000, the GSPC was closely associated with al-Qaeda and had surpassed the GIA and had become the dominant terrorist group in Algeria.

In 1997, the Islamic Salvation Army (AIS) declared a unilateral ceasefire with the government. In 1999, once it had become evident that the ceasefire was holding, newly elected President Bouteflika granted amnesty to the AIS. The AIS formally disbanded and has aided the Algerian military in capturing GIA terrorists.

In January 2000, 800 GIA members from 22 militias took advantage of Bouteflika's offer for amnesty and stated that they would abide by the ceasefire.

While weakened by the AIS-government cooperation and the GIA-GSPC split, Islamists have continued to carry out operations in Algeria. In January 2000, the GIA threatened the Dakar Road Rally and much of the race was cancelled. In 2002, the death toll in Algeria's civil war averaged over 100 per month (down from over 1,000 per month in the mid-1990s.) On July 5, 2002 at a celebration for the 40th anniversary of Algerian independence, a GIA bomb killed 38 and wounded 80. In April 2002, the GSPC ambushed and killed 21 Algerian soldiers.

During the first few weeks of 2003, over 100 people in Algeria were killed by Islamist fighters.

In March 2004, the U.S. sent Special Forces to southern Algeria to assist in counter-terror operations.

Leadership

In February 2002, Algerian security forces killed Antar Zouabri, who had been head of the Armed Islamic Group (GIA) since 1996. Zouabri was 32 years old, and had headed the GIA when it issued its statement justifying massacres and rape. Zouabri replaced Djamel Ztouni, who was killed in an internal GIA dispute. Awkali Rashid (a.k.a. al-Rashid Abu Turab), who was killed by Algerian security forces on July 28, 2002, replaced Zouabri. The Algerian security forces have targeted the GIA's leadership, thereby reducing its operational effectiveness.

The leader of the Salafist Group for Preaching and Combat (GSPC) is Hassan Hattab (a.k.a. Abu Hamza). Born in 1967, Hattab was a paratrooper in the Algerian military. He was appointed Emir of the GIA's second region in June 1995. He also directed the GSPC's overseas networks.

Organization

The Armed Islamic Group (GIA) at its peak had over 10,000 operatives. In 2000, having been targeted by the Algerian security forces and undermined by the Salafist Group for Preaching and Combat (GSPC), estimates of its strength ranged from between 800 and 2,000 operatives. The GIA divides Algeria into nine zones, each with an Emir overseeing the activities of the militias in one zone. The GIA has a loose structure, which prevents infiltration or easy dismemberment. Another consequence of the loose structure is a lack of central control over the organization.

The GSPC is more effectively organized than the GIA, with better communication and discipline. Estimates range from several hundred to several thousand operatives.

Financial Support

The GIA receives financial support from Algerians abroad and collects "taxes" from areas under its control. The GIA is known for looting and forcing civilians to provide it with supplies. The Algerian government has accused Iran and Sudan of providing support to the GIA.

The GSPC receives financial support from al-Qaeda and is heavily involved with credit card fraud and identity theft in Europe

Links to States and Terrorist Organizations

Many Algerians fought in Afghanistan, and the Algerian contingent within al-Qaeda's ranks is second only to the Egyptian one. Consequently, the Algerian Islamist movements have developed extensive links with other Islamist groups worldwide.

In the 1990s, the Sudanese government provided training facilities for the GIA. In Sudan, the GIA developed extensive relationships with other Islamist groups around the world, including Hamas, Hizbullah, Egyptian Islamist groups, and al-Qaeda. GIA ranks include Afghan veterans who have links with Islamist movements worldwide. Prior to 1996, GIA leaders met and coordinated with figures from other terrorist organizations. However, since mid-1996 when it was repudiated by other Islamist organizations, these contacts have decreased.

The GSPC is an al-Qaeda associate and its leader, Hassan Hattab, is known to be in telephone contact with Osama bin Laden. The GSPC's European apparatus is a central component of al-Qaeda's European network.

Areas of Operation

The Armed Islamic Group's and the Salafist Group for Preaching and Combat's primary theater is rural central Algeria, although they have a presence throughout Algeria and have conducted attacks in the nation's urban centers.

The Algerian Islamists have an extensive infrastructure in Europe. GIA cells have been broken up in Italy, Britain, Germany, and Belgium. The strongest presence is in France, which has a large population of Algerian immigrants and has been subject to attacks by the GIA, including a 1994 airliner hijacking and a series of bombings in 1994-1996. In Belgium, a GIA cell committed a series of bank robberies. In spring 1998, dozens of suspected GIA operatives were arrested across Europe to prevent an expected attack on the World Cup.

The GSPC took over the GIA's European network in late 1998. It directs al-Qaeda propaganda campaigns, particularly in France. A GSPC cell tied to al-Qaeda in Milan, Italy was plotting an attack on St. Peter's Square when Italian police arrested its members in March 2002. Cells have also been arrested in the Netherlands, Spain, and Germany. In 1999, British authorities discovered a GSPC cell that provided logistical support for GSPC activities on the continent. In January 2003, six Algerians in Britain were discovered producing large quantities of the poison ricin. They were arrested and are being investigated for links to al-Qaeda.

The GIA also has a presence in North America. Canada's liberal immigration laws have made Montreal an attractive destination for Francophone Algerians. In 1996 and 1997, the now-defunct American Islamic Group of San Diego, CA was the United States distribution center for GIA publications.

The GSPC is extending its activities throughout the Sahara Desert, particularly into Mali.

Targets and Tactics

For the GIA, virtually no targets or tactics are out of bounds. GIA militias are infamous for their nocturnal attacks on villages in which they murder by slitting the throats of civilians. The GIA also sets up phony checkpoints and murders those stopped. They have conducted hundreds of bombings and thousands of acts of sabotage. The organization is also known for capturing women and keeping them as slaves in mountain tunnels.

Specific GIA targets include intellectuals, journalists, and Islamist leaders who do not endorse the GIA's strict interpretation of jihad. Since 1993, the GIA has targeted European foreigners and expatriates living in Algeria. Over 100 foreigners have been killed in Algeria, including over a dozen priests and monks. The GIA also considers government employees important targets, particularly teachers. Because Algeria is a socialist state, this GIA policy put many in an untenable position because there were very few non-government jobs.

In December 1994, GIA operatives hijacked a French plane, intending to fly it into the Eiffel Tower. They have also attacked dissidents in Europe and during their wave of attacks in France in the mid-1990s, set off car bombs near Jewish schools and synagogues and in 1996 sent a letter bomb to the editor of a Jewish newspaper.

The GSPC broke from the most brutal GIA tactics of targeting Muslim civilians en masse. The GSPC has launched attacks against Algerian soldiers and has participated in al-Qaeda attacks against the West.

Chronology of Major Events and Attacks

1991

December – In the first round of legislative elections, Algiers voids the victory of the Islamic Salvation Front (FIS) – the largest Islamic opposition party – leading to the beginning of the GIA's violent activities.

1993

The GIA announces its campaign against foreigners living in Algeria.

October 19 – Terrorists kidnap a Peruvian, a Filipino and a Colombian from the cafeteria of an Italian construction firm in Tiaret. The three are found dead some fifty kilometers away from the abduction site with their throats cut. On October 26, the GIA claims responsibility for this and other attacks against foreigners.

October 24 – Three French diplomats are kidnapped as they leave their apartment in Algiers. The police officer who attempts to prevent the kidnapping is shot and killed. On October 26, the GIA claims responsibility for this incident. The three diplomats are released unharmed on the night of October 30.

December 14 – A large group of terrorists attack the work camp at a hydroelectric project in Tamezguida. Fourteen Croatian citizens are taken out of the camp. Twelve are murdered by slitting their throats, but two others escape with injuries. On December 16, the GIA claims responsibility, stating that the attack is part of an ongoing campaign to rid Algeria of all foreigners and to avenge Muslims killed in Bosnia.

1994

May 8 – Two French priests are shot and killed by two male assailants in the lower Casbah district of Algiers. In its weekly publication, the GIA claims responsibility.

August 3 – Five French embassy employees are killed and one is injured when guerrillas from the GIA attack a French residential compound in Algiers.

October 18 – Approximately 30 members of the GIA attack an oil facility, killing one French and one Italian worker.

December 24 – Members of the GIA hijack an Air France flight in Algeria. The plane arrives in Marseilles, France on December 26. A French anti-terrorist unit storms the plane, ending the 54-hour siege in which three hostages are killed by the terrorists. All four terrorists are killed during the rescue.

December 27 – The GIA claims responsibility for the murders of four Catholic priests. The murders are apparently in retaliation for the deaths of four GIA hijackers the previous day in Marseilles.

1995

January 8 – Armed assailants attempt to kill two priests, one French and one Swiss, belonging to the Order of the White Fathers. The priests escape unharmed. The GIA is suspected in the attack.

January 22 – Gunmen shoot and kill a Frenchman as he drives through a park. A woman is also injured in the attack. The GIA is suspected.

March 3 – A Palestinian student attending the Algerian Arab College is murdered by an armed group that stormed the area where he and his family lived. The GIA is suspected.

May 5 – Suspected members of the GIA attack employees of a pipeline company, killing two Frenchmen, a Briton, a Canadian, and a Tunisian. One Algerian security guard is also killed in the attack.

June 7 – Suspected members of the GIA shoot and kill a French couple in Algiers. No one claims responsibility for the attack.

July 11 – Two assailants assassinate a cofounder of the Algerian Islamic Salvation Front and his bodyguard in a Paris mosque. No one claims responsibility for the murders, but earlier the same year Algerian publications reportedly receive a communiqué from the GIA listing their priority targets. The victim is included on the list.

July 25 – Eight are killed and 86 are wounded by a bomb planted by the GIA in a Paris commuter rail station. It is part of a wave of GIA bombings in France that continue into October 1995.

September 2 – Suspected GIA militants shoot and kill an Italian national in Oran.

September 3 – Unidentified assailants shoot and kill two nuns in the Belcourt district of Algiers. One of the victims is French; the other is Maltese. Authorities suspect the GIA.

November 30 – Four suspected Islamic extremists shoot and kill two Latvian seamen and wound a third. No one claims responsibility, but the GIA is suspected.

1996

March 27 – GIA extremists kidnap seven French monks from their monastery in the Medea region. On April 26, the GIA offers to free the monks in exchange for the release of GIA members held in France. On May 21, the group states that they have killed the monks in response to the French government's refusal to negotiate with them.

August 1 – A bomb explodes at the home of the French Archbishop of Oran, killing him and his chauffeur. The attack occurs after the Archbishop's meeting with the French Foreign Minister. The GIA is suspected.

1997

June 22 – Unknown assailants kill a French woman in Bouzeguene and dump her body in a well. The GIA is suspected.

September 8 – The GIA issues a declaration justifying massacre and rape of civilians.

1998

February 23 – Eighteen people are killed and 25 are wounded in an explosion aboard a train. The bomb was hidden on the railway track or next to it and exploded when the train passed. The authorities suspect Muslim extremists.

May – The Salafist Group for Preaching and Combat (GSPC) splits off from the GIA over the GIA's policy of indiscriminate killings of civilians. The former aims its activities at only military and political targets and is led by Hassan Hattab.

August 31 – An explosion rips through a packed square, in Algiers killing at least 17 people and wounding over 60. No organization claims immediate responsibility. Authorities suspect the GIA.

2000

July 9-10 – Algerian newspapers say that more than 20 people are killed and 10 are kidnapped in a number of attacks, the highest figure for several months, both the GIA and the GSPC are suspected.

September – In the village of Bougarra, three gunmen spraying a house with automatic weapons fire, killing seven people and wounding two. The gunmen mount a fake roadblock on a main road in the same area and cut the throats of five people in two cars that stop. The gunmen cut the throats of three men in one vehicle and injure a two-year-old girl before setting the car on fire and kidnapping a young woman. The GIA is suspected.

September 24 – Reports from Algeria say 13 people are killed in attacks in Algiers, the GIA is suspected.

2001

July 7 – The security services in Algeria say that 16 people are killed on a road 120 kilometers west of Algiers. The GIA is suspected.

December 7 – Islamic militants kill 17 civilians and wound four others. The GIA is suspected.

2002

February 8 – Antar Zouabri, the head of the GIA since 1996, is reported shot and killed by security forces. He has been reported dead by newspapers several times in the past, but this is the first time the government has announced his death.

April 2 – Suspected Islamic militants in Algeria kill 20 government soldiers in an ambush. The Algerian army believes the gunmen are members of the Salafist Group for Preaching and Combat (GSPC), and that the attack is in revenge for the recent arrest of 150 people by the security forces in a sweep against suspected supporters of the GSPC in the area.

May 2 – GIA operatives kill 34 civilians in a 24-hour period in Algeria. Three are killed and a fourth is kidnapped in the northwest part of the country, just one day after 31 people are massacred in the same region. Algerian security services say two men and a woman are killed as they return from their fields near Chlef and a young woman is kidnapped.

May 23 – Ten Algerian soldiers are killed near Algeria's capital, Algiers, in the run-up to the legislative elections scheduled for one week later. The GSPC is suspected.

June 28 – GIA operatives kill 13 bus passengers and wound nine others as they riddle the bus with machine gun fire. The bus is traveling in Les Eucalyptus district in the southern outskirts of Algiers near the airport.

July 5 – GIA operatives set off a bomb in a crowded marketplace outside Algiers, killing at least 38 and injuring at least 80.

July 28 – The Algerian army, conducting military operations in the Tamezguida Forest, reportedly kill the leader of the GIA, al-Rashid Abu Turab, along with 15 other members, according to *Le Matin* newspaper.

2003

January 4 – In a massive ambush, Algerian Islamists (probably GSPC) kill 49 Algerian soldiers from an elite unit and wound at least 19, near the town of Theniet El Abed. That same night in the town of Zabana, GIA operatives kill 13 people.

January 7 – GSPC operatives kill the mayor of Chetaibi and his top assistant, wounding two others.

February- April– Several groups of Europeans, mostly German, traveling in southern Algeria without guides are taken hostage by the GSPC.

May– The kidnappers demand a 1 million Swiss Franc (about $775,000) ransom per hostage.

May 14 – Algerian Army frees 17 hostages and kills nine of the kidnappers in a raid. Later the German Foreign Minister urges Algeria not to attempt to free more hostages by force.

August 20 – The final 14 hostages are released (one died in captivity) after negotiations. The German government denies making ransom payments to the kidnappers.

Resources

Hafez, M.M. "Armed Islamist Movements and Political Violence in Algeria." *Middle East Journal* Fall 2002; Vol. 4.

Maddy-Weitzman, B. "The Islamic Challenge in North Africa." *Middle East Review of International Affairs Journal* May 1997; Vol. 1, No. 2 – available at www.meria.idc.ac.il.

Schanzer, J. "Algeria's GSPC and America's 'War on Terror'." *Policywatch* October 2, 2002; No. 666 – available at www.washingtoninstitute.org.

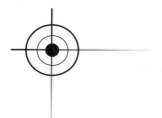

Al-Qaeda

Al-Qaeda means The Base. Al-Qaeda is technically only one part of the broader Islamic World Front for the Struggle against the Jews and the Crusaders (al-Jabhah al-Islamiyya al-'Alamiyya li-Qital al-Yahud wal-Salibiyyin). Since its formal merger with Egypt's al-Jihad (the Holy War), it has been known as Qaeda al-Jihad.

Ideology and Objectives

Al-Qaeda's ideology is expressed in the February 1998 Declaration of a World Islamic Front for Jihad against Jews and Crusaders. The declaration is motivated by, in order of priority, the American military presence in Saudi Arabia, American aggression against the Iraqi people, and the Jewish occupation of Jerusalem. This situation is viewed as the culmination of centuries of Muslim humiliation at the hands of non-Muslims. Consequently, al-Qaeda leader Osama bin Laden's Declaration calls for a holy war against the strongest non-Muslim nation, and permits the killing of Americans, civilians and military personnel, as well as their allies, including Israel, by any means possible.

Al-Qaeda also attacks and seeks the overthrow of regimes with large Muslim populations that do not install *shari'a* (Islamic holy law) as the official law. Most Muslim regimes, including the Saudi regime, have made too many compromises with non-Muslim regimes and are considered appropriate targets.

Al-Qaeda springs from the Wahhabi strain of Islam, which interprets *shari'a* strictly. This interpretation views any non-Muslim presence in Islam's holy lands (parts of the Arabian peninsula) as abhorrent. Further, Islam should eternally rule any land once under its rule.

Al-Qaeda seeks to extend the realm ruled by strict Islamic law and ultimately reinstate the caliphate, a single Islamic polity.

History

The Soviet-Afghan War

In 1979, the Soviet Union invaded Afghanistan, causing anger throughout the Muslim world. The rising Muslim fundamentalist movement, which had begun calling for jihad, focused its energies on Afghanistan, raising money for and sending volunteers to fight alongside the Afghanis. From 1980 to 1990, between 20,000 and 40,000 Muslims from around the world traveled to Afghanistan to fight with the Afghanis, and many more visited Afghanistan or volunteered with the support services in neighboring Pakistan. Many Arab governments encouraged these volunteers to go to Afghanistan, hoping to rid themselves of their own radical elements.

Saudi Arabia was the leading financial supporter of the Afghan fighters, providing approximately $3 billion in the 1980s, and at least 5,000 Saudis volunteered with the Afghan fighters. The fundamentalist Muslim Brotherhood helped recruit volunteers from across the Arab world, particularly in Algeria and Egypt. Many Islamist movements supported guesthouses for Muslim volunteers, including Sheikh Rahman of Egypt's al-Gama'a al-Islamiyya. The American Central Intelligence Agency (CIA) also contributed approximately $3 billion and provided sophisticated weapons and technical support. Most of this assistance was disseminated by Pakistan's Interservices Intelligence Agency (ISI), which supported Islamist elements among the Afghan fighters. Pakistan gave visas to anyone who wanted to join the Mujaheddin, the Afghan freedom fighters. The ISI and Pakistan's leading Islamist movement Jamaat-e-Islaami (JeI) set up reception committees for volunteers.

The leading figure in coordinating this worldwide effort was Abdallah Azzam, a Palestinian Muslim Brother renowned for his charisma, fiery rhetoric, and energy. Azzam, who had taught Islamic law at several universities in the Middle East, called for a jihad to restore the ancient Muslim caliphate and the primacy of *shari'a*. Azzam moved to Peshawar, Pakistan shortly after the Soviet invasion where he founded the Makhtab al-Khidmat or Services Office. The Services Office received recruits to the Afghan war and was the conduit for donations that poured in from across the Muslim world. Starting from Peshawar, Azzam built an international network of offices, with branches in the United States and Europe, as well as in the Arab world, for recruitment, fundraising, and disseminating his ideas. The United States branch was known as al-Khifa (The Struggle).

Prior to relocating to Pakistan, Azzam had been a lecturer at King Abdul-Aziz University in Jeddah, Saudi Arabia. While teaching in Jeddah, Azzam heavily influenced Osama bin Laden, the son of one of Saudi Arabia's wealthiest men. Bin Laden first traveled to Pakistan in 1980. He brought crews from his family's construction company with him and they built tunnels and fortifications for the Afghan fighters. Bin Laden helped Azzam set up the Services Office and became one of its primary supporters. He funded his own guesthouse for volunteers called Beit al-Ansar (House of the Supporters). Most major Islamist leaders visited Afghanistan, and many of them met with bin Laden, including Sheikh Omar Abd al-Rahman (now imprisoned in the United States for his role in the 1993 World Trade Center bombing) and Dr. Ayman Zawahiri (now second in command of al-Qaeda) of Egypt's al-Jihad. Most importantly, bin Laden devoted his efforts to spreading the Wahhabi vision of Islam to the Afghans and the volunteers from throughout the Muslim world.

At first, bin Laden traveled back and forth between Pakistan and Saudi Arabia, raising Saudi money for the Afghans. In 1986, he permanently relocated to Peshawar and built a training camp called al-Ansar near the Afghan village of Janji. In April 1987, this camp was attacked by Soviet troops. Outnumbered, the Arabs held their position for a week under intense Soviet fire before retreating. This battle was viewed as an Arab triumph in the face of a superpower and bin Laden was lionized for his bravery and for abandoning his life of ease in Saudi Arabia.

The Founding of al-Qaeda

In February 1989, Soviet forces withdrew from Afghanistan. This was viewed as a great victory throughout the Muslim world, not merely for Afghanistan, but for all Muslims. The ensuing collapse of the Soviet Union only heightened the feeling of victory. For the volunteers who had come to fight in Afghanistan, this victory was only the beginning.

While Arab financing played an important role in this victory, the military role of the international Muslim contingent was minor. However, Islamists from all over the world came into contact in Afghanistan, trained together and were further radicalized, and stayed in communication when they returned to their home countries. Afghan veterans became activists in several terrorist groups, including Egypt's al-Jihad, Algeria's Armed Islamic Group, Kashmir's Harkat-ul-Ansar, and the Philippines' Abu Sayyaf and Moro Islamic Liberation Front.

Because they were spearheading rebel movements, Arab regimes, with the exception of Sudan, were less than welcoming towards the returning Afghan veterans, and Arab intelligence agencies began monitoring their activities. In 1989, Osama bin Laden founded al-Qaeda to maintain a secure network of the Afghan veterans who continued training at bases in Afghanistan and Sudan and began appearing in other places where Muslims and non-Muslims were fighting such as Somalia, Bosnia, Kosovo, and Chechnya.

On November 24, 1989, Abdallah Azzam was assassinated, along with two of his sons, by a car bomb in Peshawar. The murder was never solved. Shortly thereafter, bin Laden returned to Saudi Arabia, where he was regarded as a hero and was in frequent demand as a speaker because of his exploits in Afghanistan. In his speeches, bin Laden called on the Saudis to boycott the United States because of its support for Israel.

When Iraq invaded Kuwait in August 1990, bin Laden offered his services and those of the Afghan veterans to the Saudi government. When the Saudis turned instead to the United States, bin Laden openly criticized the Saudi royal family. Bin Laden viewed the presence of American troops in Saudi Arabia as part of a Western plan to destroy Islam, worse than the Soviet invasion of Afghanistan because Saudi Arabia was home to Mecca and Medina – the holiest sites of Islam. When an American presence in Saudi Arabia continued after the Gulf War, bin Laden's criticism became more intense, including implying that some members of the royal family were traitors to Islam. He was placed under virtual house arrest and declared *persona non grata*.

In 1991 bin Laden left Saudi Arabia, and after spending a few months in Pakistan he settled in Sudan.

Al-Qaeda in Sudan

In June 1989, the Sudanese government was overthrown in a military coup led by General Omar al-Bashir. Behind al-Bashir's coup was the National Islamic Front, Sudan's branch of the Muslim Brotherhood, led by Hassan al-Turabi. Educated at the Sorbonne, al-Turabi became a diplomatic face for radical Islam. But beneath the Western veneer, al-Turabi was building an Islamist state in Sudan and supporting terrorist organizations in spreading jihad around the world. Al-Turabi's rise was facilitated by generous support from the Muslim Brotherhood throughout the Middle East and wealthy Saudi Islamists. While al-Turabi is a Sunni Muslim, he had cooperative relations with Iran's Shi'ite Muslim regime and allowed several thousand Pasdaran (Iranian Revolutionary Guards) and Hizbullah operatives to operate in Sudan.

When he arrived in 1992, bin Laden was an honored guest of the Sudanese regime and developed vast enterprises based in Sudan. He applied his expertise in construction when modernizing Port Sudan and a new highway from Sudan's capital Khartoum to Port Sudan. He also invested in farms, factories, and banks. These investments were not profitable; bin Laden reportedly lost tens of millions of dollars in Sudanese investments.

Bin Laden was also building the al-Qaeda network. While maintaining camps and guesthouses in Afghanistan, he also began building terrorist training camps in Sudan. Thousands of Muslims from all over the world trained in the bin Laden built training camps. In 1993, al-Qaeda completed the multi-volume *Encyclopedia of the Afghan Jihad*. Thousands of pages long and available on CD-ROM, this tome provides in-depth instruction in the weapons and tactics used in Afghanistan.

In December 1992, the United States initiated Operation Restore Hope, sending 28,000 American troops to Somalia in order to restore order and deliver humanitarian aid. Bin Laden viewed Operation Restore Hope as another American attempt to invade the Muslim world. Al-Qaeda affiliates bombed a pair of hotels in Yemen where American troops destined for Somalia were staying. The United States ceased using Yemen as a base for Operation Restore Hope.

Al-Qaeda also provided support and training to Somalis fighting the United States presence, particularly to clan leader Mohammed Farah Aidid. On October 3 and 4, 1993, 18 American soldiers were killed in fighting in Mogadishu. The battle started when Somalis using rocket-propelled grenades (RPGs) shot down a pair of American Blackhawk helicopters. Muhammad Atef, a former Egyptian policeman and al-Qaeda's military leader, had traveled to Somalia twice in 1993 to provide training. Reportedly, he taught the Somalis how to effectively target helicopters with RPGs. Shortly after the battle in Mogadishu, the United States announced it would withdraw from Somalia.

Al-Qaeda began supporting operations all over the world. The Islamist cell that perpetrated the first World Trade Center attack, a bombing on February 26, 1993, was operating out of al-Khifa, the Brooklyn branch of the bin Laden-controlled Services Office. Sheikh Rahman, who was suspected of orchestrating the World Trade Center attack and later imprisoned for plotting further terror attacks in New York City, had met bin Laden in Afghanistan. Most of the participants had a connection to the war in Afghanistan. The leader of the World Trade Center attack, Ramzi Yousef, had trained in a bin Laden camp in Afghanistan and after the bombing stayed for a time at a bin Laden supported guesthouse, Beit Ashuhada (House of the Martyrs). Yousef hastily fled the Philippines in 1994 after police learned he was plotting to assassinate Pope John Paul II, blow up 11 airliners over the Pacific, and use hijacked airliners to hit targets in the United States. Since his capture, Yousef has refused to reveal the source of his funding, but bin Laden, who was named an unindicted co-conspirator in the World Trade Center bombing trial, is suspected.

Al-Qaeda trained and dispatched operatives to fight on the fringes of the Muslim world, particularly in Bosnia, where a Services Office was opened in the early 1990s, and in Chechnya. The war between the Russians and the Chechens has a particular resonance in the Muslim world because it seemed to reprise the war in Afghanistan. Thousands of Muslims from all over the world were recruited to fight in Bosnia and Chechnya. Afghan veterans also began appearing in conflicts in central Asia, Kashmir, and the Philippines.

In 1995, al-Turabi sponsored an Islamic People's Conference in Khartoum, attended by leaders of Islamist terror organizations, including Hamas and Palestinian Islamic Jihad (PIJ), along with groups from Algeria, Egypt, Tunisia, and Pakistan. At this meeting, and at others, bin Laden forged new relations with Islamist leaders, including Imad Mughniyah, head of Hizbullah's military operations and mastermind of the 1983 attacks on the United States embassy in Beirut and the American and French barracks in Beirut. Reportedly, bin Laden told Mughniyah that he had been inspired by Mughniyah's bombings, which had led the United States to pull out of Lebanon.

Al-Qaeda also developed a close relationship with the Egyptian Islamist groups, becoming their primary donor. In 1993, Egyptian President Hosni Mubarak complained to Saudi King Fahd about bin Laden's activities. Pressured by Egypt, Pakistan cracked down on al-Qaeda activities in May 1993, arresting 800 members. Bin Laden brought several hundred others to Sudan. Al-Qaeda continued to support the Egyptian Islamists, assisting in an attempt to assassinate Mubarak in Ethiopia in June 1995 and a November 1995 suicide truck bombing of Egypt's embassy in Islamabad, Pakistan, killing 16 and injuring 60. After this bombing, Pakistan closed the Pakistani Services Office and arrested 150 Arabs linked to al-Qaeda.

Al-Qaeda was also continuing its confrontation with Saudi Arabia, although prominent members of the royal family and the Saudi elite supported al-Qaeda. In 1992, bin Laden founded the Advice and Reform Committee to advocate on behalf of change in Saudi Arabia. It criticized the Saudi regime both for corruption and for deviating from *shari'a*. In 1994, Saudi Arabia stripped bin Laden of his citizenship and froze his assets. The bin Laden family officially denounced Osama's activities in March 1994. The Saudi government sent delegations of bin Laden's relatives to urge him not to strike Saudi targets, and there is evidence that Saudi Arabia may also have tried to assassinate bin Laden in 1994.

Al-Qaeda in turn hit targets in Saudi Arabia. In November 1995, a car bombing outside of the National Guard building in Riyadh killed five Americans and two Indians. In June 1996, a truck bomb exploded outside the Khobar Towers, an American military barracks in Dahran – 19 were killed and hundreds were wounded. Bin Laden publicly denied responsibility for both attacks, although he praised the perpetrators. In both cases, there are some links to al-Qaeda. Afghan veterans, some of whom had contact with al-Qaeda operatives, planned the 1995 bombing. After the 1996 bombing, Saudi security arrested 600 Afghan veterans, although they ultimately indicted 13 members of Saudi Hizbullah, a Shi'ite Muslim group with links to Iran. Saudi Arabia beheaded the four suspects in the 1995 bombing before American investigators could interview them. Some American investigators were displeased with the level of Saudi cooperation in the investigations of both bombings. In a 1997 CNN interview, bin Laden denied any role in either bombing, but praised the courage of the perpetrators. Since the mid-1990s there have been attacks on Westerners living in Saudi Arabia. While the Saudi government claims that these attacks are connected to feuds between alcohol smugglers, al-Qaeda is suspected of orchestrating them.

In May 1996, under intense international pressure, Sudan expelled bin Laden. Reportedly, the Sudanese government offered to turn bin Laden over to both the Saudi and the American governments. The Saudi government did not want bin Laden to return to Saudi Arabia because of his hostility to the ruling Saudi faction, popularity in Saudi Arabia, and personal connections with powerful Saudis. The United States government did not feel it had sufficient evidence to make a legal case against him.

Al-Qaeda and the Taliban

Expelled from Sudan, bin Laden and his followers relocated to Afghanistan, where he developed a close relationship with the ruling Taliban. After the Soviet defeat, Afghanistan collapsed into bloody ethnic conflict. With backing from Pakistan's ISI and Saudi Arabia, the Taliban, an Islamist movement made up of students from the *madrasas* (religious schools) along the Afghanistan-Pakistan border, rose to power. In September 1996 they occupied Kabul, Afghanistan's capital, and most of the countryside and were instituting a harsh form of *shari'a*.

The Taliban welcomed bin Laden, both for his own record in the war against the Soviet Union and his affinity for the Taliban theocracy. Bin Laden also provided cash infusions that were critical to the internationally isolated Taliban regime. Well-equipped al-Qaeda fighters joined Taliban forces in the 1997-1998 offensives in northern Afghanistan against Ahmed Shah Massoud, the primary leader of the anti-Taliban forces. Al-Qaeda troops also participated in massacres of Shi'ite Azeris in northern Afghanistan. While absolutist in their religious beliefs, the Taliban were provincial. Bin Laden introduced them to the ideas of worldwide jihad. In Afghanistan al-Qaeda expanded its infrastructure, providing training for terrorists from throughout the Muslim world.

On August 23, 1996 bin Laden issued a 60-page fatwa (religious ruling) entitled, "Declaration of Jihad on Americans Occupying the Country of the Two Sacred Places." In this fatwa, he blamed a Jewish and Crusader alliance for the disaster visited on the Muslim world, particularly the American presence on the Arabian Peninsula. In it he called for a worldwide jihad against the United States and Israel and shortly after issuing it, bin Laden began permitting Western journalists to interview him.

On February 23, 1998 bin Laden issued a new fatwa that announced the formation of the Islamic World Front for the Struggle against the Jews and the Crusaders. Besides bin Laden, the signatories of the fatwa were Rifa'i Ahmed Taha, leader of Egypt's al-Gama'a al-Islamiyya, Ayman Zawahiri of Egypt's al-Jihad, Fazlul Rahman, of the Bangladeshi Jihad Movement, and Sheikh Mir Hamzah, Secretary of Pakistan's Jamaat-e-Ulema Islam (JUI). This fatwa went a step further than the previous one, explicitly calling on all Muslims to attack all Americans and their allies, whether civilian or military. In March 1998, the Afghan ulema (religious council), at bin Laden's request, validated the fatwa because bin Laden has no standing as a Muslim scholar, and his fatwas have no formal weight. On May 26, 1998 bin Laden held a press conference in which he inaugurated his World Islamic Front and implied that there would be a major attack on the United States in the near future.

On August 7, 1998 almost simultaneously, al-Qaeda attacked the American embassies in Nairobi, Kenya and Dar-es-Salaam, Tanzania with truck bombs. In Nairobi, 244 Kenyans and 12 Americans were killed and over 5,000 people were injured. In Dar-es-Salaam, ten Tanzanians were killed and 77 were injured. Bin Laden was held responsible and was placed at the top of the FBI's most wanted list.

On August 20, 1998, the United States launched over 50 cruise missiles at six al-Qaeda affiliated camps in Afghanistan and a pharmaceutical plant owned by bin Laden in Khartoum, Sudan. The strikes on the training camps, which trained militants fighting in Kashmir, killed 34 (mostly Afghani but also several Arabs). The United States government claimed that the pharmaceutical plant was being used by bin Laden to produce nerve gas. Other sources have contested that claim.

Key members of the cells that carried out the Africa bombings were arrested shortly after they occurred – they were convicted in May 2001. Their confessions revealed the truly global reach of al-Qaeda and allowed the United States to begin to effectively use electronic intelligence against al-Qaeda and its affiliates. Over 80 Islamists were arrested across the Muslim world, from central Africa to East Asia.

The American focus on bin Laden raised his status and he became an icon to Islamists worldwide. Over the next three years, al-Qaeda made numerous attempts to attack American targets in the United States, across the Middle East, in Albania, Azerbaijan, and in Africa. Al-Qaeda expanded its support for Islamist groups throughout the world.

Al-Qaeda planned a three-pronged millennium attack, to take place as close as possible to January 1, 2000. In Jordan, security forces broke up an al-Qaeda cell plotting to attack American targets and an area of the Jordan River frequented by Christian tourists. In Yemen, an al-Qaeda cell attempted to sink the destroyer USS *The Sullivans* on January 3, 2000, but the explosives-laden boat sank. On December 14, 1999, Ahmed Ressam, an Algerian who had trained in Afghanistan, was arrested at the United States-Canadian border with 130 pounds of explosives. Ressam confessed to planning to bomb Los Angeles International Airport and to having been recruited by bin Laden's deputy Abu Zubayda.

On October 12, 2000, a boat loaded with explosives, piloted by two al-Qaeda operatives, struck the destroyer USS *Cole* in the port of Aden, Yemen. Seventeen American sailors were killed and 39 were injured. The damage to the ship was approximately $250 million. The United States dispatched investigators to Yemen, but later complained about insufficient cooperation.

On September 9, 2001, Ahmed Shah Massoud, leader of the anti-Taliban Northern Alliance, was assassinated in northern Afghanistan. The assassins were posing as journalists and had arranged to see Massoud under the pretext of interviewing him. The journalists' credentials were from the Islamic Observation Center of London, which is headed by Yasser al-Sirri, a leader of Egypt's al-Jihad.

September 11, 2001

Nineteen al-Qaeda operatives hijacked four airplanes that took off from the East Coast and were bound for the West Coast of the United States. At 8:48 a.m. American Airlines Flight 11, carrying 92 passengers and crew, slammed into the North Tower of the World Trade Center in New York City. Fifteen minutes later, United Airlines Flight 175, carrying 65 people, hit the South Tower of the World Trade Center.

At 9:40 a.m. American Airlines Flight 77, carrying 64 people, crashed into the Pentagon. One hundred twenty-five Pentagon workers were killed. At 10:03 a.m., United Airlines Flight 93, carrying 45 people, crashed into a field in rural Pennsylvania. The passengers had fought the hijackers and prevented them from striking a target in Washington, D.C. – possibly the U.S. Capitol building.

At 10:05 a.m. the South Tower of the World Trade Center collapsed and at 10:29 a.m, the North Tower collapsed. Nearly 3,000 people were killed, including large numbers of rescue workers who were facilitating evacuation efforts.

Mohammed Atta, an Egyptian born citizen of the United Arab Emirates, piloted American Airlines Flight 11 and is believed to have been the operational coordinator for the 9/11 attacks. He and the other hijackers had obtained visas to reside in the United States.

American Response:
In Afghanistan, Pakistan, and Worldwide

On October 7, 2001 the United States initiated Operation Enduring Freedom (the initial name, Operation Infinite Justice, was changed on September 25) providing air support, cash, and special operations forces for the Afghani anti-Taliban Northern Alliance. With American aid, the Northern Alliance quickly defeated the Taliban and al-Qaeda. Taliban commanders, often induced by CIA-funded bribes, switched sides to the Northern Alliance rather than face American airpower. On November 10, Mazar-e-Sharif was captured by the Northern Alliance. On November 14, the Northern Alliance captured Kabul, the capital of Afghanistan. On December 7, with American support, the Northern Alliance captured the Taliban's main power center, Kandahar.

In November, an American bombing raid killed al-Qaeda's military commander Muhammad Atef. Atef, a former Egyptian police officer and a member of Egypt's al-Jihad, had been a member of al-Qaeda since the early 1990s. He was appointed head of military operations in 1996 and he orchestrated the 1998 embassy bombings. He was married to a teenaged daughter of bin Laden.

Following the defeats at their power centers, al-Qaeda and the Taliban faded into the Afghan countryside. In December 2001, Afghan forces, with American support, attacked al-Qaeda/Taliban forces in the caves of the Tora Bora Mountains in eastern Afghanistan. It is believed that bin Laden was in Tora Bora but that he and substantial numbers of al-Qaeda fighters escaped to Pakistan.

In March 2002 in Operation Anaconda, over 1,000 United States troops along with 1,000 allied Afghans and 200 soldiers from members of the American-led anti-terrorism coalition engaged in an intense battle with several hundred entrenched al-Qaeda fighters in the Shah-I-Kot Valley south of Gardez in central Afghanistan. It is estimated that between 450 and 650 al-Qaeda fighters were killed in the fighting. Eight American soldiers were killed and over 40 were wounded.

Following Operation Anaconda, there were several large-scale operations to locate al-Qaeda and Taliban forces, some spearheaded by the British Royal Marines. While they located substantial caches of weapons and documents in mountain caves throughout Afghanistan, they did not encounter Taliban or al-Qaeda forces.

Parallel to the fighting in Afghanistan, nations around the world joined American counter-terrorism efforts by arresting al-Qaeda operatives. Cells were discovered throughout Europe. In the months following the September 11 attacks over $100 million of al-Qaeda money was frozen as authorities worldwide cooperated to shut down al-Qaeda funding.

Al-Qaeda Regroups

The American attack on al-Qaeda's state sponsor, Taliban-ruled Afghanistan, substantially disrupted al-Qaeda activity. Post 9/11 al-Qaeda attempted a number of terrorist attacks. On December 22, Richard Reid, a British convert to Islam, attempted to detonate explosives planted in his shoes on American Airlines Flight 63. On April 11, 2002 in Tunisia, al-Qaeda ignited a fuel tanker outside of a synagogue, killing 20, most of whom were German tourists.

As al-Qaeda shifted to guerrilla tactics, smaller scale engagements took place both in Afghanistan and in neighboring Pakistan. Hundreds of al-Qaeda members are believed to have fled, hiding in the tribal regions along Pakistan's border with Afghanistan and in Pakistan's cities, particularly the enormous port city of Karachi From Karachi, some al-Qaeda members fled farther afield to Yemen, the Persian Gulf and beyond. It is believed that Iran has been aiding al-Qaeda members who relocated to Lebanon, where they are cooperating with Iran's proxy Hizbullah.

With the movement of al-Qaeda operatives to Pakistan, violence against foreigners and Christians increased dramatically as did terrorist violence in disputed Kashmir. On December 13, 2001 al-Qaeda affiliates Lashkar-e-Toiba and Jaish-e-Muhammad attacked India's Parliament, bringing India and Pakistan to the brink of war and complicating Pakistan's efforts to assist the American campaign against al-Qaeda.

Al-Qaeda allies within Pakistan launched a terror campaign against Westerners there. American journalist Daniel Pearl was kidnapped and murdered in January 2002. Truck bombs struck a bus carrying French technicians in Karachi on May 8, 2002, killing 14, and the United States consulate in Karachi, killing 14 Pakistanis on June 14, 2002. Churches, Christian schools, and offices of Christian organizations were attacked and Sunni Muslim violence against Shi'ite Muslims also rose.

Afghanistan was also wracked with violence intended to destabilize the new regime. Several top officials in the Afghan government have been assassinated, and car bombs have detonated in Kabul. On September 5, 2002 a powerful car bomb in the central market of Kabul killed 22 and wounded nearly 100. That day, Afghan President Hamid Karzai survived an assassination attempt. It is believed that al-Qaeda and the Taliban were behind this violence, possibly in conjunction with Afghan warlords.

In March 2002, Pakistani and American forces raided several al-Qaeda safe houses in Pakistan and captured Abu Zubayda, al-Qaeda's military commander. A Palestinian born in Saudi Arabia, Zubayda had been tried and convicted *in absentia* in Jordan for orchestrating the millennium plot. In addition to capturing Zubayda, documents and electronic records in his possession have proven to be an essential window into the inner workings of al-Qaeda.

Throughout the summer of 2002, al-Qaeda operatives were arrested throughout the United States, Western Europe, and the Middle East. However, the war against the financing of terrorism had slowed because of different banking systems and evidentiary standards. Where $100 million linked to bin Laden was frozen in the months following 9/11, for eight months of 2002 only $10 million additional funds had been frozen. In August 2002, relatives of the 9/11 victims filed a 15 count, $1 trillion lawsuit suing banks, foundations, and individuals for bankrolling the al-Qaeda network.

September 11, 2002, the first anniversary of the attacks, passed without incident – although several plots against American embassies were foiled. In Karachi, Pakistani security forces captured Ramzi bin al-Sibh, a Yemeni who masterminded the 9/11 attacks. Bin al-Sibh would have been one of the hijackers but was denied a visa to enter the United States. Bin al-Sibh wired money to the bombers from Hamburg.

A New Wave of International Terror

On October 6, 2002 *al-Jazeera* broadcast an audiotape in which bin Laden threatened more attacks on the United States and its interests, and a new wave of international terror began. Later that day off the coast of Yemen, a small boat loaded with explosives rammed the *Limburg*, a French oil tanker. One crewman was killed and 90,000 barrels of oil spilled. The Islamic Army of Aden (IAA) a Yemeni-based al-Qaeda affiliate claimed responsibility. Two days later a pair of gunmen attacked United States Marines training in Kuwait. One Marine was killed before the the gunmen was killed.

On October 12, 2002, on Bali, an island in Indonesia, a massive car bomb and a suicide bomber exploded close to nightclubs frequented by Western tourists. Over 190 people were killed; over half were British and Australian tourists. Over 300 people were injured. Al-Qaeda's Southeast Asian affiliate Jemaah Islamiyah (JI) was held responsible. The attack was on the second anniversary of the attack on the USS *Cole* in Yemen.

These attacks indicated an al-Qaeda resurgence in Yemen and Southeast Asia. Authorities in Southeast Asia cracked down on JI operatives. In November 2002, Indonesia arrested seven suspects in the Bali bombing including the Indonesian operations chief Imam Samudra. Indonesia has also detained Sheikh Abu Bakr Ba'asyir, the alleged spiritual leader of JI. In Yemen on November 4, 2002, six al-Qaeda operatives were killed when an American missile struck their car. Among the six was Qaed Salim Sunian al-Harethi, also known as Abu Ali, who was one of the organizers of the October 2000 attack on the USS *Cole* and was believed to be the al-Qaeda chief in Yemen. Another of the individuals killed in the attack was linked to a suspected al-Qaeda cell in Lackawanna, NY. In November, al-Qaeda's chief of operations for the Persian Gulf region, Abd al-Rahim al-Nashiri, was arrested. After Abu Zubayda, al-Nashiri was the highest ranking al-Qaeda operative to have been captured.

On November 28, 2002, three suicide bombers drove a car into the lobby of an Israeli-owned hotel in Mombassa, Kenya. Twelve people were killed, including three Israelis, and 80 people were injured. At almost the same time, anti-aircraft missiles were fired at an Israeli charter plane leaving Mombassa for Tel Aviv. The plane, which had 271 passengers and crew, landed safely in Tel Aviv. The serial numbers on the missile casings revealed that the missiles were from the same batch as missiles fired at a plane carrying Israeli Foreign Minister Shimon Peres near Prague in November 2001, and a those fired at an American military transport plane near Prince Sultan Air Base, Saudi Arabia in May 2002.

On March 1, 2003 Pakistani security forces captured al-Qaeda operational planner, Khalid Sheikh Mohammed. His capture led to many further arrests. According to the Federal Bureau of Investigation, over 3,000 have been captured since September 11, 2001.

Leadership
Osama bin Laden

Born in Riyadh in 1957, Osama bin Laden is the 17th son, and one of 50 children, of Muhammad bin Laden, a Saudi construction magnate. Muhammad bin Laden was born in the village of al-Rubat, in the Hadramawt region of Yemen. He immigrated to Saudi Arabia as a young man where he eventually founded a construction company that grew into the Saudi Binladen Group, which is now worth about $5 billion. In 1967,

Muhammad bin Laden was killed in a plane crash when Osama was 10 years old. Bin Laden's mother, who is Syrian, is still alive and before 9/11 was in regular contact with her son.

Osama married his first wife when he was 17 and he attended King Abdul Aziz University in Jeddah, where he took a degree in economics and public administration and was taught by leading Islamists including Abdallah Azzam and Mohammed Qutb (a brother of Muslim Brotherhood idealogue Sayyid Qutb). In 1980, he traveled to Afghanistan, where he helped the anti-Soviet resistance build installations. He also raised money in Saudi Arabia for the war in Afghanistan and participated in the 1986 battle of Jalalabad as well as other fighting.

As the only member of the Saudi elite to relocate to Afghanistan and commit himself personally to the Jihad, bin Laden became a celebrity in Saudi Arabia. While his accusations of Saudi corruption led him to be expelled from Saudi Arabia, he has personal relationships with many members of the Saudi elite.

Bin Laden has four wives and many children. His third eldest son, Saad, is about 23 years old and is taking a more prominent role in al-Qaeda's leadership. It is believed that bin Laden suffers from diabetes and possibly kidney failure. In a videotaped statement released in January 2002, he did not move the left side of his body, suggesting a stroke or a wound. It is unclear whether or not he is still alive.

Ayman Zawahiri

Ayman Zawahiri is the leading advisor to Osama bin Laden, and is believed by some to be the real leader of al-Qaeda. Born to a distinguished Egyptian family in 1951, his father was a professor of pharmacology at Cairo University and his grandfather was the Grand Imam of al-Azhar University, the most prestigious school of Sunni Islam. His great uncle was the first Secretary-General of the Arab League.

In 1966, at the age of 15, Zawahiri joined the Muslim Brotherhood and started an underground terrorist cell at his high school. He earned a medical degree in 1974 from Cairo University and practiced as a pediatrician. He is the author of several books; his best-known is *Bitter Harvest*, a critique of the Muslim Brotherhood. In the late 1970s, he took control of al-Jihad, which was responsible for the 1981 assassination of Egyptian President Anwar Sadat. Zawahiri was arrested shortly after the assassination but was released in 1984 because he could not be directly linked to the crime.

In 1980 Zawahiri worked in a clinic in Afghanistan, where he met bin Laden. Fluent in French and English, Zawahiri has acted as bin Laden's interpreter. In the mid-1990s, during a power struggle within al-Jihad, Zawahiri was temporarily displaced from his leadership role. During his hiatus, he studied medical journals looking for information relevant to constructing chemical and biological weapons.

Within al-Jihad, Zawahiri led the least compromising faction, and led endeavors to carry al-Jihad's fight beyond Egypt's borders. He was also the leading proponent of merging with al-Qaeda.

In February 1999, an Egyptian court sentenced him to death *in absentia*. He may be responsible for providing medical treatment to bin Laden.

Khalid Sheikh Mohammed

Khalid Sheikh Mohammed, a Kuwaiti-born Palestinian, is one of al-Qaeda's top operational planners and chair of al-Qaeda's military committee. He is the alleged mastermind of the September 11 attacks and is also believed to be involved in the first World Trade Center attack, the 1995 plot to hijack several airliners over the Pacific Ocean, a 1999 plot to assassinate the Pope in the Philippines, the attack on the synagogue in Tunisia, and the Bali bombing. He was arrested by Pakistani authorities on March 1, 2003 in the city of Rawalpindi.

Saif al-Adil

Saif al-Adil, chief of operations in Afghanistan and Pakistan and possibly worldwide, is a former Egyptian special forces operative and was a leader of the Egyptian al-Jihad. He moved to Afghanistan in 1988 to fight the Soviets and was a founding member of al-Qaeda. Al-Adil received training from Hizbullah and may have hidden in Iran for a time after the initial United States attack on Afghanistan, although he is believed to be back in Afghanistan.

Sheikh Said al-Sharif

Sheikh Said al-Sharif, Osama bin Laden's brother-in-law, is al-Qaeda's chief financial officer.

Abu Mohammed al-Masri

Abu Mohammed al-Masri (a.k.a. Abdullah Ahmed Abdullah) is the chief financial officer in Pakistan and Afghanistan. Approximately 40 years old, al-Masri is an Egyptian who was active in al-Jihad. He first traveled to Afghanistan in the 1980s and relocated to Sudan with bin Laden in 1991. He has contacts in West Africa, where he has traveled to purchase diamonds from the Revolutionary United Front (RUF) in Liberia.

Organization

Al-Qaeda has been described as operating like a global foundation or corporation, providing training, financing, and technical expertise for Islamist terrorists all over the world. Beneath bin Laden, the Majlis al-Shura, or consultative council, directs al-Qaeda activities. The council has four committees: military, religious, finance, and media. The top leaders select council members.

Within al-Qaeda there are several parallel structures. Brigade 055 is a guerrilla army that was founded as an elite force of about 2,000 to fight alongside the Taliban. Brigade 055 veterans often receive advanced training in order to found and lead terror cells. Al-Qaeda maintains an international network of hundreds of these cells, which usually have 2-15 members. Cells are encouraged to show initiative in their operations, and promising operations receive financial support and technical assistance. Al-Qaeda is believed to have founded sleeper cells, which integrate into the surrounding society and only become active after years and even decades of infiltration. Al-Qaeda recruits from throughout the Muslim world, but cells usually consist of members of uniform nationality. Within al-Qaeda, different nationalities specialize in different operations. For example, Algerian cells specialize in credit card fraud, Libyans forge identity documents, and Egyptians run al-Qaeda training facilities. Overall al-Qaeda membership is estimated at around 3,500.

Al-Qaeda also provides financing, training, and logistical support to other Islamist organizations throughout the world. These organizations may in turn assist al-Qaeda operations and may receive technical support from al-Qaeda for high-profile operations. Members of over two dozen Islamist organizations have received al-Qaeda training.

Central to al-Qaeda's ability to function globally, is its communications network. Al-Qaeda has made extensive use of the internet to coordinate the activities of cells on different continents. Operatives have been known to use chatrooms, websites, and e-mail to communicate. One possible method of communication is implanting coded messages in pictures posted on websites. Satellite phones, which are vulnerable to electronic eavesdropping, are restricted to the top leadership. While al-Qaeda has used commercial encryption software to foil eavesdropping, the organization also makes use of human couriers. Al-Qaeda's agent handling systems are similar to those of national intelligence agencies. Despite the fact that many of these cells operate in Muslim countries where Arabic is not spoken, Arabic remains the language of al-Qaeda communications.

Besides the multi-volume terrorist guidebook *Encyclopedia of the Afghan Jihad*, al-Qaeda has produced jihad videos featuring footage of violent combat in Chechnya, Afghanistan and elsewhere and instructional videos about explosives manufacturing to inform its operatives.

Al-Qaeda and bin Laden finance business enterprises, sometimes for potential income, but also as a cover for future terrorist activities. Al-Qaeda uses non-governmental organizations (NGOs) to funnel money and support to al-Qaeda propaganda and operational activities.

Financial Support

Al-Qaeda finances are shrouded in secrecy. There has been international cooperation in freezing the assets of several dozen organizations linked to al-Qaeda, but these may represent only a fraction of al-Qaeda's financial network. Money is transferred to al-Qaeda and within the organization through a number of untraceable means, including front corporations, secret bank accounts, and legitimate charities. Al-Qaeda's money laundering activities are aided by inconsistent regulation worldwide and particularly weak regulation of the banking centers of the Persian Gulf. Al-Qaeda also avoids the modern banking system by using the informal *hawala* banking system that is used in much of the Muslim world and by transferring funds in the form of cash or untraceable hard assets like precious stones.

The first source of al-Qaeda funds is the personal fortune of Osama bin Laden. Estimates of his personal wealth have ranged from $35 million to $250 million. According to testimony from arrested al-Qaeda operatives, in the mid-1990s al-Qaeda appeared to be low on funds, in part because the Saudi government froze bin Laden's assets in 1994 and also because of his massive investment in projects in Sudan. But after relocating to Afghanistan, al-Qaeda had replenished its resources and was launching ambitious plans worldwide. It is believed that sympathetic family members have continued to make sure that bin Laden has access to some of his inheritance. Whatever the extent of bin Laden's personal fortune, it is unlikely he could support an international network with thousands of paid operatives for nearly a decade.

In the early 1980s, bin Laden was an effective fundraiser on behalf of the Afghan fight against the Soviets. In the early 1990s, al-Qaeda's fundraising situation improved when contributions from Gulf Arabs to the PLO declined because of Arafat's support for the Iraqi invasion of Kuwait. Bin Laden's contacts within Saudi Arabia reach to the highest levels, and although he was stripped of his Saudi citizenship, it is believed that major public figures in Saudi Arabia, including members of the royal family, are sympathetic to him and continue to fund al-Qaeda. One avenue of this funding could be the Saudi Ministry of Religious Works and Saudi government-controlled charities, which distribute billions of dollars annually to promote strict Wahhabi Islam worldwide. This funding supports religious schools all over the world, including the United States. Saudi charities supported seminaries around the world, including the madrasas of Pakistan, which spawned the Taliban and from which many al-Qaeda members were recruited.

Zakat, or charity, is a central practice of Islam. Devout Muslims are required to donate 2.5 percent of their income to worthy causes. Al-Qaeda has systematically infiltrated major Muslim charitable organizations in order to raise and disseminate money. For example, the International Islamic Relief Organization provided weapons and support for Abu Sayyaf and the Moro Islamic Liberation Front in the Philippines, as well as Hamas and PIJ in the West Bank and Gaza. In Bosnia, the director of the Benevolence International Foundation was arrested in April 2002 for providing weapons to Islamists. Investigators found weapons and pictures of the director and bin Laden together handling weapons. It is believed that dozens of Islamic charities are under al-Qaeda's control and are used to funnel money to support terror activities. In some cases, these donations are not knowingly made to al-Qaeda.

While in Sudan, bin Laden founded a network of business enterprises. These businesses range from small farms and fishing operations – some of which double as providers of logistical support for terror operations – to multi-national investment and construction companies. This network allows al-Qaeda to invest money (often in the West) and facilitate its movement, without linking it directly to terrorism. Investigations have focused on al-Taqwa Management Company, an investment firm with offices in Switzerland and Panama that is accused of helping to manage bin Laden's assets.

In addition to using loopholes in international finance systems, al-Qaeda is also involved in a number of illicit activities. Al-Qaeda worked in conjunction with the Taliban to produce and distribute opium and heroin. Al-Qaeda may also extort money from Middle Eastern businessmen in order to protect their interests from attack. Al-Qaeda is believed to be heavily involved in smuggling precious stones and metal — gold, rubies, sapphires, diamonds, and Tanzanite. Its international network and secretive operations lend themselves to smuggling precious stones. The Taliban acquired weapons from Victor Bout, an international arms dealer who was a leading source of weapons for African terrorist groups. Bout was known to take payment in gold and diamonds. Al-Qaeda has been rumored to have bought diamonds from Liberia's Revolutionary United Front and to have sold them in Europe. The Saudi Binladen Group, the bin Laden family corporation (which officially disavows Osama bin Laden), acquired a major stake in Global Diamond Resources in 1997. Local al-Qaeda cells are encouraged to be self-sufficient and members often engage in illegal activities such as credit card fraud and auto theft to raise funds.

The *hawala* system, an informal traditional means of transferring money in the Muslim world, is also used extensively by al-Qaeda. Relying strictly on trust, the *hawala* system does not keep modern records and consequently financial transfers are untraceable. Centered in Dubai, the *hawala* can move money almost anywhere in the world within a few hours.

Links to States and Terrorist Organizations

Many terror groups have merged with al-Qaeda, including the two major Egyptian terrorist groups, al-Jihad and al-Gama'a al-Islamiyya, and the two major Algerian terror groups, the Armed Islamic Group (GIA) and the Salafist Group for Preaching and Combat (GSPC). They are detailed in their own entries. There is an al-Qaeda affiliated terrorist group in almost every country of the Middle East, such as the Libyan Islamist Fighting Group, which was responsible for the 1994 murder of two German nationals, Silvan Becker and his wife. Becker was German intelligence's top Arabist and his death hampered the German government's ability to monitor Islamist activity in Germany. Al-Qaeda has numerous affiliated groups in Asia, and these groups are described in the entry on Al-Qaeda Affiliates in Asia.

Al-Qaeda also has links with almost all of the major Islamist terror groups in the world. During its time in Sudan, al-Qaeda — under Sudanese leader Hassan al-Turabi's sponsorship — provided training and funding for and developed links with Islamist organizations throughout the Middle East, including Hamas and Palestinian Islamic Jihad (PIJ). Links with some major Middle Eastern states and terrorist organizations are detailed below; others are described in their individual entries.

Iran/Hizbullah

Despite al-Qaeda's strict adherence to Sunni Islam and Iran's Shi'ite orientation, Iran, and its proxy Hizbullah, have a history of cooperation with al-Qaeda. While al-Qaeda was based in Sudan, Sudanese leader Hassan al-Turabi facilitated meetings between al-Qaeda and Iranian intelligence. Bin Laden is believed to have met with Hizbullah's Special Operations Chief Imad Mughniyah in 1996. Reportedly bin Laden praised Mughniyah for his success in attacking American targets and the consequent American withdrawals. Al-Qaeda ran a guesthouse for terrorists training in Lebanon, and al-Qaeda operatives studied Hizbullah tactics. Hizbullah trained al-Qaeda bomb makers to make explosives that could destroy buildings and may have provided a counterfeit passport for one of the planners of the 1995 attack on Egypt's embassy in Islamabad, Pakistan. Iranian intelligence may have taught al-Qaeda techniques for agent handling and managing global operations.

Since relocating to Afghanistan, al-Qaeda and Iran contacts have continued. According to intelligence sources, in the period just before the 1998 embassy bombings, about 10% of the satellite phone calls from al-Qaeda leaders have been to Iran. Mughniyah, who has extensive hijacking experience, may have secretly traveled to Germany to help train the 9/11 hijackers. Since the collapse of the Taliban, Iran transferred some al-Qaeda detainees to Saudi custody, but has also helped smuggle hundreds of al-Qaeda operatives out of Afghanistan and into Lebanon, where they are linking up with Hizbullah, and providing a haven for al-Qaeda leaders such as Saif al-Adil. In August 2002 Iran reportedly helped smuggle al-Qaeda gold out of Afghanistan to Sudan.

Iraq/Abu Nidal

Iraq may have had some connections with al-Qaeda, both directly and through the terrorist group Abu Nidal. Al-Qaeda's second-in-command, Ayman Zawahiri, was reported to have traveled to

Baghdad and met with Iraqi President Saddam Hussein in 1992. Sudan's Hassan al-Turabi also facilitated meetings between Iraqi officials and al-Qaeda in the mid-1990s. Reportedly in October 1998 a delegation of Iraqi intelligence figures led by Iraqi Intelligence Chief Faruq Hijazi traveled to Afghanistan to discuss the possibility of al-Qaeda relocating to Iraq. Iraq may also have helped supply al-Qaeda with weapons, explosives, and possibly components for chemical and biological weapons. There are also reports that al-Qaeda operatives received training at a camp run by Iraqi intelligence at Salman Pak, south of Baghdad and of Iraqi intelligence operatives traveling to Afghanistan to provide training to al-Qaeda.

There are reports, partially confirmed by Czech intelligence, that Mohammed Atta, the suspected 9/11 lead hijacker, traveled twice to Prague to meet with Iraqi intelligence operatives. Before leaving for the United States, Atta traveled from Hamburg, Germany to Prague and had meetings at the Iraqi embassy. In April 2001, Atta is believed to have met Ahmed Khalil Ibrahim Samir Ani in Prague, where they may have discussed bombing a *Radio Free Europe/Radio Liberty* building. *Radio Free Europe/Radio Liberty* was broadcasting anti-Saddam programming to Iraq. Later that month, Czech authorities expelled Samir Ani for engaging in "activity incompatible with his diplomatic status."

These meetings may have been facilitated by the Abu Nidal Organization (ANO). Ziyad Samir al-Jarrah, a Lebanese citizen and one of the September 11, 2001 hijackers, lived with his uncle Assem Omar al-Jarrah in Germany for a year and a half before linking up with the Hamburg al-Qaeda cell that perpetrated 9/11. Al-Jarrah came into contact with the ANO while it was based in Libya. He was later recruited by Stasi, East German intelligence, and served as a liaison between the two. Shortly before 9/11, al-Jarrah left Germany saying that he planned to retire in Lebanon.

Iraq and al-Qaeda may be cooperating in northern Iraq, where the Iraqi Kurds have built a semi-independent polity protected by the United States. Since 1998, Islamists based in northern Iraq near the Iranian border have been attacking the nascent Kurdish democracy. In September 2001, two Islamist factions merged to form Jund al-Islam (Army of Islam) and received $300,000 in seed money from Osama bin Laden, which later changed its name to Ansar al-Islam (Partisans of Islam). The core of Ansar al-Islam's 600 fighters are Kurds and Arabs who fought in Afghanistan and came into contact with al-Qaeda.

The head of Ansar al-Islam is Mullah Krekar, a Kurd who fought in Afghanistan, and currently lives in the Netherlands and Norway. Based in the town of Beyare, Islamists in northern Iraq have conducted a wave of assassinations, including that of Fransu Hariri, a prominent Kurdish Christian politician and an attempted assassination of the Prime Minister of the eastern Kurdish region Barham Salih in April 2002. Islamists also massacred 42 captured Kurdish troops in September 2001 and have instituted strict Islamic law in the villages under their control. Captured Ansar al-Islam members have stated that Iraqi intelligence operatives help direct the group's activities. Ansar al-Islam is reportedly involved in heroin smuggling and may also receive assistance from Iran, which has facilitated the transit of people and supplies from Afghanistan to Iraq, and shares Iraq's opposition to a secular Kurdish democracy.

Jordanian-born, Abu Musab al-Zarqawi, reportedly one of the top 25 leaders in al-Qaeda, is based in the area controlled by Ansar al-Islam. After escaping from Afghanistan, al-Zarqawi received medical treatment in Baghdad before relocating to northern Iraq. He is believed to have ordered and funded the October 2002 murder of United States diplomat Laurence Foley in Jordan and to have sent ricin production instructions to the London terrorist cell arrested in January 2003.

Pakistan

The Pakistani government, and particularly the Interservices Intelligence agency (ISI), along with major Pakistani Islamist organizations all supported Muslims who traveled to Afghanistan to aid in the war against the Soviets. Jamaat-e-Islaami (JeI), Pakistan's leading Islamist organization, is similar to and has extensive links with the Muslim Brotherhood. Like the Muslim Brotherhood, JeI attempts to place its members in key roles within the national security apparatus and it has had some success cultivating an Islamist faction within the ISI. When the war against the Soviet Union ended, the ISI and the JeI helped Afghan veterans shift their focus to Kashmir, Central Asia, and beyond. Another Pakistani Islamist organization, Jamaat-e-Ulema Islam (JUI), a frequent rival of JeI, established the madrasas in Pakistan's border region that gave rise to the Taliban. JUI's leader, Sheikh Mir Hamzah, was a signatory on bin Laden's February 1998 fatwa declaring war on America.

After the attacks of 9/11, Pakistani President Pervez Musharraf committed the country to supporting the United States. He permitted American forces to operate in parts of Pakistan, arrested hundreds of al-Qaeda operatives, shared intelligence with the United States, and banned several groups affiliated with al-Qaeda. Elements of Pakistan's government and society remain aligned with the Taliban and al-Qaeda, particularly JeI and JUI along with segments of the ISI. With their help, it is believed that many al-Qaeda operatives escaped United States forces and are now based in the Pakistani region bordering Afghanistan or have moved out of Pakistan to the Middle East. While ostensibly part of Pakistan, the Pakistani government has limited control over these regions where many of the tribal leaders are sympathetic to the Taliban and al-Qaeda.

JeI and JUI, along with several other Islamist parties, formed a united front opposing Pakistan's support for the United States. Several members of the front were officially banned, including several Kashmiri groups and two domestic Pakistani terror groups, Sipah-e-Sahaba (SeS) and its more extremist offshoot Lashkar-e-Jhangvi (LeJ). SeS is a mass movement with thousands of members. LeJ is secretive and has a small number of highly skilled operatives. It is believed that the leadership of the two organizations is linked. The SeS and LeJ had traditionally targeted Pakistani Shi'ites and Iranian institutions in Pakistan. More recently, they have been linked with the string of attacks against Westerners and Christians in Pakistan. Both organizations receive support from JeI and JUI. Members of both organizations trained at al-Qaeda camps in Afghanistan and with Kashmir-based terrorist groups. Thousands of SeS members trained in Afghanistan.

In the 2002 elections in Pakistan, a coalition of Islamist parties, including JeI and JUI, won about 11% of the national election and control of the provincial government on the Afghan border. The Islamist parties have used their electoral influence to release suspected terrorists and deter authorities from investigating possible terrorist activities.

Saudi Arabia

Because of bin Laden's Saudi origins, the Saudi citizenship of 15 of the 19 September 11 hijackers, as well as Saudi support for the Taliban, the Saudi relationship with al-Qaeda has come under increasing scrutiny. While Saudi officials claim to have arrested over 100 al-Qaeda operatives in Saudi Arabia and to have frozen hundreds of millions of dollars of al-Qaeda affiliated assets, there is continuing evidence of high-level links between the Saudi royal family and prominent Saudi citizens and al-Qaeda. Several charities based in Saudi Arabia have been accused of supporting al-Qaeda activities. The World Muslim League is an umbrella organization of humanitarian organizations sponsored by the Saudi government; several of its constituent organizations and senior officials have been linked to al-Qaeda. One member organization, the International Islamic Relief Organization (IIRO), headed by bin Laden's brother-in-law, Mohammed Jamal Khalifa, channeled funds to terrorist organizations including Abu Sayyaf and Hamas. An IIRO employee in India was linked to 1999 plots to attack American consulates in India. The Kabul offices of the al-Wafa Humanitarian Organization contained a laboratory with materials for manufacturing explosives. The World Assembly of Muslim Youth (WAMY) headed by bin Laden's brother Abdullah has been linked with radical Muslim movements in Kashmir and the Philippines. The al-Haramain Islamic Foundation has been linked to financing for operatives in Chechnya and Indonesia. The Bosnian offices of the Saudi High Commission for Aid to Bosnia (founded by Saudi Prince Salman bin Abdul-Aziz) and the Bosnian Ideal Future (linked to the Benevolence International Foundation of Chicago) were both raided and found to possess materials for making fake identification and other documents and equipment relating to terrorist activity.

These charitable organizations are supported by wealthy Saudi (and other Gulf-based) businessmen, who often have personal connections with both the Saudi royal family and the bin Laden family. In November 2002, the CIA circulated a list to international bankers of 12 prominent Saudi businessmen believed to be funneling millions to al-Qaeda.

Bin Laden's own relationship with the royal family is complex. His role in the Afghanistan war had made him a celebrity in Saudi Arabia and his family was close to the royal family and the wealthy elite of Saudi Arabia. He has also supported the London-based Advice and Reform Committee, which is opposed to the rule of the Saudi royal family. While he was expelled from Saudi Arabia and stripped of his Saudi citizenship, Saudi intelligence maintained links with bin Laden. The August 15, 2002 lawsuit filed by the families of 9/11 victims against members of the Saudi royal family and Saudi businesses, individuals, and organizations alleges that after the 1995-1996 attacks against American troops in Saudi Arabia, the Saudi royal family paid bin Laden several hundred million dollars to refrain from attacking targets within Saudi Arabia.

The Saudis were key supporters of the Taliban, but they did not pressure the Taliban to hand over bin Laden. In July 1998 Saudi intelligence chief Prince Turki al-Faisal visited Kandahar and arranged for the Taliban to receive 400 new pickup trucks. After the August 1998 embassy bombings, the Saudis, under American pressure, began to ask the Taliban to hand over bin Laden. Saudi intelligence may have preferred bin Laden isolated in Afghanistan, in order to keep the links between him and members of the Saudi royal family hidden. Two weeks before 9/11, Prince Turki was replaced as intelligence chief.

Syria/Lebanon

Despite its presence on the United States' list of state sponsors of terror, Syria has provided some cooperation to the United States against al-Qaeda. Syria has arrested individuals believed to be affiliated with al-Qaeda and has provided intelligence to the United States from captured Syrian al-Qaeda operatives, particularly Mamoun Darkanzali, who was a financial conduit to the Hamburg cell, and Mohammed Zammar, a senior al-Qaeda commander.

But Syria has also permitted about 200 al-Qaeda operatives to pass through and reorganize in Palestinian refugee camps in Lebanon, particularly Ayn al-Hilweh, where an al-Qaeda affiliate, Asbat al-Ansar (Band of the Partisans), has been operating since the mid-1990s. Syria controls Lebanon and has prevented Lebanese troops from entering Ayn al-Hilweh. Asbat al-Ansar has about 200 members and is led by Abd al-Karim al-Sa'di (a.k.a. Abu Mohjen) who has been sentenced to death for the 1996 murder of a prominent Lebanese Sunni leader. Asbat al-Ansar also murdered four Lebanese judges in 1997 in revenge for sentences against their operatives. Several Asbat al-Ansar operatives fought in Chechnya, and Asbat al-Ansar has attacked Russian targets in Lebanon. Asbat al-Ansar is also linked to the London-based International Islamic Front and has arranged to send Palestinians to bin Laden's camps in Afghanistan. Although Asbat al-Ansar officially denied links to al-Qaeda, senior al-Qaeda operative Salah Hajir reportedly visited Ayn al-Hilweh in January 2002 to help coordinate the relocation of fleeing al-Qaeda members. On that trip, Hajir also met with Hizbullah leaders.

In April 2000, a Jordanian court sentenced *in absentia* Munir Maqdah, a Fatah leader in Lebanon based in Ayn al-Hilweh, to death for his role in plotting attacks on American and Israeli targets in Jordan. Jordanian prosecutors charged Maqdah with supplying explosives and weapons to the cell, which Jordanian prosecutors claimed was linked to al-Qaeda. Maqdah claimed that he did not know the cell's activities were linked to bin Laden, but that he salutes bin Laden and his achievements.

Areas of Operation

Al-Qaeda has demonstrated the ability to operate worldwide, either directly or through affiliates. Al-Qaeda or an affiliate has established itself in every predominantly Muslim nation in the world and within virtually every major Muslim community around the globe. Cells have been found in virtually every Middle Eastern state, from Morocco where in early 2002 al-Qaeda operatives were planning to attack American and British warships in the Straits of Gibraltar to the Gulf States where al-Qaeda operatives have infiltrated local security forces and have targeted American soldiers. Al-Qaeda has launched major attacks in the United States, Africa, the Middle East, and Asia and has the capacity to do so worldwide. Following are descriptions of al-Qaeda operations in major theaters around the world. Asian operations are described in the entry on al-Qaeda's Asian Affiliates.

Africa

Africa is a major front for al-Qaeda operations, both directly and through proxies. One of the major proxies is the Somali group al-Ittihad al-Islami, which is believed to have 3,000 operatives and to have carried out the 2002 attacks on Israeli tourists in Kenya. Al-Qaeda was based in Sudan in the mid-1990s, where it had a close relationship with al-Turabi's Islamist regime. From Sudan, al-Qaeda activites expanded throughout sub-Saharan Africa, where weak states and vast lawless stretches have afforded al-Qaeda opportunities to launch terrorist attacks, engage in illicit financial activity, and operate training camps and recruit operatives. Home to over 120,000 Somalis fleeing the fighting in Somalia, the Dabaab refugee camp in Kenya close to the Somali border is believed to be a major base of al-Ittihad al-Islami. Al-Qaeda has sponsored Islamist groups in Eritrea and Uganda (where they may have helped to plan an attempted assassination of President Museveni in 1999). Al-Qaeda is also infiltrating Muslim NGOs that operate in sub-Saharan Africa in order to expand its Islamist ideology.

Al-Qaeda has sponsored numerous attacks in Africa, including the 1993 downing of a United States army helicopter in Somalia, the 1998 embassy attacks, and the 2002 attacks on Israeli tourists in Kenya. Al-Qaeda has also sponsored training camps in Africa, particularly in Somalia. A major source of al-Qaeda funding comes from smuggling precious stones and metals that are purchased from local warlords throughout the continent and bartered for weapons. Both ex-Liberian President Charles Taylor and Burkina Faso President Blaise Campaore have been linked to al-Qaeda's diamond and arms smuggling operations. In August 2002, al-Qaeda was reportedly smuggling gold to Sudan in order to rebuild its financial center in Khartoum, where al-Qaeda maintains contacts. Bin Laden has also praised Nigeria's growing Islamist movement.

The Americas

Latin America's Triborder region (where Argentina, Bolivia and Paraguay meet) is known to be a major center of terrorist activity. Hizbullah is known to have a major fundraising and money laundering network there and to have carried out operations based in the area. Hamas and al-Gama'a al-Islamiyya, an al-Qaeda affiliate, have operated in the region. Local authorities claim that al-Qaeda operatives are also present and that they were plotting attacks on United States embassies in South America in May 2001. Unconfirmed reports place al-Qaeda operatives along the Colombian-Venezuelan border.

On 9/11, al-Qaeda demonstrated its ability to strike in North America. There had been previous attempts, most notably by Ahmed Ressam, a Canadian-based operative who intended to attack the Los Angeles airport in January 2000. Al-Qaeda operatives have been identified and arrested in Michigan, New York, and the Pacific Northwest. Al-Qaeda has also raised money in the United States through its Services Office (the Brooklyn branch was the base for the 1993 World Trade Center bombing) and through Muslim charities operating in the United States such as the Benevolence International Foundation's Chicago offices. Al-Qaeda leaders, including Ayman Zawahiri and founder Abdallah Azzam, traveled to the United States in order to raise money. Al-Qaeda, along with other Islamist organizations, may be attempting to recruit within American prisons. Jose Padilla, who was arrested for plotting attacks with a radiological weapon, converted to Islam and was recruited into al-Qaeda while in prison.

The Balkans

The Balkan region is a major theater of operations for al-Qaeda. In the early 1990s, the war in Bosnia, which began shortly after the war in Afghanistan ended, was a top priority for al-Qaeda. Hundreds of veterans of the Afghanistan war fought in Bosnia, particularly around Zenica. Several Muslim charitable institutions sponsored their activities and provided logistical support in Bosnia. Al-Qaeda had an office in Zagrebandt. The Third World Relief Agency in Vienna is believed to have funneled millions in donations to Islamists in Bosnia. Al-Qaeda operatives, working for international Muslim charitable organizations in Bosnia, plotted attacks on American targets, including the United States embassy in Sarajevo.

More recently, Macedonian intelligence claims that al-Qaeda is providing support to the Kosovo Liberation Army (KLA) and that KLA members have trained in Afghanistan. Albanian intelligence claims that bin Laden established an Albanian network with links to Albanian organized crime groups. On December 5, 2002 the Macedonian consulate in Karachi, Pakistan was bombed, killing three. Al-Qaeda took credit for the attack.

Al-Jihad, which merged with al-Qaeda, was very active in the Balkans, plotting numerous attacks against local and Western targets.

Chechnya

In 1994, Russia sent troops to end Chechen independence. The ensuing war in Chechnya became a major cause in the Arab world, due in great part to its echoes of the war in Afghanistan. Al-Qaeda trained and dispatched hundreds of fighters to Chechnya, sent millions of dollars of support, and opened an office in Baku, Azerbaijan to provide support for fighters in Chechnya. In 1997, an Egyptian Jihad leader and al-Qaeda's second-in-command, Ayman Zawahiri, traveled there and considered relocating his operations to Chechnya. Alleged 9/11 leader Mohammed Atta had expressed a desire to fight there. The best-known Arab-Chechen, known as Khattab, had fought with bin Laden in Afghanistan and moved to Chechnya in 1995. Khattab commanded about 1,000 troops and was allied with the Islamist

Chechen commander Shamil Basayev. In April 2002, Khattab died, possibly poisoned by the Russian intelligence agency.

Both sides adopted brutal tactics that indiscriminately targeted civilians. Arab support for Islamist factions among the Chechens increased their prominence and power, and allowed them to extend the scope of the war beyond Chechen borders. Chechen rebels carried out several operations taking hundreds of hostages, including a 1995 seizure of a hospital in southern Russia and a 1996 seizure of a town in Dagestan. Chechens were also suspected in a series of bombings of Russian apartment complexes in September 1999 in which 300 people were killed.

Chechen terrorist activity increased in late 2002. In September 2002, Chechen terrorists blew up a bus killing 19, and in October bombed a police station in Grozny, the Chechen capital, killing 25. On October 23, 2002 about 50 Chechens took control of a Moscow theater, holding about 750 hostages and demanding a Russian withdrawal from Chechnya. Movsar Barayev, nephew of the late Islamist Chechen warlord Arbi Barayev, led the attack. On October 26 Russian commandos stormed the theater after pumping an opiate type gas into the theater. All of the Chechen terrorists and almost 100 hostages were killed and many more hostages were injured from the effects of the gas. On December 27, 2002 a pair of truck bombs blasted into the regional government headquarters in Grozny, killing more than 60. This was days after 28 Chechen militants publicly surrendered their weapons and agreed to cooperate with the pro-Russian regional government.

Fighting in Chechnya has spread to neighboring countries. Islamist led incursions in neighboring Dagestan after the first Russian-Chechen war ended in 1996 led to the large-scale reentry of Russia into Chechnya. Pankisi Gorge in Georgia is believed to have become a safe haven for Islamist forces. In February 2002, the United States dispatched 200 troops to Georgia to help train the Georgian security forces in counter-terrorism.

Israel & Jordan

Al-Qaeda has attempted numerous attacks in Jordan, including the December 1999 plot to strike American hotels there. Al-Qaeda operatives assassinated United States diplomat Laurence Foley on October 28, 2002. A Jordanian and a Libyan, were arrested and accused of plotting further attacks on Western embassies and personnel in

Amman. Jordan is also being used by al-Qaeda as a staging ground for attacking Israel.

Bin Laden has been criticized for not focusing sufficiently on Israel, and in December 2002 he reportedly announced that Israel would become a priority target for al-Qaeda. There had been several attempts by al-Qaeda to infiltrate Israel. Richard Reid the shoe-bomber, visited there to scout targets for al-Qaeda in late 2001. In February 2003, Israel sentenced Nabil Okal, who was linked to Hamas and had studied bomb making in Afghanistan, to 27 years in prison. Okal had been attempting to recruit al-Qaeda operatives in Gaza and the West Bank.

United Kingdom

Al-Qaeda's European network appears to be based in Britain. One attraction for Islamist groups operating in London is its role as a major center of Arab language media. Britain's large population of Muslims from the Indian subcontinent has been a fertile ground for recruitment and fundraising for al-Qaeda-linked Kashmiri and Pakistani groups. Ahmed Omar Saeed Sheikh, accused of murdering American journalist Daniel Pearl, was a British citizen. According to British intelligence, 1,000 British citizens were recruited to fight with the Taliban. Britain has also been the target of several attempted terror attacks.

The web of British-based organizations linked to al-Qaeda is centered on the Advice and Reform Committee, which bin Laden founded in 1994. The organization's director, Khaled al-Fawwaz, was arrested in connection with the 1998 United States embassy bombings in Africa. Several prominent Muslim clerics and publishing houses linked to al-Qaeda operate in Britain. Sheikh Omar Bakri Mohammed heads the Islamist al-Muhajiroun organization in London. In October 2002, British intelligence arrested Palestinian born Sheikh Mohammed Omar Othman (a.k.a. Abu Qatada), described by Spanish authorities as the head of al-Qaeda in Europe. Othman was convicted *in absentia* in Jordan and had been living as a political refugee in Britain since 1994. With Othman's arrest, British security learned that British al-Qaeda cells had plotted to attack Heathrow Airport, the London Underground, and ferries crossing the English Channel.

On January 5, 2003, British police arrested six Algerians in London who were linked to al-Qaeda and were producing the biological toxin ricin. This arrest led to another set of arrests of Algerians in Manchester. During questioning one of the suspects broke free and stabbed a British detective to death. These arrests led British authorities to Sheikh Abu Hamza al-Masri, the Egyptian-born imam of the North London Central Mosque in Finsbury Park. Abu Hamza, who lost both hands and an eye fighting in Afghanistan, heads an organization called Supporters of Shari'a and is wanted in Yemen for his connection to the Islamic Army of Aden. Accused 9/11 accomplice Zacarias Moussaoui and shoe-bomber Richard Reid both attended his mosque. British police raided the Finsbury Mosque on Janauary 20, 2003, arrested seven and confiscated records of al-Qaeda activities in Britain. The trustees of the mosque banned Abu Hamza from continuing to preach there.

Western Europe

Al-Qaeda has an extensive European network, with numerous cells in every nation of Western Europe, and since 9/11 over 200 al-Qaeda operatives have been arrested across Western Europe, including in the United Kingdom. Al-Qaeda cells in Europe have included people from throughout the Muslim world as well as European born Muslims. The largest contingent has been of cells affiliated with the Algerian-based Salafist Group for Preaching and Combat, which is closely linked to al-Qaeda.

Most of the planning for the 9/11 attacks occurred in the Hamburg, Germany apartment of the ringleader, Mohammed Atta. Atta and two other key September 11 hijackers, Marwan al-Shehhi and Ziad Samir Jarrah, had been living in Hamburg for several years. Five other people, including Ramzi bin al-Sibh (the 9/11 chief planner) were based in Hamburg and provided logistical and financial support. Germany is also home to other Islamist cells and front organizations and about 100 operatives who received training in Afghanistan. Islamist groups in Germany are coordinated through Muslim Brotherhood offices in Munich and Aachen.

The 9/11 planners received support from an al-Qaeda cell in Spain, which may have been founded in 1994. This cell provided support for fighters in Bosnia, Chechnya and Afghanistan and engaged in credit card fraud and money laundering to support al-Qaeda activities. Cells have also been found in Italy where an al-Qaeda/GSPC cell was planning attacks on the Vatican. There are numerous cells in France, one of which plotted an attack on Strasbourg Cathedral in December 2000; another provided support for Richard Reid. A cell in the Netherlands has been accused of planning to attack the United States embassy in Paris and American military installations in Belgium. A Dublin-based charity, the Mercy International Relief Agency, was used to front al-Qaeda operations throughout Europe. As European security increases, smaller cities on the fringe of Western Europe, such as Bratislava, Slovakia are becoming potential gateways into Europe.

The January 2003 arrests in the United Kingdom revealed the presence of major al-Qaeda cells in Spain. On January 24, 2003 Spanish police raided several apartments throughout Catalonia and arrested 16 al-Qaeda operatives (15 of whom were Algerian). They were found in possession of explosives, chemicals, timers, and remote control devices and allegedly were providing communications equipment to al-Qaeda affiliates in Chechnya.

Yemen

Yemen has been a major staging ground for al-Qaeda activities. The bin Laden family is originally from Yemen and substantial numbers of Yemenis fought in Afghanistan. Many al-Qaeda operatives and leaders, including 9/11 planner Ramzi bin al-Sibh, are from Yemen. Hundreds of foreign students have studied at radical madrasas in Yemen, including American Taliban member John Walker Lindh and Richard Reid. The Yemeni government has minimal control over major portions of the country, where tribal chiefs, many allied with al-Qaeda, hold sway.

In 1991, al-Qaeda supported a camp for Afghan veterans in Yemen. The first attacks linked to al-Qaeda were the December 1992 bombings of hotels in Aden, Yemen. American troops heading for Somalia had bivouacked at these hotels, but after the bombings (in which no Americans were injured) the United States stopped using Yemen as a base for Operation Restore Hope. The suspects in this bombing were members of prominent local families and were not prosecuted.

In 1994, Afghan veterans fought in Yemen's civil war on the side of the Islamist North against the Communist South, and in 1997 bin Laden considered relocating al-Qaeda to Yemen. Al-Qaeda attempted to bomb a United States warship in Aden in January 2000, and successfully attacked the USS *Cole* in October 2000.

Al-Qaeda also supported the Islamic Army of Aden (IAA), which took 16 Westerners hostage in December 1998 in an effort to force the Yemeni government to release eight British Muslims who were suspected of plotting terrorist attacks. Abu al-Hassan, the leader of the kidnappers, had fought with bin Laden in Afghanistan and one of the kidnappers was a member of Egypt's al-Jihad. He was captured by Yemeni security forces and executed on October 17, 1999. Hatem bin Fareed took over the organization, which executed a series of bombings. He was arrested in April 2001. In June 2001, a group of IAA operatives were arrested plotting to bomb the United States Embassy in Yemen. The IAA also claimed credit for the October 6, 2002 attack on a French oil tanker and is linked to Sheikh Abu Hamza al-Masri, an Egyptian-born cleric based in London who calls himself the IAA's media advisor.

The Yemeni government has attempted to ally itself with the United States and has helped to capture some al-Qaeda leaders and operatives. But its support has been inconsistent. American investigators have complained about a lack of cooperation from Yemeni officials in the investigation of the USS *Cole* bombing and those same officials insisted the October 6, 2002 attack on the French oil tanker was an accident until October 16. This weak cooperation is due to the prominent role of Islamist factions in the Yemeni government and the lack of government control over tribal leaders. In December 2001, Yemeni troops attempted to arrest three al-Qaeda operatives. A gun battle erupted between the Yemeni soldiers and tribesmen in which 20 people were killed and the wanted al-Qaeda operatives escaped. In November 2002, the United States launched a missile strike against a car with six prominent al-Qaeda operatives. On December 30, in revenge, Yemeni Islamists linked to al-Qaeda killed three Americans working at a clinic providing free health care in Jiblah, Yemen.

Targets and Tactics

Al-Qaeda views the United States as the key obstacle to its goals of imposing strict Muslim rule. Consequently, the United States has been its primary target. When bin Laden was accused of ignoring Israel, he responded that attacking the United States was the first priority since it supported Israel. Al-Qaeda and its affiliates have also attacked a range of targets associated with the West, including European tourists, regimes allied with the United States, Russia and its allies, and Israel.

Al-Qaeda operations consistently reflect the organization's diligence in reconnoitering targets. Reportedly, operatives have practiced attacking high-profile targets at mock-ups in Afghanistan. The suicide attack has become a preferred al-Qaeda instrument because it simplifies the operation by eliminating the need for the operative to escape and allows for last minute flexibility.

Recognizing the conventional superiority of the United States, al-Qaeda has devoted extensive resources to studying non-conventional means in an effort to equalize the conflict. An article in *al-Ansar*, an online journal affiliated with al-Qaeda, revealed their familiarity with the discussion of fourth generation and asymmetric warfare in the West. These concepts focus on striking high-profile critical targets and using the mass media to undermine the target society's will to fight. Al-Qaeda's target selection reflects this strategy. The attack on the USS *Cole* in Yemen sent a message of the vulnerability of American military assets. The 9/11 attack on the World Trade Center and Pentagon were attacks on prominent symbols of American commercial and military prowess. More recent attacks on an oil tanker off the coast of Yemen and on tourist destinations in Bali and Tunisia also fit this profile. The tanker attack highlighted the vulnerability of the world's oil supply and the attacks on tourist destinations maximized casualties of vacationing Western civilians and also damaged the economies of the target states by frightening tourists.

Another aspect of al-Qaeda's strategic doctrine has been its attempts to acquire unconventional means of attack. Obtaining nuclear weapons was one of al-Qaeda's a primary goals. Captured documents indicate extensive study of the issue and attempts to acquire material and expertise from outside sources. Notes taken by al-Qaeda operatives revealed sophistication on certain aspects of nuclear weapons production and ignorance of others. Al-Qaeda made efforts to acquire nuclear material through its ally, the Islamic Movement of Uzbekistan (IMU), in former Soviet Central Asia. Al-Qaeda also attempted to hire outside experts, particularly from Pakistan's nuclear weapons program. A pair of Pakistani nuclear scientists is suspected of providing al-Qaeda technical information on building nuclear weapons.

As far back as 1994, while based in Sudan, al-Qaeda was trying to acquire chemical and biological weapons. Ayman Zawahiri, al-Qaeda's second-in-command and a medical doctor, surveyed medical textbooks for methods of producing biological weapons. Some of these efforts bore fruit as videotapes captured in Afghanistan in 2002 showed al-Qaeda testing chemical weapons. Reportedly, al-Qaeda operatives in Central Asia have attempted, without success, to acquire nuclear weapons and material from former Soviet scientists.

Al-Qaeda also explored the possibility of building a "dirty bomb," a radiological bomb in which a conventional explosive is used to disperse radioactive material. On May 8, 2002, Jose Padilla, an American convert to Islam, was arrested in Chicago for plotting to construct a radiological weapon. There were also attempts to construct a radiological bomb in Afghanistan.

In Pakistan, investigators found an al-Qaeda training camp that focused on cyberwarfare. Captured documents revealed plans to hack into the computer programs that control critical infrastructure, such as dams, power systems, and mass transportation networks.

Arms recovered from Afghanistan reveal that al-Qaeda also had a substantial ability to wage conventional warfare, possessing enormous amounts of munitions, mortars, and rockets. Al-Qaeda is believed to possess Stinger anti-aircraft missiles, originally distributed by the CIA and Pakistan to Afghan forces fighting the Soviets. The Stinger is a highly effective, man-portable system. Al-Qaeda affiliates have used older Soviet SA-7 shoulder-launched anti-aircraft missile in Saudi Arabia to target American military planes and in Africa and Prague against Israeli planes.

Chronology of Major Events and Attacks

1979

Soviet forces invade Afghanistan. The United States government, Pakistan, and Saudi Arabia provide funding to support Afghan forces resisting the Soviet invasion. Over the next decade, they contribute several billion dollars to this effort. Thousands of Muslims from around the world are recruited to fight in Afghanistan.

1980

Osama bin Laden makes his first visit to Afghanistan.

Abdallah Azzam founds the Makhtab al-Khidmat (Services Office) to raise money and recruit fighters for the war in Afghanistan. By the end of the decade, it will have offices all over the world, including more than 30 offices in the United States.

1986

Osama bin Laden relocates from Saudi Arabia to Peshawar, Pakistan. Bin Laden is the largest funder of the Makhtab al-Khidmat.

1989

Osama bin Laden founds al-Qaeda.

February – The last Soviet troops withdraw from Afghanistan.

November 24 – Al-Qaeda co-founder Abdallah Azzam is assassinated in Pakistan.

1991

After being declared *persona non grata* for criticizing the Saudi royal family, bin Laden leaves Saudi Arabia for Pakistan in April. A few months later, in 1992, he settles in Sudan.

1992

December – Al-Qaeda bombs hotels in Aden, Yemen that are being used by U.S. troops participating in Operation Restore Hope in Somalia. After the bombings, the United States stops using Yemeni facilities.

1993

February 26 – World Trade Center I - A minibus containing 1,100 pounds of explosives detonates in the garage beneath the World Trade Center complex. The blast kills six people, injures 1,000, and causes $500 million worth of damage. In the 1995 trial, blind Egyptian cleric and al-Gama'a al-Islamiyya spiritual leader Sheikh Omar Abd al-Rahman and nine others, including Sudanese, Egyptian, Jordanian, and American citizens, are convicted of conspiracy and related charges. In 1998, Ramzi Yousef, leader of the WTC I bombing, receives a life sentence plus 240 years in prison. The cell that carried out the bombing is based in the Brooklyn branch of Makhtab al-Khidmat. Osama bin Laden is named an unindicted co-conspirator.

October 3-4 – In Mogadishu, Somali militiamen shoot down a pair of American Blackhawk helicopters during Operation Restore Hope. In the ensuing battle, 18 American soldiers are killed. Al-Qaeda helped train the militias. Shortly afterward, the United States announces that it will withdraw its forces from Somalia.

1994

The Advice and Reform Committee is founded in London to act as al-Qaeda's primary front group in Great Britain and Europe.

April – Saudi Arabia revokes bin Laden's citizenship.

December – World Trade Center bomber Ramzi Yousef is captured in the Philippines after a bomb he is preparing explodes. Further investigations reveal Yousef has plans to use hijacked airliners to strike American targets including the CIA headquarters in Langley, Virginia, the Pentagon and the World Trade Center. Yousef is also planning to assassinate the Pope and destroy 11 airliners over the Pacific.

1995

June 26 – Al-Qaeda is suspected of involvement in an assassination attempt on Egyptian President Hosni Mubarak in Ethiopia by Egyptian Islamists.

November 19 – Al-Qaeda provides logistical support for a suicide bomb attack by Egyptian Islamists against Egypt's embassy in Pakistan. Sixteen are killed and over 60 are wounded.

November 13 – A car bomb explosion damages a United States military installation in Riyadh, Saudi Arabia killing five Americans and two Indians and wounding 42. The Islamic Movement for Change claims responsibility. The bombers state that they were inspired by bin Laden.

1996

May – Sudan expels Osama bin Laden, who relocates to Afghanistan.

June 25 – A fuel truck carrying explosives detonates just outside the Khobar Towers, a United States military facility in Dhahran, Saudi Arabia. Nineteen American military personnel are killed and over 500 people are injured, including several hundred American personnel. Hundreds of Saudi Afghan veterans are arrested, although 13 members of Saudi Hizbullah, a Shi'a Muslim group, are indicted. Al-Qaeda involvement is suspected and bin Laden praises the bombings.

August 23 – Bin Laden issues his "Declaration of Jihad on Americans Occupying the Country of the Two Sacred Places," a 60-page religious ruling calling for Jihad against the United States and Israel.

1998

February 23 – Bin Laden issues a fatwa (religious ruling) announcing the formation of the Islamic World Front for the Struggle Against the Jews and the Crusaders, which includes the Egyptian Islamist groups al-jihad and al-Gama'a al-Islamiyya, as well as Bangladeshi and Pakistani Islamist groups.

March – Aghanistan's religious council validates bin Laden's *fatwa*, which calls for targeting both military and civilian targets of the United States and its allies.

May 26 – Osama Bin Laden holds a press conference to inaugurate the Islamic World Front.

August 7 – The United States embassies in Nairobi, Kenya and Dar-es-Salaam, Tanzania are almost simultaneously destroyed by al-Qaeda truck bombs. In Dar-es-Salaam, ten Tanzanians are killed and 77 are injured. In Nairobi, 254 people are killed, including 12 Americans, and over 5,000 are injured.

August 20 – The United States launches over 50 cruise missiles at training camps in Afghanistan affiliated with al-Qaeda and at a pharmaceutical plant in Sudan allegedly owned by bin Laden.

2000

January 3 – An al-Qaeda cell attempts to sink the USS *The Sullivans* in Yemen by ramming it with a boat loaded with explosives. The attack fails when the boat sinks.

October 12 – An al-Qaeda cell damages the USS *Cole* while it is docked in the Yemeni port of Aden by ramming it with a boat loaded with explosives. Seventeen American sailors are killed and 39 are injured. The damage to the *Cole* is estimated at $250 million.

2001

September 9 – Ahmed Shah Massoud, leader of the anti-Taliban Northern Alliance is assassinated in a suicide bombing in northern Afghanistan.

September 11 – Four airliners, taking off from the East Coast and bound for the West Coast of the United States, are hijacked by al-Qaeda terrorists. Two are flown into the two towers of the World Trade Center in New York, which collapse about an hour later. A third plane is crashed into the Pentagon. The fourth plane, possibly destined for the United States Capitol, crashes in rural Pennsylvania after the passengers fought the hijackers. Over 2,800 people are killed.

October 7 – The United States begins bombing Taliban forces and providing massive support to the Northern Alliance. Within two months, the Northern Alliance is in control of Afghanistan's major cities.

October 28 – Al-Qaeda gunmen open fire on worshippers at a church in Bahawalpur, Pakistan. Eighteen are killed and the gunmen escape.

December – Afghan forces, with American support, battle al-Qaeda/Taliban forces in the Tora Bora Mountains of Afghanistan.

December 13– Gunmen with Lashkar-e-Toiba and Jaish-e-Muhammad, Kashmir-based terrorists allied with bin Laden, attack India's Parliament Building in New Delhi, killing 12.

December 22 – An al-Qaeda bombing is averted over the Atlantic when passengers on American Airlines Flight 63 overwhelm the bomber.

2002

January – An al-Qaeda affiliate kidnaps and murders American newspaper reporter Daniel Pearl.

March – American forces in conjunction with Afghan and European allies launch Operation Anaconda against al-Qaeda forces in Afghanistan's Shah-I-Kot Valley. Several hundred al-Qaeda operatives are believed to be killed in several days of intense combat.

March – Pakistani police capture al-Qaeda military chief Abu Zubayda.

March 17 – An al-Qaeda affiliate attacks a church in Islamabad, Pakistan with hand grenades, killing five, including an American diplomat and her daughter.

April 11 – An al-Qaeda fuel tanker filled with propane explodes outside of the ancient Ghriba synagogue on the Tunisian island of Djerba. The blast kills 16: ten German tourists, a French citizen, and five Tunisians.

May 8 – An al-Qaeda car bombing outside a hotel in the southern port city of Karachi, Pakistan kills 15 people, including 11 French technicians working on a Pakistani-French naval project. Twenty-three others are injured.

June 14 – Fourteen Pakistanis are killed by an al-Qaeda car bomb explosion outside the United States Consulate in Karachi, Pakistan.

July – Trial of accused twentieth 9/11 hijacker Zacarias Moussaoui, an al-Qaeda operative, begins.

August – Relatives of 9/11 victims file a $1 trillion lawsuit against banks, foundations, charities, and Saudi officials for bankrolling the al-Qaeda network.

August 5 – Al-Qaeda gunmen kill six in an attack on a Christian school near Islamabad, Pakistan.

August 9 – Four are killed and 25 are injured in an al-Qaeda grenade attack on a church on the grounds of a Presbyterian hospital in Taxila, Pakistan.

September 5 – An al-Qaeda car bomb in Kabul kills 22 and wounds nearly 100. In Kandahar, Afghan President Hamid Karzai survives an al-Qaeda assassination attempt.

September 11 – Pakistani security forces capture Ramzi bin al-Shibh, believed to be a central figure in planning the 9/11 attacks.

October 6 – *Al-Jazeera* broadcasts an audiotape believed to be bin Laden. An explosives- laden boat rams an oil tanker off the coast of Yemen and an al-Qaeda affiliate, the Islamic Army of Aden, claims credit.

October 8 – Al-Qaeda gunmen attack United States Marines training in Kuwait. One Marine is killed.

October 12 – A car bomb and a suicide bomber attack a pair of popular nightclubs on the Indonesian island of Bali. More than 190 people are killed and over 300 people are injured. An al-Qaeda affiliate, Jemaah Islamiyah, is suspected.

November 4 – An American missile strikes a car carrying six al-Qaeda operatives, including al-Qaeda's chief officer in Yemen. The United States also captures al-Qaeda's chief of operations for the Persian Gulf, Abd al-Rahim al-Nashiri.

November 28 – A pair of attacks are launched against Israeli targets in Kenya. Three al-Qaeda suicide bombers drive into an Israeli-owned hotel in Mombassa, Kenya, killing 12. Two anti-aircraft missiles are fired by al-Qaeda operatives at an Israeli airliner carrying 271 people. The missiles miss and the plane lands safely in Tel Aviv, Israel.

December 5 – Three are killed when the Macedonian consulate in Karachi, Pakistan is bombed by al-Qaeda operatives.

Resources

Bergen, P.L. *Holy War, Inc.: Inside the Secret World of Osama bin Laden.* New York: Touchstone, 2002.

Davis, A. "Attention Shifts to the Moro Islamic Front." *Jane's Intelligence Review* 2002; Vol. 14, No. 4.

Dettmar, J. "Al-Qaeda's Links in the Balkans." Insight Magazine July 22, 2002.

Galeotti, M. "Eastern Watch: Al-Qaeda and the Chechens." *Jane's Intelligence Review* 2001; Vol. 13, No. 12.

Gambrill, G.C., and Endrawos, B. "Bin Laden's Network in Lebanon." Middle East Intelligence Bulletin September 2001; Vol. 3, No. 9 – available at www.meib.org.

Goldberg, J. "The Great Terror." *The New Yorker* March 25, 2002 – available at www.newyorker.com.

Gunaratna, R. *Inside al-Qaeda: Global Network of Terror.* New York: Columbia University Press, 2002.

Gunaratna, R. "The Singapore Connection." *Jane's Intelligence Review* 2002; Vol. 14, No. 3.

Iraqi National Congress. German Authorities Investigate Relationship between Ziyad al-Jarrah and Abu Nidal. Available at www.inc.org.uk.

Lewis, B. "License to Kill: Osama bin Laden's Declaration of Jihad." *Foreign Affairs* Nov/Dec.; Vol. 77, No. 6.

Middle East Media Research Institute. Bin Laden Lieutenant Admits to September 11 and Explains al-Qaeda's Combat Doctrine. *Special Dispatch* February 20, 2002; No. 344 – available at www.memri.org.

Raman, B. "Harkat ul-Mujahedin – An Update." Available at the South Asia Analysis Group website www.saag.org.

Rashid, A. *Taliban*. New Haven: Yale University Press, 2001.

Rashid, A. "They're only Sleeping." *The New Yorker* January 14, 2002 – available at www.newyorker.com.

Roule, T.J., Kinsell, J., and Joyce, B. "Investigators Seek to Break up al-Qaeda's Financial Structure." *Jane's Intelligence Review* 2001; Vol. 13, No. 11.

Schanzer, J. "Behind the French Tanker Bombing: Yemen's Ongoing Problems with Islamist Terrorism." *Policywatch* October 21, 2002; No. 670 – available at www.washingtoninstitute.org.

Smith, P.J. "Transnational Terrorism and the al-Qaeda Model: Confronting New Realities." *Parameters* Summer 2002; Vol. 32, No. 2, pp. 33-46 – available at carlisle-www.army.mil.

South Asia Terrorism Portal website www.satp.org. This website provides information on terrorist groups in India, Pakistan, Bangladesh, and Kashmir.

Al-Qaeda

Asian Affiliates and Operations

Central Asia

East Turkestan Islamic Movement

The East Turkestan Islamic Movement, also known as the East Turkestan Islamic Party, fights for independence for the Uighers, a Muslim minority concentrated in the western Chinese province of Xinjiang. Uighers, who are ethnically related to the Turkic peoples of Central Asia, claim that the Chinese government oppresses them. In the 1980s, China trained Uighers to fight the Russians in Afghanistan and many came back radicalized, and, in 1990, Uigher veterans of Afghanistan led an uprising in the village of Barin. Since then, according to the Chinese government, the East Turkestan Islamic Movement has committed over 200 attacks including several suicide bombings, which have resulted in the deaths of over 160 people and injuries to 440. The Chinese government claims that the East Turkestan Islamic Movement has links to al-Qaeda and has 1,000 militants. In August 2002, under pressure from the Chinese government, the United States labeled the East Turkestan Islamic Movement a terrorist organization and vowed to freeze of the group's American assets. Outside of official Chinese statements, little information is available about the East Turkestan Islamic Movement, and it is believed that it may be one of several Uigher groups fighting the Chinese government. Former leader, Hahsan Mahsum, (who was killed by Pakistani soldier in October 2003) denied any links with al-Qaeda. Other Uighers have stated that they trained with al-Qaeda, but only to obtain combat skills.

Islamic Movement of Turkestan

Operating throughout central Asia, including Uzbekistan, Kyrgyzstan, Tajikistan, Afghanistan, Kashmir and Pakistan, the Islamic. Movement of Turkestan also known as the Islamic

Movement of Central Asia, and initially known as the Islamic Movement of Uzbekistan is dedicated to creating an Islamic religious state that includes the former Soviet republics of Central Asia and Xinjiang province in China. Their rhetoric is also anti-American and anti-Israeli.

The catalyst for the Islamist phenomenon in the former Soviet republics of Central Asia lies with the 1979 Soviet invasion of Afghanistan. Many Muslims from these predominantly Muslim Soviet republics fought in Afghanistan, where they came into contact with Islamism. Madrasas in Pakistan began reserving spots for Soviet Muslims and providing them with living allowances. Money from Saudi Arabia began funding mosques and madrasas propagating Islamism in the Central Asian Soviet republics.

Formed in 1990, the Islamic Renaissance Party had branches throughout the predominantly Muslim former Soviet republics of Central Asia. A group of Islamic Renaissance Party members in Namangan, Uzbekistan was dissatisfied with the group's failure to advocate for an Islamic state and started the Adolat (Justice) Party. In December 1991, led by Tohir Abdukhalilovich Yuldashov and Jumaboi Ahmadjonovich Khodjiyev, Adolat members clashed with the local authorities and seized the Communist Party headquarters in Namangan. Adolat began instituting *shari'a* in Namangan – and called on Uzbekistan's President, ex-Communist Islam Karimov, to declare the country an Islamic state.

Karimov cracked down on Adolat. Yuldashov fled to Pakistan, and then traveled to Saudi Arabia, Turkey, and Chechnya. Yuldashov met with Pakistan's ISI intelligence agency, Osama bin Laden, and Turkish intelligence – all of which were seeking new contacts in the new independent Central Asian republics. Khodjiyev, who had been a paratrooper in the Soviet Army during the war in Afghanistan, became a guerrilla leader known by the *nomme de guerre* Juma Namangani. Namangani set up operations in neighboring Tajikistan with about 30 Uzbeks and a few Arabs. His force quickly grew to over 200 and, in 1993, he relocated to the Tavildora Valley. Namangani's forces fought on the side of the Islamic Renaissance Party in the Tajik Civil War, but objected to the 1997 peace settlement and refused to stop fighting. Namangani developed fame as a guerilla fighter and became involved in the heroin trade.

By 1997, prominent Islamic Renaissance Party members belonged to the Tajik cabinet but, in Uzbekistan, President Karimov was cracking down on Muslims, not only jailing extremists, but effectively making any practice of Islam grounds for arrest. Yuldashov and Namangani met and decided to focus efforts on Uzbekistan.

In 1998, Yuldashov settled in Afghanistan and built an alliance with Taliban leader Mullah Omar and Osama bin Laden. Yuldashov and Namangani announced the formation of the Islamic Movement of Uzbekistan. On February 16, 1999 the Islamic Movement of Uzbekistan set off six car bombs in Uzbekistan's capital, Tashkent, in an attempt to assassinate President Karimov. Karimov was unhurt, but 16 were killed and over 100 were injured.

In August 1999, the Islamic Movement of Uzbekistan kidnapped four Kyrgyz officials. Kyrgyzstan reportedly paid ransom to have them released. The Islamic Movement of Uzbekistan continued taking hostages, holding 20, including four Japanese geologists, by the end of August. The hostages were released, and it is believed Japan paid the ransom. In winter 1999, the Islamic Movement of Uzbekistan returned to Afghanistan, escorted by Russian forces. Osama Bin Laden provided the Islamic Movement of Uzbekistan with $20 million, weapons and helicopters. In return, the Movement attempted to procure fissionable material from Russia on bin Laden's behalf. The Islamic Movement of Uzbekistan agreed to help the Taliban in their offensive against the Northern Alliance. At its peak, the Islamic Movement of Uzbekistan had about 2,000 operatives.

With these new resources plus the continuing income from the heroin trade, the Islamic Movement of Uzbekistan paid recruits $100-$500 per month and grew rapidly. Recruits included Uzbeks, Tajiks, Pakistanis, Chechens, and Uighurs from China. In summer 2000, the Islamic Movement of Uzbekistan was better equipped than the Uzbek army. In August 2000, the Islamic Movement of Uzbekistan kidnapped 10 mountain climbers, including four Americans. The Kyrgyz army rescued them and the United States declared the Islamic Movement of Uzbekistan a terrorist organization.

In autumn 2002, Namangani and Yuldashov were sentenced to death *in absentia* by an Uzbek court. At this point, the Islamic Movement of Uzbekistan had 2,000 fighters. Namangani returned to Afghanistan in January 2001.

The Islamic Movement of Uzbekistan launched another offensive in the summer of 2001, demonstrating a flexible command structure that allowed units to operate independently.

Islamic Movement of Uzbekistan forces fought alongside the Taliban in the fall and winter of 2001, including the fierce fighting at Shah-I-Kot Valley. It is likely that Namangani was killed fighting American forces. The Islamic Movement of Uzbekistan reestablished itself into the Islamic Movement of Turkestan and is now based in the Ferghana Valley from which it can attack Kyrgyzstan, Tajikistan, and Uzbekistan. However, Namangani's death and the defeat of its Taliban and al-Qaeda patrons have hampered the Islamic Movement of Turkestan and Western assistance has helped the Central Asian republics to combat the Islamic Movement of Turkestan more effectively. The Islamic Movement of Turkestan's 2002 offensive was negligible.

In March 2004, the IMU was linked to a wave of violence in Uzbekistan's capital that included clashes with police and suicide bombings.

Kashmir

Pakistan had long supported violent Kashmiri separatist groups in order to advance its claims on Indian-controlled Kashmir. But with the Soviet defeat in Afghanistan in 1989, the Pakistani government, and particularly its intelligence agency, the Interservices Intelligence (ISI), encouraged al-Qaeda's recruits in Afghanistan to focus their efforts on Kashmir. To evade international scrutiny, retired ISI members trained al-Qaeda members to fight in Kashmir.

Native Kashmiri separatist groups were frequently willing to consider ceasefires and agreements with Indian authorities, but the al-Qaeda linked groups in Kashmir brought a new level of violence to the Kashmiri conflict because of their unbending goal of liberating Kashmir from non-Muslim rule. These groups also took the conflict into India proper, launching bombings and kidnappings throughout India. The Kashmiri terrorist groups are also linked to violent extremist Islamist groups within Pakistan.

In addition to the support they receive from Pakistan, the Kashmiri groups receive support through al-Qaeda from Muslims around the world, particularly from the Gulf States and the Pakistani Muslim diaspora in Great Britain. One prominent feature of the Kashmiri front in al-Qaeda's international campaign is how specific terrorist groups are formed and de-emphasized in order to evade international scrutiny. Several of the major groups are profiled below.

Harakat-ul-Mujahedin

Harakat-ul-Mujahedin, the Islamic Freedom Fighters Group, was founded in the early 1980s to recruit Pakistanis to fight in Afghanistan.

Initially, support came from wealthy Pakistanis and Gulf Arabs, including Osama bin Laden. Harakat-ul-Mujahedin may have recruited as many as 5,000 Pakistanis to fight in Afghanistan and later extended its efforts and recruited thousands of Muslims from across Asia and Europe to fight in Afghanistan. Harakat-ul-Mujahedin fighters made substantial contributions to the Afghan war against the Soviets.

Harakat-ul-Mujahedin is affiliated with Tabligi Jamaat, an Islamist charity and missionary organization based in Pakistan that is active worldwide, particularly in the Philippines. Inspired by the Wahhabi and Deobandi forms of Islam, Harakat-ul-Mujahedin advocates the implementation of a strict interpretation of *shari'a*.

As the war in Afghanistan came to an end, Harakat-ul-Mujahedin became involved with militant Muslim causes worldwide, training fighters at its camps in Afghanistan, Kashmir, and Pakistan and dispatching them to Bosnia, Algeria, and Chechnya; providing combat training to Muslims in Burma and the Philippines; and fighting in Tajikistan's civil war. But forcing Kashmir's accession to Pakistan became a new focal point for Afghan veterans because of its proximity and Pakistan's support for an Islamist insurgency in Kashmir.

In 1993, Harakat-ul-Mujahedin merged with Harakat-ul-Jihad al-Islami to form Harakat-ul-Ansar. It was based in Muzaffarabad, capital of Pakistani-controlled Kashmir and led by Maulana Saadatullah Khan. Harakat-ul-Ansar had close relations with the Taliban and maintained bases in Afghanistan and at its peak, had 5,000 members. Of its several hundred core members, the majority were not native Kashmiris, but Afghanis and Pakistanis, along with a substantial contingent of Arabs.

In May 1994, Harakat-ul-Ansar stopped several buses and killed some of the passengers, including a 14-year-old boy. Shortly after the merger, Indian security forces captured three top Harakat-ul-Ansar leaders.

Harakat-ul-Ansar conducted a series of kidnappings in order to force the Indian government to release these leaders and in December 1994 captured four Western tourists in New Delhi. Indian security forces rescued the hostages and captured two Harakat-ul-Ansar members including Ahmed Omar Saeed Sheikh. In July 1995, al-Faran, which is suspected of being a Harakat-ul-Ansar front group, kidnapped five Western tourists and demanded the release of their jailed leaders. One of the hostages was killed in August 1995 and the others were allegedly murdered in December 1995 after the Indian government refused to release the jailed leaders.

Harakat-ul-Ansar's links to bin Laden and the international publicity of the kidnapping led the United States to place Harakat-ul-Ansar on its list of terrorist organizations in 1997. Shortly thereafter, Harakat-ul-Ansar changed its name back to Harakat-ul-Mujahedin. Because of this unfavorable attention, the ISI began to shift its support to another Kashmiri militant group, Lashkar-e-Toiba.

In February 1998, Harakat-ul-Mujahedin leader Fazlur Rehman Khalil was a signatory to Osama bin Laden's fatwa calling for attacks on American and Western interests and Harakat-ul-Mujahedin is a member of bin Laden's Islamic World Front for the Struggle against the Jews and the Crusaders. In August 1998, nine Harakat-ul-Mujahedin operatives were killed by American cruise missiles fired at terrorist training camps in Afghanistan in retaliation for al-Qaeda's attacks on American embassies in Tanzania and Kenya.

In May 1999, Harakat-ul-Mujahedin units fought in the Kargil operation in which Pakistani units and Kashmiri terrorist groups seized a mountainous portion of Indian-controlled Kashmir.

In December 1999, Harakat-ul-Mujahedin operatives hijacked an Indian Airlines plane, stabbing one passenger and demanding the release of Islamists held in Indian prisons. Taking the plane to Kandahar, Afghanistan, the hijackers negotiated with the Taliban and the Indian government. The Indian government acquiesced to the hijackers' demands, releasing (among others) Maslana Masood Azhar and Ahmed Omar Saeed Sheikh. The hijackers escaped to Pakistan. Azhar founded another terrorist group, Jaish-e-Muhammed, recruiting many of Harakat-ul-Mujahedin's veterans and reducing Harakat-ul-Mujahedin's operational capabilities. Harakat-ul-Mujahedin's operations have also been severely curtailed by the ISI's shifting its support to Lashkar-e-Toiba and Jaish-e-Muhammad. Lashkar-e-Toiba is profiled below in a separate entry.

Jaish-e-Muhammad has been involved in numerous terror attacks. Ahmed Omar Saeed Sheikh, who is also affiliated with Jaish-e-Muhammad, was tried for the murder of American journalist Daniel Pearl. Jaish-e-Muhammad has also been held responsible for the October 1, 2001 attack on Kashmir's Legislative Complex in Srinagar. Over 30 people, including the four terrorist attackers, were killed. The Indian government holds Jaish-e-Muhammad and Laskhar-e-Toiba responsible for the December 13, 2001 attack on the Indian Parliament that nearly brought India and Pakistan to war.

Lashkar-e-Toiba

Lashkar-e-Toiba, which means Army of the Pure, was founded in 1990 in Afghanistan as the armed wing of the Pakistani Wahhabi Muslim organization, Markaz-ud-Dawa-wal-Irshad. Originally operating with the Afghan Mujahedain, Lashkar-e-Toiba now operates primarily in Jammu and Kashmir — the portion of Kashmir controlled by India. Lashkar-e-Toiba and Markaz-ud-Dawa-wal-Irshad's ultimate goals are the restoration of Islamic rule over all of India. Lashkar-e-Toiba was based near Lahore, Pakistan but is believed to have shifted its headquarters to Muzaffarabad. Lashkar-e-Toiba is believed to be heavily supported by Pakistan's ISI and its 300 members are primarily Pakistanis and Afghanis.

Lashkar-e-Toiba's first known infiltration of terrorists into Jammu and Kashmir was in 1993 and, since 1996, Lashkar-e-Toiba's prominence has been increasing. The ISI has been reducing its support for its previous leading Kashmiri proxy Harakat-ul-Ansar (later Harakat-ul-Mujahedin), which was placed on the United States terrorism list in 1997. Lashkar-e-Toiba's membership is drawn primarily from Pakistani Punjabs, and Punjabi is closely related to the language of the Jammu region of Indian-controlled Kashmir. This linguistic affiliation has facilitated Lashkar-e-Toiba's infiltration and allowed the ISI to refocus its efforts on the Jammu region.

Lashkar-e-Toiba has carried out a number of massacres and suicide attacks on civilian, military, and political targets. Since 1996, Lashkar-e-Toiba operatives have committed over a dozen large scale massacres of civilians, primarily Hindus and Sikhs. In June 1998, 25 members of a wedding party were killed, including small children. There were two other civilian massacres by the Lashkar-e-Toiba that year as well. On March 20, 2000, Lashkar-e-Toiba operatives attacked and killed 35 Sikhs. Lashkar-e-Toiba is suspected in a May 2002 attack on an Indian army barracks that killed 34, mostly women and children, and in a July 2002 attack on a neighborhood in Jammu that where 27 people were killed. On November 24, 2002 Lashkar-e-Toiba operatives launched an attack on a pair of Hindu shrines in Jammu, killing 13 and injuring 45.

Lashkar-e-Toiba has also attacked Indian security forces directly, both storming garrisons and, on August 10, 2000, exploding a car bomb in Srinagar, killing 12 Indian security personnel and two civilians. On December 22, 2000 Lashkar-e-Toiba operatives attacked the army garrison at the Red Fort in New Delhi, India's capital. The attackers escaped and three Indian security personnel were killed.

On December 13, 2000, five Kashmiri gunmen attacked India's Parliament in New Delhi, killing seven Indians. This attack brought India and Pakistan to the brink of war. The Indian government blamed Lashkar-e-Toiba and Jaish-e-Muhammad. The Pakistani government outlawed the two terrorist groups, arrested their leaders, and froze their assets.

The United States designated Lashkar-e-Toiba a terrorist organization on December 26, 2001. Shortly afterwards, Markaz-ud-Dawa-wal-Irshad announced that it had reorganized its operations and was no longer linked with Lashkar-e-Toiba. Professor Hafiz Muhammad Saeed, leader of both organizations, resigned as Lashkar-e-Toiba's leader and was replaced by Maulana Abdul Wahid Kashmiri. Although Markaz-ud-Dawa-wal-Irshad was renamed Jamaat ud-Dawa, it is possible to make donations to Lashkar-e-Toiba from Jamaat ud-Dawa's website.

Lashkar-e-Toiba receives support from al-Qaeda, a number of organizations in Pakistan, donations from citizens of the Gulf States, and possibly from the ISI. Lashkar-e-Toiba cooperates with al-Qaeda and Jaish-e-Mohammed. Lashkar-e-Toiba trained operatives to fight in Chechnya and Bosnia, as well as Kashmir.

Lashkar-e-Omar

Lashkar-e-Omar, or the Army of Omar, is the latest incarnation of al-Qaeda linked Kashmiri terrorist organizations. In the last few years, Harakat-ul-Mujahedin, the oldest of the Kashmiri terrorist groups, was in the process of being de-emphasized and its operatives were switching to Jaish-e-Muhammad. When Pakistan's President Pervez Musharraf declared Jaish-e-Muhammad and Lashkar-e-Toiba illegal on January 12, 2002, their cadres began switching to Lashkar-e-Omar.

The leader of Lashkar-e-Omar is Qari Abd al-Hai, who was a leader of Lashkar-e-Jhangvi, an outlawed Pakistani terrorist organization that primarily targets Pakistan's Shi'ites. He has incorporated Lashkar-e-Jhangvi operatives into Lashkar-e-Omar. Most of its operatives trained in Afghanistan, and the organization is closely linked to and modeled after al-Qaeda.

Lashkar-e-Omar's first major attack was on October 28, 2001 against Christians in Bahawdpur that left 17 dead, including five children. Lashkar-e-Omar was also responsible for the May 8, 2002 car bombing that killed 11 French citizens and three Pakistanis in Karachi and for the June 14, 2002 attack on the American consulate in Karachi that killed 10 and injured 51.

East Asia
Bangladesh

Bangladesh is a growing area of operations for al-Qaeda. The Bangladesh wing of Jamiat-e-Islaami along with another Islamist party, Islamic Oikya Jote, are members of the governing coalition that took office in October 2001, under Prime Minister Zia of the Bangladeshi National Party (BNP).

In 1992, Osama bin Laden helped found Harakat-ul-Jihad-al-Islami, which calls itself the Bangladeshi Taliban and seeks to establish Islamic rule in Bangladesh and ultimately in the Muslim areas in India and Myanmar bordering Bangladesh. Harakat-ul-Jihad-al-Islami belongs to the Jihad Movement of Bangladesh, an association of Bangladeshi Islamist organizations. Its leader, Abdul Salam Mohamed (a.k.a. Fazlul Rahman), was a signatory of Osama bin Laden's 1998 fatwa declaring war on America. It is believed that Harakat-ul-Jihad-al-Islami's funding is through the Saudi-based charity al-Haramain, which has several dozen offices in Bangladesh. Reportedly, 150 al-Qaeda/Taliban operatives fled to Bangladesh in late 2001, possibly including al-Qaeda's second-in-command Ayman Zawahiri.

Harakat-ul-Jihad-al-Islami is believed to receive support from Pakistan's Interservices Intelligence and possibly from elements of Bangladeshi intelligence that have links to the ISI.

Many of Harakat-ul-Jihad-al-Islami's estimated 2,000 operatives trained in Afghanistan and have fought in Kashmir. Their leader is Shawkat Osman (a.k.a. Sheikh Farid). Harakat-ul-Jihad-al-Islami is believed to receive support from the ISI and is believed to operate at least 19 training camps around the country with six in the Chittagong region of Bangladesh.

Bangladesh's Islamists cooperate with the Muslim Liberation Tigers of Assam, which operate in the Indian province of Assam and have bases just over the border in Bangladesh. The Bangladeshis are ethnically related to the Muslim Rohingyas of Myanmar, and Bangladeshi Islamists support the growing Islamist groups in Myanmar, particularly Mahaz-e-Islami, and helped Rohingya Muslims to travel to Afghanistan for training.

Bangladesh has been wracked with violence. Islamists have attacked the Hindu and Christian minorities, as well as moderate Muslim figures. On June 3, 2001, a church in Baniachar was bombed killing 10 and wounding 25. The Awami League, the BNP's main political rival, has been a frequent target of violence. Its offices in Narayanganj in Bangladesh were bombed on June 15, 2001, killing 21 and injuring over 100. There were assassination attempts on the Awami League leader Sheikh Hasina in July of 2000. Theaters have also been bombed and Islamists are suspected. On December 8, 2002, during the post-Ramadan Eid al-Fitr holiday, four bombs exploded in theaters in Mymensigh killing 117 and wounding over 200. On September 28, 2002, a theater in Satkhira was bombed, killing 10 and wounding over 100.

In May 2001, the various Islamist groups in Bangladesh and their Rohingyan and Indian allies formed a Bangladeshi Islamic Manch, a united council, under Harakat-ul-Jihad-al-Islami's leadership.

Moro Islamic Liberation Front

The Moro Islamic Liberation Front (MILF) is an Islamist insurgency group based on the southern Philippine island of Mindanao. The Moro Islamic Liberation Front split from the secular Moro National Liberation Front in 1977. MILF founder, Selamat Hashim, who studied in Saudi Arabia and at Cairo's Al-Azhar University, died in August 2003. He was replaced by Al Haj Murad Ebrahim, head of MILF's military wing. The Moro National Liberation Front entered a peace deal with the Philippine government in September 1996. The Moro Islamic Liberation Front negotiated with the government between 1997 and 2000, but did not reach a peace accord. After extensive cease-fire violations the Philippine government launched an offensive against the Moro Islamic Liberation Front in April 2000, forcing it to retreat from its major bases, but the Moro Islamic Liberation Front armed wing remained intact with between 10,000 and 15,000 fighters. In August 2001, a cease-fire was signed, but attempts to restart negotiations have not been successful. While the Philippine Army has been operating against Abu Sayyaf, it has established mechanisms with the MILF to avoid accidental confrontations.

Links between the Moro Islamic Liberation Front and al-Qaeda were forged in the mid-1990s. Al-Qaeda provided funding and expertise, the MILF brought al-Qaeda into contact with other Islamist groups in East Asia. MILF members trained in Pakistan and fought in Afghanistan in the 1980s. More recently, Pakistanis, Afghans, Arabs, and Indonesians have trained at the Moro Islamic Liberation Front's Abu Bakr camp. Philippine authorities sentenced Indonesian-born, Jemaah Islamiyah explosives expert, Fathur Rothman al-Ghozi, to 10 years in prison for his role in a December 2000 wave of bombings in Manila that killed 22 and injured over 100. Local Muslim extremists, who were known to have visited Moro Islamic Liberation Front camps to provide training, aided al-Ghozi. In July 2003 al-Ghozi escaped from prison and was killed in a shootout with Philippine police in October 2003.

Abu Sayyaf

Abu Sayyaf split from the Moro Liberation Front in 1991. Abduragak Abubakr Janjalani founded the group and took the name Abu Sayyaf (Bearer of the Sword) in honor of Osama bin Laden's ally Abdul Rasoof Sayyaf with whom he fought in Afghanistan. Philippine police killed Janjalani in 1998. After a power struggle, his brother, Khadafy Janjali, took control of the organization. Abu Sayyaf is believed to have about 200 members and seeks to create a strict Islamic state and rejects any negotiations with the Philippine government.

Since its founding, Abu Sayyaf has carried out several terror attacks, including a January 1999 grenade attack on the southern Philippine island of Jolo that killed 10 and injured 74. Abu Sayyaf was also behind a series of bombings on April 21, 2002, in the southern Philippine city of General Santos, which killed 15 and injured over 70. In April 1995, Abu Sayyaf attacked a Christian town and massacred 53 civilians and soldiers.

Abu Sayyaf has achieved its greatest notoriety for it kidnappings, frequently targeting foreigners. In spring 2000, Abu Sayyaf began perpetrating mass kidnappings and in March 2000 took 53 hostages, mostly children, from two schools in Basilan. The army rescued 15 of the hostages in a massive operation. Twenty hostages had previously been freed and the hostage takers shot four. On April 23, 2000, Abu Sayyaf operatives captured 21 tourists in Malaysia. Libya paid $10 million in ransom and negotiated the freedom for most of these hostages. Libya has a long history of supporting Islamist groups in the Philippines, particularly the Moro Islamic Liberation Front. Ransom from kidnappings has been a leading source of Abu Sayyaf's income and has raised its status in the impoverished southern Philippines.

Abu Sayyaf is closely connected to al-Qaeda and its affiliates. Bin Laden's brother-in-law, Mohammad Jamal Khalifa, ran businesses in the Philippines and helped finance Abu Sayyaf. World Trade Center bomber Ramzi Yousef lived in the Philippines before and after the 1993 attack on the World Trade Center, and in 1991 he had joined Abu Sayyaf. While in the Philippines, Yousef plotted to assassinate Pope John Paul II and American President Clinton during their visits to the Philippines and to simultaneously detonate bombs on 11 United States airliners flying over the Pacific. Yousef fled the Philippines on January 6, 1995 when he started a fire in his Manila apartment while manufacturing explosives. He was arrested a month later in Islamabad, Pakistan and extradicted to the United States   Abu Sayyaf has demanded Yousef's release from prison in its hostage negotiations.

Because of Abu Sayyaf's al-Qaeda connections and because they had kidnapped and killed Americans, in January 2002, the United States deployed several hundred troops to the Philippines to train and support the Philippine army's counter-terrorist experts. In June 2002 Philippine forces, with American technical support, located and, in the ensuing firefight, killed Abu Sabaya, a top Abu Sayyaf leader. Abu Sayyaf is still an operational threat, holding several hostages. In August 2002, Abu Sayyaf beheaded a pair of Christian hostages and was responsible for several October bombings in which 15 were killed, including an American soldier, and over 100 were injured. In December 2003, Philippine troops captured top Abu Sayyaf leader Galib Andang, better known as Commander Robot, who was responsible for the beheading.

Jemaah Islamiyah

Founded in the early 1990s by Abdullah Sungkar, Jemaah Islamiyah (JI), or the Islamic Group, is al-Qaeda's main affiliate in Southeast Asia. Jemaah Islamiyah's core ambition is *Daulah Islamiah Raya*, creating a Southeast Asian Islamic superstate that includes Malaysia, Singapore, Indonesia, the southern Philippines, Thailand, and Cambodia. Most of its leaders have been to Afghanistan and Sungkar met Osama bin Laden before forming Jemaah Islamiyah. After Sungkar's death, Abu Bakr Bashir took over as the spiritual leader of Jemaah Islamiyah. The head of the *shura* (council) was an Indonesian national residing in Malaysia, Riduan Ismuddin (a.k.a. Hambali). Hambali, 37, fought in Afghanistan and is the only non-Arab to have a seat on al-Qaeda's Majlis al-Shura. Hambali was arrested in August 2003 by Thai authorities who turned him over to the Central Intelligence Agency. Al-Qaeda helped build Jemaah Islamiyah into a pan-Asian terrorist group and   command structure is modeled on al-Qaeda's, with regional *shuras* guiding most activity, and, like al-Qaeda, focusing on covert activity.

Jemaah Islamiyah has hundreds of members spread between cells in Malaysia, Indonesia, and Singapore, and has been building a terrorist infrastructure in Australia. Since 1993 it has been sending members to get training in Afghanistan and cooperates closely with Kampulan Mujahedin Malaysia, which was founded by Zainon Ismail, another Afghanistan veteran, in 1995 and seeks to overthrow the Malaysian government and replace it with an Islamist regime. Kampulan Mujahedin Malaysia recognizes Abu Bakr Bashir as its spiritual leader and is a small organization with possibly only a few hundred members, many of whom trained in Afghanistan. Kampulan Mujahedin Malaysia has attacked churches and Hindu temples, committed assassinations and robbed banks to raise funds. Kampulan Mujahedin Malaysia may be linked to Malaysia's Islamist political party, Parti Islami Se Malaysia. Jemaah Islamiyah also has links to Abu Sayyaf, the Moro Islamic Liberation Front, and Laskar Jihad, an Islamist organization in Indonesia that has massacred local Christians in Sulawesi and the Moluccas. Muslim-Christan fighting in Indonesia over the last several years has resulted in thousands of deaths. Jemaah Islamiyah has training camps in Indonesia where Islamists from all over the world train.

Jemaah Islamiyah has actively extended its regions of operation to Australia and Thailand. In Australia, Jemaah Islamiyah attempted to found terror cells. A cell in Perth trained with weapons and planned attacks on Israeli missions in Australia's capital Canberra. Thailand has had lax security and has served as a logistical center for Jemaah Islamiyah, and is a potential target for Islamist attacks. In southern Thailand, which is predominantly Muslim an Islamist group, Jemaah Salafiyya, has emerged, murdering local police and bombing Buddhist temples. It is believed that Jemaah Salafiyya is linked to Jemaah Islamiyah.

Jemaah Islamiyah conducted a wave of church bombings that struck throughout Indonesia on Christmas Eve 2000. Twenty-two people were killed and almost 100 were wounded in spite of the fact that   dozens of bombs failed to explode.

Yazid Sufaat, a Jemaah Islamiyah operative, met with two of the 9/11 hijackers in January 2001 and gave accused twentieth hijacker Zacarias Moussaoui $35,000 in January 2000 and $2,500 a month thereafter. While with Jemaah Islamiyah Hambali also helped Ramzi Youssef escape to the Philippines and was working with him on "Operation Bojinka," his plan to hijack and blow up several American airliners over the Pacific. Al-Qaeda leaders Muhammad Atef and Ayman Zawahiri may have visited Indonesia in 2000.

In December 2001 Singapore's Intelligence Services Department arrested 15 suspected Jemaah Islamiyah members (two were later released, four had been trained by al-Qaeda) who were plotting six suicide truck bomb attacks on American, Israeli, and Australian targets in Singapore. Videotape detailing these plans was captured in Kabul, Afghanistan. Al-Qaeda had sent specialists to assist the Singapore cells. Plans to attack Western targets in Singapore date back to 1993 and reportedly, the attacks were supposed to look like they were committed by Malaysia, leading to conflict between Malaysia and Singapore.

On October 12, 2002 on Bali, an island in Indonesia, a massive car bomb and a suicide bomber exploded close to nightclubs frequented by Western tourists. Over 190 people were killed; more than half were British and Australian tourists. Over 300 people were injured. Al-Qaeda's Southeast Asian affiliate Jemaah Islamiyah was held responsible. Australians were particularly targeted because of Australia's role in East Timor's secession from Indonesia, which Islamists viewed as a Western plot to break up a Muslim state. It is believed that the initial planning for the bombing took place at a February 2002 meeting in Bangkok, Thailand.

In the months after the Bali bombing, Indonesian security forces have made several arrests, including Abd al-Aziz, a.k.a. Imam Samudra, who is reportedly the head of Jemaah Islamiyah in Indonesia.

Abu Bakr Bashir, the group's spiritual leader was arrested and jailed for 18 months after the Bali bombing. Jemaah Islamiyah remains active, in August 2003 it bombed a Marriott hotel in Jakarta.

Al-Qaeda Operations in Asia
Al-Qaeda in Australia and New Zealand

Al-Qaeda operations extend throughout Asia and the Pacific. In March 2000 a suspected al-Qaeda cell consisting primarily of Afghan refugees, based in Auckland, New Zealand was discovered planning an attack on a nuclear reactor in Australia during the summer Olympics in Sydney, Australia.

Links to the Tamil Tigers

Al-Qaeda is believed to cooperate with the Liberation Tigers of Tamil Eelam (LTTE) which fights for an independent Tamil state on the island of Sri Lanka. The LTTE is not an Islamist organization and shares no common ideological ground with al-Qaeda. LTTE is however a highly effective terrorist organization that uses suicide tactics has an international network, and a fleet of sea-going ships. The LTTE came into conflict with India in the late 1980s and allied itself with Pakistan. This alliance is believed to have brought the LTTE into contact with the Kashmiri and Afghani Islamists, and ultimately with al-Qaeda. LTTE is believed to have provided forged documents to al-Qaeda operatives and may have transported weapons to Abu Sayyaf in the Philippines.

Resources

In-depth profiles of terrorist groups of the Indian subcontinent are available at the South Asia Terrorism Portal – www.satp.org.

An overview of al-Qaeda's Asian activities is found in Rohan Gunaratna's *Inside al-Qaeda: Global Network of Terror.* New York: Columbia University Press, 2002.

Islamic Movement of Turkestan

Rashid, A., "They're only Sleeping." *The New Yorker,* January 14, 2002 - available at www.newyorker.com.

Fighel, J., "Jihad in Uzbekistan ." The International Police Institute for Counter-Terrorism website March 30, 2004 - available at www.ict.org.il.

Harakat-ul-Mujahedin

Raman, B., *"Harkat-ul-Mujahedin – An Update." South Asia Analysis Group Papers* March 1999 - available at www.saag.org

Bangladeshi Islamist Groups

Perry, A., "Deadly Cargo." *Time* October 14, 2002 – available at www.time.com.

Abu Sayyaf

Shahar, Y., "Libya and the Jolo Hostages: Seeking a new image, or polishing the old one?" The International Policy Institute for Counter -Terrorism website August 20, 2000 – available at www.ict.org.il.

Moro Islamic Liberation Front English Language website - www.luwaran.com.

Al-Qaeda

Egyptian Affiliates

The two major Islamist terrorist groups in Egypt are al-Gama'a al-Islamiyya or the Islamic Group (IG) and Egyptian Islamic Jihad or al-Jihad. Both organizations are signatories of Osama bin Laden's February 23, 1998 fatwa forming a united Islamist front and are integrated into al-Qaeda. The IG is also known as The Jihad against the Crusaders and the Jews. Al-Jihad is also known as New Jihad Group or the Jihad Group.

Ideology and Objectives

Both the Islamic Group (IG) and al-Jihad were inspired by previous generations of Egyptian Islamists, particularly Sayyid Qutb of the Muslim Brotherhood. Qutb in the 1950s and 1960s wrote that the world was divided between those who submit to Islamic religious law, *shari'a,* and those who do not. According to Qutb, Islam cannot tolerate a situation in which *shari'a* does not direct human affairs and calls for jihad to implement *shari'a.* Qutb was revolutionary in his readiness to declare individual Muslims and governments of predominantly Muslim nations, particularly secular Arab regimes, apostates and, consequently, legitimate targets of jihad.

Both the IG and al-Jihad revere Qutb and are devoted to overthrowing the Egyptian government and installing a fundamentalist Muslim theocracy, governed by the laws of *shari'a.* Neither organization seeks to achieve this goal through elections. Overthrowing the Egyptian government is the preliminary step to waging a global jihad that will create worldwide Muslim rule. As efforts to overthrow the Egyptian government stalled, the IG and al-Jihad sought other theaters where Muslims were in conflict with non-Muslims, such as Afghanistan, Bosnia, and Kashmir. Because the United States is the most powerful non-Muslim state, both groups view the United States as the archenemy of Islam and an important target for Jihad. Both groups also embrace Qutb's anti-Semitic belief that Jews are responsible for the tragedies that have befallen Islam. Consequently, not only is Israel an appropriate target for Jihad, so are Jews worldwide.

Later, al-Jihad founder Abd al-Salam Faraj wrote that violent Jihad is the sixth pillar of Islam, joining the five pillars recognized in mainstream Islam.

Although rivals and allies at different times, the ideological differences between al-Jihad and the IG are minimal; their differences are primarily strategic. Both organizations respect Sheikh Omar Abd al-Rahman as their spiritual leader. The IG is a mass movement, which seeks to affect society as a whole. Al-Jihad is more focused on attacking the Egyptian government and attempting to seize power. While this has led the two organizations to pursue different targets, it has not prevented them from cooperating operationally.

History
The Muslim Brotherhood and the Foundations of Egyptian Radicalism
In 1928, an elementary school teacher named Hassan al-Banna founded the Muslim Brotherhood (MB), an Islamist organization devoted to establishing an Islamic state. At the time, Egyptians were disappointed in their recent experiments in democracy and frustrated with the continuing British control of Egypt. The MB, which included a political party and a social organization, grew rapidly in virtually all sectors of society.

MB leaders were in touch with similar movements in Iran and Pakistan from their conception, and the MB supported local affiliates throughout the Arab world. The MB built a clandestine arm, and attempted to infiltrate the army.

At the beginning of 1945, the MB launched a terror war against the Egyptian government. The MB assassinated Prime Minister Ahmed Maher prominent Egyptian citizens, intimidated judges trying MB members, and planted bombs and threw hand grenades in public places. When the Israeli War of Independence broke out, on Dec. 8, 1948 the MB attacked Jewish and foreign-owned businesses in Egypt. The Egyptian government dissolved the MB and arrested hundreds of members. The MB responded by assassinating Prime Minister Mahmed Fahmi Nugrashi. On February 12, 1949, Hassan al-Banna, was assassinated, presumably by the Egyptian government.

When the Free Officers overthrew the Egyptian government, the MB was hopeful that it would share in power because of its connections to the Free Officers. When Nasser emerged as the President of Egypt and did not share power the MB attempted to assassinate him on October 26, 1954. Nasser responded by arresting tens of thousands of MB members, placing them in detention camps, and keeping a tight lid on MB activity. Thousands of MB members fled abroad where they spread the MB's influence.

In the mid-1960s, Nasser again cracked down on the MB. Sayyid Qutb, the MB's leading ideologue was executed August 29, 1966.

Sadat and the Formation of the Egyptian Terror Groups

With the death of Nasser in 1970, Anwar Sadat assumed the Egyptian presidency. To counterbalance the Egyptian Communists, Sadat released Muslim Brotherhood (MB) leaders from prison, placed minimal restrictions on their activities, and even armed them. The reactivated MB found fertile ground for recruitment to radical Islam. Egypt in the 1970s was suffering a period of economic stagnation and had high rates of unemployment. Egypt lost a devastatingly quick war to Israel in 1967. While Egypt's military standing improved in the October War of 1973, its outcome led to negotiations with Israel, which were fundamentally unacceptable to the Islamists.

In this environment, many Egyptians, particularly in the universities where Islamist groups dominated student politics, found radical Islam appealing. Hundreds of violent Islamist cells formed and Islamist violence, particularly against Egypt's Coptic Christian minority, increased. Islamist groups also attempted, with some success, to recruit from within the military. In 1974, an Islamist revolt at the Technical Military Academy was put down with heavy casualties. In July 1977 the Minister of Islamic Endowments was kidnapped and murdered by Islamists. By the mid-1970s, the Islamic Group (IG) had been formed when Sheikh al-Rahman brought many local "Islamic groups" together. A few years later several terror cells coalesced into al-Jihad.

In 1979, Egypt signed a peace treaty with Israel. While the treaty returned all captured territories to Egypt, it also required Egypt to recognize Israel's existence — a condition unacceptable to the Islamists. Increased Islamist violence led Sadat to launch his most extensive crackdown on Egyptian Islamist terrorists in September 1981, when over 1,500 were arrested.

On October 6, 1981 at a military parade, a group of soldiers assassinated President Sadat. The soldiers, led by Second Lieutenant Khalid Ahmad Shawqi al-Islambouli, were members of al-Jihad. It is believed that al-Jihad received assistance from the IG in this operation, although an Egyptian court acquitted IG leader Sheikh Omar Abd al-Rahman of charges that he was involved in the assassination.

Two days later, there was an Islamist uprising in Asyut, in Upper Egypt, that was crushed after bloody clashes with Egyptian security forces.

In the crackdown that followed, hundreds of Islamist operatives were arrested and tortured. Key leaders, including al-Islambouli, were executed and others sentenced to life imprisonment. Islamists of Palestinian origin were expelled to Gaza where they played a key role in building Hamas and Palestinian Islamic Jihad and many IG and al-Jihad members who were not directly involved with the assassination served several years in prison and were released. Ayman Zawahiri, one of al-Jihad's leaders, met Sheikh Rahman in prison where they argued over how to achieve an Islamist revolution. Zawahiri was serving a three year sentence, while Sheikh Rahman was awaiting his trial.

Egyptian Islamists and the War in Afghanistan

With their leaders executed or imprisoned, the Egyptian Islamist groups sustained relatively low levels of activity in Egypt throughout the 1980s (albeit with brief flare-ups such as a wave of Islamist attacks on video stores and Western-style shops in 1986). However, the Egyptian terrorist groups were deeply involved in the war against the Soviets in Afghanistan. Thousands of Egyptians, and other Arabs, traveled to Central Asia to join in the war in Afghanistan. The Muslim Brotherhood sought and dispatched recruits with the blessing of the Egyptian government. Besides allowing Egypt to curry favor with the United States by supporting the American interest in stopping the Soviet advance in Afghanistan, sending Egyptian Islamists to Afghanistan reduced radical activity in Egypt.

However, while in Afghanistan, Egyptian Islamists were further radicalized and came into extended contact with Islamists worldwide. The most important link forged was between al-Jihad leader Ayman Zawahiri and Osama bin Laden. Based together in Pakistan, Zawahiri and other al-Jihad leaders reorganized al-Jihad, forming a faction of al-Jihad loyal to him, Vanguards of the Conquest (Tala'i al-Fatah), and placed al-Jihad advisors around bin Laden. The first two military commanders of al-Qaeda, Ali al-Rashidi (who drowned in Africa's Lake Victoria in 1996) and Muhammad Atef (who was killed by American bombing in November 2001) were Egyptian al-Jihad operatives.

Islamic Group (IG) operatives were also based in Pakistan and sought to win bin Laden's favor. Sheikh Rahman visited Pakistan during the war in Afghanistan. When al-Qaeda founder and spiritual leader Abdallah Azzam was killed by a car bomb in November 1989, Sheikh Omar Abd al-Rahman took his place. Bin Laden attempted to reconcile the IG and al-Jihad and, by 1989, was a main source of financial support for both groups.

Egyptian Islamists, in general, and Zawahiri, in particular, played a major role in the formation of al-Qaeda after the Soviet retreat from Afghanistan. Zawahiri helped persuade bin Laden to extend the jihad worldwide.

Egyptian Islamists in America and the First World Trade Center Attack

In 1990, after being acquitted of attempting to assassinate Egyptian President Hosni Mubarak, Sheikh Rahman fled to the United States, arriving in July. An Islamist network had been operating in the United States since the early 1980s under the auspices of Osama bin Laden's support services for the war in Afghanistan. Sheikh Rahman became the leader of a Jersey City mosque and began to take control of the North American network. According to evidence unearthed during Sheikh Rahman's 1995 trial, he may have been planning terror attacks against America before he arrived.

On November 5, 1990 in New York, Egyptian-born El Sayyid Nosair murdered Rabbi Meir Kahane, founder of the Jewish Defense League and head of an extremist anti-Arab political party in Israel. Nosair was not convicted on a technicality, but was jailed on firearms charges. From prison, he continued to plan terror attacks. Documents found at his apartment, when examined several years later, linked Nosair to Sheikh Rahman.

On February 26, 1993, a van exploded in the garage of the World Trade Center in New York City, killing six Americans, wounding over a thousand others, and causing an estimated $500 million in damage. One of the main conspirators of the operation was Ramzi Yousef, who entered the United States on an Iraqi passport in 1992. Yousef was arrested in 1995 in Pakistan. Based on intelligence gathered in Egypt and through informants in the United States, the attackers were pursued, arrested and tried. In 1994, four men – Mahmud Abu Halima, Mohammed Salama, Nidal 'Ayyad and Ahmad Ajjaj – each received a 240-year sentence. Prosecutors could not link Sheikh Rahman directly to the World Trade Center bombing. But, in 1995, Sheikh Rahman along with several co-defendants, including Nosair, were tried and sentenced to life in prison for plotting a series of bombings in New York.

Renewed Terror in Egypt

With the end of the war in Afghanistan in 1989, Arabs who had trained and been radicalized there returned to their home countries. Egyptian veterans of Afghanistan reinvigorated the Islamist movements. Sudan's 1989 Islamist revolution gave the Egyptian terrorists a nearby base for operations. While the Islamic Group (IG) and al-Jihad's rivalry never exploded into bloodshed, it hampered their effectiveness. By the mid-1990s, under Osama bin Laden's guidance, the two organizations began to cooperate more effectively.

The IG attacked all elements of secular Egypt, including Egypt's Coptic Christian minority, government figures ranging from policemen to President Mubarak, and Egyptian intellectuals who supported a secular state. The 1992, assassination of Faraj Foda and the attempted 1994 assassination of Egyptian Nobel Laureate Naguib Mahfouz are the two most prominent examples of IG attempts to silence voices advocating a modern secular Egypt at peace with Israel. Foda had founded a political party to advance the concept of a secular state.

In attacking the government, the IG launched innumerable attacks on Egyptian policemen, killing dozens over the course of the 1990s, including several high-ranking police commanders. In 1993, IG militants attempted to assassinate the Egyptian Minister of Information, injuring him and his bodyguard. In June 1995, two IG operatives were killed when they and several others attempted to assassinate President Mubarak during a state visit to Ethiopia.

In 1992, the IG began targeting foreign tourists in Egypt, attempting countless shootings and bombings. Sheikh Rahman, who issued a fatwa approving attacks on tourists, stated that they brought corruption and low morals to Egypt. Tourism is also a multi-billion dollar industry and a mainstay of the Egyptian economy. In attacking this crucial industry, the IG was hoping to undermine the Egyptian government. A February 4, 1993 attack on a group of Korean tourists visiting Cairo, damaging their bus but causing no injuries, was typical of the early attacks on foreign tourists. As IG operatives acquired greater proficiency, their attacks became more deadly. In 1994, a series of IG attacks on trains used by tourists caused numerous injuries to foreigners visiting Egypt. In September of that year, IG operatives fired into a crowded tourist pavilion in the city of Hurghada, killing two Egyptians and a German tourist. Another train attack in November 1995 resulted in the wounding of a Dutchman, a French woman, and an Egyptian. The attacks became more deadly. In 1996, four IG militants opened fire on Greek tourists congregating in front of the Europa Hotel in Cairo, killing 18 and injuring 12 as well as two Egyptians. In September 1997, IG operatives shot at and bombed a tour bus outside the Egyptian Museum in Cairo, killing nine German tourists and the bus driver.

The IG's most notorious attack on tourists in Egypt was the November 17, 1997 massacre at the Hatshepsut Temple in the Valley of the Kings near Luxor. Gunmen captured and executed 58 tourists and four Egyptians and wounded 26 others. Thirty-four Swiss, eight Japanese, five Germans, four Britons, one French, one Colombian, a dual-national Bulgarian/Briton and four unidentified persons were among the dead. Twelve Swiss, two Japanese, two Germans, one French and nine Egyptians were among the wounded. The militants claimed the attack was intended to spur the release of Sheikh Rahman, the IG spiritual leader imprisoned in the United States. These attacks more than halved Egypt's income from tourism.

Egyptian security forces responded aggressively to Islamist violence, arresting thousands of suspects and often trying them in special security courts. Human rights groups estimate that in 2002 at least 15,000 Islamists were being held in Egyptian prisons. There were also large-scale battles between Islamists and Egyptian security forces. In December 1992, Egyptian security forces fought a pitched battle to reclaim the Cairo neighborhood of Imbada which IG had taken over and declared an Islamic Republic; 14,000 Egyptian troops were mobilized to reclaim Imbada, occupying it for six weeks and hunting down IG terrorists. On March 10, 1994, security forces stormed a mosque in Upper Egypt. In the ensuing battle, 11 police and 29 suspected Islamists were killed. The government's fight against the Islamists increased after the 1995 attempt on Mubarak's life and again after the 1997 Luxor Massacre. Even before the Luxor Massacre, elements of the IG leadership had been discussing a ceasefire. By the end of 1998, the IG had been reduced substantially and the leadership, which was primarily in Egyptian prisons, agreed to a ceasefire with the Egyptian government. Over 1,200 people were killed between 1990 and 1998 in terrorist attacks and in the fighting between Egyptian forces and Islamist terrorists.

Al-Jihad in Egypt and Abroad

In contrast to the Islamic Group (IG), al-Jihad focused almost exclusively on high profile attacks on the Egyptian government. On Friday October 12, 1990, al-Jihad operatives killed Rifat Mahjub the Speaker of Egypt's Parliament. The attack was aimed at Egypt's Interior Minister. On August 18, 1993, al-Jihad attempted to assassinate him again, but was unsuccessful. On November 25 of the same year, al-Jihad attempted, unsuccessfully, to assassinate the Prime Minister Atef Sedki with a car bomb. The bomb killed a teenage girl and injured 21 others. Egyptians were outraged and about 280 al-Jihad operatives were arrested.

Also in 1993, the Egyptian government captured Ismail Nassir, a top al-Jihad official. Al-Jihad had functioned as a secretive, clandestine organization. However, Nassir's computer had a database of al-Jihad members, allowing Egyptian intelligence to roll up al-Jihad networks. Over 1,000 al-Jihad operatives were arrested.

With the Egypt-based leadership in jail, Ayman Zawahiri took over the direction of al-Jihad from Sudan, and later Afghanistan, focusing his efforts on targets outside of Egypt. In 1995, al-Jihad helped the IG in its attempt to assassinate President Mubarak. Al-Jihad responded to the ensuing crackdown on al-Jihad in Egypt by assassinating an Egyptian diplomat in Switzerland and truck bombing the Egyptian embassy in Pakistan.

In 1996, al-Jihad, along with Osama bin Laden, was forced to leave the Sudan, which was trying to improve its international standing. Zawahiri traveled ceaselessly, setting up new cells and searching for a new base for al-Jihad. He spent late 1996 and early 1997 in Chechnya, where he was arrested by Russian authorities and released after they failed to identify him as a wanted terrorist.

Drawing Closer to Al-Qaeda

Since 2000, over 1,500 suspected and convicted Islamic Group (IG) extremists have been released early in exchange for renouncing violence, although crackdowns on newly discovered Islamist cells also occur. In

January 2003, 43 Islamists in three al-Jihad cells were arrested for planning to attack foreign targets in Egypt. Most of the top leadership of the IG and al-Jihad were in prison in Egypt and had called for an end to violence against the Egyptian regime.

Those leaders remaining outside of Egypt, particularly Sheikh Rahman, IG's Rifa'i Ahmed Taha Musa and al-Jihad's Ayman Zawahiri have rejected these calls for a ceasefire. However, unable to find secure bases for funding of their own, both organizations have drawn closer to al-Qaeda. On February 23, 1998, Zawahiri and Taha joined bin Laden's International Front for Jihad on the Jews and Crusaders, effectively merging with al-Qaeda. In June 2000, Sheikh Rahman rescinded the IG's 1998 ceasefire.

In July 1998, the United States learned of an al-Jihad plot against the American embassy in Tirana, Albania. With American help, Albanian security broke up the al-Jihad cell and deported its members to Egypt.

Al-Jihad and the IG's assets have played a key role in al-Qaeda operations since the declaration of the International Front. In June 2001 al-Qaeda and al-Jihad formalized their merger, becoming Qaeda al-Jihad.

Leadership

Ayman al-Zawahiri

Ayman al-Zawahiri, head of al-Jihad, is profiled in the al-Qaeda entry.

Sheikh Omar Abd al-Rahman

Born in 1938, Sheikh Rahman was blinded by diabetes as an infant. He mastered a braille Koran when he was 11 and studied Islamic law at Cairo's al-Azhar University, the leading educational institution of Sunni Islam. His doctoral thesis was on Jihad. Originally affiliated with the Muslim Brotherhood, Rahman became increasingly extremist, criticizing the Egyptian government and al-Azhar for not adhering sufficiently to Islamic law. He was imprisoned in 1970 for declaring that praying for the late Egyptian President Nasser was a sin.

As Islamism rose in Egypt in the 1970s, Rahman, known as the Blind Sheikh, emerged as its leader, helping to forge many local groups into a national – and international – organization. As the spiritual leader of the Islamic Group (IG), Rahman ruled on whether intended actions were acceptable or not under *shari'a*.

He taught in Saudi Arabia for three years in the 1970s to avoid being imprisoned in Egypt. When he returned to Egypt in 1980, he issued a ruling that a heretical leader should be killed by the faithful. After Sadat's assassination, he was jailed but not convicted because his ruling had not mentioned Sadat by name.

With the 1989 death of Abdallah Azzam, Sheikh Rahman became the spiritual leader of al-Qaeda. In 1990, acquitted of conspiring to assassinate Egyptian President Mubarak, Rahman fled Egypt, arriving in the United States, despite being on the American list of wanted terrorists. In the United States, Rahman began preaching at a mosque in Jersey City, New Jersey and taking control of the United States offices of the al-Qaeda-affiliated Makhtab al-Khidmat (MAK), the worldwide network to recruit Muslims to fight in Afghanistan. It is believed that Rahman ordered the assassination of local MAK head Mustafa Shalabi.

From the United States, Rahman directed IG activities and raised money traveling around the United States speaking to Islamist groups. Egyptian police confiscated millions of audiotapes of Rahman's lectures.

Several of the 1993 World Trade Center bombers attended Rahman's mosque. While prosecutors could not link Rahman to that bombing, he was implicated in a conspiracy to bomb public places throughout New York and a plot to assassinate Mubarak on a trip to the United States.

On October 1, 1995, Sheikh Rahman was convicted in a federal court in New York of conspiracy to destroy United States public buildings and structures. He is currently serving a life sentence. The IG operatives who committed the 1997 Luxor massacre claimed that they were attempting to force the United States to release Rahman. Abu Sayyaf, an Islamist group in the Philippines, also demanded Rahman's release as part of its conditions for releasing hostages.

Although imprisoned, Rahman may still be playing an active role in directing Islamist terrorism. In April 2002 Attorney General John Ashcroft announced the indictment of four associates of Sheikh Rahman: Lynne Stewart, his attorney; Mohammed Yousry, Rahman and Stewart's Arabic language interpreter; Ahmed Abd al-Sattar, whom the indictment describes as a "surrogate" for Rahman; and Yasser al-Sirri, the former head of the London-based Islamic Observation Center. The indictment charges that these defendants worked together to help Rahman direct IG activities from his prison cell. Rahman rejects the call by other IG leaders for a ceasefire with the Egyptian government.

Northern Alliance forces captured Sheikh Rahman's son, Ahmed, at a Taliban position during Operation Enduring Freedom in Afghanistan on November 29, 2001. Another son is a scholar at al-Azhar University in Cairo, Egypt.

Rifa'i Ahmed Taha Musa

With most of the Islamic Group's (IG) leadership imprisoned, Taha Musa is the effective commander of the IG. Trained as an accountant, he masterminded the Luxor massacre and was a signatory to bin Laden's 1998 declaration of an International Islamic Front for Jihad. In 2001 he wrote a book justifying terrorism and operations intended to achieve mass civilian casualties. Taha Musa is believed to be based in Afghanistan or Pakistan.

Imprisoned Leaders

Since Sheikh Rahman's incarceration in the United States, the recognized leader of the Islamic Group is Karam Zhody, who has been in prison in Egypt since 1981, serving a 25-year sentence for ordering the assassination of President Anwar Sadat. The Egyptian government is considering an early release for Zhody, discounting five years from his sentence as part of the Government's anti-terrorism incentive. In an interview in early June 2002, Zhody was asked if he felt remorse for ordering the assassination of Egypt's president. His response, "No use crying over spilled milk."

Al-Jihad's top imprisoned leader is Abbud al-Zumar, an original founder of al-Jihad. He has been in an Egyptian prison since 1981, also for organizing the assassination of Sadat.

Organization

The Islamic Group (IG) began as a loose affiliation of militant Islamist cells. It operated semi-openly, collecting money at mosques, fielding slates of candidates in university elections, and attempting to recruit large numbers of members. At its peak membership, it is believed to have had tens of thousands of members. Currently, its membership is estimated in the thousands. While the group holds influence over schools and mosques, it is not clear whether the IG is actually responsible for operating these entities. The IG recruits predominantly students from poorer urban and rural areas, and those who have recently moved to large cities. Al-Qaeda adopted IG's structure of loosely affiliated regional wings.

In contrast, al-Jihad is a smaller, more clandestine and tightly disciplined organization. At its peak, al-Jihad had, perhaps, a few thousand members. The group was comprised of a leadership structure that oversaw strategy, and was complemented by a ten-man advisory committee, known as a *majlis al-shura*. The al-Jihad leader instituted a complex web of blind cells, an arrangement whereby no cell knew the members or activities of any other cell. This approach was designed to minimize the vulnerability of any individual cell, and has proven difficult to penetrate. A three-department supervisory apparatus managed day-to-day operations. Al-Qaeda adopted al-Jihad's cell structure in which cells are kept secret from each other to reduce losses if one cell is penetrated. Before it was shattered by a series of arrests in 1993, Zawahiri's faction, Vanguards of Conquest, was considered the elite faction of al-Jihad.

Al-Jihad recruits young males, usually ranging in age from 15 to 30. The young men are selected for their willingness to commit suicide/homicide in attacks against "infidel" targets.

Financial Support

The Islamic Group (IG) receives funding from several sources. One of the IG's first sources of funding was crime, particularly robbing Coptic Christian jewelers. Rahman ruled that this activity was acceptable under Islamic law because Christians and Muslims are in a state of war. Iran funded IG activity through its Islamic Revolutionary Council, a body established to "export" Iranian revolutionary dogma. This funding decreased when Iran sought to improve its relationship with Egypt in the late 1990s. The IG raises funds through its overseas network in Europe and North America and has received funding from Saudi Arabia because Rahman taught there in the 1970s. During the 1980s and the war in Afghanistan, the IG began receiving support from Osama bin Laden and al-Qaeda became the primary source of support in the 1990s. In addition to external support, IG cells in southern or Upper Egypt impose "Islamic taxes" on local businesses to fund their operations.

Al-Jihad has similar sources of support to the IG. Al-Jihad's primary source of support is Osama bin Laden, who provided between $250,000 and $500,000 a year for most of the 1990s. Iran also supported al-Jihad. Al-Jihad has supporters in the United States and Europe who funnel money through local Muslim charities to fund operations overseas. Following the attacks of September 11, 2001, the Federal Bureau of Investigation cracked down on many fraudulent and terrorist-supporting charities, such as the Benevolence International Foundation and the Holy Land Foundation.

Links to States and Terrorist Organizations

The Islamic Group (IG) and al-Jihad are integrated into al-Qaeda's international network. Egyptians hold five of the nine positions on al-Qaeda's Shura Council and more than half of its core personnel are Egyptian. Consequently, like al-Qaeda itself, the IG and al-Jihad are linked to Islamist terror groups throughout the world. For more information see the al-Qaeda entry.

Hamas and Palestinian Islamic Jihad share IG and al-Jihad's origins with the Egyptian Muslim Brotherhood and may be involved in smuggling weapons to Palestinian terrorist groups via tunnels under the Egyptian-Gaza border.

While based in Sudan, in the early 1990s, al-Jihad and the IG received training from Hizbullah and Iran's Revolutionary Guards. In the late 1970s and early 1980s, IG and al-Jihad may have received support from Libya.

Areas of Operation

Within Egypt, the Islamic Group (IG) and al-Jihad's greatest strength was in the southern part of the country known as Upper Egypt. Some neighborhoods in Cairo and university campuses were also fertile grounds for Islamist recruitment.

The Americas

With the exception of the 1993 World Trade Center attack and possibly two other murders in New York City (Meir Kahane and Mustafa Shalabi), Egyptian Islamists primarily limit their activities in the United States to fundraising. In the early 1990s, Islamic Group members set up a firearms training camp in Connecticut. Ayman Zawahiri made a pair of fundraising trips to the United States in the 1980s but they were unsuccessful.

The IG has a presence in Latin America's Tri-Border region. In January 1999, al-Sa'id Hasan Hussein Mokhless, a participant in the 1997 Luxor massacre, was arrested in Ciudad del Este in Paraguay.

Since then, four other IG members, linked to the Luxor massacre or the 1995 attempt to assassinate President Mubarak, have been arrested. Egyptian Islamists may also be present in Ecuador.

The Balkans

In the early 1990s, the Egyptian Islamist organizations first became active in the Balkans, attempting to spread Islamist ideology in Bosnia. Al-Jihad and IG operatives worked at Muslim charities where they disseminated propaganda and provided support for terrorist operations. From 1993 to June 1998, when he was handed over to Egyptian authorities, longtime al-Jihad operative Ahmed Ibrahim al-Najjar, worked at the Tirana, Albania office of the Saudi-based al-Haramain Foundation.

The Third World Relief Agency (TWRA) was used to fund and support Islamist activity in Bosnia and Croatia. In 1995, Croatian security arrested a senior IG member who was employed by the TWRA. The IG responded with a suicide bombing of a Croatian police station in October 1995.

The IG worked with al-Qaeda to plan attacks on NATO forces in Bosnia. Al-Jihad planned an attack on the American embassy in Tirana, Albania in 1998. Albanian authorities broke up the cell planning the attack.

In October 2001, the Bosnian government deported Sheikh Imad al-Misri to Egypt where he had been sentenced *in absentia* to ten years hard labor. Sheikh al-Misri is a leading figure in the IG and was one of the top Islamic missionaries in Bosnia. He is also alleged to have given his approval to terrorist acts in Bosnia.

London

Yasser al-Sirri, who lives in West London and is director of the Islamic Observation Center, is a top leader of the Egyptian Islamists. He faces a death sentence in Egypt for his role in a 1993 attempt to kill the Prime Minister of Egypt that resulted in the death of a young girl. His organization issued the press credentials to the assassins of Ahmed Shah Massoud. He has been living in Britain since 1994, as Britain has refused to extradite him to Egypt. He is one of the Egyptian Islamist leaders who calls for a ceasefire with the Egyptian government.

Egyptian Islamists also occupy top positions in the extensive London-based al-Qaeda apparatus, centered at the Advice and Reform Committee.

Targets and Tactics

Both the Islamic Group (IG) and al-Jihad have targeted civilians and used suicide tactics. However, the IG has traditionally favored mass action, using violence to create a more Islamist society. Ultimately, such a society will overthrow its secular government. Consequently, the IG has attacked video stores and other outlets selling Western goods. The IG targeted Egypt's Christian Copts, looting their stores to raise money for the IG. The attacks on tourists were aimed at ridding the society of non-Islamic influences, as well as an attempt to destroy Egypt's economy and create more favorable conditions for an Islamist revolution.

Al-Jihad was less interested in mass action, preferring coups to the IG's revolution. Al-Jihad focused on assassinating high-level government officials, with mixed success.

In 1987 Mohamed Makkawi, a retired Egyptian Army officer, suggested that al-Jihad hijack a passenger jet and crash it into the Egyptian People's Assembly.

Chronology of Major Events and Attacks

Late 1970s

The Islamic Group is founded in Egypt. It intends to establish Islamic rule in Egypt by force.

Al-Jihad becomes active, operating out of Cairo, Egypt.

1981

October 6 – Egyptian President Anwar Sadat is assassinated during a military parade by four soldiers who are al-Jihad operatives. The Islamic Group is suspected of having a role in the assassination as well.

October 8-10 – An Islamist uprising in Asyut in Upper Egypt is crushed by Egyptian government forces.

1990

October 12 – The Speaker of the Egyptian Parliament is assassinated by al-Jihad operatives. The target of the assassination attempt was the Minister of the Interior.

1992

May 4 – Fifteen people, including 13 Copts, are killed in an attack by the Islamic Group in the Upper Egyptian village of Manshiet Nasser.

June 8 – Islamic Group operative, Abel-Shafi Mohamed Ramadan, assassinates prominent writer and intellectual, and supporter of Israeli-Egyptian peace, Faraj Foda.

October – One foreign tourist is killed and five are wounded in the Upper Egyptian city of Asyut in an attack by Islamic Group operatives.

1993

February 4 – A Molotov cocktail bomb is hurled at a tour bus as South Korean passengers wait to embark at a hotel outside Cairo. The Islamic Group claims responsibility.

February 26 – WTC I - A minibus containing 1,100 pounds of explosives detonates in the garage beneath the World Trade Center complex. The blast kills six people, injures 1,000, and causes $500 million worth of damage. In the 1995 trial, Islamic Group spiritual leader Sheikh Omar Abd al-Rahman and nine others, including Sudanese, Egyptian, Jordanian, and American citizens, are convicted of conspiracy and related charges. In 1998, Ramzi Yousef receives a life sentence plus 240 years in prison.

February 26 – There are several shooting attacks on tour buses and a bomb explodes in a central Cairo café, killing four.

March 10 – Government forces storm the Rahman Mosque in Aswan. Forty-three are killed, including 29 suspected Islamist operatives and 11 policemen, and 87 are reportedly arrested. The raid follows several months of increasing Islamist violence. The Islamic Group releases a statement calling for the expansion of Jihad.

March 27 – TheIslamic Group plants a time bomb in Cairo killing a police officer and wounding seven others.

March 28 – In Aswan, three separate bombs kill a policeman and injure six.

April – The Islamic Group assassinates a senior security official, his bodyguard, and his driver, in Asyut.

April 20 – Islamic Group operatives fail in their attempt to assassinate Egyptian Information Minister Safw Cairo, firing shots at his motorcade. The Minister is slightly injured and his bodyguard is seriously wounded.

August 7 – Three villagers in the area near Asyut are murdered by al-Jihad for collaborating with Egyptian security forces.

August 18 – A motorcycle bomb kills five people and wounds fifteen others on a road in Cairo. The bomb is directed at Egyptian Interior Minister Alfi, who is slightly injured. Al-Jihad claims responsibility.

November 25 – A car bomb explodes near the motorcade of Prime Minister Atif Sedki; the Prime Minister is unhurt but a nearby teenage girl is killed and 21 people are wounded. Al-Jihad claims responsibility.

December 18 – The Islamic Group assassinates an Egyptian police commander in a suburb of Cairo, reportedly in revenge for several Islamic Group members executed on December 16.

December 27 – A bus carrying tourists is fired on. Eight tourists and eight Egyptian bystanders are wounded.

1994

January 13 – Gunmen attack a police checkpoint, killing three policemen, near Al-Qusiya in Upper Egypt.

February 6 – Islamic Group operatives assassinate a police brigadier in Asyut.

February 19 – Unknown assailants fire upon a passenger train and wound a Polish woman, a Thai woman and two Egyptians in Asyut. The Islamic Group claims responsibility.

February 23 – A bomb explosion aboard a passenger train in Asyut injures six foreign tourists and five Egyptians. The Islamic Group claims responsibility.

March 4 – Unknown gunmen open fire at a Nile cruise ship and wound a German tourist near the Sohag Governate. The Islamic Group claims responsibility.

March 7 – A series of attacks on Egyptian trains injures 11 Egyptians.

April 20 – Islamic Group operatives assassinate an Egyptian police brigadier in Asyut.

May 1 – Egyptian police arrest 80 suspected Islamic Group members in Asyut.

May 13 – The Islamic Group kills three policemen in Asyut.

May 17 – Dozens of suspected Islamic Group operatives, along with weapons and video tapes of Islamic Group preachers, are seized by police.

September 27 – Three people are killed and two are wounded when an assailant fires on a downtown tourist area in Hurghada. Two Egyptians and one German are killed in the attack. The Islamic Group claims responsibility.

October 14 – An Islamic Group operative stabs and partially paralyzes novelist Naguib Mahfouz, Egypt's Nobel Laureate in literature.

1995

January 12 – Suspected members of the Islamic Group open fire on a passenger train. Six passengers, including two Argentinian tourists, are injured.

June 26 – The Islamic Group claims responsibility for a failed assassination attempt against Egyptian president Hosni Mubarak in Addis Ababa, Ethiopia. As his motorcade heads from the airport to a meeting of the Organization of Africa Unity, two vehicles try to block the road and several gunmen fire at his armored limousine. President Mubarak is not injured. Two Ethiopian military guards die and one is wounded in the exchange of gunfire. Two operatives are killed and two others are captured. The Palestinian envoy to Ethiopia also is injured.

October 20 – A car bomb detonates outside the local police headquarters building in Rijeka, Croatia killing the driver and injuring 29 bystanders. The Islamic Group claims responsibility, warning that the attacks would continue unless authorities release an imprisoned Islamic Group operative, Tala'at Fuad Kassem, who had been arrested in September 1995.

November 8 – The Islamic Group claims responsibility for an attack where Islamic extremists open fire on a train en route to Cairo from Aswan, injuring a Dutchman, a French woman and an Egyptian.

November – An Egyptian diplomat in Switzerland is assassinated by the al-Jihad.

November 19 – A suicide bomber drives a vehicle into the Egyptian embassy compound in Islamabad, killing at least 16 persons and injuring some 60 others. The explosion destroys the entire compound, damaging structures and injuring bystanders within a half-mile radius. The Japanese and Indonesian embassies, the Canadian High Commission, the UK housing compound, and Grindlays Bank are among the damaged buildings. The Islamic Group, al-Jihad, and the International Justice Group all claim responsibility for the bombing.

1996

April 28 – Four Islamic Group operatives open fire on a group of Greek tourists in front of the Europa Hotel in Cairo, killing 18 Greek tourists and injuring 12 Greeks and two Egyptians. The Islamic Group claims that they intended to attack a group of Israeli tourists they believed were staying at the hotel, as revenge for Israeli actions in Lebanon.

1997

September 18 – Egyptian Islamists shoot and bomb a tour bus outside of the Egyptian Museum in Cairo, killing nine tourists and the bus driver.

July – Six members of the Islamic Group's Shura Council call for a halt of violent operations.

November 17 – Islamic Group gunmen shoot and kill 58 tourists and four Egyptians and wound 26 others at the Hatshepsut Temple in the Valley of the Kings near Luxor. Thirty-four Swiss, eight Japanese, five Germans, four Britons, one French, one Colombian, a dual national Bulgarian/Briton and four unidentified persons are among the dead. Twelve Swiss, two Japanese, two Germans, one French and nine Egyptians are wounded. The Islamic Group militants leave a leaflet at the scene calling for the release of Sheikh Omar Abd al-Rahman, the Islamic Group spiritual leader imprisoned in the United States.

December – In the week of the Luxor massacre, conflicting statements are released, with part of the Islamic Group's leadership calling for a cease-fire and part calling for the continuation of violent jihad.

1998

February 23 – Al-Jihad leader Ayman Zawahiri and Islamic Group leader Rifa'i Ahmed Taha join Osama bin Laden in forming the International Islamic Front for Jihad on the Jews and Crusaders.

July – An attack is planned on the American embassy in Albania by al-Jihad but the plot is thwarted before it can be carried out.

1999

March – Most of the Islamic Group leadership agrees on a cease-fire, but its spiritual leader, Sheikh Omar Abd al-Rahman, incarcerated in the United States, rescinds his support for the cease-fire in June 2000.

2001

In early 2001, Islamic Group leader Rifa'i Ahmed Taha Musa publishes a book in which he attempts to justify terrorist attacks that result in mass civilian casualties.

June – Al-Jihad merges with bin Laden's al-Qaeda organization.

November – Al-Jihad leader Ayman al-Zawahiri publishes a book entitled *Knights Under the Prophet's Banner*.

2002

April 9 – Four individuals, including Sheikh Rahman's attorney and translator, are indicted for helping Rahman communicate with the Islamic Group.

Resources

Alterman, J.B., "The Luxor Shootout and Egypt's Armed Islamic Opposition." *Policywatch* November 17, 1997; No. 279 – available at www.washingtoninstitute.org.

Fighel, J., "Radical Islam in the UK: The 'Stagnation Syndrome'." The International Policy Institute for Counter-Terrorism website October 2002 – available at www.ict.org.il.

Ganor, B., "The Islamic Jihad." The International Policy Institute for Counter-Terrorism website January 1, 1993 – available at www.ict.org.il.

McCarthy, A., "Prosecuting the New York Sheikh." *Middle East Quarterly* March 1997.

Mylroie, L., "The World Trade Center Bomb: Who is Ramzi Yousef and Why it Matters." *The National Interest* Winter, 1995/96.

Wright, L., "The Man Behind Bin Laden." *The New Yorker* September 16, 2002.

Zeidan, D., "Radical Islam in Egypt: A Comparison of Two Groups." *Middle East Review of International Affairs Journal* September 1999; Vol. 3, No. 3 - available at meria.idc.acc.il/journal/ previousj.html.

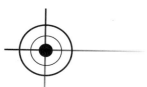

Abu Nidal Organization

Fatah al-Qiyadah al-Thawriyyah, or Fatah Revolutionary Council, is best known as the Abu Nidal Organization (ANO) after its founder Sabri al-Banna (a.k.a. Abu Nidal – Father of Struggle). It has also been known as the Arab Revolutionary Council, the Arab Revolutionary Brigades, the Revolutionary Organization of Socialist Muslims, New Black September, and Black June – which refers to June 1976 when Syrian forces entered Lebanon and attacked the PLO.

Ideology and Objectives

The ANO was one of the most violent and active terrorist groups of the Middle East. It broke away from the Fatah when Arafat began to limit Palestine Liberation Organization (PLO) terror activities. It is ideologically committed to violence. According to the ANO's principles, there can be no substitute for the violent destruction of Israel. The ANO is devoted to Arab unity, believing that expanding the conflict with Israel will unite the Arab people. They also attack pro-Western regimes and PLO figures whom the organization deems moderates.

The ANO has been accused of being a mercenary organization, carrying out attacks at the behest of its host countries. It has also used terror attacks and the threat of terror attacks against Gulf States as tools for extortion.

History
Origins and Early Operations

In 1973, with support from Iraqi leader Saddam Hussein, Abu Nidal, the Palestine Liberation Organization's (PLO) representative in Baghdad, broke off from the PLO over opposition to Arafat's acceptance of the "strategy of phases" and his limitations on terror attacks. Abu Nidal expressed his disagreement by trying to assassinate Fatah officials. Fatah tried Abu Nidal *in absentia* and sentenced him to death in October 1974. The official charge was embezzlement; Abu Nidal had, with the help of Iraqi intelligence, seized PLO assets in Iraq and also attempted to murder high-level PLO official Abu Mazen.

From 1974 to November 1983, the ANO was based in and supported by Iraq and carried out attacks throughout the Middle East and Europe. In the late 1970s, the ANO twice tried to assassinate the Foreign Minister of Syria. The ANO attacked PLO offices and officials, and diplomats of other Arab countries, particularly Kuwait. Attacks on Syrian and Jordanian targets reflected Iraqi rivalries with those states while attacks on the Gulf states were due to late payments of financial support.

The ANO also attacked Jewish community centers and synagogues and Israeli targets. On June 3, 1982 the ANO attempted to assassinate Shlomo Argov, Israel's ambassador to the United Kingdom, leaving him paralyzed. The attack triggered Israel's 1982 invasion of Lebanon to wipe out Palestinian terror forces based there.

Hosting the ANO became a political liability for Iraq in the early 1980s when Iraq began receiving American support in its war against Iran. In November 1983, Iraq expelled the ANO, which relocated to Syria. Under Syrian sponsorship, the ANO expanded its terror activities, carrying out dramatic, murderous attacks throughout Europe and the Middle East, including hijackings and an attack on a synagogue in Turkey. Syria used the ANO to fight a proxy war with Jordan over King Hussein's policies towards the Palestinians. These attacks were organized under the auspices of the New Black September, a Syrian-ANO front group. The name referred to Jordan's September 1970 expulsion of the Palestine Liberation Organization (PLO). The ANO continued to attack PLO figures, particularly those who expressed a willingness to negotiate with Israel. In 1987, Syria expelled the ANO to reduce international scrutiny of Syrian sponsorship of terrorism and the ANO moved to Libya and continued launching attacks.

The Decline of the ANO

Throughout its history, the ANO has drawn most of its support from the Palestinian refugee camps in Lebanon. In 1987, the ANO began expanding its networks in Lebanon, shifting from a clandestine organization building a political network and conventional militia. On the ground, the ANO cooperated with other Palestinian factions, including the PLO and Fatah, in the fight between the Palestinian refugees in Lebanon and the Lebanese Shi'ites, who were backed by Syria.

In the late 1980s, Abu Nidal became convinced that his organization had been penetrated by Western intelligence agencies and personally tortured and murdered several of the ANO's top leaders. In November 1989, two high-level ANO members accused Abu Nidal of murdering 150 ANO members on a single night. Over 150 other ANO members were later murdered. Reportedly, the CIA sparked these purges by attempting to recruit ANO members thereby playing on Abu Nidal's paranoia.

In the late 1980s and early 1990s, as Arafat began engaging in peace talks with Israel, the ANO and Fatah fought extensive battles in Southern Lebanon. Senior figures of both organizations as well as hundreds of members were killed. Abu Nidal also, briefly, attempted to reconcile with Arafat, but no results came of their 1987 meeting.

In the 1990s, ANO activity declined, although there were several attempts to infiltrate Israel. The war with Fatah continued, as the ANO assassinated several prominent Fatah and PLO officials. On January 14, 1991, in Tunisia, the ANO assassinated Abu Iyad, number two in Fatah and the PLO, and Abu Hol, a primary PLO commander of the first Intifada. Jordan had long been a primary ANO target, and Jordan responded ruthlessly – reportedly threatening the families of ANO militants. On January 29, 1994 the ANO assassinated a Jordanian diplomat in Beirut. The assassination led to a Lebanese crackdown on the ANO, beginning in April 1994 when the Lebanese army closed an ANO camp in eastern Lebanon.

Since then, the ANO's activities have been severely curtailed, although the ANO may have continued to serve as a terror hub, providing logistical support and intelligence for other terrorist groups. In April 1998, the ANO was expelled from Libya secretly relocating to Egypt. Rumors were that Abu Nidal was in Egypt receiving treatment for leukemia. When his presence in Egypt became public in December 1998, he left again, reportedly returning to Iraq. Egypt closed ANO offices in October 1999.

In the late 1990s, several dozen ANO members defected and joined Arafat's Fatah. In January 2000, ANO former treasurer Nimer Halima was arrested in Austria trying to withdraw over $7 million from a frozen account. It is not clear whether this withdrawal was part of the ANO's regular operations, or if it was evidence that, with Abu Nidal gravely ill, the ANO was disintegrating and its remaining leaders were feuding over the group's financial resources.

In June 2001, a Jordanian military court convicted *in absentia* Abu Nidal and three other ANO figures for the 1994 murder in Beirut. The prime suspect, Yasser Mohammad Salameh Shennar, was in Jordanian custody and was later executed.

Death of Abu Nidal

On August 16, 2002, Abu Nidal's body was discovered by Iraqi intelligence agents at his apartment in Baghdad. Iraq stated that Abu Nidal committed suicide, although the corpse showed several gunshot wounds to the chest and head. Iraq claimed that it had not been aware of Abu Nidal's presence in Iraq and attempted to arrest him when his presence became known. Iraq also claimed that Abu Nidal was conspiring with a foreign power, possibly Kuwait, against the Iraqi regime.

Leadership

The leading figure in the ANO was its Secretary-General, Sabri al-Banna, better known as Abu Nidal (Father of the Struggle.) Abu Nidal was born in Jaffa in 1937 to a wealthy family. With Israel's War of Independence, his family relocated to Gaza and then Nablus. He trained as an electrician. He was originally a Ba'athist, and founded his own liberation group in the mid-1960s. He joined Fatah in 1967 and was its representative in Khartoum, Sudan in 1969. In 1970, he was the Fatah representative in Baghdad but in 1974, displeased with Arafat's limitations on attacks against Israel, Abu Nidal formed his own terrorist group. He was aided by Iraqi intelligence, which also helped him seize PLO assets in Iraq.

Since founding the ANO, personal information about Abu Nidal has been limited. He was wanted by, among others, the United States, Israel, and Jordan which sentenced him to death *in absentia*. He frequently created rumors of his demise in order to facilitate his relocations. It is unclear, after his August 2002 death, who will take control of his organization or if the organization will continue to function.

Organization

The ANO is estimated to have a few hundred active members, including a small militia based in Lebanon. They have offices in major Palestinian refugee camps, particularly Ain al-Hilweh and Nahr al-Barel.

Financial Support

At its peak in the 1980s, the ANO received extensive financial and operational support from throughout the Arab world and had close relationships with many other international terrorist groups. Even after the ANO's expulsion from Iraq, the Iraqi government funded the ANO with tens of millions of dollars per year. The Gulf States, particularly Saudi Arabia and Kuwait also provided tens of millions of dollars in support as protection money. Iran and Libya have also, at times, provided support at similar levels.

Part of the ANO's ideology was to have complete freedom of operation. Consequently, the ANO husbanded its resources and invested them carefully. It is believed that the ANO controls hundreds of millions of dollars.

Links with States and Terrorist Organizations
Al-Qaeda

The ANO may have facilitated the operations of al-Qaeda's Hamburg cell, which plotted the 9/11 attacks. Ziad Samir Jarrah, a Lebanese citizen and one of the 9/11 hijackers, lived with his uncle, Assem Omar al-Jarrah, in Germany for a year and a half before linking up with the Hamburg al-Qaeda cell that perpetrated 9/11. Since 1985, Assem Omar al-Jarrah served as a liaison between East German intelligence and the ANO. Shortly before 9/11, Assem Omar al-Jarrah left Germany saying that he planned to retire in Lebanon. Al-Jarrah may have helped to arrange lead hijacker Mohammed Atta's reputed meeting in Prague with Iraqi intelligence.

Fatah

Officially, the ANO was an enemy of Arafat and Fatah and was responsible for the assassination of many high-ranking Fatah leaders. However, Ion Mihai Pacepa, a Romanian intelligence chief under Ceausescu who defected to the West, claimed that the split was fabricated in order to allow Arafat to pose as a moderate and to eliminate possible rivals within the Palestine Liberation Organization.

State Supporters

Syria, Iraq, Libya, and Sudan all provided training bases for the ANO. In return, the ANO targeted those nation's enemies. In the 1980s, the ANO used training bases in East Germany, and had relationships with the radical East-bloc supported terror organizations in Europe and the Japanese Red Army.

Areas of Operation

During the 1970s and 1980s, the ANO struck throughout Europe, the Middle East, and into Asia. Attacks against Israel itself have been limited, due to strong Israeli counter-intelligence. The ANO was reportedly permitted to operate in certain Western European countries in exchange for refraining from violent attacks on their soil.

An ANO cell also operated in the United States in the late 1980s. Based in St. Louis, Missouri, several ANO members ran a food coupon redemption fraud ring. In November 1989, the cell leader, Zein Isa, murdered his teenage daughter for threatening to reveal his activities to authorities.

Targets and Tactics

The ANO is held responsible for over 100 operations which have killed over 200 people and wounded 700. The ANO has employed a wide variety of tactics, including hijackings, bombings, mass shootings, assassinations, and kidnappings.

Attacks on public gathering places, such as airports, mass transit, and hotels are standard ANO operations. Another favored ANO tactic is to target the diplomats of enemy countries. The ANO has targeted Jordanian diplomats throughout its existence, and Syrian diplomats were targeted when the ANO was under Iraqi sponsorship. In the late 1980s, the ANO assassinated four British diplomats in response to Britain's permitting the U.S. to use of air bases in Britain to bomb Libya in 1986.

Chronology of Major Events and Attacks

1973

The Fatah Revolutionary Council, later known as the Abu Nidal Organization, is founded when the Fatah representative in Iraq, Abu Nidal, broke with the Palestine Liberation Organization (PLO) over the PLO's acceptance of the strategy of phases.

September 5 – Abu Nidal occupies the Saudi embassy in Paris, demanding the release of Abu Dawud, a Fatah operative imprisoned in Jordan during the September 1970 Palestinian-Jordanian confrontation.

1974

October 26 – Abu Nidal is sentenced to death *in absentia* by Fatah.

1976

September 26 – ANO operatives take over the Semiramis Hotel in Damascus, Syria. Two of the participating operatives are publicly hanged.

October 11 – ANO operatives attack the Syrian embassies in Islamabad, Pakistan and Rome, Italy.

November 17 – ANO operatives attack the Intercontinental Hotel in Amman, Jordan.

December 13 – ANO attempts to assassinate Syrian foreign minister Abdel Halim Khadam in Damascus, Syria and attack the Syrian embassy in Istanbul, Turkey.

1977

October 25 – ANO attempts to assassinate Syria's foreign minister Khadam, in Abu Dhabi. The United Arab Emirates state minister for foreign affairs, Saif Ben Goubash, is killed during this attack

1978

January 4 – Said Hammami, the Palestine Liberation Organization representative in London, is assassinated by ANO operatives.

February 18 – Egyptian journalist Youssef al-Seba'i, President of the Conference of the Organization for the Solidarity with the Peoples of Africa, Asia and Latin America is killed during an ANO attack on the conference hall.

June 15 – ANO operatives assassinate Ali Yassin, the Palestine Liberation Organization representative in Kuwait.

August 3 – ANO operatives assassinate Izz al-Din al-Kalak, the Palestine Liberation Organization representative in Paris, France as well as one of his assistants.

August 5 – ANO operatives attack Palestine Liberation Organization offices in Islamabad, Pakistan.

1980

January 17 – ANO operatives assassinate Yussouf Mubarak, director of the Palestinian Library-Shop in Paris, France.

July 27 – ANO operatives throw a grenade at children at a Jewish school in Antwerp, Belgium resulting in one person dead and 16 injured. The ANO claims responsibility for the murder of the Israeli commercial attaché in Brussels.

1981

May 1 – ANO operatives assassinate Heinz Nittel, President of the Austrian-Israeli Friendship Association in Vienna, Austria.

June 1 – ANO operatives assassinate Naim Khader, the Palestine Liberation Organization representative in Brussels, Belgium.

August 29 – ANO operatives carry out a machine gun attack on a Vienna synagogue, killing two and wounding 17 persons.

1982

June 3 – ANO operatives attempt an assassination of Shlomo Argov, Israeli ambassador to the United Kingdom. The attack triggers Israeli invasion of Lebanon to expel the Palestine Liberation Organization.

August 9 – ANO operatives carry out a machine gun attack on the Jewish restaurant Goldberg in Paris, France. Four are killed and over 30 are wounded.

August 26 – ANO operatives attempt to assassinate the United Arab Emirates' consul in Bombay, India, and attempt to assassinate another Kuwaiti diplomat in Karachi, Pakistan.

September – ANO operatives assassinate a Kuwaiti diplomat in Madrid, Spain.

September – ANO operatives attack a synagogue in Brussels, Belgium.

October 9 – ANO operatives carry out a grenade and machine gun attack on the central synagogue in Rome, Italy; one child is killed and another ten people are injured.

1983

April 10 – ANO operatives assassinate Palestine Liberation Organization official Issam Sartawi at the Socialist International conference in Lisbon, Portugal.

ANO operatives attempt to assassinate the Jordanian ambassador to Italy, in Rome.

October 25 – ANO operatives assassinate the Jordanian ambassador in New Delhi, India. The next day, ANO operatives kill the Jordanian ambassador in Rome, Italy.

November – The ANO is expelled from Iraq and relocates to Syria.

November 7 – A security guard is killed during an ANO attack on the Jordanian embassy in Athens, Greece.

December – The ANO is believed to be responsible for bombing the French Cultural Center in Izmir, Turkey.

December 29 – ANO operatives assassinate the Jordanian ambassador in Madrid, Spain.

1984

February 8 – ANO operatives assassinate the UAE ambassador in Paris, France.

March – ANO operatives assassinate a British diplomat in Athens, Greece.

March 24 – An ANO planted bomb is discovered in the Intercontinental Hotel in Amman, during the visit of England's Queen Elizabeth II to Jordan.

June 5 – ANO operatives attempt to assassinate an Israeli diplomat in Cairo, Egypt.

October 27 – ANO operatives attempt to assassinate an UAE diplomat in Rome, Italy.

November 27 – ANO operatives assassinate the British High Commissioner in Bombay, India.

November 29 – ANO operatives bomb the British Airways offices in Beirut, Lebanon.

ANO operatives attempt to assassinate a Jordanian diplomat in Athens, Greece.

December 4 – ANO operatives (New Black September) assassinate a Jordanian diplomat in Bucharest, Romania.

December 26 – ANO operatives (New Black September) bomb Palestine Liberation Organization leader Hani al-Hassan's home in Amman, Jordan.

December 29 – ANO operatives (New Black September) assassinate PLO activist and former mayor of Hebron, Fahed Kawasmeh in Amman, Jordan.

1985

March 21 – ANO operatives (New Black September) bomb ALIA (the Royal Jordanian Airlines) offices in Rome, Athens and Nicosia.

April 3 & 4 – ANO operatives fire rockets at an ALIA airliner as it takes off from Athens airport (although the rocket does not detonate, it leaves a hole in the fuselage) and against the Jordanian embassy in Rome.

July 22 – ANO attempts to bomb the American embassy in Cairo.

July 1 – ANO operatives bomb the British Airways office in Madrid (one person is killed and 27 are wounded); five minutes later, ANO operatives attack ALIA offices, two blocks away (two persons wounded).

September – ANO grenade attack at the Café de Paris in Rome, results in 38 people wounded.

November 23 – ANO operatives hijack an Egyptian plane to Malta, where 66 people are killed during a rescue attempt by the Egyptian military forces.

December 27 – ANO operatives attack El Al ticket counters at the Rome and Vienna airports, killing 19 and wounding 119. Twenty-two are killed during an attempted ANO hijacking of a Pan Am flight at Karachi airport.

September 6 – ANO operatives attack the Neve-Shalom synagogue in Istanbul, killing 22 worshippers.

1988

March – An ANO operative fires upon an Alitalia crew aboard a commuter bus in Bombay, seriously wounding the crew captain.

May – ANO operatives carry out simultaneous attacks on the Acropole Hotel and the Sudan Club in Khartoum (eight are killed and 21 are wounded).

July – Following the premature detonation of a car bomb at an Athens pier, in which two operatives die, ANO operatives aboard the Greek ferry *The City of Poros* fire upon the passengers, killing nine and wounding 98.

1991

January 14 – Palestine Liberation Organization deputy chief Abu Iyad, the most senior official of Fatah after Yasser Arafat, and Abu Hol, commander of the Western Sector forces of Fatah, are assassinated by an ANO operative in Tunis, Tunisia.

1994

January 29 – A Jordanian diplomat is shot and killed outside his home in Beirut. The government of Lebanon arrests and prosecutes ANO operatives for the attack.

2002

August 16 – Abu Nidal is killed when Iraqi intelligence agents come to his Baghdad apartment to arrest him. Iraqi intelligence calls the death a suicide although Abu Nidal's corpse bears several gunshot wounds.

Resources

Ledeen, M., "Dead Terrorist in Baghdad." *National Review Online* August 20, 2002 – available at www.nationalreview.com.

Pipes, D., "Review of Patrick Seale's *Abu Nidal: A Gun for Hire*." *The Wall Street Journal* February 18, 1992 – available at www.danielpipes.org.

Steinberg,M., "The Radical Worldview of the Abu-Nidal Faction." *The Jerusalem Quarterly* Fall 1988; No. 48 – available at www.ict.org.il.

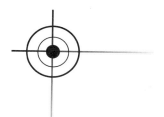

Hamas

H amas is an acronym of Harakat al-Muqawma al-Islamiyya, which is Arabic for Islamic Resistance Movement. The Arabic word Hamas can mean zealot, strength or bravery.

Ideology and Objectives

Hamas is an Islamist organization devoted to the destruction of the "Zionist entity" through jihad. Hamas views Islamic awakening as essential to the fight against Israel, considers Israel's existence an affront to Islam and views Islamic awakening as essential to the fight against Israel. Consequently, no compromise with or recognition of Israel is possible. Hamas opposes the Middle East peace process. However, because of the paramount religious importance of destroying Israel, Hamas strives to maintain Palestinian unity in order to marshal forces to confront the "Zionist entity." While Hamas has clashed with secular Palestinian organizations, it has also cooperated with them. Although motivated by radical Islam, Hamas readily adopts the language of leftist extremism, referring to Israel as a neo-colonialist entity. Hamas-sponsored media has published vicious anti-Semitic and anti-American vitriol and the Hamas charter cites the anti-Semitic forgery *The Protocols of the Elders of Zion*.

History

Origins

Hamas sprang from the original modern Muslim fundamentalist movement, the Muslim Brotherhood (al-Ikhwan al-Muslimun), which was founded in Egypt in the 1920s by Sheikh Hasan al-Banna to foster a return to the original precepts of the *Koran*. The Muslim Brotherhood spread beyond Egypt, creating a particularly strong presence in Jordan.

While always adhering to extremist politics and in many places having clandestine armed wings, the Muslim Brotherhood was best known for its religious, social, and educational works. After 1967, the Muslim Brotherhood in Gaza and the West Bank focused on these charitable works and did not take an active role in the violent struggle against Israel.

In 1973, Gaza-based Muslim Brotherhood activist Sheikh Ahmed Yassin founded al-Mujamma al-Islami (The Islamic Assembly) which did social and religious work. Yassin also began building an underground organization that would become Hamas. In 1982, with colleagues from al-Mujamma al-Islami, Yassin founded al-Majahodoun al-Falestinioun (The Palestinian Holy Fighters) to lay the groundwork for violence – first against Palestinian rivals, and later against Israel. In 1984 Israeli investigators unearthed this activity. Yassin was sentenced to 13 years in prison but he was released in May 1985 as part of a prisoner exchange. Yassin continued stockpiling weapons and attacking collaborators.

In early 1986, Yassin and his associates established Jehaz Aman (The Security Section) to monitor those suspected of collaborating with Israel or of profane, anti-Islamic activity (such as dealing in drugs or pornography). Shortly thereafter, Yassin organized an enforcement arm, the MAJD (an Arabic word for glory, it is also an acronym for the Holy War and Sermonizing Group) to murder collaborators.

The First Intifada

On December 8, 1987, a truck driven by an Israeli accidentally hit a car in the Jabalia Refugee Camp and killed four Palestinians. This sparked a wave of demonstrations that grew into the Intifada. On December 15, 1987, Hamas issued its first communiqué. Due to Sheikh Yassin's years of preparation, Hamas quickly took a leading role in organizing demonstrations and strikes. Within a few months, Hamas began targeting Israeli soldiers and civilians.

In September 1989, Israel declared Hamas an illegal organization. Sheikh Yassin and several other Hamas leaders were arrested. Yassin was sentenced to life imprisonment. Hamas reorganized around new leadership and continued its terror attacks. In 1991, the Izz al-Din al-Qassam Battalions were formed. Al-Qassam was a Palestinian terrorist who attacked Jews in the 1930s during the British Mandate period. The Izz al-Din al-Qassam Battalions carried out kidnappings, murders, and bombings.

As Hamas grew in popularity and power, it became a rival to the nationalist Palestine Liberation Organization (PLO) factions. In June of 1992 there were large-scale clashes between Hamas and Fatah militants in Gaza.

In December 1992, Israel deported 400 Hamas and Islamic Jihad members to Lebanon. While the deportations weakened Hamas' infrastructure, the organization continued to garner Palestinian support. Terrorist attacks by the al-Qassam Battalions did not abate and became more daring, such as an April 16, 1993 suicide bombing in the Jordan Valley.

In June of 1993, Hamas called for redoubling the efforts of Palestinian militants in order to derail the negotiations between Israel and the PLO. Attacks against Israeli soldiers were escalated and mass protests were organized.

On September 9, 1993, Palestinian deportees, including Hamas members, were permitted to return to their homes after nine months of exile in Lebanon. Nineteen had returned previously and the remaining 207 were permitted to return in mid-December 1993. During their Lebanese exile, Hamas and Islamic Jihad activists developed contacts with Hizbullah and began developing support in the Palestinian refugee camps in Lebanon.

Under the Palestinian Authority

With the PLO's signing of the Declaration of Principles with Israel in September 1993 and the establishment of the Palestinian Authority (PA) in June 1994, Hamas was placed in a difficult position. It had previously refused to join the PLO unless it was allotted 40 percent of the seats of the Palestinian National Council (the PLO's legislative body), and could not embrace the PA because that would have entailed tacit recognition of Israel.

At first it attempted to challenge the PA, but the PA responded quickly to these efforts. On November 18, 1994, PA security forces fired on rioting Hamas worshippers. In the ensuing battle, 13 people were killed and 200 were wounded. In preparation for the 1996 PA elections, Hamas formed a political party Hizb al-Khalas al-Watani al-Islami (National Islamic Salvation Party). When it recognized that the elections were being manipulated to ensure a massive majority for Arafat's Fatah movement in the Palestinian Legislative Council, Hamas declined to formally participate. A few independent legislators affiliated with Hamas were elected. By refusing to participate formally, Hamas avoided being marginalized by a poor electoral showing.

Ultimately, Hamas adopted the policy of respecting the PLO's role in the national struggle and not confronting it in order to avoid a Palestinian civil war. Hamas figures argued that such a conflict would in fact fulfill Zionist ambitions of dividing the Palestinian people.

On February 25, 1994, Baruch Goldstein, an Israeli extremist murdered 29 Palestinians praying at a mosque in Hebron. In revenge, Hamas, sometimes in cooperation with Palestinian Islamic Jihad (PIJ), launched a series of massive suicide bombings primarily targeting Israeli buses in Jerusalem and Tel Aviv. Hundreds were injured or killed. These attacks, while ostensibly in revenge for the massacre at Hebron, were also intended to derail the peace process. On October 19, 1994, a suicide bomber attacked a bus in Tel Aviv, killing 22 and injuring 56; a pair of attacks in 1995 killed 10 and wounded 130. On January 5, 1996, an explosive device in his cell-phone killed a leading Hamas bomb maker, Yehiye Ayyash, "The Engineer." On February 25, 1996. Hamas perpetrated the suicide bombing of a Jerusalem bus that killed 26 and wounded 80 and claimed it was in revenge for the assassination of Ayyash. Hundreds of thousands of Palestinians attended Ayyash's funeral.

The Hamas and Islamic Jihad attacks of 1994-1996 were a major factor in Likud's Binyamin Netanyahu's electoral victory over Labor's Shimon Peres in the June 1996 elections for Israeli Prime Minister.

In September 1997, Israel attempted to assassinate Hamas Political Chief Khalid Mash'al in Jordan, but the Mossad agents failed and were arrested. To extradite the agents, Israel was forced to release Sheikh Yassin from prison in October 1997. Shortly after his release, Sheikh Yassin traveled to Iran, where he consolidated Hamas's growing relations with the Iranian regime.

In 1998, there was a decline in Hamas activity. To a great extent, this was due to improved cooperation between Israeli and Palestinian security forces. Several Hamas bomb makers including the Awadallah brothers and Muhi al-Din al-Sharif, who led the Hamas military wing in the West Bank, were killed in 1998.

In the summer of 1999, Hamas terrorist incidents began to increase. In September 1999 Hamas was linked to a pair of car bomb explosions that killed three people. The three victims, apparently the perpetrators, were Arab citizens of Israel and members of Israel's Islamic Movement. They had been recruited by Hamas.

In August of 1999, Hamas offices in Jordan were shut down and top Hamas officials were arrested. The Jordanian government, which had granted Hamas relative freedom of action, had been asking Hamas to curtail its activities in Jordan since the signing of the Wye Accords between Israel, the PA, and Jordan in October 1998.

Since the founding of the PA, Hamas was permitted to operate as long as it did not directly challenge the PA. The PA permitted Hamas terrorism and Hamas activists were employed by PA security forces. At certain points, PA security forces prevented specific attacks. But Hamas infrastructure was left intact and arrests of Hamas figures by the PA were temporary and characterized by frequent "escapes." In May 2000 after five years of Israeli requests, the PA arrested Mohammed Deif, the head of the Hamas military organization in Gaza.

Throughout this period, PA misrule led to deteriorating social and economic conditions in Gaza and the West Bank. Hamas filled this gap by expanding its charitable activities and thereby expanding its influence among the Palestinians.

The al-Aqsa Intifada

In the summer of 2000, the Camp David summit failed to bring a final settlement to the Palestinian-Israeli conflict. Then on September 29, 2000, the West Bank and Gaza erupted in violence. Supposedly sparked by then Likud chief and later Prime Minister of Israel Ariel Sharon's visit to the Temple Mount, the violence was orchestrated and controlled by PA officials. By October 2000, Hamas and PIJ leaders were meeting daily with their Fatah counterparts and with PA officials, as well as receiving technical support from Hizbullah. That month, the PA released Hamas activists it had arrested including several notorious bombers. In December Mohammed Deif, one of Hamas' leading bomb makers, "escaped" with the help of his guards.

Hamas engineered a series of bloody bombings throughout Israel, including the June 1, 2001 bombing at Tel Aviv's Dolphinatium disco, which killed 21 teenagers and injured over 100 and the August 9, 2001 bombing of a Sbarro restaurant in Jerusalem that killed 15 people and injured over 90. Most of the suicide bombings emanated from the West Bank since Gaza was not as proximate to Israeli population centers, and the flat terrain aided Israeli efforts to prevent infiltrations. In Gaza, the joint Hamas-Fatah Saladin Brigades, with guidance from Hizbullah, attacked Israeli military targets. On January 9, 2002, Hamas assaulted an Israel Defense Forces (IDF) outpost in Gaza, killing four Arab soldiers in the IDF. On February 14, 2002, the Saladin Brigades adopted Hizbullah tactics for using roadside bombs and destroyed an Israeli Merkava tank. Hamas has orchestrated innumerable attacks on Israeli soldiers and settlers in the West Bank and Gaza.

Israel attempted to prevent and retaliate for these bombings by targeted killings of Hamas militants. Most of the targets of these attacks are terrorists who have an operational role in the attacks. Bomb makers are particularly targeted. Israel struck the Hamas political leadership with the July 31, 2001 assassination of Hamas Political Bureau member Jamal Mansour and the November 24, 2001 assassination of Mahmoud Abu Hanoud, the head of the Izz al-Din al-Qassam Battalions.

Throughout the al-Aqsa Intifada, there have been brief declarations of cease-fires between Israel and the PA. Hamas, along with other Palestinian factions, did not abide by these cease-fires and continued its operations. One of Israel's primary complaints has been that the PA does not crack down sufficiently on Hamas.

Sheikh Yassin condemned the September 11 bombings, saying that Islam forbids the killing of civilians, but added that American support for Israel was the source of Arab anger and the ultimate cause of the terrorist attacks. In Gaza in October 2001, Hamas-organized demonstrations celebrating Osama bin Laden and 9/11 became protests against the PA and its corruption. Rioters attacked PA police offices. PA security forces crushed the riots, firing on the crowds and killing three rioters (including a 13-year-old boy) and wounding 120.

In December 2001, after a series of terror attacks, including Hamas' December 1, 2001 double suicide bombing in Jerusalem which killed 11 and injured 180 and a December 2, 2001 bus bombing in Haifa in which 15 were killed, under international pressure, Arafat cracked down on Palestinian terrorist groups. Arafat arrested over 100 Hamas operatives, although Israel claimed that the leadership was left untouched and that Hamas members were released from prison too quickly. In late December 2001, Hamas operatives and PA security fought when PA security threatened to arrest Sheikh Yassin. Seven Hamas operatives were killed and over 100 were injured.

Hamas agreed to consider refraining from attacks within Israel's pre-1967 boundaries, although attacks on Israeli settlers and soldiers in the West Bank and Gaza continued. Hamas stated that this ceasefire was to preserve national unity. Hamas declared this cease-fire void after Israel assassinated Ra'id al-Karmi, a Tulkarm-based Fatah operative in January 2002.

Operation Defensive Shield

In March 2002, Israel was struck by a wave of devastating suicide bombings. The most deadly were launched by Hamas: the March 9 bombing of the Moment Café in Jerusalem, which killed 11 and injured 54, and the March 27 bombing at a Passover seder in Netanya that killed 29 and injured 140.

Israel responded with a massive incursion into the PA-controlled cities of the West Bank. The Israeli operations were intended to disrupt terrorist infrastructure, which included capturing and killing terrorist leaders, locating caches of supplies, and destroying workshops and laboratories that produce weapons and explosives.

The center of Hamas activity in the West Bank was the town of Nablus. Several major attacks had originated in Nablus, including the June 2001 Dolphinarium bombing which killed 21, the August 2001 Sbarro restaurant bombing which killed 15, and the December 2001 bombing in Haifa which killed 15. Hamas' West Bank leadership was based in Nablus and major Hamas weapons factories were located there. Most of the explosives used in Hamas suicide bombings and the Qassam 2 rockets were manufactured in Nablus. In Operation Defensive Shield, Israeli forces disrupted the Hamas infrastructure in Nablus by destroying several weapons factories, unearthing caches of stored weapons, and arresting or killing over a dozen major Hamas leaders. Husam Afaf Ali Badran, head of Hamas' military wing in the West Bank, was arrested on April 18; he was linked to attacks that killed over 100 Israeli citizens.

On March 30, 2002, after learning that many suspected terrorists were hiding there, the IDF surrounded the headquarters of the Palestinian Preventive Security Service in Betunia, near Nablus. On April 2, 2002 after negotiations, 184 Palestinian suspects, including four senior Hamas operatives surrendered to the IDF.

Another major IDF target was the Palestinian town of Jenin, which had been the home of 23 of the 100 suicide bombers who attacked Israel between October 2000 and April 2002. Hamas' Jenin network worked closely with Fatah and the PIJ, and carried out several attacks including the March 31 attack on a bus in Haifa, which killed 15. At least six Hamas leaders were killed in the intense fighting in Jenin, and dozens were captured.

Because of its proximity to Israel's major population centers, Tulkarm is a major zone for Palestinian terrorism. The Hamas organization in Tulkarm played a central role in several attacks, including the March 27, 2002 Passover Seder attack in Netanya that triggered Operation Defensive Shield. Tulkarm was also the base from which Hamas intended to launch its Qassam missiles.

Throughout the West Bank, dozens of Hamas operatives were arrested in the course of Operation Defensive Shield and four of the 13 terrorists deported after the May 2002 standoff at the Church of the Nativity were Hamas operatives.

Operation Defensive Shield was not extended to Gaza, where the Hamas infrastructure remained intact.

Terror Resumes

While its infrastructure was severely damaged, Hamas continued to launch terror attacks against Israel. On May 7, 2002, 16 were killed and 55 were wounded in a suicide bombing at a club in Rishon Lezion near Tel Aviv. Hamas continued targeting Israeli buses, including a June 18, 2002 suicide bombing on a Jerusalem city bus that killed 19 and wounded 70, and attacking a bus in northern Israel on August 4, 2002 killing 10 and wounding over 40.

Hamas also expanded its operations against West Bank settlements such as the July 16, 2002 ambush of a bus near the settlement of Emmanuel, nine were killed and 20 wounded.

On July 31, 2002, a bomb planted by a Hamas operative in the cafeteria of the Frank Sinatra student center of Hebrew University in Jerusalem exploded, killing nine (including five Americans) and wounding 85. In August, the leaders of the Hamas cell that conducted the attack were captured. The bomber was employed by the university. The cell members were East Jerusalem residents and unlike Palestinians living in the West Bank could travel freely throughout Israel. They used this freedom to reconnoiter targets for other terrorist cells and had helped smuggle bombers across the Green Line. This cell was also responsible for the March 9, 2002 bombing of the Moment Café.

Israel continued to attempt to capture or kill Hamas leaders. On July 22, 2002, the IDF killed Salah Shehadeh, the military commander of Hamas. IDF fighters bombed Shehadeh's residence, killing 15 other people, including nine children. Shehadeh had been linked to dozens of attacks on Israeli civilians and soldiers in the Gaza Strip, was a key link between Hamas leaders in Damascus and operations in Gaza and the West Bank, and helped recruit children to attack Israeli forces. Israel had made numerous requests that the PA arrest him. Shortly after Shehadeh's assassination, Sheikh Yassin appointed master bomb maker Mohammed Deif as the Hamas military commander. Deif may have been injured when the Israelis attempted to assassinate him in September.

In August, Israeli forces arrested two Hamas operatives who were rebuilding Hamas infrastructure in Jenin. They were linked to numerous attacks that had killed over 50 Israelis and wounded hundreds, including the March 31, 2002 attack in Haifa and the bombing of the Sbarro restaurant in Jerusalem.

In October 2002, Palestinian Authority (PA) Colonel Rajah Abu Lehiya was killed in Gaza. Colonel Lehiya had led the crackdown on the Hamas uprising of October 2001 in which three people were killed. His death sparked another round of Fatah-Hamas fighting in which five were killed. A massive show of PA-Fatah force forestalled further fighting. Hamas and Fatah began negotiations in Cairo under Egyptian auspices. The negotiations were designed to maintain national unity and determine the best strategy for continuing the Intifada. In these meetings, Hamas remained committed to attacking Israeli civilians.

As of December 2002, Israel had captured hundreds of Hamas operatives, primarily in the West Bank, and there was a corresponding decline in the number and effectiveness of Hamas attacks. The Gaza branch remained intact and Hamas leaders were, with limited success, attempting to transfer their expertise to the West Bank in order to rebuild those networks.

Leadership
Sheikh Ahmed Yassin – Founder and Spiritual Leader
Born in Ashkelon Israel in 1936, Yassin was partially paralyzed at the age of 14 from an injury received during a soccer game. He joined the Muslim Brotherhood in Gaza in 1955 and taught at religious schools. Gaza was then under Egyptian control, and the Muslim Brotherhood was an underground, outlawed organization in Egypt. In 1966, the Egyptian authorities imprisoned Yassin for a month.

After 1967, Yassin built the infrastructure of the Muslim Brotherhood in the Gaza Strip. Focusing on social, educational, and charitable works, Yassin became a leader of the Muslim Brotherhood in Gaza. In the 1970s, Yassin began building an underground.

He was arrested by Israel in 1984 and imprisoned for possessing weapons, forming a military organization, and incitement. After 11 months in prison, Yassin was freed in an exchange of prisoners along with terrorists from Ahmad Jibril's Popular Front for the Liberation of Palestine-General Council (PFLP – GC) organization.

Arrested in May 1989, an Israeli military court sentenced Yassin to life imprisonment plus 15 years in October 1991. That he was successfully prosecuted for the crimes of incitement, kidnapping, and murder, indicated that Yassin's centrality to Hamas operations. He was released in an October 1997 deal between Jordan and Israel to allow the extradition of two Israeli agents arrested in Jordan after the failed assassination attempt on Khalid Mash'al, Chairman of Hamas' Political Bureau, in Amman.

Yassin was killed by the IDF on March 22, 2004.

Musa Mohammed Abu Marzuq – Deputy Head of the Political Bureau

Musa Mohammed Abu Marzuq was born in 1951 in the Rafah refugee camp in the Gaza Strip. He studied engineering in Egypt and became a close associate of Sheikh Ahmed Yassin when he returned to Gaza. In 1988, Abu Marzuq helped found the Hamas movement.

In 1974, he left Gaza for the United States, where he continued his studies in engineering. Between 1981 and 1992, he and his family lived in Falls Church, Virginia and Ruston, Louisiana, while he pursued a Ph.D. in industrial engineering. While in the United States, he helped found the Islamic Association for Palestine and the United Association of Studies and Research. The organizations were the cornerstones of an extensive Hamas fundraising and recruitment network in the United States.

In 1989, Abu Marzuq was elected head of the Political Bureau of Hamas, the movement's central leadership body. With the arrest of Sheikh Yassin, Abu Marzuq became the effective head of Hamas and oversaw its reorganization. Abu Marzuq selected and coordinated terrorist operations, transferring funds for operations, and organizing and appointing leaders for Hamas divisions and units. In 1992, he headed a Hamas delegation to Tehran that concluded several cooperative agreements with Iran. That same year he also served as the chief Hamas representative in negotiations with the PLO in Tunis.

From 1992 to 1995, Abu Marzuq lived in Jordan but was expelled after the May 1995 Jordanian-Israeli peace agreement. Abu Marzuq was arrested in New York on July 25, 1995. Israel requested his extradition for transferring money to the military wing of Hamas and an American judge ruled in May 1996 that Abu Marzuq could be extradited for trial in Israel. Fearing a possible wave of terror in 1997, the Israeli government elected not to try Abu Marzuq, who instead returned to Jordan.

In September, on returning to Jordan from a trip to Iran, Abu Marzuq (along with several other Hamas leaders) was arrested by Jordanian authorities and deported. Since then, Abu Marzuq has operated out of the Hamas office in Damascus, Syria.

Khalid Mash'al – Chairman of the Political Bureau

Khalid Mash'al, born near Ramallah in 1956, lived in Kuwait from 1967 until the 1990 Gulf War. Mash'al received a degree in physics from Kuwait University and taught physics in Kuwait. Also at Kuwait University, Mash'al was a leading activist for Islamic organizations within the Palestinian Student Union. In 1990, he moved to Jordan, where he has focused on building Hamas.

One of the founders of Hamas, Mash'al was an original member of the Political Bureau. In 1996, after the detention in the United States of Abu Marzuq, Mash'al was elected chairman of the Hamas Political Bureau.

On September 25, 1997, Mash'al escaped an assassination attempt by the Mossad in Amman, Jordan. Israel was forced to release Sheikh Yassin, Hamas' spiritual leader, from prison as a result of this failed attempt.

In September 1999, on his return from a trip to Iran, Jordanian authorities arrested Mash'al and several other Hamas officials. He was expelled from Jordan and relocated to Qatar. He is now based in Syria.

Ibrahim Ghousheh - Hamas Spokesman

Ibrahim Ghousheh was born in Jerusalem on November 26, 1936 and joined the Islamic Movement in Jerusalem in 1950. He earned a bachelor of science degree in civil engineering from Cairo University in 1961 and as a student at Cairo University, he was an Islamic activist in the Palestinian Students League in Egypt.

Ghousheh worked as an engineer in the Jordan Valley and Kuwait, but since 1989 he has devoted all of his efforts to political work for Hamas. He is a member of the Hamas Political Bureau and has been the Hamas spokesman since 1992.

In September 1999, along with several other Hamas officials, Ghousheh was arrested on returning to Jordan from a trip to Iran. He was deported to Qatar. In June 2001, Ghousheh attempted to return to Jordan and was detained at the airport for several weeks before being allowed to reenter Jordan.

Abdel Aziz Ali al-Rantisi – Hamas Leader in Gaza

Abdel Aziz al-Rantisi was born in Yabna village (between Ashkelon and Jaffa) in 1947. His family fled to the Gaza Strip during the 1948 war and he was raised in the Khan Yunis refugee camp. He earned a medical degree from Alexandria University in Egypt and worked as a resident pediatrician at Nasser Hospital in Khan Yunis. Al-Rantisi has been a lecturer in science at the Islamic University in Gaza since its founding in 1978 and was arrested in 1983 for refusing to pay taxes to Israel. In 1987, he helped found Hamas.

In January 1988, he was detained for 21 days. In March 1988, Israel arrested him and detained him for 30 months. He was released in September 1990 and in December 1990 he was placed in administrative detention for one year.

In December 1992, he was deported, along with 400 Hamas and Islamic Jihad activists, to South Lebanon. He was the spokesman of the deportees in Marj Al Zuhour camp (Return Camp). On his return to Gaza in 1993, he was arrested and remained under administrative arrest until mid-1997. Rantisi was killed by the IDF on April 17, 2004.

Mohammed Nazzal – Political Bureau Member

Mohammed Nazzal, born in Amman, Jordan in 1963, attended secondary school in Kuwait and studied chemistry at Karachi University in Pakistan. He was elected Secretary-General of the Muslim Students Union in Pakistan, a coalition of Islamist expatriate students in Pakistan. While there, Nazzal made contact with extremist Pakistani Islamist organizations.

Nazzal joined the Hamas Political Bureau and was appointed its representative in Jordan in 1992. In September 1999, when Jordan cracked down on Hamas, Nazzal, a Jordanian citizen, went into hiding.

Imad al-Alami - Member of Hamas Political Bureau

Imad al-Alami holds a bachelor's degree in civil engineering from Alexandria University in Egypt. He was arrested by Israel in September 1988 for inciting and organizing violence through the Hamas information committee and was released in September 1990. In January 1991, Israel deported him to Lebanon. In the early 1990s, al-Alami was the Hamas liaison to Iran. More recently, he has been based in Damascus.

Organization

The primary division of Hamas operations is between the overt and covert branches. The covert and overt wings are not divided ideologically, they exist to support the others' activities and work in harmony. There are several parallel overt branches that run charities, support social activities and conduct religious outreach. They are referred to as *da'wa*, which literally translates as sermonizing. These branches broaden the Hamas presence in Palestinian society, foster greater observance among the Palestinians, and recruit members to the covert wing. The overt branches organize general protests and strikes. Individuals who distinguish themselves in this arena are recruited into the covert wing.

Hamas has an active youth wing that is particularly strong at al-Najah University in Nablus, where the student council is dominated by a Hamas-PIJ coalition. The university laboratories have been used to make explosives and poison for use in terror attacks. Several suicide bombers have been recruited from al-Najah's student body and al-Najah students staged a reenactment of the 2001 Sbarro's bombing. Hamas also runs summer camps where children are indoctrinated in Islamist ideology and trained how to participate in violent protests.

Hamas has several hundred to a few thousand military operatives and thousands of active supporters who are involved in its social networks. Overall, 15-30 percent of Palestinians support Hamas. While Hamas' leadership is Islamist, many members are not. Many are drawn to Hamas because of its effectiveness, by its social services and because it represents the most credible opposition to Fatah.

Besides being divided by function, Hamas is also divided by geography. The West Bank and Gaza units operate independently and are divided into smaller districts and subdistricts. Due to Israeli arrests, Hamas leadership has been based in Jordan and, later, Syria and other areas outside of the West Bank and Gaza since the early 1990s.

Hamas was virtually incapacitated by the Israeli arrest of Sheikh Yassin and other top Hamas leaders in the late 1980s and early 1990s. Abu Marzuq developed the current compartmentalized structure with extensive unit autonomy to ensure that the loss of a single individual would not endanger the movement. In the wake of Operation Defensive Shield, the Hamas network in the West Bank was severely damaged. The Gaza network remains substantially intact. IDF intelligence keeps tabs on the Gaza network by monitoring graffiti in the refugee camps and towns of the Gaza strip.

Financial Support

Zakat (or charity) is one of the five basic principles of Islam. Hamas diligently and, in some cases, forcibly collects this tithe from its supporters in the West Bank and Gaza. Hamas also runs profitable business enterprises in the West Bank and Gaza and engages in criminal activity – particularly producing counterfeit music compact discs and other multimedia material. Intellectual property piracy is believed to earn Hamas millions of dollars annually.

Hamas raises funds from individuals throughout the Arab world, particularly from the Gulf States, which have not restricted Hamas activities. Hamas opposed the 1990 Iraqi invasion of Kuwait, and, consequently, Kuwait has proven a particularly fertile ground for Hamas fundraising endeavors. While there is little data on Hamas' efforts in the Gulf States, anecdotal evidence suggests that Hamas raises tens of millions of dollars annually from the Gulf Arabs. Reportedly, in his 1998 tour of Saudi Arabia Sheikh Yassin raised $300-400 million.

Hamas members also benefit from grants made by Saudi Arabia and Iraq under Saddam Hussein to the families of those killed fighting in the Intifada.

As an offshoot of the Muslim Brotherhood, Hamas receives financial and political support from branches of the Muslim Brotherhood throughout the Middle East, including the Islamic Movement in Israel, which has helped to transfer funds to Hamas under the auspices of charitable organizations. The Muslim Brotherhood in Jordan has been a staunch ally of Hamas, particularly during Jordanian crackdowns on Hamas activities.

Iran also provides financial support to Hamas. Exact data is unavailable, but it is at least $3 million annually and may be as much as $10-20 million annually.

Hamas has fundraising operations throughout the United States, Britain, and Europe. Often, the money is raised under the auspices of seemingly legitimate charities that are front groups for Hamas. While the money may go to underwrite Hamas' charitable activities, Hamas' social and military endeavors are integrated. Charitable donations to Hamas free other funds to support terrorist activities and support Hamas' recruitment and social objectives, which underpin the terrorist activity.

The four central Hamas charities in the West are: The Palestine Relief and Development Fund (Interpal) in Great Britain, The Holy Land Foundation in the United States, The al-Aqsa Foundation in Germany with branches in Belgium and Holland, and Comité de Bienfaisance et Solidarité avec la Palestine in France. It is estimated that tens of millions of dollars a year are raised for Hamas in the United States and Britain – between one-third and three-quarters of Hamas' total budget. In the year 2000, the Holy Land Foundation raised about $13 million. In the wake of 9/11, the FBI closed the Holy Land Foundation in November 2001.

Links to States and Terrorist Organizations
Hizbullah

The Hamas-Hizbullah relationship originated in the early 1990s but has expanded since the beginning of the al-Aqsa Intifada. Hamas was inspired by Hizbullah's long war with Israel in Lebanon, which ultimately culminated in Israel's complete withdrawal from Lebanon in May 2000. Hamas has adopted Hizbullah's strategy of attrition and has received training from Hizbullah in tactics. A pair of Hamas-Fatah operations in Gaza – a January 9, 2002 attack on an IDF outpost in Gaza, killing four Arab Israeli soldiers and the February 14, 2002 destruction of a Merkava tank – used tactics developed by Hizbullah. The bomb used in the Passover Seder massacre in Netanya may have employed Hizbullah bomb making techniques. Hizbullah has also assisted Hamas in producing Qassam rockets.

Iran

When Hamas was first founded, its Sunni Muslim ideology was a barrier to cooperation with the Iranian Shi'ites. But relations began to warm after Hamas and Hizbullah came into contact. The Hamas militants deported to Lebanon in 1992 helped further this relationship and Hamas' continued growth made it an appealing partner for the

Iranian regime. Iran has become a major source of financial and technical support for Hamas, both directly and through Hizbullah. In April 2001 Iran sponsored a conference on intensifying the Intifada where Hamas was represented by Khalid Mash'al.

PA-Fatah

Secular Fatah and Islamist Hamas were rivals as Hamas opposed the establishment of the Palestinian Authority (PA) and the Oslo process. After the establishment of the PA, PA-Fatah dominated Palestinian politics. In November 1994 PA security fired on a rioting Hamas crowd in Gaza. Violence has since flared between Fatah and Hamas, but Hamas avoids an open confrontation and insists on maintaining Palestinian unity. Nor does the PA seek to eliminate Hamas. Throughout the Oslo process, Israel called for the PA to crack down on the Palestinian terror infrastructure. The PA would arrest Hamas activists but release them shortly thereafter. Hamas operatives were also hired to work in Palestinian security services.

With the outbreak of the al-Aqsa Intifada, Hamas and Fatah have cooperated closely, including forming "cocktail" cells that have members of several terrorist organizations. Reportedly, the PA helps ensure that Fatah has a steady supply of weapons. In Gaza, Hamas has begun to challenge the PA as its control has broken down.

Other Palestinian Terrorist Organizations

Hamas was initially reluctant to cooperate with the various PLO factions due to their secularism and viewed the PIJ as a rival. By rejecting the Oslo peace process, Hamas had common ground with the secular rejectionist front, including the Popular Front for the Liberation of Palestine (PFLP), the Popular Front for the Liberation of Palestine-General Command (PFLP-GC) and the Democratic Front for the Liberation of Palestine (DFLP). The PIJ's failure to develop as a rival to Hamas has led to closer relations between the two Islamist organizations.

With the outbreak of the al-Aqsa Intifada, Hamas and the PIJ have closely coordinated activities with each other and other Palestinian organizations. Hamas has been outspoken in its support for the activities of various secular Palestinian leaders, for example condemning the PA's arrest of Ahmed Sa'dat the Secretary General of the PFLP. Hamas operatives have trained with the PFLP-GC in Lebanon.

Sudan

Since the 1989 military coup, Sudan has been dominated by Hassan al-Turabi's National Islamic Front, which was linked to the Muslim Brotherhood. Hamas terrorists were welcomed and trained in Sudan. After 1999, al-Turabi's influence was limited since losing a power struggle with Sudan's President Omar Hasan Ahmad al-Bashir in 1999 and in Sudan's overt support for external terrorist organizations has declined.

Syria/Lebanon

Since the temporary expulsion of Hamas leaders to Lebanon in 1993, Hamas has had close relations with the Syrian regime. When the Hamas leadership was forced to leave Jordan in 1999, Khalid Mash'al and Abu Marzuq directed Hamas affairs from Damascus. Damascus now serves as the headquarters and planning center for Hamas. Orders to launch an operation usually come from the Damascus office.

Having faced an armed rebellion from the Muslim Brotherhood, the secular Syrian regime limits armed Hamas activities with Syria, but facilitates Hamas training and cooperation with Hizbullah and the PFLP-GC in Lebanon. Hamas has also, at Fatah's expense, garnered popular support in the Palestinian refugee camps of Lebanon.

Other States and Terrorist Organizations

Hamas also has links to other terrorist organizations throughout the world. In June 2001, Hamas reportedly bought explosives from ETA, the Basque separatists and Colombian officials claim that Hamas terrorists train with the FARC in Colombia.

Hamas opposed Iraq's invasion of Kuwait in 1990, and since falling into the Iranian orbit has never built a relationship with Iraq. However, Hamas has benefited from Iraqi funding of suicide bombers. In late 2002 and early 2003, Hamas organized pro-Iraq rallies and Hamas leaders threatened to target American interests if Iraq were attacked.

Al-Qaeda and the Islamist Terror Network

Hamas has links with Islamist terrorist organizations throughout the world. Tracing its origins to the Muslim Brotherhood, Hamas maintains links with the organization and its armed factions throughout the Arab world, particularly in Egypt and Algeria. These links were cemented when Hamas members trained in Sudan, where they came into contact with Islamist movements from all over the world. Hamas is closely aligned with the Islamic Action Front in Jordan. Since 1998, Hamas representatives have attended international conferences of Islamic organizations where they have made contact with terrorist organizations based in Pakistan and throughout the world, including al-Qaeda.

A Hamas operative in the United States helped provide components for the bomb used in the 1993 attack on the World Trade Center.

While Hamas has links with al-Qaeda, Hamas leaders have been careful to keep a certain distance in order to avoid being absorbed into al-Qaeda the way the Egyptian terrorist organizations were. However, Abdallah Azzam, the founder of al-Qaeda, was a Palestinian from Jenin and provided funds for Hamas in the 1980s.

Hamas and al-Qaeda also have linked financial networks. Hamas' American fundraising operations are intertwined with the International Islamic Relief Organization (IIRO), a Saudi-based charity that operates worldwide and has been linked to al-Qaeda. Saudi businessman Yassin al-Qadi used the Virginia office of the IIRO to funnel donations to Hamas. Al-Qadi is also suspected of funding al-Qaeda. The Holy Land Foundation handles the West Bank and Gaza operations of the Benevolence International Foundation, which has been linked to al-Qaeda as well.

Areas of Operation

Hamas was initially strongest in Gaza, but is now also prominent in the West Bank, although Operation Defensive Shield and other Israeli actions disrupted its networks there. It has attacked Israeli soldiers and civilians both in the West Bank and Gaza, and also within Israel proper. It officially eschews expanding the conflict to areas outside of "historic Palestine."

Much of the Hamas leadership was based in Jordan, but, after Jordanian crackdowns, moved to Damascus, Syria. Hamas has offices around the globe – openly in the Middle East and under the cover of front organizations in the United States and Europe.

The Americas

Taking advantage of the civil liberties offered by the United States, Hamas pioneered the development of an American infrastructure to support terror. Several major organizations that represent American Muslims, including the Muslim Arab Youth Association and the American Muslim Council, have held conferences featuring Hamas leaders who have called for the destruction of Israel and published anti-Semitic material.

Abu Marzuq, one of Hamas' top officials, lived in the United States for almost a decade and developed a support network, and for a time directed American Hamas operations. Besides developing a fundraising network, he recruited Hamas militants and helped found several organizations that furthered Hamas goals. While living in the United States, Abu Marzuq founded the United Association for Studies and Research (UASR) and headed the consultative body governing the Islamic Association for Palestine (IAP), which served as a public relations vehicle for Hamas and other Islamist organizations. The IAP publishes newspapers, produces videos for terrorist training and recruitment as well as other videos for general American consumption, and has sponsored summer camps and retreats.

Founded in 1994, the Council on American-Islamic Relations (CAIR) ostensibly advocates for Muslim civil rights in the United States. But much of CAIR's leadership was drawn from the IAP. CAIR's executive director edited a newspaper published by the IAP. Rafeeq Jabar, a founding director of CAIR, is the president of the IAP in Chicago. Mohammed Nimer, director of CAIR's research center, was a director of (UASR) in 1992.

Abu Marzuq also founded the Holy Land Foundation for Relief and Development (HLF), which is at the center of a widespread fundraising network. The HLF is based in Richardson, TX and has several offices around the country. The organization shared office space in Richardson with Infocom, a technology company that was closed by the United States government in December 2002 for funneling money to Abu Marzuq and his wife and for selling computers to Syria and Libya without a license. Abu Marzuq and his wife contributed $250,000 to Infocom's start-up which was managed by cousins of Abu Marzuq's wife.

The United States network extended to Canada where authorities, until November 2002, did not consider Hamas a terrorist entity. Throughout the 1990s, Hamas raised hundreds of thousands of dollars annually in Canada.

In December 2003, Israeli authorities arrested Jamal Akkal, a Canadian citizen of Palestinian descent. Akkal confessed that he had been training with Hamas in Gaza to attack Israeli targets in North America.

Hamas is one of several Islamist organizations building an infrastructure for terror and criminal activities in the Tri-Border region of South America where Brazil, Paraguay, and Argentina meet. In the

Tri-Border region, Hamas raises money both through donations and criminal activities including drug smuggling. Reportedly, the region serves as a logistical hub for Hamas operations, and Hamas runs training camps and recruits operatives there. Hamas operatives are also suspected of working with the FARC in Colombia.

Targets and Tactics

Hamas has used a variety of tactics, including ambushing soldiers and Israeli civilians in the West Bank, fomenting violent demonstrations and strikes, and kidnapping. In its efforts to achieve mass casualties, Hamas has used suicide bombers and planted bombs, but Hamas operatives have also fired on, thrown grenades at, and driven cars and buses into crowds.

The major suicide bombings have mostly originated from the West Bank. But Hamas operatives in Gaza have launched hundreds of lower level attacks against soldiers and civilians in and bordering Gaza, especially the IDF base at Rafah on the Egyptian border. Tunnels under Rafah are used to smuggle weapons, people, and goods into and out of Gaza.

Major attacks are coordinated by the Hamas organization. But through continuing incitement, Hamas urges Palestinians to carry out individual attacks against Israelis by whatever means possible and has organized children to attack Israeli soldiers.

Hamas does not differentiate between Israeli soldiers and civilians. To maximize casualties, Hamas has struck Israeli buses, bus stops, and restaurants. Hamas also targets Israeli "collaborators." Collaboration with Israel is broadly defined and can include working for the Israeli Civil Administration or doing business with Israelis. Hamas has been linked to the murder of at least 85 Palestinians suspected of "collaboration."

In a January 2003 rally on behalf of Iraq, Hamas officials stated that the United States would be a target of Hamas attacks if the United States attacked Iraq.

Hamas has workshops and factories throughout the West Bank and Gaza to produce the explosives, mortars, anti-tank weapons, and most recently the Qassam I, II and III rockets. These rockets, similar to Katyushas, with a range of 1.5 to 12 km, will allow Hamas to strike strategic targets within Israel. Mohammed Deif, who became the military leader of Hamas in July 2002, is believed to be personally directing the Qassam project.

Hamas has attempted to augment the lethality of its attacks with chemical weapons. Hamas engineers have tried to design a chemical warhead for the Qassam rockets and have immersed bomb components used in suicide bombings in rat poison to maximize victims' bleeding. Reportedly Hamas is trying to manufacture nerve gas, and the Hamas website includes an Arabic language manual that explains how to make poisons. In September 2002, Israeli authorities broke up a Hamas cell in East Jerusalem that was planning to poison the food at a restaurant where one of the members of the cell worked.

Chronology of Major Events and Attacks

1973

Sheikh Yassin founds al-Mujamma al-Islami (The Islamic Assembly) as a social organization in Gaza. Yassin also begins building a terrorist infrastructure.

1984

Sheikh Yassin is arrested by the Israeli authorities and is sentenced to 13 years in prison. He is released in 1985 as part of the 1985 Ahmed Jibril prisoner exchange.

1987

December 8 – In a traffic accident in the Jabalia Refugee Camp in Gaza, an Israeli truck driver accidentally kills four Palestinians when he loses control of his vehicle. Protests spread across Gaza and the West Bank and erupt into the Intifada.

December 15 – Hamas issues its first communiqué.

1989

February 16 – An Israeli soldier is kidnapped and shot to death by Hamas operatives while hitchhiking at the Hodaya junction.

May 3 – An Israeli soldier is kidnapped and murdered by Hamas operatives.

September – Israel declares Hamas an illegal organization. Sheikh Yassin and several other Hamas leaders are arrested and Yassin is given a life sentence. Musa Abu Marzuq takes charge of Hamas and reorganizes it.

1990

December 2 – Three Hamas operatives stab and kill an Israeli and wound three others on a bus between Petah Tikva and Tel Aviv.

December 14 – Two Hamas operatives stab to death three employees, one a woman, in a Jaffa metal works factory. Following this incident, Israel arrests more than 1,500 Hamas activists in Gaza and the West Bank.

1991

October 11 – Hamas claims responsibility when a Palestinian drives a van into a group of soldiers at a suburban Tel Aviv bus station, killing two and injuring 11.

October 30 – The Madrid Arab-Israeli peace conference opens. The conference lays the groundwork for future bilateral negotiations between the PLO and Israel.

1992

May 17 – An Israeli merchant is shot and killed by members of Hamas' Izz al-Din al-Qassam Battalions in Bet Le'he'ya in the Gaza District.

May 27 – The rabbi of Darom village, in Gush Katif, Shimon Biran, is stabbed to death by Hamas operatives.

June 25 – Two Israelis are stabbed to death by Hamas operatives in their place of business near the Saja'i'a neighborhood in the Gaza District.

July 7 – Over the course of one week, Hamas and Fatah loyalists in Gaza clash, fighting with fists, guns, and clubs. Eight people are shot and wounded, 20 are beaten in a melee at the Rafah Refugee Camp.

September 18 – Members of Hamas' Izz al-Din al-Qassam Battalions kidnap a hitchhiking IDF soldier. He is stabbed, and then thrown from the vehicle.

December 7 – In Gaza, three IDF reserve soldiers are killed in a Hamas drive-by shooting.

December 12 – An Israeli border guard is kidnapped and murdered near Lod. Shots are fired at an army Jeep in Hebron, killing an IDF reserve soldier and injuring two others, one of them critically. This attack precipitates the Israeli arrest and deportation of 400 Hamas and Palestinian Islamic Jihad members to Southern Lebanon.

1993

April 16 – A suicide bomber driving an explosives-laden van sets off his explosives between two buses outside of a restaurant near Mekholah in the Jordan Valley. One Palestinian passerby is killed, as is the driver of the van. Five soldiers are lightly injured. Hamas and two factions of the Palestinian Islamic Jihad claim responsibility for the attack. The investigation proves that Hamas carried out the operation.

May 16 – Hamas and Fatah cooperate to ambush and kill two Arabs and two Israelis.

July 1 – A Hamas operative infiltrates Israel and stabs and kills two women and wounds one man.

September – PLO Chairman Yasser Arafat sends Israeli Prime Minister Yitzhak Rabin a letter recognizing the right of Israel to exist. Israel replies by recognizing the PLO as the representative of the Palestinian people. On

September 13, Israel and the PLO sign the Declaration of Principles, which outlines Palestinian self-government.

September 9 – Over two hundred of the Hamas and Palestinian Islamic Jihad operatives that Israel had deported to Lebanon return to Israel. In Lebanon they forge links with Hizbullah.

November 7 – Near Hebron, Hamas operatives fire on the car of Rabbi Chaim Druckman, a former member of the Israeli Knesset, killing his driver. The Damascus-based DFLP also claims responsibility for the attack.

December 24 – The commander of the IDF Special Forces in the Gaza area is shot and killed by Hamas operatives in an ambush in Gaza. Also in December 1993 six Israelis are killed in three ambushes in the West Bank and Gaza.

1994

February 19 – An Israeli woman, five months pregnant, is killed on the trans-Samaria highway in a Hamas ambush by shots fired at her car.

April 6 – A Hamas car bomb detonates at the No. 348 bus stop in the center of Afula, Israel. Eight people are killed and 51 are injured.

April 13 – A Hamas suicide bomber attacks the Central Bus Station in Hadera, killing five and injuring 30.

May 4 – Israel and the PLO sign the Gaza-Jericho Agreement, which brings the Palestinian Authority into being. Hamas, which opposes any recognition of Israel's existence, launches a massive terror campaign against Israel.

October 9 – Hamas operatives open fire with automatic weapons in Jerusalem's Nahalat Shiva'a business district. An off-duty soldier and an Israeli Arab are killed in the attack and 14 people are wounded. Bystanders shoot one of the attackers and capture the other.

October 19 – A Hamas suicide bomber attacks the No. 5 bus on Dizengoff Street in Tel Aviv. Twenty-one Israelis and a Dutch national are killed and 56 are injured.

November 18 – PA security forces fire on rioting Hamas worshippers. Thirteen people are killed and over 200 are injured in the riots.

December 25 – A Hamas suicide bomber attacks a bus stop outside the International Convention Center in Jerusalem. Thirteen people are hurt, and the bomber, a Palestinian policeman affiliated with Hamas, is killed.

1995

July 24 – A Hamas suicide bomber attacks a bus at the "Elite" Intersection in Ramat Gan, Israel, killing six and injuring 31.

August 21 – A Hamas suicide bomber targets a bus in Jerusalem, killing four and wounding nearly 100.

1996

January 5 – An explosive device planted in his cell phone by Israeli Intelligence kills Yehiye Ayyash, "the Engineer," a leading Hamas bomb maker.

February 25 – In Jerusalem a suicide bomber blows up a bus, killing 26 people and injuring 80. Hamas' Izz al-Din al-Qassam Battalion claims the bombing is in retaliation for the Hebron massacre two years before, but later denies involvement. Hamas also claims the attack is in revenge for the assassination of Yehiye Ayyash. Also that day, in Ashdod, an Israeli soldier is killed in an explosion set off by a suicide bomber at a hitchhiking post outside Ashkelon.

March 3 – A suicide bomber detonates a bomb on a No. 18 bus in Jerusalem, killing 19 persons, including six Romanians, and injuring six.

June – Israeli voters elect Likud's Binyamin Netanyahu Prime Minister. The spate of Hamas and Islamic Jihad attacks is cited as a crucial factor in the defeat of Shimon Peres.

1997

March 21 – A Hamas operative detonates a bomb on the terrace of the "Apropo" restaurant in Tel Aviv. Three young women are killed and 48 people are injured.

July 30 – Two Hamas suicide bombers detonate themselves in the Mahane Yehuda Market in Jerusalem, killing 16 people and wounding 178.

September – Israel tries, unsuccessfully, to assassinate Hamas Political Chief Khalid Mash'al. The Mossad agents are captured and Israel is forced to release several imprisoned Hamas figures, including Sheikh Yassin, in order to free the Mossad agents.

September 4 – Five people are killed and 200 are wounded in three Hamas suicide bombings on the Ben-Yehuda pedestrian mall in Jerusalem.

1998

July 19 – A Hamas van loaded with explosives fails to explode. A policeman extinguishes the fire and the bomber is rushed to the hospital in critical condition.

August – The Jordanian government closes Hamas offices and expels Hamas leaders from the country.

August 20 – Rabbi Shlomo Raanan is stabbed to death by a Hamas operative in his home in Tel Rumeida in Hebron. The attacker enters the house through a window and escapes after throwing a Molotov cocktail, which sets fire to the house.

August 27 – A small Hamas bomb planted in a garbage dumpster near Allenby Street in Tel Aviv, explodes injuring fourteen people, one seriously.

October 1 – In Hebron, 13 soldiers and five Palestinians are injured when a Hamas supporter throws two grenades at a group of soldiers. Two border policemen and one soldier suffer moderate injuries, while ten others are slightly hurt. Five Palestinians are taken to Hebron hospitals.

October 19 – A Hamas member hurls two grenades into a crowd at the Central Bus Station in Beersheva. At least 59 people are wounded, two seriously. Bystanders apprehend the attacker and turn him over to civil guard policemen.

October 29 – A Hamas suicide bomber targets a school bus in Gaza carrying children from the community of Kfar Darom to a regional school near the Gush Katif Junction. Driving an explosives-laden vehicle, the suicide bomber attempts to collide head-on with the bus. The driver of an escorting jeep blocks the car from reaching the bus; one person in the jeep is killed, along with the suicide bomber. Two passengers of the jeep are seriously injured, six of the school bus passengers receive moderate injuries.

1999

August 10 – Six people are wounded when a Hamas operative twice steers into a crowd at a bus stop at the Nahshon junction in central Israel. The car veers onto the sidewalk and into the crowd, hits two women soldiers and then speeds off. Five minutes later, the driver returns and attempts to run over the wounded women and several soldiers who are giving first aid, injuring four others. Police shoot and kill the assailant.

September 5 – Three Israeli Arabs, believed to be connected with Hamas, are killed trying to carry out car bombings in Haifa and Tiberias in northern Israel. A pedestrian in Tiberias is seriously injured.

November 7 – Three Hamas-planted pipe bombs explode at a busy intersection in Netanya. Police sappers defuse a fourth pipe bomb. Twenty-seven people are hospitalized with primarily light to moderate injuries.

2000

September 28 – Likud leader Ariel Sharon visits the Temple Mount (al-Haram al-Sharif to Muslims). The next day massive riots break out, which soon spread and are dubbed the al-Aqsa Intifada.

2001

January 1 – A Hamas car bomb explodes near a busy intersection in Netanya injuring 20 people.

February 14 – A Palestinian affiliated with Hamas drives into a group of soldiers and civilians waiting at a bus stop in Azor south of Tel Aviv, killing eight and injuring 20. Three female soldiers are critically injured.

March 4 – Three people are killed and 50 are wounded in a Hamas suicide bombing in the city center of Netanya, close to the bus station.

March 27 – There are two Hamas suicide attacks on buses in Jerusalem. Twenty-eight people are injured, two seriously, in a suicide bombing directed against a northbound No. 6 bus at the French Hill junction. In the second bombing on a bus in Jerusalem's French Hill, the bus driver is critically injured and 27 others sustain light to moderate injuries.

March 28 – A Hamas suicide bomber blows himself up near a bus stop in Neve Yamim. Two children are killed, along with the bomber. Four youths, aged 13 to 15, are injured, one critically.

April 22 – A Hamas operative detonates a powerful bomb near a group of people waiting at a bus stop on the corner of Weizman and Tchernichovsky streets in Kfar Sava. The operative and one other person are killed and about 60 are injured in the blast, two severely.

May 18 – A Hamas suicide bomber detonates his explosives at the entrance to HaSharon Shopping Mall in Netanya. Five people are killed and 100 are injured.

June 1 – On a Friday night, a Hamas suicide bomber detonates an explosives belt amid a crowd outside Tel Aviv's Dolphinarium beachfront nightclub killing at least 20 and injuring more than 120.

August 9 – A Hamas suicide bombing at a Sbarro's pizzeria restaurant in the center of Jerusalem at the corner of King George and Jaffa streets kills 15 people, including six children, and wounds more than 90.

September 9 – Three people are killed and 90 are injured, most lightly, in a Hamas suicide bombing near the Nahariya train station in northern Israel. The operative, who is killed in the blast, detonates the bomb after the train arrives from Tel Aviv and people are exiting the station.

October 2 – A Hamas terrorist cell infiltrates the northern Gaza District community of Alei Sinai, opening fire on residents and hurling grenades into homes. Two are killed and 15 are wounded in the attack.

November 26 – A Hamas suicide bomber kills himself and lightly wounds two Border Policemen at the Erez crossing point in the Gaza Strip. The bomber was joining workers waiting to be cleared for entry into Israel.

December 1 – Eleven people are killed and about 180 are injured when explosive devices are detonated by two Hamas suicide bombers close to 11: 30 p.m. Saturday night on Ben-Yehuda Street, the pedestrian mall in the center of Jerusalem.

December 2 – Fifteen people are killed and 40 are injured, several critically, in a Hamas suicide bombing on an Egged bus No. 16 in Haifa shortly after 12:00 a.m.

December 12 – A double Hamas suicide attack in Gaza kills three Israeli civilians.

2002

February 10 – A drive-by terrorist shooting at the entrance to the IDF Southern Command base in Beersheva kills two female soldiers and injures four others. One of the Hamas operatives is killed at the scene; the second, wearing an explosives belt, flees in the direction of a nearby school when he is shot and killed by a soldier and police officer.

March 7 – Five high school students are killed and 23 people are injured, four seriously, when a Palestinian gunman affiliated with Hamas attacks a school in the Gush Katif settlement of Atzmona in Gaza.

March 9 – Eleven people are killed and 54 are injured, 10 of them seriously, when a Hamas suicide bomber explodes in a crowded café in Jerusalem's Rehavia neighborhood.

March 27 – Twenty-nine people are killed and 140 are injured, 20 seriously, in a Hamas suicide bombing at the Park Hotel in the coastal city of Netanya, in the midst of the Passover seder attended by 250 guests.

March 29 – Israel launches Operation Defensive Shield, a massive campaign to destroy the terrorist infrastructure on the West Bank. Over the next six weeks, the IDF enters major Palestinian towns and arrests hundreds of terrorists, including dozens of Hamas members.

March 31 – Fifteen people are killed and more than 40 are injured in a Hamas suicide bombing in a Haifa restaurant.

April 10 – Eight people are killed and 22 are injured in a suicide bombing on Egged bus No. 960, en route from Haifa to Jerusalem, which explodes near Kibbutz Yagur, east of Haifa.

April 27 – Three Palestinian gunmen disguised as Israeli Army soldiers cut through the perimeter fence of Adora, in the West Bank, and enter several homes, shooting residents in their bedrooms. Four people, including a 5-year-old girl, are killed in the attacks. Another seven are injured, including one seriously. Both Hamas and the PFLP claim responsibility.

May 7 – Sixteen people are killed and 55 are wounded in a crowded game club in Rishon Lezion, southeast of Tel Aviv, when a suicide bomber detonates a powerful charge in the third floor club, causing part of the building to collapse.

June 8 – Three Israelis, including a pregnant woman, are killed, and five are injured when an armed Hamas operative infiltrates the community of Carmei Tzur, south of Jerusalem.

June 18 – More than19 people, including many high school students, are killed, and over 70 are wounded, many grievously, when a Hamas operative detonates a suicide bomb full of nail-studded explosives on a Jerusalem city bus.

June 30 – Muhanad Taher, a mastermind behind many Hamas attacks, is killed in Nablus. The 26-year-old headed Israel's most wanted list.

July 16 – Nine are killed and 20 wounded when several terrorists attack a bus near Emmanuel, in the West Bank. The terrorists escape. Although four Palestinian factions claim responsibility for the attack, the IDF determines that a Hamas cell, probably the one that committed the December 12, 2001 attack on a bus near Emmanuel, is responsible.

July 23 – Salah Shehadeh, the Gaza leader of Izz al-Din al-Qassam, the military wing of Hamas, is killed in an airstrike carried out by Israeli forces in Gaza City.

July 31 – Nine people, including five Americans are killed and 85 are injured when a bomb planted by Hamas explodes in a cafeteria at the Mt. Scopus campus of the Hebrew University in Jerusalem.

August 4 – Ten people are killed and over 40 are wounded in a Hamas bombing on bus No. 361 at the Meron intersection in northern Israel.

August 4 – The IDF captures Hamas leader Mazan Fukha, head of the Hamas military unit in the town of Tubas.

September 19 – A Hamas suicide bomber strikes bus No. 4 on a busy street in Tel Aviv. The explosion kills five and wounds more than 50.

October 10 – One person is killed and some 30 are wounded when a Hamas suicide bomber blows himself up while trying to board a bus across from Bar-Ilan University.

2003

March 5 – Seventeen people are killed and 53 wounded by a Hamas suicide bomber on a bus in Haifa.

June 11 – Seventeen people are killed and more than 100 wounded by a Hamas suicide bomber on a bus in central Jerusalem.

August 19 – Twenty-three people are killed and more than 130 are wounded by a Hamas suicide bomber on a Jerusalem bus.

September 9 – Hamas carries out two suicide bombings within six hours, one at a hitchhiking post outside an IDF base and the other at a Jerusalem cafe. Sixteen people are killed and over 80 are wounded.

2004

March 22 – Sheikh Ahmed Yassin is killled in an IDF airstrike.

Resources

Barsky, Y. " Focus on Hamas: Terror by Remote Control." *The Middle East Quarterly* June 1996; Vol. 3, No. 2 - available at www.meforum.org.

Barsky, Y. Hamas - The Islamic Resistance Movement of Palestine. Briefings: The American Jewish Committee, February 7, 2002.

Gambrill, G. "Sponsoring Terrorism: Syria and Hamas," *Middle East Intelligence Bulletin* October 2002; Vol. 4, No. 10 - available at www.meib.org.

Hamas official website www.palestine-info.com, has an English language section.

The Islamic Association for Palestine, www.iap.org,a U.S.-based Hamas front.

Karmon, E. *Hamas' Terrorism Strategy: Operational Limitations and Political Constraints.*

Middle East Review of International Affairs Journal March 2000; Vol. 4, No. 1 - available at meria.idc.ac.il/.

Katzman, K. "Hamas's Foreign Benefactors." *The Middle East Quarterly* June 1995; Vol. 2, No. 2 - available at www.meforum.org.

The Palestine Times is a Hamas English language publication with extensive online archives, website www.ptimes.com.

Paz. R. "Why Did Arafat Arrest Muhammad Deif, and Why Now?" *Middle East Intelligence Bulletin* June 2000; Vol. 2, No. 5 - available at www.meib.org.

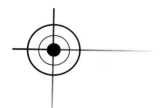

Hizbullah

Hizbullah is Arabic for Party of God. It is also known as Islamic Jihad, Revolutionary Justice Organization, Organization of the Oppressed on Earth, and Islamic Jihad for the Liberation of Palestine.

Ideology and Objectives

Hizbullah is an Islamist Shi'ite organization inspired by the Iranian revolution of 1979. Its ultimate goals are the extension of its Shi'ite Islamist ideology worldwide. An important aspect of Hizbullah's ideology is an openness to cooperating with Sunni Islamist groups. Hizbullah's immediate goals are the expulsion of the Western and Israeli presence in Lebanon, the establishment of an Islamist state in Lebanon modeled on the Iranian Islamic Republic, the destruction of Israel, and the capture of Jerusalem and placing it under Muslim rule. Despite its oft-stated antipathy towards Israel, Hizbullah leaders view the United States as the real enemy. While Hizbullah adheres to an Islamist theology, its rhetoric includes references to colonialism, Western imperialism, and other Marxist concepts.

Islamic law governs Hizbullah activities, and particularly tactics and strategy have to be justified under Islamic law by an acknowledged scholar. Because Islam forbids suicide, Hizbullah's suicide attacks require a religious ruling classifying them as martyrdom operations against an enemy of Islam. Hizbullah's participation in the Lebanese government is also the subject of debate among its religious leaders because there is no precedent for democracy within Islam. Some Hizbullah leaders advocate immediate steps by Hizbullah to transform Lebanon into an Islamist theocracy. For these clerics, participation in Lebanese elections is an unacceptable recognition of a secular state.

History

Origins

Hizbullah is rooted in the Shi'ite community of Lebanon, which traditionally was the least powerful faction there. In the 1960s and 1970s, the traditional order within the Shi'ite community and within Lebanon as a whole began to fracture, ultimately resulting in the Lebanese Civil War. Initially Shi'ite politics were channeled into the moderate religious Amal movement, founded by Musa Sadr. By the late 1970s, Shi'ite politics had become more radical. Musa Sadr disappeared during a 1978 trip to Libya. Nabih Berri emerged as the head of Amal and adopted a secular orientation.

In the 1960s and 1970s, Lebanese Shi'ite clerics had studying at the seminaries of southern Iraq, encountered Shi'ite Islamists, including the Ayatollah Khomeini and other architects of the Iranian revolution. Lebanese Shi'ite clerics began building a radical underground Islamist movement known as al-Da'wa (The Call), under the guidance of Sheikh Husayn Fadlallah. Al-Da'wa members attempted to join Lebanese Shi'ite institutions, particularly Amal, and obtain high-level positions in them in order to push them towards Islamism. Sheikh Fadlallah also headed the Association of Muslim Students, which acted as a cover organization for the clandestine al-Da'wa cells. The Lebanese al-Da'wa was linked to extremist factions of Iraq's al-Da'wa.

In 1982, in response to Palestine Liberation Organization (PLO) terrorism, Israel launched a full-scale invasion of southern Lebanon to expel the PLO. The south Lebanese Shi'ites, who had been brutally mistreated for over a decade by the PLO, initially welcomed Israeli soldiers. Syria, which sought to control Lebanon, became concerned about the possibility of an Israeli-Shi'ite alliance. To forestall this development, Syria permitted Iran to sponsor Islamist Shi'ite groups in Lebanon. Previously, Ba'athist Syria had kept its distance from Islamist Iran.

With Iranian support, Husayn al-Musawi led a group of Islamists to found Islamic Amal. In November 1982, Islamic Amal took over a Lebanese Army barracks and invited Iran to make use of the facility. Iran sent over 1,000 Pasdaran (Revolutionary Guards) to Lebanon in the early 1980s to provide training for the radical Shi'ite groups. In late 1982, Islamic Amal then merged with the Association of Muslim Students and incorporated al-Da'wa members to form Hizbullah. Fadlallah became the spiritual leader. The Iranian ambassador to Syria, Ali-Akbar Mohtashemi, coordinated these activities.

The PLO also played a central role in founding Hizbullah. The PLO had a long-standing relationship with the Iranian Islamists; many Iranian Islamist leaders trained in Lebanon with the PLO. Forced out of Lebanon by Israel in the summer of 1982, the PLO left an extensive network of operatives who became operatives for Hizbullah. The most notable was Imad Mughniyah, a Lebanese Shi'ite who had been a member of the Fatah's elite Force 17. Mughniyah joined Hizbullah and became a bodyguard of Sheikh Fadlallah. He later became Hizbullah's Director of Special Operations and masterminded Hizbullah's most notorious terror attacks.

Hizbullah's War against the Western Presence in Lebanon

In 1982, an international peacekeeping force led by the United States and with contingents from Britain, France, and Italy entered Beirut to oversee the Palestine Liberation Organization's withdrawal and to help stabilize the situation in Lebanon. With support from Iran and Syria, Hizbullah's armed wing, Islamic Jihad, launched a war against the Western presence in Lebanon, initially targeting Western embassies and installations with truck bombs and car bombs, and kidnapping Westerners residing in Lebanon. The first of these attacks was an April 1983 suicide car bombing against the United States embassy in Beirut that killed 63 and injured 120, including several of the CIA's top Middle East specialists.

In October 1983, twin suicide truck bombers struck the United States Marine barracks in Beirut, killing 242 Americans, and a French base, killing 58 French troops. In the next few months, a series of Hizbullah car bombs strike the French Multinational Forces Command in Lebanon, killing dozens. On November 4, 1983, Hizbullah bombed Israel's military headquarters in Tyre. In September 1984, a Hizbullah truck bomb struck the relocated United States embassy, killing 23 people including two Americans. In 1984, beleaguered by the terrorist attacks, the peacekeeping forces withdrew from Lebanon.

The Western Hostage Crises

On July 19, 1982, Islamic Amal, with the support of the Iranian Pasdaran, kidnapped David Dodge, President of the American University in Beirut (AUB) and one of the most prominent Westerners in Lebanon. Dodge was later transferred to Iran. His kidnapping was an attempt by the Iranians to pressure the United States to force the

Lebanese Christian Phalangist militia to release four Iranian embassy officials they had kidnapped. Dodge was released in July 1983, the Iranian captives were not released but Iran and Islamic Amal were not subject to any American repercussions. This was the beginning of the Western Hostage crises of the mid- and late-1980s. Hizbullah, with Iranian support, kidnapped American, French, and British citizens in Lebanon and used them as bargaining chips to extract concessions from those countries. The kidnappings were also motivated by Hizbullah's ambition of ridding Lebanon of Western influences, and were intended to gain support domestically in Hizbullah's rivalry with the Amal militia, which dominated Shi'ite politics in Lebanon.

In January 1984, in retaliation for shelling by American ships and fighting with United States Marines, Hizbullah members murdered Malcolm Kerr, the new President of the American University in Beirut and a prominent scholar of the Middle East.

In Kuwait, after a spate of terrorist attacks by the Iraqi al-Da'wa (which received support from Iran) in December 1983, over 20 Iraqi and three Lebanese Shi'ites were arrested. One of the Lebanese arrested was related to Husayn al-Musawi and another was related to Imad Mughniyah. In February 1984, Hizbullah kidnapped an American and a Frenchman in an attempt to pressure these governments to force Kuwait to improve its treatment of the Shi'ite prisoners. Hizbullah continued to kidnap Americans and other Westerners in Lebanon throughout 1984 and into 1985. In 1984, the Central Intelligence Agency (CIA) station chief in Beirut, William Buckley, was kidnapped, tortured, and killed. In December 1984, Hizbullah, with Iranian help, hijacked Kuwait Airline, flight 221. Besides pressuring Kuwait, these kidnappings were coordinated by Iran to discourage the United States and France from supporting Iraq in the Iran-Iraq war.

On March 8, 1985, a car bomb in Beirut exploded near the home of Sheikh Fadlallah. At least 80 people were killed and over 200 were injured, but Sheikh Fadlallah was unharmed. The CIA was suspected of involvement and Hizbullah retaliated by kidnapping American Associated Press reporter Terry Anderson on March 16, 1985. Two British citizens were also kidnapped a few days after the bombing, but they were released only two weeks later. Anderson was held for over six years.

In June 1985, the Islamic Jihad Organization, a front for Hizbullah, hijacked TWA flight 847 in Athens and flew to Beirut. The hijackers killed an American navy diver who was on the flight and dumped his body on the runway. The attack was masterminded by Imad Mughniyah. Israel released several hundred Shi'ite prisoners to secure the release of the 39 Americans held captive.

From August 1985 through November 1986, the United States was involved in a clandestine negotiation with Iran in which the United States provided weapons to Iran in exchange for the release of hostages and the cessation of hostage taking. The exposure of this clandestine arrangement resulted in the Iran-Contra affair.

In late 1986, Hizbullah began taking Western hostages again. In January 1987, four Americans, a Frenchman, and Briton Terry Waite, special envoy of the Archbishop of Canterbury who was playing an informal role in negotiations over hostages, were kidnapped. These kidnappings were, in part, a reaction to arrests of Hizbullah members in Europe. They were also a response to the Iranian-American arms for hostages arrangement.

On February 17, 1988, Hizbullah kidnapped U.S. Marine Lt. Colonel William "Rich" Higgins, an American with the United Nations observer group. The kidnapping was orchestrated both to pressure Israel into releasing Shi'ite prisoners and to undermine Amal in South Lebanon. Higgins was killed in captivity. In 1989, in an effort to force Hizbullah to negotiate prisoner exchanges with captured Israelis, particularly captured pilot Ron Arad, Israel kidnapped Sheikh Obeid, the chief of Hizbullah operations in southern Lebanon and planner of the Higgins kidnapping. In January 2004, Israel released Obeid as part of a prisoner exchange with Hizbullah.

On April 5, 1988, Hizbullah hijacked Kuwait Airlines Flight 422, again attempting to force Kuwait to release the Iraqi al-Da'wa prisoners. Ultimately, these prisoners were released from Kuwaiti a prison by Iraq during their occupation of Kuwait.

In November 1989, the United States released $567 million of frozen Iranian assets and, in April 1990, two Americans were released.

On March 22, 1985, three French embassy employees were kidnapped. Hizbullah, partially on Iran's behalf, was attempting to pressure France into curtailing its arms sales to Iraq and to repay an Iranian loan made to the French government by the deposed Shah. Hizbullah was also trying to obtain the release of Anis Naccache, a Force 17/Hizbullah operative who had attempted to assassinate the Shah's last Prime Minister Shapour Bakthiar in Paris.

In 1986, Hizbullah expanded its operations against France, kidnapping eight French citizens between February and May. Hizbullah also launched a bombing campaign in Paris between December 1985 and September 1986 during the French national elections, which killed 13 and wounded 303. Hizbullah also targeted the French United Nations Interim Force in Lebanon (UNIFIL) contingent in Southern Lebanon. In March 1987, French authorities arrested key members of the Hizbullah network in France and an Iranian diplomat who coordinated them.

In May 1988, the last French hostage was released on the eve of France's Presidential elections. France had made substantial concessions in order to secure the release of French hostages, including repaying the billion-dollar loan the Shah had made to France, with interest. The last of three payments was made in 1991. In 1990, French President Mitterrand pardoned Anis Naccache.

On December 4, 1991, Terry Anderson, the longest held and last American hostage, was released, effectively ending the hostage crises. Over the decade of Hizbullah hostage taking, almost 100 Westerners, mostly American and French, but also some British and German, were kidnapped and held by Hizbullah.

Hizbullah and Lebanese Politics

Along with fighting the Western and Israeli presence in Lebanon, Hizbullah was attempting to displace Amal as the leading Shi'ite organization in Lebanon. With the partial Israeli withdrawal of 1985, Hizbullah began building a political infrastructure and providing social services in Southern Lebanon, which had previously been dominated by Amal. Hizbullah used its credentials of Jihad against Israel and the West to gain popular support against Amal. This rivalry eventually escalated into armed clashes. Hizbullah supported the Palestinians in the 1985-1987 "War of the Camps" between Amal and the Palestine Liberation Organization. Syria, while supportive of Hizbullah's war with Israel, saw a rise in Shi'ite radicalism as a threat to its own control over Lebanon and supported Amal in its conflict with Hizbullah. In February 1987, Syrian forces clashed with Hizbullah forces, killing 23 Hizbullah members. At another point, Hizbullah took 14 Syrian soldiers hostage.

In 1988, Amal and Hizbullah came into direct conflict and began assassinating each other's leaders. Syria supported Amal, while

Iran supported Hizbullah. Lebanese Christian militias opposed to Syria's continued presence in Lebanon also provided some support for Hizbullah. With Iranian help, Hizbullah had defeated Amal in Beirut by spring 1988, although it was losing ground to Amal in South Lebanon. Syria intervened on Amal's behalf in June 1988.

In January 1989, in the Tufah region of Southern Lebanon, Hizbullah launched a large-scale assault slaughtering hundreds of Amal loyalists. Hizbullah religious leaders had to issue a fatwa forbidding the desecration of bodies. By the time Syria brokered a truce between Hizbullah and Amal in 1990, over 1,000 Lebanese Shi'ites had died in the fighting.

In the summer of 1992, Hizbullah ran in the Lebanese parliamentary elections, winning 12 seats and becoming the largest single bloc in Lebanon's fractious 128-member parliament.

The War with Israel

In 1985, Israel withdrew from most of Lebanon (at least in part because of Hizbullah's successful attack on Israel's headquarters in Tyre), holding a small area in South Lebanon as a buffer to limit Hizbullah attacks on Israel. Israel patrolled its security zone in conjunction with the South Lebanon Army (SLA), a 2,500-man militia supported by Israel consisting of Christians, Shi'ites, and some Druze. The security zone was approximately 328 square miles and 10 to 12 miles deep into Lebanese territory. This depth minimized the efficacy of Hizbullah's Katyusha rocket attacks on northern Israel and complicated terrorist efforts to infiltrate Israel. In the 15 years of the Israeli security zone, only two terrorist infiltrations crossed Israel's northern border and both were eliminated before they could attack civilian targets. During that period more than 4,000 Katyusha rockets were fired by Hizbullah into northern Israel, killing seven civilians. Casualties could have been much higher, but the security zone forced Hizbullah to launch the Katyushas beyond their most effective range of six to eight miles and denied Hizbullah forward observation posts for directing the rocket fire.

Within the Israeli controlled zone of Southern Lebanon, Hizbullah fought a guerrilla war of ambushes and booby traps with the Israel Defense Forces and the SLA. From 1985 on, Israel lost 10 to 30 soldiers per year in the fighting in Lebanon.

Throughout the early 1990's, the quality and quantity of Hizbullah attacks on the Israel Defense Forces (IDF) and the SLA in the security zone of Southern Lebanon increased. In 1990, there were 19 Hizbullah attacks on the IDF and the SLA. In 1991, Hizbullah surpassed Amal as Israel's leading adversary in Lebanon, launching 51 attacks against the IDF and SLA. By 1993, there were over 158 such attacks, and these attacks became an almost daily occurrence by 1995. The ratio of Hizbullah to Israeli dead also changed in Hizbullah's favor, from 5: 1 in 1990 to 1.5:1 by the middle of the 1990s. Israeli and Hizbullah casualties also began to mount.

1990s
The War with Israel and International Terror Attacks Escalate

Frustrated with deadlocked negotiations over Israeli prisoners, Israel killed Hizbullah Secretary-General Sheikh Abbas al-Musawi on February 17, 1992 in a missile attack. Sheikh Hassan Nasrallah, who had run for the post in the May 1991 elections, was quickly elected to the post of Secretary-General. Hizbullah responded to the assassination with the March 17 car bomb attack on the Israeli embassy in Buenos Aires, Argentina which killed 30 and injured 252. Intelligence officers at the Iranian embassy in Buenos Aires helped to coordinate the attack. Argentine security services never made any arrests in connection with this attack.

In July 1993, in response to hundreds of Katyushas fired into northern Israel, Prime Minister Yitzhak Rabin launched Operation Accountability, a massive military strike intended to turn the civilian population of Southern Lebanon against Hizbullah. Israeli operations caused over 100,000 Lebanese to flee north, but did not destroy Hizbullah's military capacity and ultimately the civilian population returned. In the wake of Operation Accountability, the United States brokered an agreement that Hizbullah and Israel would agree to refrain from targeting civilian populations.

In 1994, Hizbullah launched a worldwide terror campaign against Israeli and Jewish targets. In March 1994, an attempted truck bombing of the Israeli embassy in Bangkok, Thailand was aborted when the truck broke down. On July 18, 1994, a Hizbullah car bomb destroyed the Buenos Aires offices of the Argentine Israeli Mutual Association (AMIA), the central communal organization of the Argentine Jewish community. Eighty-six people were killed and over 200 were wounded in the attack. In 1998, Argentine prosecutors identified Mohsen Rabbani, who had been the cultural attaché at Iran's Embassy in Buenos Aires, as being directly involved in the attack. The attack may have served a dual purpose, to reply to Israeli attacks on Hizbullah bases in Lebanon, but also to punish Argentina's President Carlos Menem who had long been courted by Iran but failed to provide the diplomatic and military support Iran had requested. The ensuing investigation of the AMIA bombing was plagued with charges of corruption and cover-up that extended throughout Argentina's security forces and possibly included President Menem.

Hizbullah, in conjunction with Iran, is suspected of orchestrating the November 13, 1995 car bombing of a Saudi National Guard building (7 were killed, including several Americans, and 42 were injured) and June 25, 1996 truck bombing of the Khobar Towers which housed U.S. personnel in Saudi Arabia. In the Khobar Towers bombing 19 Americans were killed and 515 (including 240 Americans) were injured. The Saudi investigation focused on the Saudi Hizbullah, a Saudi Shi'a group linked to Hizbullah and Iran. American investigators complained about inadequate access to the evidence and in June 1998 most of the U.S. investigators departed Saudi Arabia. In June 2001, 13 Saudi Shi'a and a Lebanese were indicted by the United States for their participation in the Khobar Towers bombing.

In April 1996, in response to hundreds of Katyusha rockets launched by Hizbullah into the security zone and northern Israel, the IDF, under the orders of Prime Minister Shimon Peres, initiated Operation Grapes of Wrath, a massive artillery and bombing campaign against Hizbullah positions in South Lebanon. In May 1996, Israeli artillery accidentally killed 107 civilians at Kafr Kana in South Lebanon. Operation Grapes of Wrath ended with an understanding between Hizbullah and Israel that neither side would target civilians.

The Israeli public was becoming increasingly frustrated with the casualties in South Lebanon. In August 1996, new Israeli Prime Minister Binyamin Netanyahu offered to withdraw from Southern Lebanon if the Lebanese government would secure the border and prevent attacks on Israel. The Lebanese and Syrian governments refused.

In February 1997, two Israeli helicopters ferrying troops to Southern Lebanon collided and 73 soldiers were killed. In September of that year, a botched commando raid against Hizbullah resulted in 12 Israeli soldiers killed. In 1998, Israel and the SLA withdrew from the town of Jezzine and several surrounding outposts. In February 1999, Hizbullah killed IDF Brigadier General Erez Gerstein, commander of the IDF liaison unit with the SLA.

As Israel struggled with the insurgency in South Lebanon, Hizbullah's stature in the Arab world grew. Public statements by Hizbullah leaders referred to Israel's weakness before Hizbullah fighters.

Israeli Withdrawal from South Lebanon

In Israel's 1999 elections, all major candidates promised to end Israel's presence in Lebanon. Under the winner, former IDF Chief of Staff Lt. Gen. Ehud Barak, Israel attempted to arrange a phased withdrawal to be completed by July 7, 2000. Hizbullah stepped up attacks and responded ambiguously about whether it would launch attacks on Israel proper after an Israeli withdrawal.

The South Lebanon Army (SLA), which had long been plagued by issues of ineffectiveness and disloyalty, was severely undermined by the discussions of withdrawal. The Lebanese government refused to offer a general amnesty to SLA members, instead threatening to try them as traitors. Hizbullah threatened to murder SLA members. In late May 2000, as the SLA was taking control of crucial outposts in South Lebanon, Hizbullah attacked the predominantly Shi'ite battalion of the SLA which controlled the center of the security zone. The attacks came in the wake of a flood of civilian refugees and the central battalion collapsed leaving the other SLA positions vulnerable. Large numbers of SLA troops deserted their posts in the face of Hizbullah assaults, some defecting to Hizbullah and others fleeing towards Israel. The Israel Defense Forces (IDF) accelerated its withdrawal schedule and on May 24, 2000 the last IDF soldier left Lebanon. Several thousand Lebanese who had served in or who were related to someone who had served in the SLA fled to Israel, where they were resettled. Hizbullah attacked people suspected of collaborating with Israel, and substantial numbers of SLA soldiers joined Hizbullah.

Israel's withdrawal was greeted with jubilation throughout the Arab world, and Hizbullah was lauded for reversing decades of Arab defeats by Israel. The Lebanese-Israeli border, particularly Fatma Gate, became a tourist attraction where Lebanese and other Arabs could go and throw stones at Israel. The Israeli withdrawal particularly inspired the Palestinians to believe that Israel could be defeated. Less than four months later, the Palestinians launched the al-Aqsa Intifada.

On July 24, 2000, the United Nations recognized that Israel had fully implemented United Nations Resolution 425, which called for

Israel to withdraw from Lebanon. Both Israel and the UN called on the Lebanese Army to deploy along and secure the Lebanese side of the border. Rock throwing from the Lebanese side had disrupted work and injured Israelis but under Syrian orders, the Lebanese army did not deploy in Southern Lebanon and Hizbullah was not disarmed.

Continuing Fighting over Shebaa Farms

After Israel's withdrawal, public sentiment in Lebanon, while favorable to Israel's withdrawal, was that Hizbullah should not continue attacks on Israel because of possible Israeli reprisals. There was also speculation that Hizbullah would capitalize on its popularity within Lebanon to expand its social services and its role in Lebanese electoral politics. However, Syria required another avenue for attacks on Israel in order to continue its own occupation of Lebanon. Shortly before the Israeli withdrawal, the Lebanese government began advancing claims on the area known as Shebaa Farms.

The United Nations and virtually all maps of the region recognize the Shebaa Farms (a 25 square kilometer adjacent to the Lebanon-Israel border) as being south of the Lebanese border and part of the Golan Heights, which Israel captured from Syria in 1967. Desiring to preserve a rationalization for Lebanese hostility toward Israel, Syria promoted the idea that Shebaa Farms was occupied Lebanese territory and not Syrian In order to support the Lebanese title to this area, Syrian officials claimed that they had given the Shebaa Farms to Lebanon in 1951. There was no documentation to support this claim and the UN has not recognized Lebanese claims to the Shebaa Farms.

Nonetheless, shortly after the al-Aqsa Intifada erupted, Hizbullah began operations in the Shebaa Farms. On October 7, 2000, Hizbullah abducted three Israeli soldiers patrolling the area. The Hizbullah operatives were disguised in the uniforms of UN peacekeepers. In June 2001, the UN peacekeeping force revealed that it possessed a videotape of the incident, and, in August 2001, the existence of a second videotape was disclosed.

Hizbullah launched more than 80 rocket and mortar attacks against Shebaa Farms. Many of these attacks occurred shortly after anti-Syrian incidents in Lebanon. Over the next two years, seven Israel Defense Forces soldiers were killed and 42 civilians and eight soldiers were wounded.

Hizbullah and the Intifada

Hizbullah has provided large-scale aid to the Palestinian Intifada. Hizbullah's satellite television station *al-Manar* (The Beacon), which had been used to broadcast footage of Hizbullah attacks on Israeli soldiers in Lebanon, has been broadcasting similar material from the Palestinian-Israeli fighting.

Hizbullah has also been involved directly, providing training and logistical support to Hamas, Palestinian Islamic Jihad, and Fatah. There have been increasing numbers of Palestinian attacks, which use tactics Hizbullah developed during its fighting with Israel in Lebanon. On February 15, 2002, an Israeli Merkava tank was lured into a trap and destroyed by a mine, which it is believed was designed by Hizbullah. Hizbullah may have also provided guidance in building the bomb used in the March 27, 2002 Passover Massacre in which 29 were killed, and that sparked Operation Defensive Shield.

In conjunction with Arafat's bodyguards, Force 17, Hizbullah has set up terrorist cells in the West Bank and Gaza that were responsible for mortar attacks against Israeli villages. Hizbullah is also building its own infrastructure in Israel by recruiting Arabs to gather intelligence and cultivating operatives with European citizenship to travel to Israel and carry out attacks.

Hizbullah has attempted to smuggle weapons to the Palestinians both by sea and overland through Jordan. The *Karine-A*, a ship captured by Israeli naval commandos on January 3, 2002 while smuggling heavy weapons to Gaza was a joint Palestinian Authority-Iranian-Hizbullah operation. The weapons, which included anti-tank missiles, anti-aircraft systems, and artillery, came from Iran, and it was reported that the operation was overseen by Hizbullah Special Operations chief Imad Mughniyah.

In March 2002, terrorists infiltrated northern Israel and killed five civilians and a soldier near Kibbutz Metsuva. Hizbullah is suspected, although it denied responsibility and claimed a Palestinian group carried out the attack. Hizbullah has also shelled northern Israel, outside of the Farms, causing several injuries. Israel has responded to Hizbullah attacks with carefully targeted attacks on Syrian installations in Lebanon.

Since spring 2002, Hizbullah received additional advanced equipment from Syria and Iran, including the Iranian-built 240mm Fajr missiles. It is also believed that Hizbullah has stockpiled over 5,000 Katyusha artillery rockets.

On October 16, 2002, Lebanon opened a new pumping station on the Wazzani River, a source of Lake Kinneret, Israel's leading water reservoir. Israel warned Lebanon not to exceed established limits on Lebanese use of the Wazzani River. The project was initiated by the Amal, but Hizbullah leaders announced their readiness to respond to Israeli attack.

Leadership
Mohammed Husayn Fadlallah

Ayatollah Mohammed Husayn Fadlallah, the spiritual leader of Hizbullah and the Lebanese Shi'ite community, was born in Najaf, Iraq, in 1935. His father was a religious leader from Southern Lebanon who had moved to Najaf to study. While studying in the seminaries of Najaf, Fadlallah made several trips to Lebanon. In 1966, he relocated permanently to an impoverished Shi'ite neighborhood in Beirut. He quickly established himself as a religious leader, founding a social service organization and a journal to circulate his ideas more broadly and delivering lectures to secular Shi'ites. The neighborhood's residents fled from the violence of the Lebanese Civil War in 1975. Fadlallah reestablished himself in another Beirut neighborhood and in the late 1970s was made the head of an internationally funded charitable institution devoted to relieving the suffering of Lebanon's Shi'ites. In 1977, when the Iraqi regime began cracking down on the seminaries in Najaf, many Lebanese Shi'ite religious leaders returned to Lebanon, and became followers of Fadlallah. In 1978 Musa Sadr, the Shi'ite leader in Lebanon, disappeared while on a trip in Libya, leaving a power vacuum among the leadership of the Lebanese Shi'ites. Fadlallah allied himself with the 1979 Iranian Islamic Revolution, for which he received material and ideological support from Iran. He helped to set up clandestine networks and built the foundations for Hizbullah, although he claims to have no formal relationship to it.

Fadlallah is the author of several books, including volumes of poetry and "Islam and the logic of power," written in 1975, which urged Lebanon's Shi'ites to lead the Islamic struggle against Imperialism. While Fadlallah was loyal to Iran's Ayatollah Khomeini, he is not loyal to his successor, Ayatollah Khameini. Fadlallah is believed to be attempting to extend his own reputation as a spiritual leader to Shi'ites beyond Lebanon.

Sheikh Hassan Nasrallah

Hassan Nasrallah was born in 1960 in the Southern Lebanese village Bazuriyah. Nasrallah was elected to the Amal delegate from his village at the age of 15 and at 16, traveled to Iraq to study in the Shi'ite seminaries of Najaf, where he came into contact with many Lebanese Shi'ite Islamists and became close to Abbas al-Musawi, his predecessor as Secretary-General of Hizbullah. In 1978 the Iraqi regime began cracking down on the Najaf seminaries and Nasrallah fled back to Lebanon. He founded a religious school and became head of Amal in the Beqaa Valley. When Hizbullah formed, Nasrallah and his followers joined. He was the first Hizbullah head in Baalbek and then in the Beqaa Valley. He also directed Hizbullah activities in Beirut.

Nasrallah was elected Secretary-General of Hizbullah in February 1992 after Abbas al-Musawi was assassinated by Israel. Nasrallah had received a majority of the votes in the May 1991 elections, but because of violent factionalism within Hizbullah, had yielded the Secretary-General post to al-Musawi. Nasrallah has been reelected to the Secretary-General position several times and his long-time assistant, Naim Kassem, is the Deputy Secretary-General. His son, Hadi, was killed in a firefight with Israeli troops in Southern Lebanon.

Imad Mughniyah

Imad Mughniyah was born in July 1962 to a Shi'ite family in the village of Tir Dabbi in Southern Lebanon. He and his family moved to Beirut when Mughniyah was a boy. Head of Hizbullah's Special Security Apparatus, Mughniyah is the suspected mastermind of most of Hizbullah's major terrorist activities, including the car bombings and kidnappings in Beirut in the 1980s, the 1985 hijacking of TWA 847, and the attacks in Buenos Aires. As a teenager, Mughniyah joined Force 17, Arafat's bodyguards. When the Palestine Liberation Organization was forced out of Beirut, Mughniyah stayed behind and became active in the Hizbullah movement. He was a bodyguard for Sheikh Fadlallah, and, as his operational talent for terrorism surfaced, he rose in the Hizbullah organization. His brothers, Fuad and Jihad, were both killed in car bombings. He is believed to divide his time between Lebanon and Iran. He reportedly met with Osama bin Laden in the mid-1990s. Bin Laden expressed his admiration for Mughniyah's attacks on U.S. targets. In September 2000, with the outbreak of the al-Aqsa Intifada, Iran assigned Mughniyah to liaise between Iran and Hizbullah and Hamas and Palestinian Islamic Jihad. He directed the January 2002 arms shipment on the *Karine-A* captured by Israel.

Organization
Governing Bodies

Hizbullah is governed by the Majlis al-Shura (Consultative Assembly) which consists of 12 senior Shi'ite religious leaders including the Secretary-General who is elected every two years. The Consultative Assembly began meeting regularly in 1986. The Majlis al-Shura also has seven standing committees to address judicial, ideological, military, financial, informational, political, and social affairs. In December 1989, Hizbullah reorganized and the Majlis al-Shura al-Karar (Deciding Assembly) which consists of nine senior clerics, was founded in order to oversee Hizbullah's administration.

Each of Hizbullah's major operating regions in Beirut, the Beqaa Valley, and Southern Lebanon has a regional Majlis al-Shura with seven standing committees.

Armed Units

Hizbullah's armed division has two units, the al-Muqawana al-Islamiyya (Islamic Resistance), which is the militia that fought Israel and the SLA in South Lebanon and now fights along the Lebanese-Israeli border, and the Special Security Apparatus (SSA), which is responsible for intelligence, internal security, and international terror.

The Islamic Resistance has several hundred full-time fighters and as many as 5,000 fighters total. They are paid a few hundred dollars a month and receive educational and health benefits. These wages were competitive with the SLA and are superior to the rival Amal militia, allowing Hizbullah to induce Amal members to defect.

The Special Security Apparatus has three units, the central apparatus that operates in Beirut and attempts to infiltrate Amal, the preventative apparatus that provides security for Hizbullah leaders, and the overseas apparatus that conducts international terror. The central and overseas units overlap in operations and personnel. Because the Mughniyah and Hamadi clans dominate it, the SSA has resisted to Israeli attempts at infiltration.

Social and Political Operations

Hizbullah runs extensive social and propaganda activities in Lebanon, all of which exist to support its armed struggle and its long-term political ambition to create an Islamic state in Lebanon. Hizbullah's external communications include newspapers, a radio station, and, most notable, *al-Manar* (The Beacon), a satellite television station. *Al-Manar* is particularly popular in the West Bank and Gaza where its programming focuses on the conflict with Israel.

Hizbullah provides social services, running several hospitals and over a dozen medical centers in Lebanon. The organization pays millions of dollars annually to the dependents of Hizbullah members who were killed and wounded fighting with Israel. Between 1988 and 1991, Hizbullah helped reconstruct over 1,000 homes damaged in fighting with Israel. Hizbullah also makes small loans to its members. The social service activities are coordinated by the Jihad al-Bina' (Holy Reconstruction Organ).

Hizbullah is also active as a political party, holding 12 seats in Lebanon's parliament. As a political party, Hizbullah capitalizes primarily on its success against Israel and also on the modest lifestyles of its leaders in contrast to the rampant corruption in Lebanese politics.

Financial Support

Hizbullah's initial source of financial support was the Islamic Republic of Iran. In the early 1980s, this support was estimated at about $30 million annually. It is currently estimated that Iran contributes more than $100 million annually. This support is funneled through official channels such as the Iranian Ministry of Foreign Affairs and the Pasdaran. Semi-official foundations, controlled by Iranian clerics, also provide support for Hizbullah. Iranian support underwrites both military equipment and social services.

Hizbullah also has substantial independent sources of income. It cooperates with Syria in cultivating opium and hashish in the Beqaa Valley and Hizbullah cells in the Americas and Europe engage in criminal activities to raise money. Hizbullah also receives donations, many made involuntarily, from areas under its control in Lebanon and also worldwide. It is estimated that Hizbullah operatives raise over $10 million annually through extortion and smuggling in the Tri-Border region of South America. This region is so-named because it is where the three countries, Argentina, Brazil and Paraguay meet. Hizbullah also operates commercial businesses in Lebanon including supermarkets, gas stations, department stores, and construction companies.

Links to States and Terrorist Organizations
Iran

Iran and Hizbullah have a deep and complex relationship. Of all Iran's attempts to export the Islamic revolution, Hizbullah is by far the most successful. Iran played a crucial role in Hizbullah's formation, providing the radical Islamist ideology, funding, weapons, and training necessary to build the organization. Many of Hizbullah's clerics had studied with Iranian leader Ayatollah Khomeini in Najaf, Iraq where they absorbed his Shi'ite Islamist vision. They brought Khomeini's ideology with them to Lebanon when they were forced out of Iraq in 1977-1978. In the wake of the 1982 Israeli invasion of Lebanon, Syria permitted Iran to station a unit of Pasdaran in the Beqaa Valley, where they took over a Lebanese Army barracks and began providing military training to Lebanese Shi'ite fighters, and religious guidance for the clerics. By July 1984, there were six training centers in the Beqaa Valley. There have been as many as 1,500 Pasdaran in Lebanon providing training. Iran has also provided extensive weaponry. In April 1996, 30 Iranian planes loaded with weapons and ammunition intended for Hizbullah landed at Damascus airport.

Iranian organizational support was essential to the foundation and later effectiveness of Hizbullah. Iran's ambassador to Syria from 1982 to 1986, Ali Akbar Mohtashemi, played a crucial role in bringing the different Lebanese Shi'ite Islamist factions together. The governing Majlis al-Shura was founded with Iranian guidance, and one or two Iranians belong to the council (originally Iran was represented by Mohtashemi). Mohtashemi was later appointed Minister of Interior and served in that post from 1986 to 1989, where he continued to provide support for Hizbullah.

Hizbullah has been an effective proxy for Iran, advancing its position in the Arab world, both through its confrontation with Israel and by forging links with Sunni and Shi'ite terrorist organizations. Hizbullah has conducted many of its operations in close cooperation with Iran, particularly the hostage taking of the 1980s. Westerners taken hostage were selected based on their nationality to force their governments to change their policies toward Iran. For example, kidnapping French citizens and carrying out bombings in Paris in 1985-1986 led France to make payments to the Iranian government. American attempts to free American hostages taken by Hizbullah led the United States to supply Iran with weapons. Particular hostages were transferred to Iran, such as the CIA Station Chief in Beirut, William Buckley, where they were tortured. Hizbullah has also carried out proxy assassinations on Iran's behalf. In September 1992, Hizbullah operatives murdered four Iranian Kurdish leaders in Berlin. Hizbullah has also curtailed activity, such as the hostage taking, when it no longer served Iranian interests.

As Hizbullah has developed its own resources, it has, within the context of a close alliance, acted independently of Iran and pursued its own interests. However, Hizbullah and Iran remain closely linked. Hizbullah has been the primary conduit for Iranian support for Palestinian terror organizations in the al-Aqsa Intifada.

Al-Qaeda and Its Affiliates

Hizbullah, in conjunction with Iran, made great efforts to forge links with Sunni terrorist groups. Al-Qaeda and its affiliates made use of these opportunities and ultimately forged a strategic partnership. The relationship began in Sudan, where Hassan al-Turabi's Islamist regime was a leading sponsor of terrorism, providing bases for Islamist groups from all over the world. Al-Turabi facilitated meetings between Osama bin Laden, Iranian intelligence, and Hizbullah leaders. Bin Laden reportedly met with Hizbullah's Special Operations Chief Imad Mughniyah in 1996 and praised Mughniyah for his success attacking American targets and the subsequent American withdrawals. Al-Qaeda ran a guesthouse for terrorists training in Lebanon, and al-Qaeda operatives studied Hizbullah tactics. In particular, Mughniyah helped al-Qaeda develop networks to manage long-distance operations that were resistant to infiltration. Hizbullah also taught al-Qaeda explosives experts how to destroy large buildings, and coached them in surveilling a target and planning massive simultaneous attacks. Hizbullah training videos were used to train al-Qaeda operatives.

In Sudan, Hizbullah also forged links with and provided training to al-Qaeda affiliates, such as Egypt's al-Jihad and al-Gama'a al-Islamiyya and Algeria's Armed Islamic Group. Hizbullah may have provided a fake passport for one of the planners of al-Jihad's 1995 attack on Egypt's embassy in Islamabad, Pakistan.

Hizbullah and al-Qaeda also cooperate in Southeast Asia, where al-Qaeda affiliate, the Moro Islamic Liberation Front (MILF), is in contact with Asian-based Hizbullah operatives. Also in Southeast Asia, Hizbullah has received support from the same Muslim charity organizations that have been linked to al-Qaeda.

Mughniyah, who has extensive hijacking experience, may have secretly traveled to Germany to help train the 9/11 hijackers. Since the collapse of the Taliban, Iran has helped smuggle al-Qaeda operatives including Abu Musab al-Zarqawi out of Afghanistan and into Lebanon where they are linking up with Hizbullah.

Shi'ite Islamist Organizations

There are "Hizbullahs" in Shi'ite communities throughout the world. The Lebanese Hizbullah has links with and provides support to militant Shi'ite organizations throughout the Middle East and beyond, but particularly among the Shi'ite populations of Saudi Arabia, Bahrain, and Iraq. Saudi Shi'ite Islamists, known as Saudi Hizbullah, are believed to be responsible – possibly in conjunction with al-Qaeda – for the 1995 and the 1996 bombings of American bases in Saudi Arabia. They are reportedly linked to Iran and Hizbullah.

The founders of Hizbullah were linked to the clandestine al-Da'wa network in Iraq. Some of Hizbullah's operations, such as the December 1984 hijacking of a Kuwaiti airliner, were intended, at least in part, to free captured al-Da'wa operatives. While the al-Da'wa network has been strongly repressed by the Iraqi government of Saddam Hussein, Hizbullah is believed to have links with whatever remains of the al-Da'wa network. Since Saddam Hussein's removal Hizbullah has opened several offices in Southern Iraq.

In Pakistan, Hizbullah has provided assistance to Sipah-e-Mohammed (Army of Mohammed), a militant Shi'ite organization that battles militant Sunni organizations that attack Shi'ites.

Fatah/Palestine Liberation Organization

The Fatah/Palestine Liberation Organization, and, particularly its elite unit Force 17, played a central role in the founding of Hizbullah. Fatah networks, particularly in Europe supported Hizbullah operations. This relationship was strained when Arafat chose to support Iraq in the Iran/Iraq war. With the outbreak of the al-Aqsa Intifada, this relationship has been reestablished.

Hizbullah has provided training for Force 17 officers while using them as a means to build their own cells in Israel, Gaza, and the West Bank. Force 17 Lt. Colonel Massoud Ayad had been trained by Hizbullah and was setting up the first Hizbullah cell in Gaza. Colonel Mahmoud Damra, commander of Force 17 in the West Bank, is suspected of setting up the first Hizbullah cell in the West Bank. Hizbullah has also worked closely with Iran to ship weapons to the Palestinian Authority, such as the *Karine-A* arms shipment, which was directed by Imad Mughniyah.

Hamas and Palestinian Islamic Jihad

Both Hamas and Palestinian Islamic Jihad (PIJ) have extensive links to Hizbullah. The PIJ's links are deeper, extending to 1988 when Israel deported to Lebanon the PIJ's leaders, Fathi Shqaqi and Sheikh Odeh. In Lebanon, they came into contact with Hizbullah and Iran. Hizbullah provided training and served as a conduit for Iranian aid. The PIJ, which had limited financial resources and was ideologically sympathetic, was drawn closely into Hizbullah's orbit. Effectively becoming a unit of Hizbullah and receiving its funding through them, the PIJ-Hizbullah relationship was a leading example of Shi'ite and Sunni cooperation. Hizbullah used the PIJ to establish its own presence in the West Bank and Gaza, and among the Arab citizens of Israel. Hizbullah supports PIJ efforts to recruit and expand its influence among Palestinian refugees in Lebanon.

When Hamas was first founded, its Sunni ideology was a barrier to cooperation with the Iranian Shi'ites. But relations began to warm after Hamas and Hizbullah came into contact. The Hamas operatives deported to Lebanon in 1992 helped further this relationship and Hamas' continued growth and success heightened its appeal to Hizbullah and Iran.

This cooperation has expanded during the al-Aqsa Intifada. Hamas was inspired by Hizbullah's long war with Israel in Lebanon, which culminated in Israel's complete withdrawal from Lebanon in May 2000. Hizbullah has provided guidance and training for Hamas, which has adopted Hizbullah's strategy of attrition and has also adopted many Hizbullah tactics. A pair of Hamas-Fatah operations in Gaza a January 9, 2002 attack on an Israel Defense Forces (IDF) outpost in Gaza, killing four Arab Israeli soldiers and the February 14, 2002 destruction of a Merkava tank — used tactics developed by Hizbullah. The bomb used in the Passover Seder massacre of March 27, 2002 may have used Hizbullah bomb making techniques. Hizbullah has assisted Hamas in producing the Qassam rockets, and with Iran produces how-to videos for bomb-makers.

Syria

The Hizbullah/Syria relationship is complex. Although officially secular, Syria helped found Hizbullah in the early 1980s in order to prevent Lebanon's Shi'ites from making peace with Israel, thereby protecting Syria's control over Lebanon. Hizbullah's war with Israel was a useful outlet for Syria's anti-Israel rhetoric and a useful bargaining chip in negotiations. Hizbullah's attacks on Westerners in Lebanon helped establish Syria as the only party that could keep peace in Lebanon.

At other points, Syria stymied Hizbullah actions to prevent it from becoming too powerful or from taking actions that would damage Syrian interests. Syria placed limits on Hizbullah hostage taking – threatening to kill Hizbullah leaders if necessary. In the late 1980s, Syria intervened in the Hizbullah-Amal war on the side of Amal. In February 1987 Syrian soldiers killed 23 Hizbullah operatives and in March 1994 Syria ordered the arrest of 11 Hizbullah operatives for their role in violent protests that threatened to become anti-Syrian. After the 1989 Ta'if Accord, which stabilized the situation in Lebanon, Syria forced Hizbullah into coalitions with Amal in order to limit the number of seats Hizbullah would hold in the Parliament in both the 1992 and 1996 elections.

Overall, Syria has permitted Hizbullah to carry out its international terrorist activities and its war against Israel. Massive shipments of weapons were transferred from Iran to Lebanon via Damascus. Hizbullah has opposed calls within Lebanon for Syria to end its occupation of Lebanon. Long-time Syrian President Hafez al-Assad kept Hizbullah at arm's length, only holding limited meetings with its representatives. Bashar al-Assad, his successor and son, is much closer to the leaders of Hizbullah. He has met with Sheikh Nasrallah and has allowed Hizbullah to hold rallies in Syria.

Under Syrian auspices, Hizbullah has worked with the secular Palestinian factions based in Damascus, particularly Ahmed Jibril's Popular Front for the Liberation of Palestine-General Command (PFLP-GC) which also has extensive training facilities in Lebanon.

Areas of Operation
Lebanon

Hizbullah's primary bases of operations are in the Shi'ite sections of Lebanon: the Beqaa Valley, South Lebanon, and the Shi'ite suburbs of Beirut. Southern Lebanon, where Hizbullah fought with Israel and the South Lebanon Army for over a decade, has become known as

Hizbullahstan. Hizbullah enforces strict Islamic law in this region and the Lebanese Army and police are not permitted to deploy there in substantial numbers. This region is also the base for Hizbullah infiltration of and missile attacks on Israel. South Lebanon has also been the location of fierce fighting between Amal and Hizbullah.

The Beqaa Valley was Hizbullah's initial base. A detachment of Iranian Pasdaran continues to be based there and provide training for Hizbullah. Hizbullah is also linked to the cultivation of opium and hashish in Beqaa.

Beirut has been the locale for many of Hizbullah's operations, including attacks on Western embassies and soldiers, and the kidnapping of Westerners in Lebanon. The impoverished Shi'ite neighborhoods of Beirut have been Hizbullah's leading recruiting grounds. Hizbullah's headquarters, the *al-Manar* satellite television station, and Hizbullah's spiritual leader Sheikh Fadlallah are all based in Beirut.

Israel, the Palestinian Authority, and Jordan

In its attempts to continue its confrontation with Israel, Hizbullah has attempted to establish operations in Jordan, the West Bank, Gaza, and Israel itself. In addition to setting up terrorist cells in the West Bank and Gaza, particularly in conjunction with Force 17, Hizbullah has attempted to infiltrate Israel directly. On April 12, 1996, Mohammed Hussein Mikdad, a Lebanese Hizbullah operative who traveled to Israel on a false passport, mishandled his bomb and severely injured himself. In November 1997, Israeli police arrested Stephen Smyrek, a German convert to Islam with links to Hizbullah, who admitted to traveling to Israel in order to undertake a suicide bombing. In January 2001, Israeli security arrested Jihad Aya Latif "Gerard" Shuman, a Lebanese Hizbullah activist who entered Israel with a false British passport. Hizbullah has also recruited some Israeli Arab citizens, primarily those involved in the illegal drug trade across the Israeli-Lebanese border. In October 2002, ten Israeli Bedouins involved with the drug trade, including a retired IDF Lieutenant Colonel, were accused of spying for Hizbullah.

Hizbullah and Iran have attempted to launch rockets at Israel and smuggle weapons to Palestinian terrorists from Jordan. In the summer of 2001, three Hizbullah members arrested in Jordan had two dozen Katyusha rockets in their possession. Reportedly, there have been over a dozen Iranian-backed attempts to launch Katyushas at Israel from Jordan

Europe

Hizbullah has operated throughout Europe. In April 1984, Hizbullah bombed a restaurant frequented by United States servicemen in Spain. In 1985, Hizbullah bombed a synagogue in Copenhagen. In 1986, Hizbullah carried out a series of bombings in Paris during the French election campaign.

Hizbullah has also perpetrated a number of assassinations in Europe, at Iran's request. An Iranian dissident in Switzerland was assassinated in the early 1990s, and Hizbullah in Germany killed four Kurdish Democratic Party leaders in 1992.

Hizbullah has also recruited members from European Shi'ites and European converts to Islam. Hizbullah raises funds in Europe and has attempted to infiltrate Israel via Europe.

Mughniyah is also suspected in a November 2003 wave of suicide bombings in Turkey that targeted synagogues and British institutions that left dozens dead.

Americas

South America has been a major theater of Hizbullah operations, carrying out two major terror attacks in Buenos Aires, the March 1992 bombing of the Israeli Embassy and the July 1994 bombing of the AMIA Building that housed the offices of Argentina's Jewish communal organizations. According to Argentine intelligence, these attacks were directed from Hizbullah's primary center of operations in South America, the Tri-Border region where Paraguay, Brazil, and Argentina meet. The Tri-Border region's poorly regulated frontiers have made it a haven for criminal activity and an attractive base of operations for terrorists. There are approximately 30,000 Muslims in the region, most of whom are Lebanese Shi'ites. The region, and particularly the Paraguayan city of Ciudad del Este, is a fundraising and money laundering center for Hizbullah. It is also believed that training camps have been set up in the nearby wilderness. Hizbullah operatives may have set up private call switching centers in homes to evade American satellites that can monitor telephone traffic. Since 9/11, Argentina, Brazil, and Paraguay have all made terrorist related arrests in the area, however, their counter-terrorism efforts have been hampered by loose, and in Paraguay's case, non-existent laws prohibiting the financing of terrorist operations.

However, Hizbullah operations in South America are not limited to the Tri-Border region. Free trade zones throughout the region, particularly Iquique in Chile, Maicao in Colombia, and Isla Margarita in Venezuela, are reportedly becoming centers for Hizbullah and other terrorist groups. In June 2002, Brazilian authorities arrested Assad Ahmed Barakat, a leading Hizbullah operative based in the Tri-Border region. He was in Rio de Janeiro, attempting to recruit members from Brazil's Shi'ite community.

Hizbullah also operates a North American network that extends throughout the United States and Canada. These networks raise money through criminal activity and purchase dual use technology such as blasting caps, night vision goggles, GPS systems, scuba gear, and laser range finders. In North Carolina, two Hizbullah operatives were convicted in June 2002 of providing material support for a terrorist group. They were members of a cell that was engaged in cigarette smuggling. Canadian Hizbullah operatives took out life insurance policies on Hizbullah operatives likely to be killed in terrorist attacks. On December 11, 2002, Canada outlawed Hizbullah.

There are unconfirmed reports of Hizbullah sleeper cells in the Houston area, that are preparing to target the U.S. oil industry.

Asia

Hizbullah has operations throughout Asia, and has recruited members from the local Shi'ite populations, particularly in Malaysia, Indonesia, and most importantly India, where there are millions of Shi'ites.

In March 1994, Hizbullah attempted a truck bombing on the Israeli embassy in Bangkok, Thailand. The attack failed because the truck broke down on the way. In the late 1990s, Singapore's Internal Security Department broke up a Hizbullah cell that was planning to attack American and Israeli ships in that country. In the Philippines in 1999 and 2000, Hizbullah operatives with links to the Moro Islamic Liberation Front (MILF) were arrested.

Africa

Hizbullah has a presence in the Lebanese Shi'ite diaspora in central and western Africa. Hizbullah has also trained and collaborated with other terrorist organizations in the Sudan.

Targets and Tactics

Hizbullah opposes all Western presence in the Middle East, so that it has targeted both Israeli and Western influence in Lebanon. Professors and administrators at the American University in Beirut are particularly targeted, both because of their local prominence and because the AUB symbolizes the secular Western culture that Hizbullah despises.

Many of Hizbullah's targets have been military installations or soldiers. But Hizbullah has also made innumerable attacks on civilians, including its frequent Katyusha launches against northern Israel, its attack on the AMIA building in Buenos Aires, Argentina, and its kidnapping of journalists and Western civilians.

Hizbullah has also targeted Lebanese Christians and Muslims and Hizbullah's long running conflict with Amal has given rise to massacres. In 1985, in the course of fighting with Amal in the Tufa region of Southern Lebanon, Hizbullah fighters massacred and desecrated the corpses of hundreds of people. Since Israel's withdrawal from Southern Lebanon in May 2000, Lebanese Christians in South Lebanon and anyone suspected of collaborating with Israel is harassed. Bombings, abductions, and arson are becoming frequent occurrences there.

Hizbullah pioneered many terrorist tactics, including suicide bombing and the massive simultaneous truck or car bomb attack. Hizbullah also developed expertise in constructing highly effective explosive devices.

Hizbullah developed competence at guerilla war fighting Israel in South Lebanon throughout the 1980s and 1990s, carrying out innumerable ambushes and using roadside bombs effectively. Hizbullah has also successfully targeted Israeli tanks. In the late 1990s, Iran, with Syria's permission, gave Hizbullah more sophisticated weapons such as AT-3 Sagger and AT-4 Spigot anti-tank missiles and SA-7 anti-aircraft missiles. With Israel's withdrawal, substantial numbers of South Lebanon Army personnel defected to Hizbullah, bringing with them intimate knowledge of Israeli tactics and capabilities.

Since the Israeli withdrawal, Hizbullah has reportedly received enormous amounts of military equipment from Iran. Among this ordnance are an estimated 10,000 rockets, including the Fajr-3 and Fajr-5 with ranges of 25 and 45 miles, respectively, and a 200-pound warhead. Hizbullah views these rockets as a strategic asset that puts more than a third of Israel in its striking range.

Chronology of Major Events and Attacks

1982

June 4 – Israel invades Lebanon and lays siege to Beirut, intending to drive the PLO out of the country.

July 19 – Iranian-linked Islamic Amal kidnaps David Dodge, acting President of the American University in Beirut. Dodge was released in July 1983.

August 21– PLO begins evacuating Lebanon.

November 21 – Islamic Amal takes control of a Lebanese Army barracks in Baalbeck. It is later used to house Iranian Revolutionary Guards.

1983

April 18 – A suicide car bomb attack against the United States embassy in Beirut kills 63 and wounds 120. This attack is claimed by the Islamic Jihad, which is later revealed as Hizbullah's military wing.

October 23 – A suicide truck bombing of the United States Marine Headquarters and barracks and a French base in Beirut, Lebanon results in the deaths of 241 American Marines and 56 French soldiers. The Islamic Jihad claims responsibility for this incident.

November - December – Several dozen are killed and wounded in a series of Hizbullah car bomb attacks against the French Multinational Forces Command in Lebanon.

November 4 – A Hizbullah suicide bomber attacks Israel Defense Forces headquarters in Tyre, Lebanon killing 60 soldiers and General Security Service officers and injuring more than a dozen others.

1984

January 18 – Malcolm Kerr, the president of AUB is murdered by Islamic Jihad.

February – Hizbullah kidnaps an American citizen, Professor Frank Reiger of AUB, in Beirut and French citizen Christian Joubert. Both were freed on April 15, 1984.

February 26 – United States Marines complete their withdrawal from Beirut.

March 7 – Hizbullah kidnapped American journalist Jeremy Levin in Lebanon. He escaped in February 1985.

March 8 – A car bomb in Beirut explodes near the home of Hizbullah spiritual leader Sheikh Fadlallah. Over 80 people are killed and over 200 injured, Fadlallah survives. The United States is suspected.

March 16 – Hizbullah kidnaps William Buckley, the United States Central Intelligence Agency Station Chief in Beirut. He is reported killed in 1985. Buckley's remains are returned to the United States embassy in December 1991.

April 12 – Eighteen American servicemen are killed and over 80 others are injured in the Hizbullah bombing of a restaurant in Torrejon, Spain near a United States military base.

May – Hizbullah kidnaps the Reverend Benjamin Weir, an American citizen, in Lebanon. He is released in September 1985.

September 20 – The Islamic Jihad claims responsibility for a suicide truck bombing of the American embassy Annex in East Beirut. Twenty-three persons, including two Americans, are killed.

December – Hizbullah hijacks a Kuwaiti airliner en route to Tehran, Iran. The hijackers murder two passengers, both of whom are United States Agency for International Development officials.

1985

January – Hizbullah kidnaps Father Lawrence Jenco, an American citizen, in Lebanon. He is released in July 1986.

February – Hizbullah publishes its first political manifesto.

March – Hizbullah kidnaps Terry Anderson, a United States citizen and an Associated Press journalist, in Beirut. He is released in December 1991.

In a Hizbullah car bomb attack at the Egel Gate crossing point near Metulla, Israel, 12 Israeli soldiers are killed and 20 are wounded.

May – Hizbullah kidnaps an American citizen, an official at the American University of Beirut, in Lebanon. He is released in November 1986.

June – Hizbullah kidnaps a U.S. citizen, the director of the of AUB in Lebanon. He is released in November 1991.

TWA Flight 847 en route to Athens, Greece is hijacked. One passenger, a United States Navy diver, is murdered. Hizbullah and a faction of the pro-Syrian Shi'ite militia, Amal, hold 39 passengers hostage for 17 days in Beirut before they are released.

July – The Islamic Jihad claims responsibility for the simultaneous bombings of a Northwest Orient Airlines plane and a synagogue in Copenhagen, Denmark. In these bombings, one person is killed and 26 are injured.

December – Hizbullah initiates a series of bombings in France that continue through the end of the French elections in September 1986. Thirteen are killed and 303 are injured.

1986

September – Hizbullah kidnaps two American citizens in Beirut. One is released in April 1990 and the other is released in December 1991.

October – Hizbullah kidnaps an American citizen in Beirut. He is released in August 1991.

1987

January – Hizbullah kidnaps Anglican Church Envoy Terry Waite as well as three AUB professors in Beirut. All are released by 1991.

June – Hizbullah kidnaps an American journalist Charles Glass in Beirut. He escapes in August 1987.

1988

February – Hizbullah kidnaps United Nations military observer Lt. Colonel William Richard Higgins, USMC. He is reported killed in 1991 and his remains are handed over to the American Embassy in Beirut in December 1991.

October – Hizbullah claims responsibility for an attack near an Israeli checkpoint, just north of the Israeli border with Lebanon, in which a suicide bomber drives a van loaded with explosives into an Israeli Defense Forces convoy. Eight Israeli soldiers are killed and nine are injured.

1989

January – Hizbullah fighters massacre hundreds of Amal loyalists in the Tufah region of Southern Lebanon.

March 29 – Hizbullah operatives murder the Imam of a mosque in Brussels, Belgium, and his assistant. The Imam had taken a moderate stance towards Salman Rushdie's novel *Satanic Verses*, which Islamists accused of defaming Islam.

June 11 – A Saudi diplomat is assassinated and the Saudi embassy in Beirut is bombed. It is believed Hizbullah carried out these attacks to avenge the execution of 16 Kuwaiti Shi'ites who were involved with bombing plots in Mecca.

1990

November – Hizbullah claims responsibility for the murder of a Saudi diplomat in Beirut.

1991

October – Three Israeli soldiers are killed when a bomb explodes under their armored vehicle in Israel's security zone in Southern Lebanon.

The Hizbullah-affiliated Islamic Resistance Movement claims responsibility for the attack. Hizbullah also claims responsibility for a bomb attack in the security zone nine days later, in which two Israeli soldiers are killed and a third is injured.

1992

January — Hizbullah bombs the Lebanese village of Tayr Harfa in Israel's security zone in Southern Lebanon. The village's mayor is killed.

February 17 — Israel assassinates Hizbullah Secretary-General Sheikh Abbas al-Musawi.

March 17 — Hizbullah claims responsibility for the bombing of the Israeli embassy in Buenos Aires, Argentina. Twenty-nine people are killed and 252 are injured. Most of the casualties are Argentines. Hizbullah claims that the attack was carried out to avenge the death of Sheikh al-Musawi.

April — The Hizbullah-affiliated Islamic Resistance Movement and the Palestinian Islamic Jihad (PIJ) claim to have carried out a joint attack in Israel's security zone in Southern Lebanon that kills two Israeli soldiers and wounds five others.

July — Hizbullah operatives kill one Israeli soldier and injure three with a bomb that detonates under a tank in the Israeli security zone in Southern Lebanon.

October — Five Israeli soldiers are killed and five are wounded in a Hizbullah ambush in Southern Lebanon.

1993

April — A roadside bomb kills three Israeli soldiers and injures two in Southern Lebanon. Hizbullah's military wing, the Islamic Jihad, claims responsibility.

June — Five Katyusha rockets are fired at the Israeli city of Qiryat Shmona. The fusillade injured six Israeli civilians and destroyed six houses. In retaliation Israel launches Operation Accountability, a massive artillery assault on Hizbullah positions in Lebanon.

August – In two separate bomb attacks in southern Lebanon, eight Israeli soldiers were killed and one was injured.

October – Six Katyusha rockets were fired into positions held by the SLA in the security zone.

1994

February – An Israeli patrol in the security zone in South Lebanon was attacked with automatic weapons fire, rocket-propelled grenades, and anti-tank missiles. Four Israeli soldiers were killed and five were wounded.

March – Security officials in Bangkok, Thailand announced that a Hizbullah plot to blow up the Israeli embassy with a large truck bomb was foiled when the truck broke down and was abandoned on a Bangkok street.

An IDF patrol was ambushed in the security zone in Lebanon. Two Israelis and two SLA soldiers were killed.

June – Katyusha rockets were fired at Israeli targets in northern Israel and in the security zone in Southern Lebanon. Three rockets hit the town of Nahariya, on the Israeli coast and three others landed in the Hamra passageway in the security zone. No casualties were reported. Katyusha rockets were fired into Israel. There were no casualties. Israeli retaliation includ air raids that killed 26 Hizbullah operatives.

Hizbullah operatives clash with the Fijian United Nations Interim Force in Lebanon (UNIFIL) peacekeepers when they prevent Hizbullah forces from moving into a zone southeast of the Port of Tyre. During a machine gun and anti-tank rocket battle, one Hizbullah fighter is killed and two Fijian peacekeepers injured.

Hizbullah operatives ambush an IDF patrol and kill three Israeli soldiers and injure three others near Beaufort Castle in the security zone. Hizbullah fire anti-tank missiles, mortars, and machine guns at Israeli and Lebanese army positions stationed in the Tallousah region of the central sector of the security zone.

July 18, 1994 – A large car bomb destroyes the AMIA building, housing many Jewish agencies, in downtown Buenos Aires, Argentina. Hizbullah is strongly suspected of carrying out the attack although a group calling itself Ansarollah (Partisans of God) claims responsibility. Eighty-six people a killed and 206 a wounded.

August – One Israeli soldier is killed and 13 others injured during battles between Israeli forces and Hizbullah operatives in Southern Lebanon. On the same day, an IDF officer is killed and five soldiers injured when Hizbullah fighters attack their vehicle with anti-tank missiles in the security zone. Hizbullah also fires 12 Katyusha rockets that land near the South Lebanese town of Kfar Kila, near the Israeli border.

August – Hizbullah fires Katyusha rockets into northern Israel, injuring three Israeli children.

Hizbullah attacks an Israeli patrol and kills two Israeli soldiers and wounds three others. An Israeli tank is also destroyed.

1996

April – Israel launches Operation Grapes of Wrath, a massive assault of artillery and airpower, in response to hundreds of rockets fired into the security zone and northern Israel. In May 1996, Israel accidentally shells the refugee camp at Qana, killing 107 Lebanese civilians.

1997

September 5 – Twelve Israeli soldiers are killed in an unsuccessful commando mission.

1998

March – A roadside bomb kills six Lebanese construction workers and wounds two. The men were doing construction work at an SLA outpost near Marjayoun. The attack reportedly occurrs shortly after a visit to the nearby SLA headquarters by Israeli Defense Minister Yitzhak Mordechai. Hizbullah claims responsibility for the attack.

1999

February – Hizbullah operatives kill Brigadier General Erez Gerstein, head of the IDF liaison unit in Lebanon.

December – A Hizbullah suicide bomber drives a car loaded with explosives into the southern Lebanese town of Klaiyat and blows it up near an Israeli convoy, injuring 12 local residents and one Israeli soldier.

2000

May 24 – Israel completes its withdrawal from Lebanon.

July 24 – The UN certifies that Israel has fully complied with UN Resolution 425, calling for a complete withdrawal from Lebanon.

October 7 – Hizbullah operatives capture three Israeli soldiers in the Shebaa Farms region, which Hizbullah claims is part of Lebanon. Shortly thereafter an Elhanan Tannenbaum Israeli businessman in Europe is lured to Lebanon and taken hostage.

2002

March 13 – A pair of Hizbullah operatives wearing IDF uniforms infiltrate northern Israel and fire on vehicles. Six Israelis are killed and seven are wounded before security forces locate and kill the terrorists.

2004

January 29 – Israel and Hizbullah carry out a large-scale prisoner exchange. Israel released more than two dozen Lebanese prisoners including senior Hizbullah leader Sheikh Obeid, 400 Palestinian prisoners, and the bodies of 54 Lebanese killed in fighting with Israel. Israel, in turn, received Tannenbaum and bodies of the three soldiers killed by Hizbullah in October 2003.

Resources

Al-Manar, Hizbullah's affiliated satellite channel, website www.manarty.com

Eisenberg, L.Z. Israel's South Lebanon Imbroglio. *Middle East Quarterly,* June 1997; Vol. 4, No. 2 – available at www.meforum.org
Gambrill, G., and Abdelnour, Z. "Hizbullah: Between Tehran and Damascus." *Middle East Intelligence Bulletin*, February 2002; Vol. 4, No. 2 – available at www.meib.org

Gambrill, G.,"Dossier: hassan Nasrallah." Middle East Intelligence Bulletin, February- March 2004; Vol. 6, No. 2/3– available at www.meib.org

Hassan Nasrallah, The Hizbullah Secretary-General, website www.nasrollah.net

Hizbullah official website www.hizbollah.org. It has an extensive English language section.

Kramer, M. website www.martinkramer.org Martin Kramer is a Professor at the Moshe Dayan Center for Middle Eastern and African Studies at Tel Aviv University and his website has several articles on Hizbullah, including a biography of Sheikh Fadlallah.

Levitt, M. "Hezbollah's West Bank Terror Network." Middle East Intelligence Bulletin, August - September 2003; Vol. 5, No. 8-9–available at www.meib.org

Ranstorp, M. Hizb'allah, *Lebanon: The Politics of the Western Hostage Crises.* New York: St. Martin's Press, 1997.

Zisser, E. Hizballah, "Lebanon: At the Crossroads." *Middle East Review of International Affairs Journal,* September 1997; Vol. 1, No. 3 – available at meria. idc.ac.il/journal/previousj.html.

Kurdistan Workers' Party

Partiya Karkeren Kurdistan (PKK) translates as the Kurdistan Workers' Party.

Ideology and Objectives

The PKK is a Marxist revolutionary organization devoted to liberating the Kurds from colonialism by founding an independent Kurdish state in southeastern Turkey. It views itself as part of the world Marxist movement, however, with the collapse of the Soviet Union, the PKK has been de-emphasizing class struggle and emphasizing the Kurdish national struggle. The PKK has also made references to Islamist doctrine and has attacked the Turkish-Israeli alliance as a plot to undermine the Iranians and the Arabs.

History

Origins

The PKK grew out of Marxist and Maoist debate clubs at Turkish universities. In 1965, these clubs merged into the Federation of Debate Clubs and, in 1970, reorganized as the Revolutionary Youth Federation. Several far-left revolutionary groups grew out of these organizations, most notably the Turkish People's Liberation Army. Within these organizations, there were large numbers of Kurds who had aspirations for an independent Kurdistan.

On November 27, 1978, Abdullah Ocalan formed the PKK. At first, its existence was clandestine. It was devoted to communist revolution, but, since it had no funds, its first operations were robbing jewelry stores and drug trafficking.

On December 12, 1980, on the eve of a military coup, the PKK fled to Lebanon where they trained with the Palestine Liberation Organization (PLO). In 1982, they fought against Israel. While in Lebanon, the PKK received Syrian support and began building a support network among the Kurdish diaspora. They were particularly successful in recruiting Kurdish businessmen, Kurdish workers in Libya, and the Iraqi Kurds. Ocalan also began consolidating power and taking complete control of the organization.

Initiating Anti-Turkish Terror

In 1982, the PKK infiltrated back into Turkey and initiated a war against Turkey. Ocalan established the Kurdish National Liberation Front and started a hit-and-run guerrilla war but had difficulty forging popular support. In 1985, Ocalan changed the identity of the armed wing, calling it the Kurdish Popular Liberation Army, and attempted to include the religious and rural populations that did not find PKK Marxism appealing.

In 1984, Turkey responded to PKK activity by arming and organizing the Kurdish tribes that had good relations with the Turkish state. By 1987, Turkey had recruited 70,000 well-paid Kurdish village guards and in 1985 the PKK began murdering women and children related to village guards. This strategy was effective; Kurds became unwilling to support the Turkish government. The PKK grew during the late 1980s, due to the efficiency of their tactics and to Turkish Prime Minister Turgat Ozal's underestimation of the threat posed by the PKK from 1983-1989.

Turkey and Syria signed an agreement in which Syria agreed to stop supporting the PKK in 1987. Ocalan moved from Syria to Lebanon (which was controlled by Syria and used as a staging area for many Syrian-supported terrorist organizations). This agreement was the first of many Turkish-Syrian agreements in which Syria committed to limiting its support for the PKK.

In 1988, the PKK expanded the role of its overseas organizations, particularly in Europe, to advance the Kurdish cause. The overseas wing operated through Kurdish cultural associations and emphasized Turkish human rights violations against the Kurds.

Turkish Crackdown Begins

In 1989, Turkey began cracking down on the PKK, which responded by offering amnesty to village guards and claiming that it would focus on Turkish military targets. At about the same time, Islamist terrorists appeared in Kurdish areas of Turkey and began targeting the PKK. The Islamists believed that the PKK was opposed to Islam and sought to divide the Muslim world by building an independent Kurdish state. This shadowy, clandestine organization or group of organizations also attacked Turkey proper. Because of its attacks on PKK members, there was speculation that the Turkish government secretly backed it. It was also believed that the Islamists received support from Iran. In 1993, the PKK and the Islamists came to the conclusion that the real enemy was Turkey and that the infighting did not benefit Islam.

At about this time, the PKK began making more explicit Islamic references in its literature and began establishing links with Iran. The organization also established links with Turkish leftists, particularly DHPK-C (Dev-Sol), although this alliance did not hold up over time.

The Gulf War in 1990 to 1991 and the ensuing chaos in Kurdish northern Iraq, was advantageous to the PKK. The PKK had long operated in northern Iraq, often with Iraqi support, although, from 1987 to 1988, Iraq allowed Turkey to hit PKK targets in northern Iraq. But the factionalism among the Iraqi Kurds allowed the PKK to establish an extensive infrastructure in northern Iraq. Combined with growing support from Iran and continued support from Syria, the PKK expanded its operations to Turkey's Black Sea regions and began abducting tourists. In the early and mid-1990s, the PKK had virtual control over large parts of southeastern Turkey and at its peak, the PKK had nearly 15,000 operatives.

The PKK was also orchestrating violence in Europe, particularly Germany, which has a large Kurdish population. Turkish diplomatic and commercial offices were attacked throughout Europe and the PKK was banned in several European countries.

In tandem with its military success, the PKK pressed forward on the political front. In 1994, the PKK began calling for a dialogue, and in late 1994, announced its intent to focus its attacks on Turkish security forces and pro-Turkish guerrillas. In early 1995, the PKK Congress attempted to drop the hammer and sickle from the PKK insignia but instead renewed them and in 1995, the PKK founded a parliament-in-exile.

Turkey responded with large-scale incursions into northern Iraq in 1992, 1993, and 1995. In May 1997, Turkey launched Operation Steel, its largest anti-PKK operation involving 35,000 troops – 965 PKK operatives were killed along with 113 Turkish soldiers. By this point, the war in Turkey had cost an estimated 27,000 lives, including over 5,000 civilians. Hundreds of villages in southern Turkey had been evacuated because of PKK activity, causing massive economic and social disruption.

Pursuit and Capture of Ocalan

In the fall of 1998, Turkey threatened to declare war on Syria if it did not cease supporting the PKK. On October 20, 1998, Syria signed an agreement with Turkey designating the PKK as a terrorist organization. Ocalan was forced to leave Syria.

Seeking a safe haven, Ocalan went to Italy. Italy, which opposes the death penalty, would not grant Ocalan asylum, but also would not extradite him to Turkey where he was likely to be sentenced to death.

Leaving Italy on January 16, 1999, Ocalan continued seeking asylum. No European country would grant it, but Greece, a rival to Turkey and a supporter of the PKK, permitted him to land on the island of Corfu. From Corfu, Ocalan flew to Nairobi, Kenya, where he found refuge in the Greek diplomatic compound. On February 15, he left the Greek diplomatic compound, was seized by Turkish commandos, and brought to Turkey. A Turkish court charged him with treason on February 23, 1999 and he was sentenced to death on June 29, 1999. The sentence was not carried out and Ocalan was held in a Turkish prison.

Ocalan's arrest and conviction was accompanied by a wave of terror in Turkey, including the assassination of a regional governor and a firebombing in Istanbul that killed thirteen. This was accompanied by protests in Europe by Kurdish immigrants.

From prison, Ocalan called for a PKK-Turkish dialogue. The PKK stated that it had renounced armed conflict. In September 2000, a PKK Congress called for an end to the war with Turkey, and in April 2002 the PKK relaunched itself as the Kurdistan Freedom and Democracy Congress (Kadek).

Turkey has refused to negotiate, and in May 2002 the European Union added the PKK to its terror list.

In August 2002, Turkey outlawed the death penalty, effectively commuting Ocalan's sentence to life imprisonment, in order to improve its chances of being accepted into the European Union, which opposes the death penalty.

In October 2002, Turkish intelligence reported that the PKK was purchasing weapons, particularly SA-7 anti-aircraft missiles, from Iran, Iraq, and Armenia. As of January 2004, about 5000 armed PKK fighters remain in strongholds in the mountains of northern Iraq.

Leadership

The PKK was a highly centralized Marxist-Leninist organization, and, consequently, Ocalan's arrest was a critical blow to the organization's ability to function. In the wake of his absence, a power vacuum developed. Ocalan's brother, Osman, attempted to fill it but was unsuccessful. A rivalry has developed between Cemil Bayih and Kani Yilmaz, head of the ERNK (National Liberation Front of Kurdistan-PKK international wing). Bayih was elected PKK high authority, making him titular head without displacing Abdullah Ocalan.

Organization

The PKK is under the control of the Chairman and the Chairman Council, which is elected by the Central Committee. The Central Committee governs PKK activities and the Central Disciplinary Board monitors internal discipline. These bodies are elected by the Party Congress, which meets every four years to vote on the PKK program. This structure is replicated at the provincial, regional and local levels within Kurdish areas.

The military arm is the ARGK, which is an acronym for Arteshen Rizgariya Gelli Kurdistan (Kurdistan People's Liberation Army). It has had bases in Armenia, Azerbaijan, Iran, Iraq, Syria, and Turkey. The ARGK is believed to have between 4,000 and 5,000 operatives, and has had as many as 15,000 operatives in the past.

The international wing of the PKK is the ERNK, an acronym for Rizgariya Netewa Kurdistan (National Liberation Front of Kurdistan). The ERNK handles the diplomatic and propaganda operations, particularly in Europe. It is an umbrella group that includes student groups and cultural institutions, and it often operates through these fronts. In advocating the Kurdish cause, it highlights Turkish human rights abuses. The ERNK has also instigated violent demonstrations by Kurds in Europe.

The PKK has an intelligence and counter-intelligence organ and specialized terror units, such as the Metropolitan Teams for Terror. The PKK runs *Med-TV*, a satellite channel popular with Kurds.

Financial Support

The PKK's primary source of income is from drug trafficking, which represents approximately 40% of its annual budget, which in the mid-1990s was between $80 and $90 million.

Additional sources of income include other criminal activity, such as robbery, arms and people smuggling, and extortion. When the PKK controlled areas of Turkey, businesses and individuals were forced to pay them a tax. The PKK raises money in the Kurdish diaspora through fundraising, publication sales, and extortion. The PKK also operates commercial enterprises.

At different times the PKK has received financial support from Syria, Iraq and Iran.

Links to States and Terrorist Organizations

Greece

Greece and Turkey have several important areas of contention. In the past Greece supported the PKK in order to strengthen its position vis-à-vis its more powerful neighbor and has offered diplomatic support to the PKK and allowed PKK fundraising and propaganda to be launched from its territory. Turkey alleges that Greece has also trained PKK militants.

More recently, Greece's ambassador to Kenya provided a haven for Ocalan when he was fleeing capture.

Iran

Despite the PKK's secular stance and Iran's Islamist ideology, they have been cooperating since at least 1993. In 1994, Iran turned 14 PKK terrorists over to Turkey. In exchange, Turkey cracked down on Mujahedin-e Khalq, a radical Islamist-Marxist group that turned against the Iranian Muslim revolution. However, Iranian support for the PKK has grown. In 1997, Iran supplied the PKK with missiles, transportation, and medical supplies. Iranian missiles enabled the PKK to shoot down a pair of Turkish helicopters and in 1999 the PKK had 50 bases in Iran and Iran was training 1,200 PKK fighters annually. Iran was also supporting PKK operations in northern Iraq. In exchange, the PKK killed 11 leading members of the Iran Kurdistan Party, which opposes the Iranian government and its policies toward the Kurds of Iran.

Iran's support for the PKK may in part be in exchange for Syria's support for Hizbullah in Lebanon.

Iraq

In the past, Iraq has been a supporter of the PKK. Since the removal of Iraqi authority in northern Iraq in the wake of the first Gulf War, the

PKK has had substantial operations in northern Iraq, with the support of Iran and Syria. The PKK is unpopular among the Iraqi Kurds and many times has clashed violently with the Iraqi Kurdish organizations, but the local Kurdish organizations are unable to defeat the PKK as long as it receives outside support. The PKK is used as a proxy by Syria and Iran to prevent the Iraqi Kurds from achieving a political union that could support their own Kurdish minorities.

Syria

Syria was the leading supporter of the PKK, allowing Ocalan to reside in Damascus and providing training and logistical infrastructure for the organization. Syria supported the group in order to influence Turkish policy in three areas: Turkish control of the Euphrates river, which is a primary source of water for Syria; Turkey's growing strategic alliance with Israel; and advancing Syria's claim to Turkish territory.

PKK facilities were often located in Lebanon, which while controlled by Syria, allowed Syria to claim that it did not support the PKK. In the fall of 1998 Syria expelled Ocalan when Turkey threatened to go to war over Syrian support for the PKK. Some reports indicate that Syria may not be abiding by its agreement with Turkey, allowing the PKK to operate under a new name — Democratic Union of the Homeland.

Other Terrorist Organizations

When it was first founded, the PKK trained with the PLO in Lebanon. While in Syria they trained with the various secular Palestinian organizations based in Syria: Popular Front for the Liberation of Palestine (PFLP), Democratic Front for the Liberation of Palestine (DFLP), and Popular Front for the Liberation of Palestine – General Command (PFLP-GC).

The PKK briefly had an alliance with the radical left terrorist group DHPK-C. But this alliance did not last and, in 1998, the groups announced they were no longer cooperating. The PKK may be cooperating with TIKKO, a Maoist organization based primarily in Turkey's Tunceli province with about 100 operatives. TIKKO carried out a number of violent attacks after Ocalan was arrested.

Areas of Operation

The PKK's primary focus is southeastern Turkey, but it also has launched attacks on major Turkish cities and at Turkish tourist sites.

The PKK has operated from bases in Iran, Iraq, Syria, and Lebanon.

The PKK has an extensive infrastructure in Europe and Canada where there are large Kurdish communities. Besides diplomatic, propaganda, and fundraising activities it has committed terrorist acts and incited riots and vandalism in Western Europe. Britain, France, and Germany have banned the PKK.

Targets and Tactics

The PKK attacks Turkish security forces, but has also struck Kurds who are willing to cooperate with Turkey. Besides the armed village guards, the PKK targeted teachers in Kurdish areas because they spread Turkish propaganda to the Kurds. Hundreds of schoolteachers were murdered. In the mid-1990s, the PKK planted mines on roads frequented by tractors hauling villagers to work and forced young men to join by threatening to fine their parents.

They have also used suicide bombers, including women, and targeted government officials. While the PKK has focused on the rural front in southeastern Turkey, it has also engaged in urban terror in Turkey's major cities. For example in an effort to attack Turkey's tourism industry, the PKK has targeted Westerners for kidnapping.

The PKK has also used anti-aircraft weapons effectively. In 1997, PKK operatives shot down a pair of Turkish helicopters using SA-7 shoulder-launched anti-aircraft missiles.

Chronology of Major Events and Attacks

1978

November 27 – Abdullah Ocalan forms the PKK as a clandestine organization.

1980

December 12 – In the wake of a military coup, PKK operatives and leadership flee Turkey for Lebanon where they train with the PLO.

1982

PKK fights alongside the PLO against Israel in Lebanon, and begins infiltrating Turkey.

1988

April 1 – The Kurdish National Liberation Front, affiliated with the Kurdistan Workers' Party (PKK), claims responsibility for the shooting death of the West German consular affairs attaché in Paris.

1989

August 23 – A bomb explodes near the Israeli consulate in Istanbul, Turkey, causing no damage or injuries. The Armed People's Unit, associated with the PKK, claims responsibility for the attack. Prior to the attack, the Israeli consulate receives several anonymous calls threatening to avenge the Israeli seizure of Sheikh Obeid, senior Hizbullah official.

November 24 – The PKK claims responsibility for a massacre of 24 civilians in the village of I'kiyaka.

1991

December 25 – Eleven civilians are killed and 18 are injured in a bomb attack at a department store. The PKK claims responsibility.

1992

June 10 – Eleven civilians are killed in a PKK attack on a transportation vehicle in the hamlet of Sutlu.

September 9 – Probable PKK operatives attack the Mobil exploration site near the city of Batman. Several workers are wounded.

October 1 – Forty civilians are massacred and another 40 are wounded in a PKK assault on the village of Cevizdal.

October 20 – Nineteen civilians are killed and 19 are wounded in a PKK attack on a minibus in the hamlet of Aksakalli.

1993

June 24 – Operatives from the PKK stage a wave of coordinated attacks in more than 30 cities in six West European countries. The attacks consist primarily of vandalism against Turkish diplomatic and commercial targets and include the takeover of a Turkish consulate.

June 27 – PKK operatives throw hand grenades at a number of hotels and restaurants frequented by tourists in the Mediterranean resort area of Antalya. Twelve foreigners are among the 28 persons injured. Earlier, on June 9, PKK leader, Abdullah Ocalan, threatens that his group will start to use violence against tourist facilities in western Turkey.

July 5 – Thirty-two civilians die in a PKK attack on Kemaliye.

July 18 – Twenty-six nomads are killed in a PKK attack on the plateau of Bahcesaray.

October 4 – Twenty-six civilians are killed and four are maimed as a result of the PKK mining of the Midyat-Kayapinar village road.

October 4 – Thirty-seven are killed and ten are injured in a PKK attack on Daltepe and Kalanak villages.

October 21 – Twenty-four civilians are killed and seven are injured in a PKK attack in the Derince hamlet of Baykan.

October 25 – Thirty-one civilians are massacred and 16 civilians are wounded in a PKK attack on Cat-Yavi village.

November 4 – The PKK makes a second round of coordinated attacks against Turkish diplomatic and commercial facilities in six West European countries. The assaults consist mainly of firebombings and vandalism, but one person is killed and about 20 people are injured.

1994

February 2 – Five military school students are killed and 13 students are injured in a PKK bomb explosion at Tuzla train station.

March 27 – A bomb detonates in the gardens of the Saint Sophia Church and museum in Istanbul, injuring three tourists: one German, one Spanish and one Dutch. The Metropole Revenge Team of the political wing of the PKK claims responsibility.

April 2 – The PKK claims responsibility for bombing IC Bedesten, at the Center the Grand Bazaar in Istanbul. Two foreign tourists, one Belgian and one Spanish are killed and 17 others are injured.

June 24 – In the coastal towns of Fethiye and Marmaris, bombs kill one foreign national and injure 10 others at tourist sites. German television states that the PKK claims responsibility for the attacks.

1995

January 1 – Nineteen civilians are massacred in a PKK attack on the village of Kulp-Hamzali.

April 6 – Eight civilians are killed by PKK operatives in the village of Dortyol-Ahmetceduzu.

April 22 – Two Turkish citizens are shot by Kurdish extremists affiliated with the PKK at a coffeehouse in The Hague. Four men are arrested in connection with the attack.

July 13 – Kurdish separatists abduct a Japanese tourist at a rebel checkpoint near Siirt. No demands are made, and the kidnappers release the hostage unharmed on 17 July. The PKK is suspected.

July 24 – Twelve civilians are massacred in a PKK attack on the village of Gurpnar-Atabinen.

August 20 – Assailants throw a Molotov cocktail at a building in Paris that houses a Turkish sporting and cultural association, injuring six persons and causing minor damage. Witnesses report seeing three people flee the scene. The PKK may be responsible for the attack.

September 7 – Nine civilians are killed in a PKK attack on the village of Samandag.

1996

June 12 – Four Kurdish militants occupy a Reuters news agency office in Vienna and hold two employees hostage for several hours before surrendering. The attackers are suspected PKK sympathizers.

June 22 – Seven civilians are killed and 11 are injured as a result of the PKK attack on a tourist establishment in Altindag.

August 12 – Eight civilians are killed in a PKK attack on the Kangal-Demiriz train station.

September 30 – Four teachers are killed in a PKK attack on the village of Hantepe.

November 8 – Sixteen people are killed and 12 people are injured as a consequence of a PKK attack on a transportation bus running between villages.

1997

January 21 – At the Atrush refugee camp in northern Iraq, approximately 400 militants take 1,500 Turkish male refugees hostage and flee to Garo Mountain after the United Nations High Commission for Refugees (UNHCR) closes the camp. There are approximately 5,000 to 8,000 persons remaining at the camp. UNHCR and Turkish Government officials believe the PKK is responsible.

March 21 – Suspected members of the PKK detonate an improvised explosive device next to propane/butane gas tanks outside a Turkish-owned fast food restaurant in Bad Vilbel, injuring one person and causing extensive damage.

March 25 – Suspected members or sympathizers of the Turkish Grey Wolves organization of the PKK set a fire at a home in a predominantly Turkish neighborhood in The Hague, killing a mother and her five children, and causing extensive damage.

May – Turkey launches Operation Steel, a large-scale incursion against PKK bases in northern Iraq. According to Turkish sources, 965 PKK operatives are killed, along with 113 Turkish soldiers.

October 13 – Nine PKK operatives kidnap two Bulgarians and a Turk from a coal mine. The Turkish engineer is found dead, but the Bulgarians are released unharmed on 16 October.

October 19 – One civilian is killed and 15 are maimed in a PKK bomb attack on a transportation vehicle.

December 11 – Ten civilians are killed and four are maimed when a minibus hits a PKK planted mine in Dargecit.

1998

April 10 – Two members of the PKK throw an explosive device into a park near the Blue Mosque in Istanbul, injuring two Indian tourists, one New Zealander, four Turkish civilians, and two Turkish soldiers. Two PKK members, who are suspected of the attack, are arrested by security forces on 12 April 1998.

April 24 – Four people are killed and six are wounded in a PKK attack on a cafeteria in Diyadin county.

June 1 – PKK rebels kill ten members of a village guard militia in a clash near the mountainous Iraqi border.

June 3 – One civilian is killed and three people are injured in a PKK attack on a commuter train.

July 10 – Seven people are killed and 118 are injured as a result of an explosion of a bomb planted by the PKK in the famous covered bazaar Misir Cars.

July 14 – Four people are killed and five are injured in a PKK attack on the village of Cayozu.

October 20 – Syria signs an agreement with Turkey pledging to cease supporting the PKK forcing Ocalan to flee Syria.

October 30 – A Turkish airliner carrying 34 passengers and six crew members is hijacked by PKK operatives after taking off from Adana. The hijacking ends in Ankara early Friday morning when an elite Turkish anti-terrorist team storms the plane and kills the hijacker. None of the passengers are hurt.

November 17 – A PKK suicide bomber kills herself with a bomb strapped to her body. The blast wounds six people outside of a police station in southeast Turkey. The attack comes as a response to the detention in Italy of PKK leader, Abdullah Ocalan.

November 27 – A PKK planted bomb explodes on a bus in central Turkey, killing four passengers and injuring seventeen. The bomb, apparently on a timer, is hidden in the luggage rack above the bus door. It goes off just after midnight when the Istanbul-bound bus is about 14 kilometers from the town of Kirikkale, east of Ankara.

December 1 – A Kurdish woman affiliated with the PKK blows herself up in a suicide attack in the Turkish town of Lice. Fourteen people are injured in the attack, which takes place at a small supermarket frequented by Turkish soldiers. Some of the casualties are civilians, including a small child.

December 24 – A woman affiliated with the PKK sets off a bomb outside of an army barracks in east Turkey, killing herself and a passer-by. Twenty-two people, including 14 soldiers are injured in the blast.

1999

February 15 – Turkish commando capture Ocalan in Nairobi, Kenya. Since his expulsion from Syria, he had been traveling around Europe seeking asylum.

February 23 – A Turkish court indicts Ocalan. The PKK responds by threatening a wave of violence.

February 25 – Three people are killed and five others are injured in an attack believed to have been carried out by the PKK in the eastern province of Bingol. Four PKK members open fire on buildings and vehicles in a street. They also spray bullets on people sitting at a local coffee bar on the same street.

April 9 – A PKK suicide bomber throws himself in front of a provincial governor's car in southern Turkey, killing himself and the driver of the car. Hakkari province governor, Nihat Canpolat, is injured in the attack, along with a paramilitary police chief and a bodyguard. Several bystanders are also injured.

June 29 – A Turkish court sentences Ocalan to death.

July 20 – A 49-year-old man is killed and seven people are wounded when a group of PKK terrorists open fire on an open-air restaurant.

July 24 – One person is killed and 24 are wounded, five of them seriously, when a PKK planted bomb goes off in an Istanbul park.

2000

September – The PKK Congress calls for an end to the war with Turkey.

2002

April – PKK renames itself the Kurdistan Freedom and Democracy Congress (Kadek).

May – The European Union (EU) names the PKK as a terrorist group.

August – Turkey outlaws the death penalty, effectively commuting Ocalan's sentence to life imprisonment.

Resources

Gunter, M.M., "Turkey and Iran Face off in Kurdistan." *Middle East Quarterly* March 1998; Vol. 5, No.1 – available at www.meforum.org.

"Iran and Turkey Sign Border Security Agreement." *Middle East Intelligence Bulletin* September 1999; Vol.1, No. 9 – available at www.meib.org.

Karmon, E., "Terrorism in Turkey: An Analysis of the Primary Players." The International Policy Institute for Counter-Terrorism website March 16, 1999 – available at www.ict.org.il.

Turkish Foreign Ministry has extensive material online about the PKK - www.mfa.gov.tr/grupa/ac/acf/default.htm.

The International Policy Institute for Counter-Terrorism has an in-depth section on the PKK, including analyses and documents – www.ict.org.il.

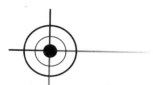

Palestinian Islamic Jihad

Harakat al-Jihad al-Islami al-Filastini in English means Palestinian Islamic Jihad Movement (PIJ).

Ideology and Objectives

The PIJ is a radical Islamic organization that seeks to create an Islamic polity governed by shari'a (Islamic Law) and is committed to violence as the means of achieving this goal. The destruction of Israel is, in the PIJ worldview, the essential first step towards a greater Jihad and, ultimately, Islamic governance. The PIJ views any compromise with Israel as impossible. Inspired by the 1979 radical Muslim revolution in Iran, the founders of the PIJ were disaffected members of the Muslim Brotherhood who felt that the Muslim Brotherhood's gradualist approach was ineffective and that more active, violent means were necessary to achieve Islamist goals. The PIJ is one of the few Sunni Muslim movements inspired by the Shi'ite Iranians. Sunni Islam views Shi'ite Islam as heresy, and the PIJ has long sought a formula to downplay that schism.

History

Origins

In 1979-1980, Palestinian students in Egypt who had split from the Palestinian Muslim Brotherhood in Gaza founded the PIJ. They were disappointed by the "moderation" of the Egyptian Muslim Brotherhood and felt that the Egyptian Islamists had made a mistake in not giving first priority to the Palestinian problem.

The leaders of this movement, Dr. Fathi Abd al-Aziz Shqaqi, Abd al-Aziz Odeh and Bashir Musa, were inspired by the 1979 Iranian Islamist revolution which provided a model that they felt was more appropriate to the Palestinian problem. Dr. Fathi Shqaqi, who became the Secretary-General of the PIJ, was born in the Gaza Strip in January 1951. He studied mathematics at Bir-Zeit University in the West Bank where he was active in the Muslim Brotherhood and in 1974, went to Egypt to study medicine at Zaqaziq University. He left the Muslim Brotherhood in 1974 because of ideological disputes. In 1979, Shqaqi wrote a pamphlet entitled *Khomeini: The Islamic Solution and the Alternative*, which supported the Islamic revolution and praised Khomeini's position on uniting the Sunni and Shi'ite Muslims. Egyptian authorities banned Shqaqi's work and imprisoned him for three months.

In 1980, Shqaqi returned to Gaza and began to organize a group of young Islamic radicals. Their ranks were reinforced in 1981 when many Palestinian Islamic radicals were expelled from Egypt for having links to Sadat's assassins. Under Shqaqi's leadership, Palestinian Islamic Jihad began building an infrastructure for terror and carried out several attacks prior to the Intifada. In 1986, Israeli authorities arrested Shqaqi.

Shqaqi's faction became the dominant faction of the PIJ, but there were several other Palestinian Islamist factions that embraced the Iranian revolution. For example, Sheikh As'ad Bayoud al-Tamimi who began building a parallel terrorist organization in the West Bank in 1982, led the most prominent of the PIJ's other factions. He received assistance from Fatah and the Iranian government and in 1983, this faction murdered an Israeli in Hebron. Ultimately, al-Tamimi died in Jordan in 1998 at the age of 86.

The First Intifada

When the Intifada broke out in 1987, the PIJ had about 250 militants, and took the lead in launching attacks and instigating riots. In 1988, Shqaqi, who had spent the previous two years in an Israeli prison, and Sheikh Odeh were deported to Lebanon. In Lebanon, they made contact with Hizbullah, Iran, Syria, and the Damascus-based Palestinian organizations. Since then, the PIJ has coordinated with and received support from Hizbullah. Iran became the sponsor of the PIJ, and Syria provided operational support. Shqaqi directed PIJ operations from Damascus.

The PIJ continued to launch attacks on Israeli soldiers and civilians and extended its attacks to Egypt. On February 4, 1990, the PIJ attacked a tour bus near Ismailia in Egypt killing nine

Israeli tourists, two Egyptian security guards, and injuring 20 tourists. In February 1991, the PIJ bombed an American Express office in Cairo.

Under Oslo

The PIJ opposed Palestine Liberation Organization (PLO) negotiations with Israel and the founding of the Palestinian Authority. On February 25, 1994, an Israeli extremist murdered 29 Palestinians worshipping at a mosque in Hebron. In retaliation, the PIJ launched a series of deadly bombings, including the March 4, 1996 suicide bombing on Tel Aviv's Dizengoff Street in which 20 were killed and 75 were wounded. The PIJ also began to coordinate with Hamas. The January 22, 1995, suicide bombing at Beit Lid, Israel in which 21 were killed and 69 were injured and the April 9, 1995 suicide attack in Gaza, which killed eight and wounded 50 were joint Hamas-PIJ efforts. These bombings, officially in revenge for the massacre at Hebron, were also aimed at derailing the peace process.

On October 26, 1995, Fathi Shqaqi was assassinated by the Israeli Mossad in Malta. Ramadan 'Abdallah Shalah took over as Secretary-General of the PIJ. Shqaqi's death was a major blow to the PIJ, as Shalah did not possess Shqaqi's charisma, organizational abilities, or intellect. The effectiveness and frequency of PIJ operations declined dramatically.

While still a major Palestinian movement, polls showed the PIJ a distant third behind Fatah and Hamas in popular support. Hamas had built a social infrastructure to expand its influence and increase its base of supporters and potential operatives, but the Palestinian Islamic Jihad had not engaged in social activities, instead focusing its efforts on terrorism.

Under the PA, the PIJ did not challenge PA authority openly, but also did not disarm or desist from terror attacks and there were times when the PA cooperated with Israeli security forces to prevent terror attacks. Sometimes the PA arrested PIJ militants – usually releasing them later. The case of Iyad Harden, the PIJ commander in Jenin, is an instructive example. After months of Israeli requests, PA police arrested Harden for his role in orchestrating several suicide bombings in November 1998. In October 1999, Harden escaped. Terrorists wanted by Israel frequently escape from PA prisons and are often aided by the guards. In May 2001, Harden was being held in a PA prison "for his own protection" but was permitted to come and go as he pleased. He was killed when the phone booth he was using outside the prison exploded.

Al-Aqsa Intifada

With the outbreak of the al-Aqsa Intifada in September 2000 the PIJ coordinated activities with Hamas and Fatah. Expanded funding from Iran allowed it to increase its activities and in October 2001, the PIJ participated in meetings in Damascus that included Hamas, Hizbullah, and other Palestinian terror groups on expanding their cooperative efforts. In late 2001, the PIJ began cooperating with Fatah and began providing funds for joint PIJ-Fatah operations. Palestinian security services were also cooperating with them providing early warning of crackdowns so PIJ operatives could avoid arrest.

In Israel's ongoing attempts to dismantle the PIJ infrastructure by eliminating its leadership, Israeli military forces on April 1, 2001 killed Mohammed Abdel-A'ael, a leading operative of the PIJ's al-Quds Brigades.

Despite this action, Palestinian Islamic Jihad operations grew in effectiveness. In August 2001, Israel released its list of most wanted Palestinians; three of the seven were PIJ operatives. In December 2001, Arafat called for a cease-fire by Palestinian organizations. The PIJ stated that it would not abide by these orders.

The Battle in Jenin

After the March 27, 2002 Passover massacre, Israel launched Operation Defensive Shield, which attempted to destroy the terrorist infrastructure in the West Bank. The city of Jenin, which had long been a center for Palestinian radicalism (bin Laden mentor Abdallah Azzam was born there) and had a strong PIJ presence, was a primary target of Israeli Defense Force (IDF) operations. Of the 100 suicide bombings between October 2000 and April 2002, 23 originated in Jenin.

The head of the PIJ's military operations in Jenin, Mahmud Tu'albe was killed in the battle, and several senior PIJ operatives were arrested, including Ali Safuri and Thabet Mardawi, who between them were responsible for dozens of deaths in several suicide bombings. The IDF also discovered large caches of weapons, explosives laboratories, and extensive documents outlining the activities and relationships between the different organizations. Thirty-three IDF soldiers were killed in the fighting in Jenin.

While the PIJ's operational abilities were curtailed by Defensive Shield and by other IDF operations, it remained capable of carrying out large-scale terror attacks. In October 2002, the PIJ attacked an Israeli bus with a car bomb, killing 14. In November, the PIJ ambushed a group of Israelis in Hebron and killed 12 Israeli civilians and soldiers. After the November attack, the United States and Israel urged Syria to close the PIJ offices in Damascus. Syria insisted that the Damascus office was only a media relations office.

Leadership

Ramadan 'Abdallah Shalah

The Secretary-General of the Palestinian Islamic Jihad is Dr. Ramadan 'Abdallah Shalah. Born in the Saja`iyah refugee camp in Gaza, Shalah was one of the first militants in the PIJ and was close to PIJ founder Fathi Shqaqi. While studying in London from 1986 to 1990, he headed the PIJ's London office, which directed the organization's military, propaganda and information activity in the West Bank and Gaza. After completing his doctorate on Islamic economics at the UK's University of Durnham in 1990, he moved to Tampa, Florida where he was a director of the PIJ front group, the World and Islam Studies Enterprise (WISE). From 1994-1995, he was an adjunct professor at the University of South Florida in Tampa, but he left the United States after Shqaqi's killing in October 1995 to become the head of the major faction of the PIJ and de facto leader of the movement. He is currently based in Damascus.

Sheikh Abd al-Aziz Odeh

The spiritual leader of Palestinian Islamic Jihad is Sheikh Abd al-Aziz Odeh, who co-founded the PIJ with Shqaqi and worked as a teacher in Gaza. In 1984, he was arrested by Israel for incitement and sentenced to 11 months in prison. He was deported from Israel to Lebanon in 1988 and is now based in Damascus.

Ahmed Ma'ana

Ahmed Ma'ana was born in Khan Yunis, Gaza and was an officer in the Palestine Liberation Army (PLA). While in Israeli prison, he became a radical Islamist. In 1985, he was released within the framework of the Ahmed Jibril prisoner exchange and he became a major activist in Dr. Shqaqi's faction later serving as an assistant to Sheikh al-Tamimi in Jordan. Ma'ana used his Syrian connections to arrange Islamic Jihad broadcasts on the PFLP-GC radio station, al-Quds, which broadcasts to the West Bank from southern Syria. In 1990, he relocated to Syria after angering Jordanian security forces and having a falling out with al-Tamimi.

Organization

Unlike Hamas, the PIJ has no overt social component — it is strictly a military operation with only a few hundred core militants and a broader base of supporters. PIJ operatives function in small, secret cells with a high level of autonomy. In Jenin, the PIJ had a highly developed terrorist infrastructure that, according to captured documents, was directly linked to the PIJ leadership in Damascus. Bassam Ragheb al-Sa'ad was the official in charge of disbursing money granted by the Damascus headquarters and those documents attest to his disbursal of $31,000 for a terrorist operation and $127,000 to aid the families of terrorists.

The PIJ faction founded by Shqaqi and now led by Shalah remains dominant, but there are several other factions. Two of the more notable are the al-Jihadi al-Islami – Bait al-Maqdas and the Tanzim al-Jihad al-Islami.

The al-Jihadi al-Islami – Bait al-Maqdas (Islamic Jihad – The Temple) was founded by Fatah and has served to link Fatah with the PIJ. It carried out a pre-Intifada terror attack on October 15, 1986 when several terrorists threw hand grenades at Israeli soldiers and their families during a swearing in ceremony at the Western Wall. The leaders of this faction were killed by a car bomb in 1988 in Cyprus.

The Islamic Jihad Squad (Tanzim al-Jihad al-Islami) was a small group of Islamic Jihad militants led by Ahmed Ma'ana that masterminded the terrorist attack in Egypt against an Israeli tourist bus in northern Sinai, on February 4, 1990.

Financial Support

The PIJ receives most of its financial support from Iran. With the onset of the al-Aqsa Intifada, Iran instituted an incentive system, paying millions of dollars for successful attacks. In June 2002, Iran separated its support for the PIJ from its support for Hizbullah. With its offices headquartered in Damascus, the PIJ receives extensive logistical assistance from Syria and with its increased use of suicide bombing attacks, PIJ members' families received stipends from Saddam's Iraq and Saudi Arabia.

Links to States and Terrorist Organizations
Iran and Hizbullah

Iran is the PIJ's primary benefactor and the PIJ is generally considered to be the Iranian proxy in the Palestinian-Israeli conflict. During the Iran-Iraq war, the PIJ was one of the few Sunni Muslim organizations to support Iran over Iraq. Initially, Iran was ambivalent about the PIJ, but in the late 1980s, the Iranian government expanded its efforts to export its radical Islamist ideology. This decision coincided with the outbreak of the Intifada, in which the PIJ played a major role. Seeing the PIJ as a possible bridge into the Sunni world, Iran provided them with funds, weapons, and training. When the PIJ's leadership was deported to Lebanon in 1988, they expanded their contacts with Iran and Hizbullah. Shortly after Israel's withdrawal from Lebanon in May 2000, the Iranian government encouraged the PIJ to expand its attacks against Israel. Iran has also been instrumental in encouraging cooperation between PIJ, Hamas, Fatah, Hizbullah, and other terrorist organizations.

Hizbullah and the PIJ coordinate actions and train together, and for a time the PIJ was effectively under Hizbullah's command. In June 2002 Iran, pleased with the PIJ's activity in the al-Aqsa Intifada, granted it an independent budget.

Hizbullah allegedly carried out the attack on the Jewish Agency in Buenos Aires, but the PIJ took responsibility for the attack. Their statement read, "The war will continue until Israel ceases to exist and the last Jew is eliminated from the world. Israel is entirely evil and must be wiped off the face of the earth." Reportedly, Hizbullah is using the PIJ to establish its own presence in the West Bank and Gaza, and among the Arab citizens of Israel. Hizbullah supports PIJ efforts to recruit and expand its influence among Palestinian refugees in Lebanon.

Syria

Syria is the PIJ's other major benefactor. The PIJ's leadership is based in Damascus and carries out operations in Lebanon in conjunction with Hizbullah and with Syrian approval. Syria facilitates communications and the transfer of money between the leadership in Damascus and PIJ operatives in the West Bank and Gaza, and PIJ fighters train in Syria and Lebanon.

Sudan

Since the 1989 coup, which placed the National Islamic Front and its ideologue Hassan al-Turabi in power, Sudan has been a leading state backer of terror. Sudan provided support, training camps, and a haven to many Islamist terror groups including PIJ and al-Qaeda. Al-Turabi also provided diplomatic passports to PIJ leaders Sheikh Abd al-Aziz Odeh and Fathi Shqaqi. While in Sudan, PIJ operatives received training from Iran's Revolutionary Guard, and came into contact with Osama bin Laden. Al-Turabi fell from power and was arrested in February 2000 and in May 2000 Sudan entered into a dialogue with the United States on terrorism and has taken some steps toward cracking down on terrorists.

Fatah

In the early 1980s, Fatah provided extensive training, financial, and organizational support to the PIJ in an attempt to take advantage of the rising Islamist trend in the West Bank and Gaza. This cooperation continued through the beginning of the Intifada in 1987. As Arafat began to negotiate with Israel, this relationship broke down because the PIJ could not accept any recognition of Israel. Exacerbating this breakdown, in 1988, Abu Jihad, the patron of the Islamist movements within the PLO, was assassinated by Israel.

Under the PA, PIJ militants were, because of Israeli pressure, occasionally arrested occasionally and later released. With the outbreak of the al-Aqsa Intifada, the PIJ has coordinated closely with Fatah. One aspect of this cooperation are the "cocktail" cells which include members of the PIJ, Fatah, and Hamas. With its expanded revenues, the PIJ has funded Fatah operations and provided financial support for the families of Fatah operatives killed in the al-Aqsa Intifada.

Hamas

Founded at approximately the same time, the early relationship between Hamas and the PIJ was characterized by intense ideological and practical rivalry. Both organizations competed for the same base of support. While the PIJ was inspired by the Iranian Shi'ite Muslim revolution, Hamas grew out of the Sunni Muslim Brotherhood, which was traditionally antipathetic towards Shi'ite Islam. Hamas viewed building infrastructure and developing the Muslim character of the Palestinian people as the first priority. The PIJ, taking the Iranian revolution as its model, believed that launching a violent jihad against Israel was urgent. At times, the competition between the two groups was violent, characterized by beatings and stabbings.

The outbreak of the Intifada in 1987 made the ideological disputes between Hamas and the PIJ irrelevant. Both organizations played key roles in orchestrating demonstrations and planning terrorist attacks. They continued to compete for support, but ultimately Hamas' better-developed social infrastructure led it to become more prominent than the PIJ. Because of the PIJ's decline in influence, Hamas no longer viewed it as a rival. Also as Hamas developed a closer relationship with Iran, ideological disputes between Hamas and the PIJ became less consequential. In the al-Aqsa Intifada, the two organizations have cooperated closely. An example of the close cooperation between the two groups is the use of Hamas' website and publications to announce plans for further terrorist attacks against Israel by the PIJ.

Other Terrorist Organizations

While ideologically opposed to the secular Palestinian organizations, the PIJ respects their militant commitment to the Palestinian cause. The PIJ cooperates with the Damascus-based organizations that reject the Oslo process, particularly the Popular Front for the Liberation of Palestine-General Command (PFLP-GC), which allows the PIJ to broadcast on their Damascus-based radio station, *al-Quds*, and provides training for PIJ operatives at its camps in Lebanon.

Through Hizbullah and in its own right, the PIJ has relationships with Muslim groups throughout the world including al-Qaeda. In particular, the PIJ has connections with Egypt's al-Jihad, a cell of which assassinated Egyptian President Anwar Sadat in 1981. Future PIJ leaders ended up in Gaza after being deported from Egypt because of their relationship with Egypt's al-Jihad. Sheikh al-Aziz Odeh, the PIJ's spiritual leader, is an unindicted co-conspirator in the 1993 World Trade Center bombing. Sheikh Odeh met with followers of Sheikh Omar Abdel Rahman of Egypt's al-Gama'a al-Islamiyya — another Egyptian Islamic terror organization. This meeting took place in the United States.

Areas of Operation

The PIJ is headquartered in Damascus and its strongest support is in the Gaza Strip. There are also PIJ cells in the West Bank and Lebanon. There is a particularly strong PIJ cell operating in the West Bank city of Jenin, but as evidenced by the 1990 attack on a tour bus in Egypt, the PIJ has not limited its operations to Israel, the West Bank, and Gaza.

United States

The PIJ is classified as a terrorist organization by the United States Deparment of State, but this classification has not prevented it from creating an extensive support network in the United States. The PIJ's American operations were headquartered in Tampa, Florida where future PIJ Secretary-General Ramadan Shalah was an adjunct professor at the University of South Florida (USF)

The PIJ's presence at USF began in 1986 when Sami al-Arian, a Palestinian professor of engineering, joined the faculty. Al-Arian launched the Islamic Concern Project, which was soon renamed the Islamic Committee for Palestine (ICP), a charitable organization. In 1991, al-Arian's brother-in-law, Mazen al-Najjar, founded the World Islam Studies Enterprise (WISE). In 1992, WISE entered into a formal cooperative agreement with USF to conduct research, co-host forums, and sponsor graduate students at USF. Al-Arian served WISE as chairman of the board.

Both WISE and ICP were closely connected to the PIJ leadership. When Ramadan Shalah came to Tampa, he served on the board of ICP and worked for WISE as director of administration. Shalah also briefed military officers at MacDill Air Force Base in Tampa, location of the United States Central Command.

WISE and ICP not only raised money for the PIJ in the United States, but also played a key role in directing terrorist operations. In May 1998 WISE board member Tarik Hamdi personally delivered a satellite telephone and battery pack to Osama bin Laden. ICP has sponsored large conferences throughout the United States featuring radical Islamist leaders from terrorist organizations throughout the Middle East, including Hamas, Hizbullah, Sudan's National Islamic Front, and al-Gama'a al-Islamiyya leader Sheikh Abdal-Rahman. Terrorist leaders gave speeches calling for terrorist acts against Israel, secular regimes of the Arab world, and the United States.

In May 1997, Mazen al-Najjar was arrested for overstaying his visa and held as a national security risk. In December 2000, he was ordered released due to lack of evidence, but in November 2001 he was arrested again and later deported to Lebanon in August 2002. Professor al-Arian and several others were indicted by a federal grand jury on February 20, 2003 on charges of raising money for the PIJ. The university, which had initiated termination procedures in December 2001, completed them on February 26, 2003.

Targets and Tactics

The PIJ views Israel as the primary, but not exclusive, enemy. The United States and secular Arab regimes are also potential targets. The PIJ is waging a two-front campaign against Israel: launching guerrilla attacks against Israeli military positions and terrorist attacks on Israeli civilians within Israel. During the al-Aqsa Intifada, the PIJ has claimed responsibility for at least a dozen guerrilla attacks and 25 terror attacks, killing hundreds and maiming even more. While suicide bombings have been prevalent, in order to counter the increased vigilance of Israeli bus drivers, the PIJ has used car bombs in its attacks against buses.

With technical support from Hamas, the PIJ has begun to build rockets, similar to Hamas' Qassam rocket. On May 25, 2002 PIJ operatives fired three rockets at the Israeli town Sderot from Gaza.

The quality of the PIJ's attacks have improved because of support from Hizbullah. The November 15, 2002 ambush of Israeli forces in Hebron was one example of a well-planned and deadly attack.

Chronology of Major Events and Attacks

1979

In Egypt Dr. Fathi Shqaqi writes *Khomeini: The Islamic Solution and the Alternative*. Egyptian authorities sentence him to three months in prison for his writing and upon his release, he returns to Gaza and begins organizing Palestinian radicals.

1981

October 6 – Egyptian President Anwar Sadat is assassinated by Islamists. In the aftermath of the assassination, Palestinian Islamists studying in Egypt are expelled to Gaza, many of whom join the nascent PIJ.

1983

July 7 – An Israeli student in Hebron is stabbed to death by a PIJ operative.

1986

February – PIJ Secretary-General Fathi Shqaqi is arrested by Israel.

October 15 – One Israeli is killed and 70 are injured in a PIJ grenade attack on the IDF induction ceremony at the Western Wall in Jerusalem.

1987

September – PIJ spiritual leader Sheikh Abd al-Aziz Odeh is arrested by Israeli security forces.

December 8 – In a traffic accident in the Jabalia refugee camp in Gaza, four Palestinians are killed when struck accidentally by an Israeli truck. Protests spread across Gaza and the West Bank and erupt into the Intifada.

1988

Sheikh Odeh and Dr. Shqaqi are deported to Southern Lebanon. They develop relations with Hizbullah, Iran, and Syria.

1989

May 3 – A pair of elderly Israelis are murdered by PIJ operatives at a bus stop in Jerusalem.

July 6 – The PIJ claims responsibility for an attack on a bus on the Tel Aviv-Jerusalem Highway in which 16 are killed and 25 are injured (fatalities include one American citizen; seven American citizens are injured).

1990

February 4 – The PIJ and a group calling itself the "Organization for the Defense of the Oppressed in Egypt's Prisons" claim responsibility for killing nine Israeli tourists and two Egyptian security guards, and injuring 20 tourists on an Egyptian bus near Ismailia, Egypt.

1991

February – The PIJ claims responsibility for two small explosions inside the American Express office in Cairo, Egypt.

October 28 – The PIJ and the PFLP claim responsibility for killing two and wounding at least six Israelis, including five children, on a bus north of Jerusalem. The attack occurs days before the opening of the Madrid Arab-Israeli peace conference.

October 30 – The Madrid Arab-Israeli peace conference opens. The conference lays the groundwork for future bilateral negotiations between the PLO and Israel.

1992

October – The Fathi Shqaqi faction of the PIJ claims responsibility for a roadside bomb explosion in Israel that kills an Israeli woman and injures eight others.

1993

March – A Palestinian from the Gaza Strip stabs and kills two Israelis and injures eight others in Tel Aviv. PIJ Secretary-General Fathi Shqaqi claims that the man is a PIJ activist acting on behalf of the organization.

August 2 – An armed Palestinian believed to be a member of the PIJ hijacks a United Nations Relief and Works Agency bus in the Gaza Strip and rams two Israeli cars, killing one Israeli and injuring five others (two critically).

September – The PIJ and Hamas both claim responsibility for an attack in which two gunmen open fire on an IDF patrol in Gaza City, killing three Israeli soldiers.

September – PLO Chairman Yasser Arafat sends Israeli Prime Minister Yitzhak Rabin a letter recognizing the right of Israel to exist. Israel replies by recognizing the PLO as the representative of the Palestinian people. On September 13 Israel and the PLO sign the Declaration of Principles, which outlines Palestinian self-government.

1994

May 4 – Israel and the PLO sign the Gaza-Jericho Agreement which brings the Palestinian Authority into being.

July 8 – Two Israelis are killed in the town of Kiryat Netafim. The PIJ calls the attack "a present" given to PLO leader Yasser Arafat for the PLO's agreements with Israel.

November 11 – Three IDF officers are killed at the Netzarim junction in the Gaza Strip by a Palestinian bicyclist who detonates explosives strapped to his body. Islamic Jihad states that the attack is to avenge the November 2 assassination of Islamic Jihad leader Hani Abed.

1995

January 22 – Two suicide bombers set off their explosives at a bus stop at Beit Lid Junction. The first bomb explodes in the midst of a crowd of soldiers; the second is detonated as bystanders crowd in to attempt to assist the wounded. Eighteen people are killed and 69 are injured.

April 9 – Two suicide attacks are carried out within a few hours of each other in Gaza. In Netzarim a PIJ suicide bomber crashes an explosives-rigged van into an Israeli bus, killing an American. citizen and seven Israelis, and injuring over 30 others. In Kfar Darom a PIJ suicide bomber detonates a car bomb in the midst of a convoy of cars, injuring 12 people.

October 26 – In Malta, PIJ Secretary-General Fathi Shqaqi is assassinated by Israel. Ramadan 'Abdallah Shalah becomes the leader of the PIJ.

1996

March 4 – A PIJ suicide bomber detonates a massive explosive device outside the Dizengoff Center, Tel Aviv's largest shopping mall, killing 20 and injuring 75.

1998

November 6 – Two PIJ operatives die and more than 20 bystanders are injured in a failed car bombing terrorist attack in the Mahane Yehuda market in Jerusalem.

2000

September 28 – Likud leader Ariel Sharon visits the Temple Mount (al-Haram al-Sharif to Muslims). The next day massive riots break out, which soon spread and are dubbed the al-Aqsa Intifada.

November 2 – A car packed with explosives explodes on a side street near Jerusalem's main outdoor market, killing two and injuring 10.

November 22 – A PIJ car bomb detonates next to a crowded bus in the northern Israeli town of Hadera during the evening rush hour. Two people are killed and about 55 are injured, five of them seriously.

2001

May 27 – A PIJ planted bomb explodes in Jerusalem near the intersection of Jaffa Road and Heshin Street. The bomb includes several mortar shells, extending the radius of the explosion. Thirty people are injured, most suffering from shock.

July 16 – A PIJ suicide bomber detonates a bomb at a bus stop near the train station in Binyamina, halfway between Netanya and Haifa. Two people are killed and 11 are wounded – three seriously.

August 9 – The PIJ and Hamas collaborate on a suicide attack on a Sbarro pizzeria in Jerusalem. Fifteen people are killed, including seven children, and about 130 are injured.

August 12 – A PIJ suicide bomber attacks a restaurant in Haifa, 21 people are wounded.

September 9 – Near the Jordanian border, PIJ gunmen strike a mini-van carrying schoolteachers, two are killed.

October 28 – Two PIJ gunmen open fire in the northern Israeli city of Hadera, killing four and wounding 28 others, some critically.

November 4 – A PIJ gunman opens fire on a bus at the French Hill junction in Jerusalem. A 14-year-old boy and a 16-year-old girl returning home from school are killed, and 45 are wounded.

November 27 – Two gunmen, one from the PIJ and one from Fatah, open fire in a crowded marketplace in Afula, killing two and injuring 30. Israeli security forces kill the gunmen.

November 29 – A PIJ suicide bomber detonates a bomb on an intercity bus traveling from Nazareth to Tel Aviv. Three passengers are killed and nine are wounded.

2002

March 20 – Seven people are killed and dozens are injured when a PIJ suicide bomber detonates a powerful bomb on a bus in northern Israel. The bombing occurs on an intercity bus en route from Tel Aviv to Nazareth.

April – Operation Defensive Shield: In response to the March 27 Passover massacre, the IDF enters Palestinian cities on the West Bank with overwhelming force. Highly developed terrorist infrastructure is dismantled by Israeli troops. Mahmud Tu'albe, head of PIJ military operations in Jenin, is killed in the battle, other senior PIJ operatives are arrested.

June 5 – The PIJ takes responsibility for a car packed with explosives that explodes next to a bus near the Megiddo Junction in northern Israel. Seventeen Israelis are killed, and at least 50 are wounded – 10 of them seriously

July 17 – In a double PIJ suicide bombing in Tel Aviv, five people are killed and 40 are injured.

October 21 – A PIJ car bomb is detonated next to a bus, killing 14 and wounding 45 at the Karkur Station in northern Israel.

November 4 – Two people are killed and 70 are injured in a PIJ suicide bombing at a shopping mall in Kfar Sava.

November 9 – The PIJ commander in Samaria, Iyad Sawalaha, is killed by an Israeli missile. He is responsible for the June 5 bombing in Megiddo and the October 21 attack at Karkur station.

November 15 – Three PIJ gunmen ambush a group of Israelis in Hebron. Israeli security forces join the battle. Twelve Israelis are killed, including an IDF Colonel, and 30 are injured.

2003

October 4 – A female PIJ suicide bomber evaded the guard at Maxim restaurant in Haifa. Twenty-one were killed, including three children, a baby and three Arab-Israeli employees of the restaurant, and 60 were wounded. Among the casualties was retired IDF Admiral Ze'ev Almog and four members of his family.

Resources

Barsky, Y., "Focus on Hamas: Terror by Remote Control." *The Middle East Quarterly* June 1996; Vol. 3, No. 2 - available at www.meforum.org.

Leavitt, M.A., "Sponsoring Terrorism: Syria and Islamic Jihad." *Middle East Intelligence Bulletin*, November-December 2002; Vol. 4, Nos. 11-12 – available at www.meib.org.

Palestinian Islamic Jihad website www.qudsway.org. It includes an interview with PIJ founder Fathi Shqaqi.

Stindberg, A., "The Damascus-Based Alliance of Palestinian Forces: A Primer." *Journal of Palestine Studies* Spring 2000; Vol. 29, No. 3, pp. 60-76.

"The Movement of Islamic Jihad and the Oslo Process: An Interview with Ramadan 'Abdallah Shallah." *Journal of Palestine Studies* Summer 1999; Vol. 28, No. 4, pp. 61-73.

The St. Petersburg Times has an in-depth special report on the case of USF professor Sami Al-Arian - available online at www.sptimes.com/2003/web-specials03/alarian/.

Palestine Liberation Organization & Its Affiliates

PLO & its Affiliates
Democratic Front for the Liberation of Palestine

The Democratic Front for the Liberation of Palestine (DFLP) is also known as the Popular Democratic Front for the Liberation of Palestine. In Arabic, the group is called al-Jabha al-Dimuqratiyah Li-Tahrir Filastin. The DFLP is a member, but not an active participant, of the Palestine Liberation Organization (PLO).

Ideology and Objectives

The DFLP is a Marxist-Leninist organization that believes the goal of a Palestinian state can only be accomplished in the context of a working class revolution brought about through violence. As such, it is also devoted to fostering revolution throughout the Arab world and particularly against the Arab monarchies (the DFLP has particular animosity for the Jordanian monarchy). The DFLP considers the Palestinian cause a part of the greater international "war of liberation" in which the United States is the central enemy.

While uncompromising in its call for armed struggle against Israel, the DFLP was the first major advocate within the PLO of a political solution. These ideas translated into the 1974 PLO "Strategy of Phases," which allowed for the declaration of a Palestinian state on any territory reclaimed from Israel, without the complete destruction of Israel but as a first step toward Israel's destruction. At the same time, the DFLP opposed the Oslo process and advocated the continuation of armed struggle against Israel as being the surer path toward achieving Palestinian goals.

History
Origins and Activities through the First Intifada

On February 22, 1969, Nayef Hawatmeh's faction of the Popular Front for the Liberation of Palestine (PFLP) split to form a new faction.

Hawatmeh felt that the PFLP over-emphasized Arab nationalism at the expense of Marxist-Leninist doctrine. However, to a great extent, the split was the product of personal differences between the PFLP's leader George Habash and Hawatmeh. Originally the DFLP was named the Democratic Popular Front for the Liberation of Palestine. This name reflected Hawatmeh's criticism of Habash's autocratic tendencies. Worried about violent confrontations with the PFLP, Hawatmeh sought support from Arafat's Fatah – which in turn was seeking to limit the PFLP's growth in order to maintain its dominant position in the PLO. Habash's PFLP threatened to attack Hawatmeh's faction until, after several years, its name was formally changed to the DFLP.

In 1971, Hawatmeh, writing as a "Palestinian leftist," proposed an interim solution to the conflict with Israel. This was the Strategy of Phases, in which the PLO would negotiate with Israel in order to obtain territory on which to declare a Palestinian state as a first step to the ultimate liberation of Palestine. It was officially adopted by the DFLP in 1973 and by the Palestine National Council (PNC) in 1974. This was a break with PLO orthodoxy which held that negotiating with Israel was a tacit recognition of Israel's existence and therefore impossible.

Despite their reputed moderation, the DFLP launched murderous attacks on Israeli civilians. The best known was in May 1974 when a DFLP team took over an Israeli schoolhouse in Ma'alot and massacred 22 school children.

Along with the rest of the PLO, the DFLP was expelled from Lebanon in Israel's 1982 Peace for Galiee campaign. In the early and mid-1980s, the DFLP sought to preserve PLO unity and did not back the 1983 Fatah rebellion against Arafat.

The DFLP had a limited infrastructure in the West Bank and Gaza, but did launch several attacks during the first Intifada (1987-1993). In 1988 DFLP operatives attempted to firebomb Ariel Sharon's car and there were several unsuccessful attempts to infiltrate northern Israel from Lebanon. Hawatmeh called for escalating the Intifada to an armed struggle.

The Soviet Union had been the DFLP's greatest patron, and its collapse caused the DFLP to decline and lose influence.

Splitting over Oslo

As the PLO moved towards negotiating with Israel, the DFLP was torn. Hawatmeh supported the legality of the 18th PNC in 1988 in which the PLO prepared to negotiate with Israel – but he opposed the political direction taken by the PLO, and wanted to focus on the armed struggle. Yasser Abd Rabbo, the DFLP's representative on the PLO Executive Committee, supported negotiating with Israel.

In September 1991, Abd Rabbo won the DFLP elections and Hawatmeh declared the elections invalid. Abd Rabbo renounced Marxist-Leninist ideology and in October 1992 stated that he supported continuing PLO-Israel negotiations. In December 1992, armed supporters of Hawatmeh took over an office of Abd Rabbo supporters in the Yarmouk refugee camp outside of Damascus.

In 1993, Abd Rabbo dropped the DFLP's name and his faction became the core of the Palestinian Democratic Union (FIDA). Abd Rabbo allied with Arafat and has served as the Palestinian Authority's Information Minister.

Under Oslo and the al-Aqsa Intifada

The DFLP joined the other Damascus-based Palestinian terrorist groups in the Alliance of Palestinian Forces (APF). The DFLP suspended its participation in the PLO and operatives launched several attacks in an effort to derail the peace process. As the Oslo process continued, the DFLP began expanding its infrastructure in the West Bank and Gaza. In February 1997, the DFLP renounced its opposition to the Oslo process.

These moves led the DFLP to fall out with its allies in the APF. At a December 1998 rally in Damascus, Hawatmeh fought with the Popular Front for the Liberation of Palestine – General Command's (PFLP-GC) Ahmed Jibril over accepting a political settlement with Israel. When Hawatmeh accidentally shook hands with Israel's President Ezer Weizman at the February 1998 funeral for Jordan's King Hussein, he was accused of "normalization" with Israel by other APF factions.

In March 1999, the DFLP left the APF. The pro-Syrian factions – PFLP-GC, Sa'iqa, and Fatah-Intifada – attacked DFLP offices, killing a DFLP member and injuring several others.

In August 1999, Hawatmeh met with Arafat and they reconciled. Because of its moves in support of a political settlement and its lack of recent terrorist activity, the DFLP was removed from the United States Department of State's list of terrorist organizations in October 1999.

According to polls, less than 5% of West Bank and Gaza residents support the DFLP. Nonetheless, the DFLP has played a key role in the al-Aqsa Intifada. In January 2002, Israeli security arrested a six-man DFLP cell in the northern Jerusalem village of Issawiya. This cell had perpetrated attacks on the Jerusalem-Maale Adumim Road and on Palestinians suspected of cooperating with Israel in Issawiya. The DFLP took part in the April 2002 battle between the Israeli Defense Force and Palestinian terrorist organizations in Jenin.

A DFLP cell in Gaza has also perpetrated several attacks, including one in August 2001 on an IDF checkpoint in which three soldiers were killed. Israel had repeatedly pressed Palestinian Authority security forces to arrest the head of this cell, Talal Khalil Muhammad Zarifa.

In December 2002, the DFLP head in Ramallah, who was also the DFLP representative to the Palestine National Council, Ebrahim Abu Hijeh was arrested by Israel for his role in directing terror attacks, including plotting a suicide bombing.

Leadership

The founder and Secretary-General of the DFLP is Nayef Hawatmeh (a.k.a. Abul Nouf). Hawatmeh was born in 1937 in Salt, Jordan to a tribe of Christian Bedouins. He served in the Jordanian army, earned a degree in philosophy and psychology from Beirut University, and was a member of the Arab National Movement.

Organization

The DFLP is estimated to have 500 members with several hundred in Lebanon. The military wing of the DFLP was known as the Red Star Brigades, but since the al-Aqsa Intifada they have been known as the Palestinian National Resistance Battalions. The DFLP is affiliated with Hashd, the Jordanian People's Democratic Party. Unlike the other PLO factions, the DFLP does not pay members, which limits its appeal to potential recruits.

Financial Support

In the past, the DFLP received support from the Soviet Union and had relationships with Marxist movements around the world, including the Sandinista Liberation Front of Nicaragua and the Cuban government. The collapse of the Soviet Union severely reduced its revenues. Currently, its primary patron is Syria with substantial support coming from Libya as well. The Marxist DFLP has also accumulated investments in various businesses. In the 1980s, the DFLP invested primarily in light industries such as textiles and plastics.

Links to States and Terrorist Organizations

Despite their contentious origins, the DFLP and PFLP have cooperated extensively both within the governing circles of the PLO and also on the ground in Lebanon. Under Syrian auspices, the DFLP has cooperated with Hizbullah and during the al-Aqsa Intifada has worked in tandem with all of the other Palestinian factions.

Areas of Operation

The DFLP headquarters is in Damascus, but DFLP attacks have always focused on Israel. In the past, the DFLP attempted to infiltrate northern Israel from Lebanon but recently recently its attacks have been within the West Bank and Gaza. Besides its presence in the West Bank and Gaza, there are DFLP offices in refugee camps in Lebanon and Syria.

Targets and Tactics

In its attempts to infiltrate Israel from the Lebanese border, DFLP fighters often disguised themselves in IDF uniforms. Because of its limited activity in the 1990s and its moves toward accepting the Oslo process, the DFLP was removed from the United States State Department's list of terrorist groups in 1999. During the al-Aqsa Intifada, the DFLP initially refrained from operations within Israel's pre-1967 borders, focusing its attacks on IDF soldiers and Israeli settlers in the West Bank and Gaza.

Chronology of Major Events and Attacks

1969

February 22 – Nayef Hawatmeh's faction splits off from the PFLP to form a new organization, which becomes the DFLP.

1973

Hawatmeh's proposed interim solution to the conflict with Israel is adopted by the DFLP. This is the Strategy of Phases, in which the PLO negotiates with Israel in order to obtain territory on which to declare a Palestinian state as a first step to the ultimate liberation of all of Palestine.

1974

May 15 – Three DFLP operatives assault a school in the Galilee town of Ma'alot and take Israeli schoolchildren hostage. When Israeli soldiers storm the building the terrorists massacre 26, including 20 children and wound over 50 others. The DFLP calls the killings a response to then-Secretary of State Henry Kissinger's attempts to negotiate an Israeli-Syrian disengagement agreement. The terrorists also demand the release of 26 Arab prisoners. Before attacking the school, they attack a truck carrying Arab workers and a family in their apartment.

November 19 – Four DFLP operatives attack the town of Bet Shean in Israel, killing four.

1975

November 21 – DFLP operatives wielding axes attack Israeli students in the town of Ramat Hamagshimim, killing Michael Nadler, an American-Israeli student from Miami Beach, Florida.

1979

January – DFLP operatives attempt to seize a guesthouse in Ma'alot. Three operatives, armed with Kalashnikovs and hand grenades, are killed by a routine IDF patrol.

1984

February – DFLP operatives claim responsibility for a grenade explosion in Jerusalem that wounds 21 people.

1988

May – DFLP operatives attempt to firebomb Ariel Sharon's car.

1993

The DFLP and various other rejectionist groups form the Alliance of Palestinian Forces (APF) to oppose Israel's Declaration of Principles with the Palestinians. Yasser Abd Rabbo splits from the DFLP and his faction becomes the core of the Palestinian Democratic Union (FIDA).

1994

March 31 – Yosef Zandani, of B'nei Ayish, near Gedera, Israel, is found murdered in his apartment. A leaflet from the DFLP Red Star Brigades is found near the body. The leaflet states that the murder is in revenge for the shooting of one of its members by an Israeli citizen.

1999

October – The DFLP is removed from the United States Department of State's list of terror groups.

2001

August 25 – Two DFLP gunmen kill three soldiers and wound seven in an attack on the Marganit outpost in Gaza. Soldiers shoot and kill the two gunmen.

2002

January – Israeli security arrests a six-man DFLP cell in the northern Jerusalem village of Issawiya. This cell has perpetrated attacks on the

Jerusalem-Maale Adumim Road and on Palestinians suspected of co-operating with Israel in Issawiya.

Resources

Al-Hourriah, the DFLP Arabic language magazine website provides an English profile on the DFLP at www.alhourriah.org/dflp e.asp.

Khalil, A., "George Habash and the Movement of Arab Nationalists." *Journal of Palestine Studies* 1999; Vol. 27, No. 4.

Levitt, M., Waldoks, E., "The Return of Palestinian Nationalist Terrorism." *Peacewatch* May 3, 2002; No. 379 – available at www.washingtoninstitute.org.

Strindberg, A., "The Damascus-Based Alliance of Palestinian Forces." *Journal of Palestine Studies* 2000; Vol. 29, No. 3.

Strindberg, A. "Palestinian Nationalist Left Makes a Comeback". *Jane's Intelligence Review* 2002; Vol. 4, No 3.

# PLO & its Affiliates

Fatah

Fatah is a reverse acronym for the Arabic Harakat al-Tahrir al-Wateriyyeh al-Falestiniyyeh (Palestine Liberation Movement). In Arabic, Fatah means "conquest by Jihad."

Since 1968, when Fatah joined and effectively took over the Palestine Liberation Organization (PLO), its history has been closely intertwined with that of the PLO. Originally, Fatah's armed wing was named al-'Asifa, "The Thunderstorm." Fatah has formed and disbanded numerous front groups to carry out terrorist activities, including Black September in the 1970s, Fatah Hawks during the first Intifada, Fatah *Tanzim* (Tanzim means Organization), and the al-Aqsa Martyrs Brigades.

Ideology and Objectives

Fatah's ideology is focused on the importance of liberating Palestine by armed struggle. At its founding, it was deeply influenced by the Algerian revolution against the French and Frantz Fanon, ideologue of the Algerian revolution. The third leaflet published by Fatah consisted of quotes from Fanon's *The Wretched of the Earth*. Fanon believed that violence had a cathartic, liberating quality for oppressed peoples. These concepts underpinned the founding goals of using attacks on Israel to forge a new Palestinian identity to confront Israel.

Fatah has steered a careful line between ideological trends in order to appeal to the broadest possible Palestinian and Arab population. While it is ostensibly secular, it maintains an Islamic character — as evidenced by its name. In his speeches, Yasser Arafat makes frequent references to Muslim history, but also refers to protecting Christian holy sites. Fatah embraces Marxist rhetoric, referring to Israel as a colonialist entity and the United States as an imperialist power. But at the same time, Fatah does not focus on class struggle – doing so would alienate the Palestinian merchants and businessmen who are important supporters of Fatah. Also, devotion to a Marxist revolution would make cooperation with Arab monarchies impossible.

While focused on the Palestinian predicament, Fatah considers itself part of the international revolution against imperialism and central to the pan-Arab cause. Fatah views its struggle with Israel as the antidote to the despair prevailing in the Arab world and views the United States as Israel's sponsor and, therefore, an enemy to Palestinian aspirations.

In the early 1970s, some in Fatah accepted the Strategy of Phases. This called for the establishment of a Palestinian state on any territory acquired from Israel, either through negotiations or war, as a first step to eliminating all of Israel. Others in Fatah embraced a compromise with Israel. However, the Fatah constitution officially calls for the elimination of Israel and Fatah officials and publications frequently use anti-Semitic rhetoric.

History
Origins and Early Activities

Fatah was founded in the late 1950s by a group of Palestinians from Gaza working in Kuwait. They had been students together in Egypt, mostly at Cairo University, where they had founded the Union of Palestinian Students. Many of them had been active in the Egyptian Muslim Brotherhood. The initial group included Yasser Arafat, Salah Khalaf (a.k.a. Abu Iyad), Faruq Qaddoumi (a.k.a. Abu Lutf), Khalil al-Wazir (a.k.a. Abu Jihad), and Khaled al-Hassan (a.k.a. Abu Said). They were soon joined by three Palestinians working in Qatar, Mahmoud Abbas (a.k.a. Abu Mazen), Yousef al-Najjar, and Kamal Adwan.

Initial Fatah activity was confined to occasionally publishing *Filastinuna* (Our Palestine), which the Fatah founders financed themselves. The first issue appeared in November 1959, and called for Palestinian independence and a campaign to liberate Palestine. Fatah reversed the prevailing thinking in the Arab world, which called for Arab unity in order to confront Israel. Fatah instead called for confronting Israel as the only way to achieve Arab unity.

Fatah was a marginal organization, but it began to attract attention. Publishing in Lebanon, which at the time was the Arab world's media center, Fatah had some success at generating publicity for itself, and began to acquire a following in the Lebanese refugee camps.

In 1962, the new Algerian government became Fatah's first patron. Through Algeria, Fatah came into contact with the Soviet Union and revolutionary movements throughout the world, including the Irish Republican Army (IRA), the Basque separatist group ETA, the Baader-Meinhof Gang, and various revolutionary Latin American groups. Fatah's publications touted armed struggle with Israel, and, in the early 1960s, Fatah began building cells in the West Bank, Gaza, Syria, and Lebanon.

In part to counter Fatah's rising prominence, Egyptian President Gamal Abd al-Nasser founded the Palestine Liberation Organization in January 1964. Fatah turned to Syria, Egypt's rival for support in launching its attacks against Israel. Syria, which had claims of its own on Palestine, backed Fatah hoping to dominate Palestinian affairs. In 1966, when Fatah asserted its independence, Syria imprisoned Arafat for several months.

In January 1965, Fatah launched its first attack against Israel, placing a small explosive in Israel's National Water Carrier. This first attack and most of the dozens of attempted attacks that followed were unsuccessful. Many more were stopped by Jordanian security. Fatah's first casualty was an operative killed by Jordanian soldiers as he returned from an attack on Israel. Some attacks were more successful. In 1966, a Fatah mine killed three Israeli soldiers. Israel responded to these attacks with raids into the West Bank (then under Jordanian control).

The goal of these attacks was to unite the Palestinians, focus world attention on the Palestinian problem, and to trigger a broader Arab-Israeli confrontation. Despite their negligible military impact, Fatah's publicity machine in Lebanon issued communiqués detailing fictional, major military successes with hundreds of Israeli casualties. Fatah soon achieved prominence as the one Arab force that could succeed against Israel.

The popular cry for action against Israel, combined with the heightened border tensions resulting from Fatah's raids, was a factor in causing the Six-Day War. The 1967 war left Israel controlling the Gaza Strip and the West Bank, which had been part of the original Palestinian Mandate, and had large Palestinian populations. Fatah attempted to build a resistance to Israel in the West Bank and Gaza. But these plans collapsed in the face of efficient Israeli security, and the local population's willingness to cooperate with Israeli authorities. Fatah was forced to relocate its base of operations to Jordan.

The Battle of Karameh and Fatah's Rise to Power

From Jordan, Fatah launched a series of raids against Israel. As Arab states recovered from the massive defeat of 1967, the PLO was seen as merely an agent of these failed states, and Fatah, which was launching attacks on Israel, became increasingly prominent.

In early 1968, a Fatah mine blew up an Israeli school bus, killing two teachers and wounding several students. Israel responded on March 21, 1968 by launching a full-scale attack on Fatah headquarters in the town of Karameh in Jordan.

In planning the operation, Israel assumed that the Jordanian Army, still smarting from the 1967 defeat, would not challenge the IDF. Instead, the Jordanian Army mounted an effective defense and the Israeli operation failed. While over 100 Fatah fighters were killed and captured, Fatah was not destroyed and the IDF was forced to withdraw.

Fatah's role in this battle was minor. There were 300 Fatah members involved in the fighting while the Jordanian and Israeli forces each had about 15,000 soldiers. But, having survived a major Israeli assault in the wake of the massive Arab defeat of 1967, the battle of Karameh (which coincidentally means dignity in Arabic) became a symbolic victory.

Fatah and its leader, Yasser Arafat, who was present at the battle, became heroes and thousands of men volunteered to join the organization. Fatah was invited to join the PLO in 1968, and in February 1969, Arafat was named Chairman of the PLO Executive Committee, a position he has held since. Fatah effectively took over the PLO at that point and, since 1969, the PLO and Fatah's history and organization have been very closely linked.

Black September and Lebanon

In September 1970, the Popular Front for the Liberation of Palestine (PFLP), Fatah's main rival within the PLO, hijacked four airliners and forced them to land in Jordan. These mass hijackings brought to a head a growing conflict between the Jordanian government under King Hussein and the PLO. Fatah and the PLO had been operating independently and challenging the authority of the Jordanian government. With the hijackings and the ensuing international condemnation, Jordan expelled the PLO and all of its factions. In two weeks of fighting, several thousand Palestinians were killed.

The PLO and Fatah relocated to Lebanon where there was a large Palestinian refugee population and where Fatah had already built an extensive infrastructure. South Lebanon became known as Fatahland, because Fatah operated free of interference from the Lebanese government.

Fatah also started Black September to conduct international terror. Salah Khalaf, head of al-Rasd, Fatah's Intelligence unit, was also the head of Black September. Black September did not publish official statements and was not officially linked to the PLO or Fatah in order to protect Fatah's international image.

Black September's first targets were Jordanian. On November 28, 1971, Black September operatives assassinated Jordanian Prime Minister Wasfi al-Tal in Cairo. The assassins fled after the Egyptian government released them on a low bail. A month later Black September wounded Jordan's ambassador to London. Black September also plotted to overthrow King Hussein in 1972 and tried to assassinate him at the 1974 Arab summit in Rabat.

The organization was also responsible for the attack on Israeli athletes at the 1972 Olympics in Munich where 11 Israeli athletes were killed, and in March 1973 the group seized the Saudi embassy in Khartoum, Sudan during a party where they killed the United States Ambassador Cleo Noel, the United States chargé d'affaires Curtis Moore, and Belgian diplomat Guy Eid. Throughout the 1970s Fatah launched attacks against Israel from Lebanon and at various targets worldwide.

Israel responded to the Munich massacre by assassinating the operation's leaders. Starting in October 1972, within ten months Israeli agents had killed 12 Black September operatives. In a nighttime raid on April 10, 1973, Israeli agents killed three Black September leaders in Beirut. The campaign culminated with Israel's 1979 assassination of Black September leader Hassan Salameh. At the same time, Black September was assassinating Israeli intelligence agents and informers throughout Europe. In the 1970s, almost 200 Israelis were killed by Fatah terrorists and over 1,000 were injured. Through various means including mail bombs, and grenade and bomb attacks at Israeli diplomatic and commercial offices around the world.

The PLO and Fatah also became an important Eastern Bloc client, receiving massive aid and armaments as well as technical and diplomatic support from the Soviet Union and its allies. Many Fatah terrorists trained in camps in the Soviet Union and Fatah camps in Lebanon became centers for training terrorists from all over the world.

After the 1973 Yom Kippur War, Fatah officially renounced international terrorism – which within PLO ranks was understood to refer to airline hijacking. In 1975, Fatah became embroiled in the Lebanese Civil War, which included an internal three-way struggle for control of the PLO between Syrian and Iraqi factions and Fatah and its allies. In the late 1970s, Fatah attacked Iraqi operatives due to Iraq's support of Abu Nidal, and Syria for its support of the PLO's enemies in Lebanon.

In March 1978, after a PLO raid into Israel in which a bus was hijacked and 36 people were killed, Israel invaded Southern Lebanon up to the Litani River. In April 1978, there was a revolt within Fatah, that was put down quickly but left Arafat in a weakened position.

In 1979, Egypt and Israel signed a peace treaty. The PLO and Fatah viewed this as a betrayal and broke relations with Egypt, effectively leaving Fatah and the PLO without a major Arab ally. At the same time, Arafat and Fatah supported the Iranian revolution. The son of Iranian leader Ayatollah Khomeini had trained in a PLO camp and Fatah helped the new Iranian regime hunt down dissidents in Europe. Hizbullah special operations chief Imad Mughniyah received his initial training with Fatah's Force 17.

Attacks on Israel from Southern Lebanon continued and in June 1982, Israel invaded Lebanon, intending to end the PLO's presence. Under siege in August 1982, PLO forces evacuated Beirut under the auspices of an international peacekeeping force.

In November 1983, frustrated with Arafat's incompetence and backed by Syria, a senior Fatah officer, Abu Musa led a revolt against Fatah. The revolt forced Arafat from his bastion in Tripoli in northern Lebanon, but it failed to displace him as the head of Fatah.

Fatah in Tunis

After the retreat from Lebanon there were effectively three Palestine Liberation Organizations (PLOs). The official PLO, dominated by Fatah and based in Tunisia; the Syrian-controlled Palestinian Alliance led by the Popular Front for the Liberation of Palestine-General Command (PFLP-GC) and Abu Musa's rebel group; and the Democratic Alliance of the Democratic Front for the Liberation of Palestine (DFLP), Popular Front for the Liberation of Palestine (PFLP), and two small Iraqi groups.

Isolated in Tunisia without direct means to attack Israel, the PLO returned to international terror. The primary actor in this terror was Force 17. In 1983, Fatah tried to kill an Israeli representative in Malta and the Israeli ambassador to Greece. In 1985, Fatah launched several unsuccessful attacks, and Force 17 operatives killed three Israelis in Cyprus. Israel responded by bombing the PLO headquarters in Tunis, killing 70. In 1986, Fatah planned attacks in Paris and Stockholm but the terrorist cells were broken up before they could act.

Fatah's ongoing conflict with the Abu Nidal Organization (ANO) and its Syrian backers hampered terrorist operations. Syria was attempting to prevent Fatah and the PLO from reconciling with Jordan's King Hussein and entering into negotiations with Israel. In the late 1980s, Fatah successfully infiltrated the ANO and reduced its effectiveness.

Syria also encouraged the Lebanese Shi'ite Amal organization to attack the Palestinian refugee camps near Beirut. Clashes in May 1985 left over 600 Palestinians dead and over 1,500 missing. Fatah and the PLO were virtually eliminated as independent factors in Lebanese politics.

While in Tunis, Fatah stepped up its efforts at organizing a political wing in the West Bank and Gaza Strip. Previous attempts at organizing military activity in the West Bank and Gaza had failed. In the early and mid-1980s, Fatah established a political infrastructure in the West Bank and Gaza, including newspapers such as *al-Fajr*, the Shahiba youth wing, and the successful subsidization of Palestinian trade unions. This activity allowed Fatah to play a central role when the Intifada broke out in December 1987.

Many of the leaders of the Intifada were Fatah activists and they received instructions from the PLO headquarters in Tunis. These operations were under the command of Khalil al-Wazir, who was Arafat's top aide in Fatah. Israel responded by attempting to eliminate the leadership of the Intifada. In February 1988, three senior Fatah leaders were assassinated in Cyprus. In response, a Fatah team infiltrated Israel from the south and hijacked a bus killing three Israelis. On April 16, 1988, Israeli commandos assassinated al-Wazir in Tunis.

Within the West Bank and Gaza, Fatah built an armed wing, the Fatah Hawks, which carried out attacks on Israelis.

Abu Iyad, the former head of the Black September Organization and a founding member of Fatah, was assassinated in January 1991 by what

PLO sources identified as a bodyguard of the PLO leader Abu Hol, who was also assassinated that night. Reports suggested that the gunman belonged to the ANO.

Fatah in the Palestinian Authority

With the establishment of the Palestinian Authority (PA) in 1994, most of the Fatah leadership relocated to the West Bank and Gaza. The Fatah armed forces, al-Asifa, were subsumed into the PA security forces and Force 17 became Arafat's personal bodyguards. Fatah and Hamas activists began to clash, but Fatah activists were supported by the well-armed PA security services and achieved the upper hand.

The Fatah Hawks, an armed wing of Fatah, were disbanded under the provisions of Oslo in 1995. Shortly thereafter, the Fatah Tanzim were formed to replace them. Many members of the PA Security Services were also activists in the Tanzim which served many purposes within Fatah. They fought Hamas supporters for control of the streets and they were a counterweight to the PA security forces. Most importantly, they were armed and trained to confront Israeli forces. In the September 1996 Tunnel War and later in the May 2000 Nakba Riots, armed Tanzim members, in conjunction with PA security forces, rioted and engaged in firefights with Israeli forces.

The growing power of the Tanzim and its West Bank leader, Marwan Barghouti, led to occasional clashes with PA Security Services. The Preventive Security Force disrupted Tanzim meetings and, in 1998, PA Military Intelligence raided the Tanzim office in Ramallah. A boy was killed in the ensuing demonstration. In Palestinian public opinion, the Tanzim became associated with the "insiders," the natives of the West Bank and Gaza, who were treated unfairly by the PA, which was dominated by "outsiders" – Fatah personnel who had been based in Tunisia.

Al-Aqsa Intifada

With the outbreak of the al-Aqsa Intifada, after Israeli leader Ariel Sharon's September 28, 2000 visit to the Temple Mount, the Fatah Tanzim played a central role in orchestrating demonstrations. A frequent feature of these clashes was Tanzim operatives firing at Israeli soldiers from within the rock-throwing mob. As the conflict escalated, the Tanzim began organizing units under the name al-Aqsa Martyrs Brigades. The Tanzim and the al-Aqsa Martyrs Brigades attempted hundreds of ambushes against Israelis driving on the roads of the West Bank and Gaza, killing dozens of Israeli civilians. These units also committed hundreds of attacks on Israeli checkpoints in the West Bank and Gaza, killing dozens of Israeli soldiers. In Gaza, a major target has been the IDF outposts on the Gaza-Egypt border close to the Rafah refugee camp. Arms, drugs, contraband, and people are smuggled through tunnels under this border and these outposts are the primary obstacle to this traffic.

From the beginning of the al-Aqsa Intifada, Fatah began coordinating closely with the Palestinian Islamic Jihad (PIJ), Hamas, the Popular Front for the Liberation of Palestine (PFLP), the Democratic Front for the Liberation of Palestine (DFLP), and later Hizbullah. "Cocktail cells" which included members of several different organizations were formed. In Gaza, Fatah and Hamas cooperated, forming the Saladin Brigades. Fatah operatives received arms and support from PA security services, particularly Force 17 and the Preventive Security Force. Fatah conducted its first successful suicide bombing in the al-Aqsa Intifada on November 29, 2001 against a bus near Hadera in conjunction with the PIJ. It had also collaborated with the PIJ in orchestrating a November 27, 2001 shooting attack in Afula. On December 3, 2001 the Israeli government designated the Tanzim a terrorist organization.

Israel responded by arresting and assassinating Tanzim leaders. On January 14, 2002, the al-Aqsa Martyrs Brigades leader in Tulkarm, Raed Karmi, was killed in an explosion. Israel officially denied assassinating Karmi, although Israeli officials claimed Karmi was responsible for the shooting deaths of nine Israelis and several attempted suicide bombings. The al-Aqsa Martyrs Brigades responded to Karmi's death with a January 17, 2002, attack in Hadera. A former Palestinian Authority police officer affiliated with the al-Aqsa Martyrs Brigades opened fire on a Bat Mitzvah party, killing six. On January 27, 2002 Wafa Idris became the first female Palestinian suicide bomber, her attack outside a shoe store on Jaffa Street in Jerusalem killed one and wounded 140.

Operation Defensive Shield

In March and April 2002, Israel responded to a wave of Palestinian suicide bombings with Operation Defensive Shield. In this operation, Israel Defense Forces (IDF) entered West Bank refugee camps and cities with large terrorist infrastructures to capture terrorists and their equipment. On March 21, 2002, the United States designated the al-Aqsa Martyrs Brigades a terrorist organization.

The major center for Fatah activity was Ramallah, where Arafat's headquarters (Mukata) is located and the head of Fatah in the West Bank, Marwan Barghouti, was based. During the siege of the Mukata, the IDF captured documents detailing PA financing of Fatah activities. Fatah cells based in Ramallah carried out many attacks including the January 22, 2002 shooting and the January 27, 2002 suicide bombing in Jerusalem, as well as a number of deadly assaults on Israeli soldiers in the West Bank, and the March 5, 2002 shooting and grenade attack on a restaurant in Tel Aviv.

On March 30, 2002, the IDF surrounded the headquarters of the Palestinian Preventive Security Service in Betunia, near Ramallah, when several wanted terrorists fled into the compound. After several days the siege ended when the occupants surrendered. Among the 184 arrested were seven senior Tanzim operatives who were involved in dozens of attacks on Israelis.

Marwan Barghouti, Secretary-General of Fatah in the West Bank and head of the Tanzim and the al-Aqsa Martyrs Brigades, was arrested by the IDF in Ramallah on April 15, 2002. His deputy and cousin, Ahmed Barghouti, was arrested with him. They were the highest-ranking Palestinian leaders arrested by Israel. According to captured documents, Barghouti was responsible for providing funding for terrorist attacks and he has been linked to dozens of terror attacks. On May 19, 2004 Marwan Barghouti was convicted of four counts of murder by an Israeli court.

Nasser Abu Hamid, a Ramallah-based senior al-Aqsa Martyrs Brigades commander and ally of Barghouti's, was also arrested in Operation Defensive Shield.

In Jenin, the scene of some of the fiercest fighting, Fatah fought the IDF alongside other Palestinian terror groups. Jenin's Fatah cells, which reported to Barghouti, had over 60 members, including the head of the Preventive Security apparatus in Jenin. Fatah cells based in Jenin launched the November 27, 2001 shooting in Afula, the March 30, 2002 suicide bombing in Tel Aviv, and scores of attacks on Israelis in the West Bank.

Nablus was the base for several Fatah cells, with several dozen members, of whom at least 30 received salaries from the Palestinian Authority security apparatus. The top Fatah leader was Nasser Aweis, who was arrested in April 2002 and was an officer in the Palestinian National Security Force. The Nablus cells were responsible for at least seven attacks resulting in the deaths of 15 Israeli civilians and injuries to over 200. The Nablus command directed Fatah cells in Tulkarm, Qalqilya, and Ramallah and reported to Marwan Barghouti. In Nablus, the IDF captured five top Fatah leaders and destroyed numerous explosives factories.

Bethlehem was also a major center for Fatah activity. On October 18, 2001, the Tanzim head in Bethlehem, Atef Abiyat, was killed in an explosion. While Abiyat was supposed to be under PA detention, it was believed that he was constructing a bomb. Numerous attacks on Israeli civilians and soldiers in the West Bank emanated from Bethlehem. The March 2, 2002, suicide bombing in Jerusalem that killed 10 and wounded 50 was carried out by the Fatah organization in Bethlehem. On April 2, 2002, when Israeli troops entered Bethlehem, over 100 Palestinian terrorists fled to the Church of the Nativity. A five-week standoff ensued, in which the terrorists held nuns and priests captive. On May 10, 2002, after five weeks, a solution was negotiated. Eighty-five of the Palestinians, who were not wanted by Israel, were questioned by Israeli police and released, 26 were deported to Gaza, and a final 13 (including nine senior Fatah operatives) were deported to Europe. After the standoff ended, the IDF searched the Church of the Nativity at the request of the priests and found nearly forty explosives had been planted there.

Continuing Violence and Competition with Hamas

Fatah continued to launch terrorist attacks during and after Operation Defensive Shield. On June 19, 2002, a Fatah suicide bomber attacked a bus stop in Jerusalem, killing seven and wounding over 50. In November, Fatah operatives infiltrated a kibbutz in northern Israel where five were killed and launched a shooting attack on an Israeli polling station on the day of the Likud party primaries, killing five and wounding 20.

Israel reentered Palestinian Authority-administered territory at will to arrest and assassinate Fatah leaders. By late 2002, hundreds of Fatah operatives had been arrested and several had been killed, including top leaders.

In October 2002, PA Colonel Rajah Abu Lehiya was kidnapped and killed in Gaza. Colonel Lehiya had led the crackdown on the October 2001 Hamas uprising in which three people were killed and his death sparked another round of Fatah-Hamas fighting in which five were killed. A massive show of force by PA security forestalled further fighting, but Hamas' popularity was increasing at Fatah's expense. This rise in Hamas' popularity was due, in great part, to PA corruption. Hamas and Fatah began negotiating to maintain national unity and determine the best strategy for continuing the Intifada. In these meetings, Fatah called on Hamas to join it in renouncing attacks on Israeli civilians, particularly suicide bombings because these attacks were not effectively advancing Palestinian goals. However, al-Aqsa Martyrs Brigades commanders insisted that they remained committed to targeting Israeli civilians.

In December 2002, Israeli officials reported that wanted Palestinians were turning themselves in to Israeli authorities in increasing numbers and providing valuable information to the IDF. Several hundred Fatah members are currently held in Israeli detention.

Leadership

The political leadership of Fatah is the same as the leadership of the Palestine Liberation Organization (PLO) and the Palestinian Authority (PA). The primary leaders of the PLO and PA also have seats on Fatah's governing body, the Fatah Central Council. Eighty percent of the members of the PA cabinet are members of Fatah.

Organization

Fatah's organization is deeply intertwined with the organization of the Palestine Liberation Organization. Fatah runs various social and political programs for Palestinians both in the Palestinian Authority and for Palestinians outside of the PA — particularly in Lebanon. Fatah has also built an infrastructure to manufacture explosives and weapons in Gaza and the West Bank.

In its history, Fatah has organized district armed wings for various purposes. Black September was organized to take revenge on Jordan for the 1970 expulsion and to perpetrate acts of international terror. Fatah denied formal affiliation with Black September to maintain plausible deniability about its terrorist operations. In the late 1980s and early 1990s, the Fatah Hawks were organized out of Fatah membership to clash with Israeli forces. The Tanzim are the heir to the Fatah Hawks.

Tanzim

The Tanzim exists to indoctrinate young Palestinians and prepare them to confront Israel. The group organizes summer camps, weapons training, and courses on civil defense and first aid. The group operates in conjunction with the Fatah youth movement – Shabiba.

The Tanzim is organized by geographical sector and divided into cells. Tanzim branches exist everywhere in the Palestinian Authority –neighborhoods, villages, and schools. The strongest Tanzim branches are at Palestinian universities.

There are tens of thousands of members – including many members of the PA security services. The 2000 elections in Nablus alone had over 6,000 participants. The Tanzim also have extensive stockpiles of weapons including assault rifles, machine guns, and anti-tank missiles, primarily smuggled in from Jordan and Egypt. Many of the local leaders and activists participated in the first Intifada. The local leaders operate with a great deal of autonomy in organizing riots, suicide bombings, and ambushes.

While the local leaders have autonomy, Arafat selects the top leadership. Before his April 2002 arrest, Marwan Barghouti was the Secretary-General of Fatah in the West Bank. The head of the Tanzim in Gaza is Ahmed Chiles.

During the al-Aqsa Intifada, Tanzim cells began to include Hamas and Palestinian Islamic Jihad (PIJ) members. The Tanzim also began to offer $300 to those injured in clashes with Israeli forces, and $2,000 to the families of those killed. This was later supplemented by more substantial contributions from Saudi Arabia and Iraq.

The al-Aqsa Martyrs Brigades grew out of the Tanzim, its operatives are drawn from Tanzim ranks, and the same people lead them. Large numbers of Tanzim and al-Aqsa operatives hold full-time positions in the PA Security forces.

Fatah in Lebanon

In the 1970s and early 1980s, Southern Lebanon was known as Fatahland. Since the expulsion of Fatah/PLO leadership from Lebanon, Lebanese authorities have limited Fatah activities. However, over 350,000 Palestinian refugees remained in 13 camps in Lebanon. The largest of these camps Ayn al-Hilweh, is south of Beirut near Sidon. It has over 70,000 residents living in two square kilometers. These refugees felt abandoned when the PLO signed an accord with Israel and were attracted to Hizbullah, Hamas, and Palestinian Islamic Jihad.

The effective head of Fatah in Lebanon is Munir Maqdah, who is based in Ain al-Hilweh and has approximately 2,000 fighters under his command. Maqdah broke with Arafat, both over the Oslo Accords and because the PLO failed to pay their wages for several months. Maqdah was dismissed by Arafat in October 1993 but refused to leave his position and declared that he remained loyal to the spirit of Fatah.

Arafat began placing more emphasis on the camps in Lebanon. He visited Ayn al-Hilweh in 1999, allocated money to recruit new members and began a training course for an armed group, "Martyrs of the Return." Maqdah and Arafat reconciled in 1999 although the relationship is reportedly strained again.

In the al-Aqsa Intifada, Maqdah has been providing funds and weapons to Fatah cells in the West Bank, including Nasser Aweis' Nablus cell. Maqdah may be serving as a conduit for Hizbullah, Iran, Syria, and possibly al-Qaeda.

Financial Support

Fatah finances are inextricably linked to those of the Palestine Liberation Organization. The Tanzim, Fatah's armed wing, is financially supported by the Palestinian Authority (PA), which provides them with $2.4 million annually. Documents captured by Israel in Operation Defensive Shield and from the Orient House in Jerusalem show Arafat disbursing money to Tanzim leaders, and approving the purchase of weapons and equipment for weapons factories. Many Fatah operatives hold positions in the Palestinian Authority, particularly in the security apparatus. In many cases, these PA employees' primary activity is work on behalf of Fatah. PA security officers pay mandatory dues to Fatah equal to 1.5-2% of their salaries.

Relations with States and Terrorist Organizations
Al-Qaeda

In April 2000, a Jordanian court sentenced Munir Maqdah, Fatah leader in Lebanon and veteran of Force 17, *in absentia* to death for his role in plotting attacks on American and Israeli targets in Jordan. Jordanian prosecutors charged Maqdah with supplying explosives and weapons to the cell, which Jordanian prosecutors claimed was linked to al-Qaeda.

Maqdah claimed that he did not know the Jordanian cell's activities were linked to bin Laden, but that he salutes bin Laden and his achievements.

Maqdah is based in the Ain al-Hilweh refugee camp in Lebanon. This camp is also the main base for Asbat al-Ansar (League of

Supporters), a Sunni extremist group linked to bin Laden. There are over 100 members of Asbat al-Ansar in Ayn al-Hilweh, many of whom fought in Afghanistan, Chechnya, and Bosnia.

Reportedly, al-Qaeda has been building relations with Fatah cells in Gaza, possibly through operatives in Lebanon.

Hamas

Fatah's primary rival for control of the Palestinians is now Hamas. Hamas and Fatah activists clashed in the early days of the Palestinian Authority (PA). In November 1994, PA security forces fired on rioting Hamas worshippers, killing 14. Opinion polls usually place Palestinian support for Fatah at between 35-50%. Support for Hamas rarely rises above 20%. Hamas did not challenge Fatah in the 1996 Palestinian elections.

In the al-Aqsa Intifada, Hamas and Fatah have cooperated closely. Representatives of their respective armed wings have met daily throughout Gaza and the West Bank. In Gaza, the Saladin Brigade, that destroyed an Israeli tank in February 2002, is made up of Hamas and Fatah operatives.

The two organizations remain rivals. Support for Hamas grew on the campuses of Palestinian universities, where Islamist groups affiliated with Hamas began defeating Fatah in student elections. In October 2001, Hamas supporters organized a pro-bin Laden rally in Gaza. Fueled by popular discontent, this rally became an anti-Fatah/PA riot which was harshly put down by PA security; three people were killed. A year later Hamas kidnapped and killed PA Colonel Rajah Abu Lehiya, who commanded the PA forces that put down these protests. In late 2002 in Gaza, Fatah-Hamas tension mounted, occasionally exploding into violence, and according to some polls the popularity of Hamas outstripped that of Fatah. In Cairo, under Egyptian auspices, the two organizations were meeting in order to maintain national unity.

Iran and Hizbullah

The relationship between Fatah and the Iranian revolutionaries goes back to 1970. Iranian revolutionaries, including Ayatollah Khomeini's son, trained at Fatah camps in Lebanon before the Iranian revolution. Shortly after the revolution, Arafat visited Tehran in February 1979 and set up training camps in Iran for the Palestine Liberation Organization. Abu Mazen served as a go-between in Iranian-Soviet relations. When the revolutionaries seized Israel's embassy in Iran, they gave it to the PLO.

In 1982, after Fatah left Lebanon, Iran cultivated the radical Shi'ite movement, Hizbullah. Fatah provided operational and technical support and many Fatah members who had been recruited from the Lebanese Shi'ite community went on to join Hizbullah. Hizbullah's head of special operations, Imad Mughniyah, had been a member of Arafat's bodyguards, Force 17. Mughniyah masterminded the 1983 bombings in Beirut of the American embassy, United States Marine barracks, and the French headquarters. Over 300 people were killed in these bombings. Mughniyah then planned a series of kidnappings of American citizens.

Arafat's support for Iraq in the Iran-Iraq War, which raged throughout the 1980s, damaged their relationship, and in the late 1980s and early 1990s Iranian and Hizbullah support focused on Palestinian Islamist organizations. Recently, as evidenced by the *Karine-A* incident, in which Iran tried to send arms to the Palestinians, a rapprochement has been effected and Iran is providing support to Fatah.

In the al-Aqsa Intifada, Fatah and Hizbullah are cooperating. Since the mid-1990s, Hizbullah had been attempting to build cells in the West Bank and Gaza. Several cells were established in conjunction with Fatah members – particularly officers from Arafat's bodyguard, Force 17. These cells had launched sniper and mortar attacks against Israeli towns within the pre-1967 Israeli borderlines.

On February 14, 2002, a joint Tanzim-Hamas cell known as the al-Nasr Saladin Brigade destroyed an Israeli tank and killed three Israel Defense Forces (IDF) soldiers. The tank was destroyed with 80 kilograms of explosives buried underground and detonated by remote control. This was similar to tactics used by Hizbullah in its war with the IDF in Lebanon, and is another indication of Fatah-Hizbullah collaboration.

Munir Maqdah, head of Fatah in Lebanon, is a central conduit for Iranian funding of Fatah. Fatah cells in Nablus have been the primary beneficiaries of Iranian funding transferred through Maqdah.

Other Palestinian Organizations

After taking control of the Palestine Liberation Organization (PLO) in 1968, Fatah's main rival was the Popular Front for the Liberation of Palestine (PFLP). The PFLP was more devoted to Marxism, Arab nationalism, and secularism than Fatah. Some of the contention reflected the personal rivalry between PFLP leader George Habash and Yasser Arafat. But in spite of this, throughout the 1970s, Fatah and the PFLP cooperated in committing terrorist attacks. The collapse of the Soviet Union removed the PFLP's leading patron and left Fatah unchallenged within the PLO.

The Syrian-backed factions, such as the Popular Front for the Liberation of Palestine-General Command (PFLP-GC), Saiqa, and Fatah-Intifada, sought to supplant Fatah and Arafat as leaders of the PLO. But their close relationships with the Syrian regime prevented them from gaining a popular Palestinian following.

Throughout the al-Aqsa Intifada, Fatah has cooperated closely with other Palestinian terrorist movements.

Soviet Bloc and its Allies

Fatah's first office was opened in Algeria in January of 1963. Fatah's founders had been inspired by the Algerian war against the French. Through the Algerian National Liberation Front (FLN) movement, Fatah came into contact with the Soviet Union and its proxies throughout the world.

Even before it became the dominant force in the PLO, Fatah was receiving Soviet attention. In the mid-1960s, when Fatah was just beginning to launch terror attacks, Fatah members were receiving Soviet-sponsored training. The Arab defeat in the 1967 Six-Day War increased the utility of Palestinian organizations to the Soviet Union, and aid to Fatah increased, expanding dramatically with Fatah's ascendancy after the Battle of Karameh. In July 1968, Arafat visited Moscow to arrange arms shipments. When Arafat took over the PLO in February 1969, the PLO became a major Soviet client. Fatah members received training in camps throughout the Soviet Bloc as well as Cuba and the Soviet Union's allies in the Middle East.

Targets and Tactics

Fatah has conducted an enormous variety of terror attacks in its four decades of existence. It has planted hundreds of bombs in Israel and attempted dozens of infiltrations by land and sea. Fatah has also shelled Israel with artillery from Southern Lebanon. In the 1970s, it conducted international hijackings and assassinations, and was responsible for numerous attacks on Israeli diplomats around the world.

In the al-Asqa Intifada, Tanzim and other Fatah forces have orchestrated tactical attacks on Israel Defense Forces posts and patrols.

These attacks included planting gunmen in the midst of rock-throwing children and teenagers. The Tanzim have conducted the majority of attacks on vehicles driving on the roads of the West Bank and Gaza—these attacks were primarily aimed at the settlers, Israeli citizens living in the West Bank and Gaza.

The Tanzim have conducted suicide bombing operations, along with shooting and grenade attacks, and were the first Palestinian terrorist group to dispatch women as suicide bombers. Tanzim cells have also launched mortar attacks both at Israeli settlements and into towns within Israel's pre-1967 borders.

Fatah has long targeted Palestinians who advocated peaceful relations with Israel. During the Israeli administration of the West Bank and Gaza this included community and religious leaders. Since the establishment of the PA, collaboration with Israel included business and professional relationships with Israelis. Fatah cells in Tulkarm, for example, executed more than 20 suspected collaborators, including several women.

While ostensibly a secular organization, Fatah has frequently targeted Arab Christians. In Lebanon, the Fatah fought with Christian militia forces. In South Lebanon, which was under Fatah control in the late 1970s, large numbers of Christians were murdered, tortured and raped. (The Muslim population was not immune to these depredations). According to documents captured in Operation Defensive Shield, the Fatah targeted Palestinian Christians for extortion and systematically attempted to reduce the Christian population of Bethlehem. PA police have harassed converts to Christianity. In April 2002, Fatah terrorists took refuge in the Church of the Nativity, causing a five-week standoff with the IDF. This was a continuation of a Fatah practice from the beginning of the al-Aqsa Intifada of using Christian churches and institutions as cover in attacks on Israel. The predominantly Christian town of Beit Jala, just outside of Jerusalem was the primary base for Fatah operatives firing on Jerusalem.

In March 2002, Brig. Gen. Sultan Abul Aynayn, head of Fatah in Lebanon stated that the United States might become the target for suicide bombings because of its support for Israel.

Areas of Operation

In the past Fatah operated across the Middle East and Europe, with an extensive network in Paris. At present, its operations are focused on the West Bank and Gaza. There are substantial Fatah assets in Lebanon and elements of Fatah's leadership remain in Tunisia. Fatah has also been gathering support among Israeli Arabs, two of whom were arrested for aiding the November 10, 2002 attack on Kibbutz Metzer.

Chronology of Major Events and Attacks

1959

January – Fatah is established by Yasser Arafat and his associates, one of whom, Abu Jihad, begins publishing the Fatah magazine *Filastinuna*.

1963

January – Fatah opens its first office. Located in Algeria, it is headed by Abu Jihad.

1965

January 1 – Fatah carries out its first attack on Israel, planting a small bomb in the National Water Carrier.

May 25 – Fatah operatives, originating from terrorist camps in the Jordanian-controlled West Bank, kill three Israelis in an attack on Ramat Hakovesh.

1967

June – In the Six-Day War, Israel defeats Syria, Egypt, and Jordan and occupies the West Bank and Gaza Strip – placing their populations under Israeli administration.

1968

March 18 – An Israeli schoolbus is blown up by a mine planted by Fatah. Two teachers are killed and 28 other people are injured, including many children.

March 21 – Battle of Karameh. The Jordanian army repels an Israeli attack on Fatah headquarters in the Jordanian town of Karameh. Fatah takes heavy casualties, but in surviving the Israeli attack its status in the Arab world increases dramatically.

October 1 – Fatah spokesman, Salah Khalaf, declares that Fatah's aim is "a democratic, progressive, non-sectarian state in which Jews, Muslims and Christians would live together in peace and enjoy the same rights."

1969

February 1-4 – Fatah gains control over the Palestine Liberation Organization at the fifth Palestine National Counil (PNC) in Cairo, with Arafat declared the chairman of the Executive Committee. The PNC statement sets a goal of a democratic society for Muslims, Christians and Jews.

February 24 – Israel launches airstrikes against two Fatah camps near Damascus.

December 21-23 – The Arab summit in Rabat accepts the new Fatah-led Palestine Liberation Organization.

1970

September – PFLP operatives hijack several airliners and force them to land outside of Amman, Jordan. All of the planes are blown up after their passengers are evacuated. The international attention given the hijackings and the growing PLO threat to the stability of the Jordanian regime triggers the events of Black September. Jordanian security forces attack the PLO and expel it from Jordan. The PLO relocates to Lebanon. Fatah forms the Black September unit to conduct international terror to avenge these events.

1971

November 28 – Black September operatives assassinate Jordanian Prime Minister Wasfi al-Tal in Cairo, in revenge for Jordan's crackdown on Fatah.

1972

September 5 – Eight Black September operatives take Israeli athletes hostage at the Munich Olympics; 11 athletes, a policeman and five guerrillas are killed during a police raid at the military air base.

October – Israeli agents assassinate a Palestinian intellectual in Rome for his role in the Olympic terror attack.

1973

January 26 – An Israeli intelligence agent is killed in Madrid.

March 2 – A Black September squad attacks the Saudi embassy in Khartoum, Sudan, where the chargé d'affaires at the American embassy, Curtis Moore, is the guest of honor. Moore, Cleo Noel, the American ambassador to Sudan, and Guy Eid, the Belgian chargé d'affaires are killed, reportedly on the orders of Yasser Arafat.

March 8 – A Black September operative wounds an Israeli intelligence officer in Brussels.

April 10 – An Israeli raid on Fatah HQ in Rue Verdun in Beirut kills three PLO leaders: Kamal Nasir (the independent PLO official spokesperson), al-Najjar and Udwan (both Fatah). The three are linked to the attack at the Olympics.

August 4 – Two Black September operatives attack the Athens airport, where they kill five passengers (four American) and wound 55.

September – Two Black September operatives take three Russian Jews emigrating from the Soviet Union hostage in Austria. To secure their release the Austrian government agrees to close the transit point at Shonau Castle in Austria for Jews fleeing from Russia to Israel.

1974

June 25 – Fatah operatives land by boat near Nahariya, Israel, and attempt to take civilians hostage. Three Israelis and all the operatives are killed in a firefight.

December 1 – Fatah operatives from Lebanon attack the Israeli village of Rechanya, inhabited by Circassian Muslims. One Israeli is killed and one is wounded.

1975

March – Eight Lebanon-based Fatah operatives infiltrate Israel by rubber boat and seize the Savoy Hotel in Tel Aviv where they take hostages.

Israeli security storms the hotel. Seven of the terrorists and three Israeli soldiers are killed. Eight hostages are killed and three are wounded.

November 14 – Six civilians are killed and 38 are injured by a bomb planted by Fatah in downtown Jerusalem.

1976

June 16 – Francis E. Meloy, American ambassador to Lebanon, Robert O. Waring, United States economic counselor in Lebanon and their Lebanese driver are kidnapped and later killed by Fatah operatives.

1978

March 11 – A nine-person Fatah seaborne raiding party lands in Israel and hijacks a bus, killing 36 Israelis and wounding 82. Israeli security forces kill the operatives. The Israelis retaliate by invading southern Lebanon, under codename Operation Litani.

April – An internal revolt in Fatah is accompanied by a 3-way battle between Fatah, Syrian-backed PLO factions, and Iraqi-backed PLO factions.

June 2 – Six civilians are killed when Fatah bombs a bus in Jerusalem.

1982

June – Israeli forces launch a full-scale invasion of Lebanon, besieging Fatah and other Palestinian terrorist groups in Beirut after Palestinian terrorists attack Israeli diplomats in Europe.

August 21 – Palestine Liberation Organization forces, including Fatah, begin evacuating Beirut under international supervision.

September 16-18 – Lebanese Christian militiamen allied with Israel enter the Sabra and Shatila refugee camps near Beirut and massacre 700-800 people, primarily Palestinians.

1983

July 1 – An American-Israeli is stabbed to death in the Hebron marketplace by Fatah operatives.

November – Abu Musa, a senior Fatah officer, leads a Syrian-backed revolt against Arafat. Arafat is forced to abandon his base in Tripoli, Lebanon and move to Tunisia.

1984

April 13 – Four Fatah operatives hijack a bus traveling to Ashkelon from Tel Aviv. Israeli commandos storm the bus, killing two terrorists and one hostage. The other two operatives are killed while in Israeli custody.

1985

June 27 – A husband and wife are shot and killed near Beit Shemesh by Fatah operatives.

October 1 – Israel bombs the Palestine Liberation Organization headquarters in Tunisia, killing 70, in retaliation for the September 25 attack by Force 17, that kills three Israelis in Cyprus.

1987

December 9 – The Intifada begins when four Palestinians are killed and seven are wounded when an Israeli truck collides with two vans carrying Palestinian workers. Mass riots soon break out throughout the West Bank and Gaza Strip. Fatah takes a leading role in organizing the demonstrations.

1988

March 7 – Fatah operatives infiltrate Israel from the Sinai and hijack a bus transporting workers to Dimona, a nuclear facility. Israeli commandos kill the three terrorists and free the hostages.

April 16 – In Tunis, Israeli commandos assassinate Khalil al-Wazir (a.k.a. Abu Jihad), a founding member of Fatah and head of Fatah activities in the West Bank and Gaza.

1993

October 29 – A resident of Beit El is kidnapped from a poultry farm near Ramallah and is later killed. Three Fatah members are convicted for this murder on July 27, 1994.

2000

November 20 – A powerful blast targets a school bus carrying Jewish children in the Gaza Strip. Two people, a man and a woman, are killed and 12 are injured, among them five children. A group affiliated with Fatah, the Forces of Omar al-Mukhtar, claims responsibility although Hamas may also have used the name as a cover.

December 8 – Gunmen fire on a van carrying teachers in the West Bank. A teacher and the driver of the van are killed. Also that day, in another part of the West Bank, an Israeli soldier is killed when gunmen fire on an Israeli bus.

December 28 – A bomb on an urban bus injures 14 people in Tel Aviv. The explosion occurs at around noon on a crowded No. 51 bus, in the vicinity of the Israel Diamond Center. The bomber is later found to have links with Palestinian Authority intelligence and to have been recruited by Yasser Arafat's Fatah organization.

2001

January 17 – An Israeli teenager is murdered near Ramallah by Fatah operatives after he is lured there by a woman he meets on the Internet.

March 26 – A Tanzim sniper shoots and kills a 10-month old girl in Hebron. Her father is wounded in the attack.

May 29 – Two civilians are killed in a Fatah drive-by shooting south of Jerusalem.

June 5 – In the West Bank, an infant is critically injured and later dies when he is hit by a rock thrown at his family's car by Fatah activists.

July 30 – In the West Bank refugee camp of Fara, six Fatah operatives are killed and two are injured in an explosion. It is believed that they were constructing an explosive. Three are also members of the Palestinian Authority Military Intelligence organization, which is headed by Yasser Arafat's cousin, Moussa.

August 5 – Tehiya Bloomberg, 40, of Karnei Shomron, mother of five and five months pregnant, is killed when Fatah-affiliated gunmen open fire on the family vehicle between Alfei Menashe and Karnei Shomron. Three people are seriously wounded, including her husband, Shimon, and daughter, Tzippi, 14. Two other children in the car escape unharmed. The family is driving in a convoy with two other vehicles; the occupants of the other cars are unhurt.

November 27 – Two gunmen, one from the Palestinian Islamic Jihad and one from the al-Aqsa Martyrs Brigades, open fire on a crowded market in Afula. Two are killed and 30 are injured before Israeli police and an Israeli Defense Forces reservist kill the attackers.

November 29 – Three civilians are killed and nine are wounded in a Fatah suicide bombing of a bus near Hadera. The Palestinian Islamic Jihad also claims responsibility for the attack.

December 3 – The Israeli government designates the Tanzim as a terrorist organization.

2002

January 17 – A Palestinian gunman bursts into a bat mitzvah celebration in a banquet hall in Hadera, opening fire on the 180 guests with an M-16 assault rifle, killing six people and injuring 35. The Fatah al-Aqsa Martyrs Brigades claim responsibility for the attack.

January 22 – A Palestinian terrorist opens fire with an M-16 assault rifle near a bus stop in downtown Jerusalem, killing two women and injuring about 40 others. The Fatah al-Aqsa Martyrs Brigades claims responsibility for the attack.

January 27 – One man is killed and over 150 are wounded in a suicide bombing on Jaffa Road, in the center of Jerusalem. The female terrorist, identified as a Fatah member, is armed with more than 20 pounds of explosives.

February 18 – A policeman for the Bedouin village of Beit Zarzir in the Galilee is killed by a suicide bomber whom he has stopped for questioning. The terrorist succeeds in detonating the bomb in his car. The Fatah al-Aqsa Martyrs Brigades claims responsibility for the attack.

February 19 – Six soldiers are killed and one is wounded in an attack near a roadblock west of Ramallah. Several terrorists open fire at soldiers at the roadblock, including three off-duty soldiers inside a structure at the roadblock, killing them at point-blank range. The Fatah al-Aqsa Martyrs Brigades claims responsibility for the attack.

February 22 – A man is killed by terrorists in a drive-by shooting on the Atarot-Givat Ze'ev Road north of Jerusalem as he returns home from work. Fatah claims responsibility for the attack.

March 2 – Ten people are killed and over 50 are injured in a suicide bombing near a yeshiva in the ultra-orthodox Beit Yisrael neighborhood in the center of Jerusalem where people have gathered for a bar mitzvah celebration. The terrorist detonates the bomb next to a group of women waiting with their baby carriages for their husbands to leave the nearby synagogue. The Fatah al-Aqsa Martyrs Brigades claims responsibility for the attack.

March 3 – Ten Israelis, including two IDF officers and five soldiers, are killed and five are injured when terrorists open fire at an IDF roadblock north of Ofra in Samaria. The Fatah al-Aqsa Martyrs Brigades claims responsibility for the attack.

March 5 – Three police officers are killed and over 30 people are injured in Tel Aviv when a Palestinian opens fire on two adjacent restaurants. The Fatah al-Aqsa Martyrs Brigades claims responsibility for the attack.

March 5 – A woman is killed and her husband is injured in a shooting attack on the Bethlehem bypass "tunnel road," south of Jerusalem. The Fatah al-Aqsa Martyrs Brigades claims responsibility for the attack.

March 9 – An infant girl and a 27-year-old man are killed and about 50 people are injured, several seriously, when two Palestinians open fire and throw grenades at cars and pedestrians in the coastal city of Netanya, close to the city's boardwalk and hotels. The terrorists are killed by Israeli border police. The Fatah al-Aqsa Martyrs Brigades claims responsibility for the attack.

March 21 – Three people are killed and 86 are injured in a suicide bombing on King George Street in the center of Jerusalem. The terrorist detonates the bomb, packed with metal spikes and nails, in the center of a crowd of shoppers. Shortly after the attack, the United States government designates the al-Aqsa Martyrs Brigades as a terrorist organization.

March 29 – Two people are killed and 28 are injured, two seriously, when a 16-year-old female suicide bomber blows herself up in the Kiryat Yovel supermarket in Jerusalem. The Fatah al-Aqsa Martyrs Brigades claims responsibility for the attack.

March 30 – One person is killed and about 30 people are injured in a Fatah suicide bombing in a café on the corner of Allenby and Bialik streets in Tel Aviv.

April 1 – A police officer is killed in Jerusalem when a Fatah-affiliated suicide bomber heading toward the city center blows himself up in his car after being stopped at a roadblock.

April 12 – Six people are killed and 104 are wounded when a woman suicide bomber, affiliated with Fatah, detonates a powerful charge at a bus stop on Jaffa Road at the entrance to Jerusalem's Mahane Yehuda open-air market.

April 14 – Israeli Defense Forces arrest West Bank Fatah chief Marwan Barghouti along with his senior aide, Ahmed Taleb Mustafa Barghouti.

May 22 – A Fatah-affiliated suicide bomber, disguised as an Israeli with his hair dyed blond, kills two people and wounds 40 after detonating a powerful explosive in an outdoor market in Rishon Lezion.

May 27 – A grandmother and her infant granddaughter are killed and 37 people are injured when a suicide bomber detonates himself near an ice cream parlor outside a shopping mall in Petah Tikva. The Fatah al-Aqsa Martyrs Brigades claims responsibility for the attack.

May 28 – An Israeli man is killed in an ambush on the Ramallah by-pass road. The Fatah al-Aqsa Martyrs Brigades claims responsibility for the attack.

May 28 – Three yeshiva high school students are killed and two others are wounded in Itamar when a Palestinian gunman opens fire before he is shot dead by a security guard. The Fatah al-Aqsa Martyrs Brigades claims responsibility for the attack.

June 19 – Seven people are killed and 50 are injured – three of them in critical condition – when a suicide bomber blows himself up at a crowded bus stop and hitchhiking post at the French Hill intersection in northern Jerusalem shortly after 7:00 p.m. as people are returning home from work. The Fatah al-Aqsa Martyrs Brigades claims responsibility for the attack.

June 20 – Five Israelis, including a mother, three children and a neighbor who comes to aid the family, are killed, when a Palestinian terrorist enters a home and opens fire in the West Bank settlement of Itamar. Two other children and two soldiers are also injured in the attack. The Popular Front for the Liberation of Palestine and the al-Aqsa Martyrs Brigades claim responsibility for the attack.

August 10 – One Israeli is killed and another is seriously injured when a Palestinian terrorist infiltrates Moshav Mechora in the Jordan Valley and opens fire. The Fatah al-Aqsa Martyrs Brigades claims responsibility for the attack.

August 14 – A senior leader of Arafat's Fatah movement is indicted in an Israeli court. Marwan Barghouti, 43, is the first Palestinian political leader to be tried in Israel since the signing of the now-defunct Oslo Accords. Barghouti is indicted in Tel Aviv District Court on charges of murder, attempted murder and involvement in terrorist organizations. According to the highlights of the charge sheet released by the Justice

Ministry, he has authority over the Fatah Tanzim and the al-Aqsa Martyrs Brigades in the West Bank, and is a major participant in the decision-making process in those organizations.

November 10 – An al-Aqsa Martyrs Brigades terrorist infiltrates Kibbutz Metzer in northern Israel killing five people, including two children in their beds.

November 28 – Five people are killed and more than 20 are wounded when Palestinian gunmen attack a polling station in northern Israel. Voters are gathered to vote in the Likud Party primary election when ambushed by terrorists armed with guns and grenades. The Fatah al-Aqsa Martyrs Brigades take credit for the attacks.

Resources

Fatah website www.fateh.net

Israel Ministry of Foreign Affairs. The Arafat File: The Involvement of Arafat, PA Senior Officials, and Apparatuses in Terrorism Against Israel, Corruption, and Crime. May 2002 – available at www.mfa.gov.il.

Karmon, E., "Fatah and the Popular Front for the Liberation of Palestine: International Terrorism Strategies (1968-1990)." The International Policy Institute for Counter-Terrorism, Nov. 25, 2000 – available at www.ict.org.il.

Luft, G., and Schanzer, J., "Fatah-Hamas Relations: Rapprochement or Ready to Rumble." *Policywatch* December 19, 2002; No. 693 – available at www.washingtoninstitute.org

Schenker, D., "Inside the Fatah Tanzim: A Primer." *Peacewatch* October 6, 2000; No. 206 – available at www.washingtoninstitute.org.

Terrill, W.A., "The Political Mythology of the Battle of Karameh." *The Middle East Journal* 2001; Vol. 55, No. 1.

PLO & its Affiliates

Force 17

The official name of Force 17 is al-Amn al-Ri'asah, which means Presidential Security. However, the unit is generally understood to be the same as the PLO unit Force 17, and is generally referred to as such. There are several explanations for this name. The most popular is that, in the 1970s, Force 17 was based at 17 Faqahani Street in Beirut.

Ideology and Objectives

Force 17 is a Palestinian security unit. Prior to the foundation of the Palestinian Authority (PA), it was an elite terrorist squad within the PLO and did not espouse a particular ideology, distinct from the PLO. Force 17's distinguishing characteristic was its absolute loyalty to Yasser Arafat.

History

Origins

Force 17 was founded as an elite unit after the PLO was expelled from Jordan in 1970. Its first commander was Ali Hassan Salameh (a.k.a. Abu Hassan) who organized terror attacks throughout Europe, including the 1972 Munich massacre. He was assassinated by Israel in 1979 along with several other senior Force 17 leaders in the 1970s. Colonel Mahmoud al-Natour (a.k.a. Abu Tayeb), who had been Arafat's personal bodyguard, took command of Force 17 after Salamh's death.

In the 1982 war in Lebanon, Force 17, which had a combat strength of 3,600, participated in heavy fighting against the IDF. Al-Natour claimed that 500 Force 17 fighters were killed in action in 1982. Force 17 was evacuated with the rest of the PLO to Tunis.

In Tunisia, Force 17 focused on conducting terror operations in Europe. Much of Force 17's terrorist infrastructure was built under the auspices of PLO diplomatic missions. In 1985, Force 17 operatives killed two Israelis in Cyprus. In 1987, Force 17 killed Nagy El-Ali, a well-known political cartoonist who was critical of Arafat. In the late 1980s, a new unit was formed out of Force 17 known as the Special Forces Apparatus or the Colonel Hawari Apparatus, after its founder.

Force 17 played a minimal role during the first Intifada, although in an attempt to bolster their standing within Palestinian politics, they claimed credit for operations that never occurred.

Under the Palestinian Authority

Officially, Force 17 was disbanded with the founding of the Palestinian Authority (PA). However, the Presidential Security unit that was founded shortly after the founding of the PA consisted primarily of Force 17 members. Because of this, Palestinians generally refer to it as Force 17. The unit's uniforms have the number 17 on the arm.

Because of its absolute loyalty to Arafat, Force 17 has taken the lead on many sensitive matters. When Arafat chose to crack down on Hamas and Palestinian Islamic Jihad (PIJ), Force 17 played a key role. Force 17 also jails those Hamas and PIJ militants that the PA actually wants to keep imprisoned. In 1997, when the Palestinian Authority began a campaign against "land dealers" who sold West Bank and Gaza land to Israelis, Force 17 abducted and intimidated land dealers.

Al-Aqsa Intifada

As a professional, well-trained unit, Force 17 has played a key role in the al-Aqsa Intifada. Force 17 has conducted sniper attacks against Israeli civilians driving in the West Bank and mortar attacks against settlements in Gaza and Israeli towns in the Negev. Force 17 officers have received training from Hizbullah and have taken the lead in adopting Hizbullah tactics. Lt. Colonel Massoud Ayad, who was killed by Israeli helicopters after directing mortar attacks against Israeli settlements, set up the first Hizbullah cell in Gaza. The Force 17 commander in Ramallah started a Hizbullah cell in the West Bank.

In March 2001, after a series of suicide bombings, the Israel Defense Forces (IDF) began launching major attacks on Force 17 installations. The installations were usually empty when Israel struck, keeping Force 17 casualties to a minimum. Because of its links to terror and its close relationship to Arafat, Force 17 continued to be targeted by Israel throughout 2001 and during Operation Defensive Shield. On December 3, 2001, the Israeli government declared Force 17 to be a terrorist organization.

Force 17 continued to play a central role in coordinating and facilitating terror attacks on Israel, particularly, by providing weapons and explosives. In the wake of Operation Defensive Shield, Ziyad Younis, a Force 17 member based in Jenin, was arrested for taking part in several shootings and attempted suicide bombings perpetrated in conjunction with other Fatah members. In June 2002, a captured Tanzim operative told Israeli authorities that the explosives used in a failed May 24, 2002 car bombing in Tel Aviv had been provided by Force 17.

Leadership

Force 17 is under the direct command of Yasser Arafat (see his entry under the PLO).

The commander of Force 17 is Colonel Faisal Abu Sharah, who was deputy to long-time Force 17 commander Colonel al-Natour. Abu Sharah also serves as head of the Gaza command. The West Bank commander is Colonel Mahmoud Damra. He commands a Fatah cell which has been responsible for the deaths of at least seven Israelis and is wanted by Israel. The Presidential Guard is headed by Lt. Colonel Ali Ahmed Abdallah.

Organization

Force 17's present strength is about 3,500 men and it is divided into Gaza and West Bank regional commands. There are two attached units, the General Intelligence Unit, which collects information on Palestinian groups which oppose Arafat, and the Presidential Guard, which is responsible for Arafat's personal security and consists of a few dozen of Arafat's most loyal fighters.

The two regional commands are both divided into North and South sectors., and Force 17 is divided into five battalions. One battalion is stationed in each sector, with the fifth battalion under the Gaza command and based in Gaza City.

Financial Support

As a unit of the PA security apparatus, the PA supports Force 17 financially.

Links to States and Terrorist Organizations

Other Palestinian Security Forces

Throughout the Arab world, national security establishments have several different competing military services with different roles. This is done in order to diffuse power and prevent military coups. The PA under Arafat has been no exception. Under the agreements signed with Israel, the Palestinian Authority was to have a limited internal police force, under the command of the General Security Services. Within the General Security Services there are ten competing security apparatuses.

To balance these security services, Arafat created the Special Security Forces, which report directly to him under the command of former Force 17 commander al-Natour. He was replaced in 1995 and has not been active since.

The Special Security Forces' most important function was to covertly monitor the other Palestinian security forces. But, because of its sensitive role, it was conceivable that the Special Security Forces could become too powerful. So Force 17, which is also outside of the General Security framework and reports directly to Arafat, acts as a counterbalance.

Palestinian Terrorist Organizations

Prior to the outbreak of the al-Aqsa Intifada, Force 17's relations with other Palestinian terrorist organizations was ambivalent and occasionally hostile. Their role in crackdowns on Hamas and Palestinian Islamic Jihad (PIJ) made them unpopular with those organizations and their supporters in Palestinian society. Force 17 was also unpopular with the rank and file of Fatah. Force 17's officers were "returnees" who were based in Tunisia during the first Intifada. Many Fatah members resent the "returnees" for their arrogance and corruption.

However, in the al-Aqsa Intifada, Force 17 has lent its training and expertise to other Palestinian terrorist organizations. High-ranking Force 17 officers also hold positions in the Fatah Tanzim. Senior Fatah leader Nasser Abu Hamid, after his arrest by Israeli security forces, told them that Force 17 provided explosives for Tanzim operations.

Other Terrorist Organizations

As an elite unit within the PLO, Force 17 has operational experience with terrorist organizations throughout the world. From its base in

Beirut, Force 17 trained terrorists all over the world. One of their most successful alumni is Imad Mughniyah, head of Hizbullah's foreign operations. Mughniyah also has close relations with elements in the Iranian regime and serves as a key link between the PA and Iran.

Force 17's relations with Hizbullah are extensive. Hizbullah has provided training for Force 17 officers. Force 17 Lt. Colonel Massoud Ayad, who was killed by Israeli helicopter gunships, had been trained by Hizbullah and was setting up the first Hizbullah cell in Gaza. Colonel Mahmoud Damra, commander of Force 17 in the West Bank, is suspected of setting up the first Hizbullah cell in the West Bank.

Areas of Operations

Currently, Force 17 operations are mostly in the West Bank, Gaza, and East Jerusalem. In the past, they operated throughout Europe.

Tactics and Targets

Force 17 is an elite, well-trained, well-equipped unit that can perform a wide-range of missions. In the 1970s and 1980s, the organization carried out bombings and armed attacks. In the 1982 Lebanon War, Force 17 gained experience at conventional battle. In the al-Aqsa Intifada, Force 17 has operated as a guerrilla force, conducting small scale, targeted sniper attacks.

Because of its loyalty and experience, Force 17 has been used against high-priority targets. In 1997 and 1998, Arafat launched a campaign against "land dealers;" Palestinians who facilitated the sale of land to Israelis. Force 17 was linked to the May 1997 abduction and murder of "land dealer" Mahmoud Ali Jumhour. Force 17 is suspected of murdering several other "land dealers" and intimidating over 100 others.

In the al-Aqsa Intifada, Force 17 snipers have ambushed Israeli civilian traffic in the West Bank and attacked Gaza settlements with mortars. Attacks on settlements are a particular priority in the al-Aqsa Intifada. Force 17 also attacked the Israeli National Insurance Institute branch in East Jerusalem. This attack undermined the Israeli position in East Jerusalem and intimidated Arab East Jerusalem residents who used Israeli services.

Equipped with light anti-tank and anti-aircraft missiles, Force 17 could function as a conventional military unit.

Chronology of Major Events and Attacks

1970s

Force 17 is founded as an elite unit of the Palestine Liberation Organization after it is expelled from Jordan in 1970.

1979

January 22 – The first commander of Force 17, Ali Hassan Salameh (a.k.a. Abu Hassan) is killed by a bomb planted in his car by Israeli agents. He had helped organize the attack on the Israeli athletes at the 1972 Munich Olympics.

1982

August – Force 17 is evacuated from Beirut and relocates in Tunis. Force 17 fights Israeli forces in Beirut and north of Sidon.

1985

September 25 – Two Israelis are killed in Cyprus. two Palestinians and a British mercenary are arrested and tell Cypriot police that they are members of Force 17.

1986

March 30 – A bomb, planted by Force 17, explodes on TWA Flight 840 over Greece, killing four American citizens and wounding ten.

1987

July 22 – Palestinian caricaturist Nagy El-Ali, who is known for his political cartoons criticizing the Palestinian leadership and Arafat, is shot and mortally wounded by Force 17 operatives in Chelsea, United Kingdom.

1997

May – Force 17 abducts and murders Mahmoud Ali Jumhour, an

Israeli Arab, for facilitating sales of land in the West Bank to Jews. The killing is part of a Palestinian Authority campaign against "land dealers." Force 17 is linked to other murders and attacks on suspected "land dealers."

2000

October 19 – A Force 17 installation in Bethlehem is destroyed in an explosion. PA officials claim it is due to a gas leak. Evidence suggests that a bomb was being prepared.

October 30 – Two security guards at the National Insurance Institute's East Jerusalem branch are shot by Force 17 operatives, one is killed and the other is injured.

November 13 – Near Ofra in the West Bank, gunmen affiliated with Force 17 fire from a car at an Israeli civilian car, killing one of the passengers. After continuing for a few hundred meters, the gunmen encounter a bus transporting Israel Defense Forces personnel. They spray the military bus with automatic fire killing two and wounding six.

November 24 – An IDF civilian employee is killed by Force 17 snipers as he travels near Otzarin in the West Bank.

December 20 – Gunmen affiliated with Force 17 waiting in ambush on the road between Givat Ze'ev and Beit Horon kill one Israeli.

December 31 – An Israeli family comes under automatic rifle fire near the West Bank town of Ofra while driving toward Jerusalem. Binyamin Kahane, who is driving, is killed outright, resulting in the car's overturning in a ditch beside the road. His wife Talia dies of her injuries and five of the couple's daughters – aged two-months to ten-years -old–are wounded.

2001

January 29 – An Israeli motorist is killed by shots fired by a Force 17 affiliate fired from a passing car near the Rama junction north of Jerusalem.

February 13 – IDF helicopters kill Force 17 Lt. Colonel Massoud Ayad.

Ayad had directed mortar attacks on the Israeli settlement of Netzarim in Gaza a few days earlier and had founded the first Hizbullah cell in Gaza.

March 28 – IDF helicopters strike Force 17 headquarters in Ramallah and other Force 17 facilities in the Gaza Strip. A Force 17 member is killed and six are wounded.

May 18 – Israeli jets bomb Force 17 headquarters in Ramallah and Force 17 facilities in Gaza.

December 3 – The Israeli government declares Force 17 a terrorist organization.

December 4 – The IDF strikes several Force 17 installations, including the Force 17 headquarters in the Gaza Strip and Tulkarm.

Resources

Eshel, D., "The Burgeoning Role of Force 17." *Jane's Intelligence Review* 2002; Vol. 14, No. 3:12-15.

Paz, R., "The Renewal of Old Competition Motivates Violence." *Peacewatch* April 5, 2001; No. 316 – available at www.washingtoninstitute.org.

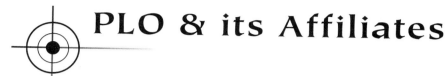

PLO & its Affiliates

Palestine Liberation Front

The Palestine Liberation Front (PLF) is also known as the Front for the Liberation of Palestine. Its Arabic name is Jabhat al-Tahrir al-Filistiniyyah. The PLF is an active member of the PLO.

Ideology and Objectives

The PLF is an Arab nationalist organization devoted to conducting terrorist actions in order to create a Palestinian state. Its leadership describes the PLF as a socialist, democratic, revolutionary movement.

History

The PLF was the original name of Ahmed Jibril's terrorist organization, which later joined and then split from the Popular Front for the Liberation of Palestine (PFLP), calling itself the Popular Front for the Liberation of Palestine-General Command (PFLP-GC). On April 24, 1977, a faction of the PFLP-GC, led by Mohammed Zaidan (a.k.a. Abu Abbas) and by Tal'at Ya'akub, split from the PFLP-GC to found the PLF. At issue was the PFLP-GC's support for Syria's intervention in Lebanon, ostensibly on behalf of the Lebanese Maronite Christians and against the PLO, but also as part of its campaign to take control of the PLO and Lebanon. The PLF was supported by Arafat and by Iraq, which was also attempting to dominate the PLO.

In 1978, the PFLP-GC bombed the PLF's headquarters in Beirut, killing over 200 people. Four of the PLF's top operational commanders were killed and millions of dollars worth of equipment were destroyed.

In April 1979, PLF operatives infiltrated northern Israel from Lebanon by sea and attacked an apartment building in Nahariya, where they killed a policeman, and a father and his daughter. PLF head Abu Abbas stated that this would be the first of many attacks.

The PLF split during the Fatah rebellion which took place from 1983-1984. Abu Abbas headed the largest faction with about 400 supporters, who remained loyal to Arafat and ultimately fled to Tunisia with him. Abd al-Fatah Ghanim took control of the organization's Damascus offices and supported Abu Musa's (a Fatah colonel) Syrian-backed rebellion against Arafat. Tal'at Ya'akub tried to steer a neutral course between Syria and the PLO, but ultimately ended up based in Damascus and allied with Syria.

In 1984, Abu Abbas became a member of the PLO Executive Committee. In November 1985, the PLF hijacked the cruise ship *Achille Lauro* and took its 545 crew members and passengers hostage. Under careful instructions from Abu Abbas, who directed the operation from Egypt, the hijackers separated Americans from the other passengers and murdered a wheelchair-bound American Jew, Leon Klinghoffer, throwing his body overboard. After two days, the hijackers forced the boat to Egypt. Abu Abbas traveled to Egypt to negotiate the hijackers' surrender. Egyptian authorities permitted the hijackers and Abu Abbas to return to Tunisia. United States warplanes forced the hijackers' jetliner to land in Italy where most of the operatives were tried and imprisoned. The United States and Italy fought over jurisdiction and Abu Abbas fled to Yugoslavia.

In response to the *Achille Lauro* attack, Tunisia banished the PLF, which relocated to Iraq. The PLF remained close to Arafat and the Fatah. In May 1990, with Libyan support, the PLF attempted to attack Israeli beachgoers. The IDF intercepted one team of operatives at sea and ambushed the other group when it landed. Arafat did not condemn the attack, and the United States broke off its dialogue with the PLO. In 1991 Abu Abbas left the PLO Executive Committee and the US-PLO dialogue resumed.

In November 1986, Abu Abbas and Tal'at Ya'akub discussed merging their factions and in 1988 Ya'akub died of a heart attack and relations between the organizations grew closer. The Syrian branch was active in the Alliance of Palestinian Forces, working with the PFLP, Democratic Front for the Liberation of Palestine (DFLP), PFLP-GC, Hamas, and PIJ. It made several attempts to infiltrate Israel.

The PLF opposed the peace process, but avoided an outright break with Arafat. In 1996, Abu Abbas entered Israel to attend the Palestine National Council (PNC) summit in Gaza. In 1998, he settled in Gaza and claimed that he supported peace, but in 2000, he returned to Iraq.

In November 2001, Israeli security uncovered a major PLF cell based in Ramallah and Jenin and headed by Abu Abbas' deputy Ali Hagin. Their weapons were smuggled by Palestinian Authority official (and later Interior Minister) Abd al-Razak Yechia, who possessed a VIP pass allowing him to bypass Israeli security. The cell had received financing from and military training in Iraq. They were planning major attacks on Ben-Gurion Airport and on downtown Tel Aviv and Jerusalem. They abducted and murdered a Jerusalemite in July 2001 and attempted several bombings. In September 2002, Israeli security forces arrested three PLF members returning to the West Bank after training in Iraq.

Leadership

Mohammed Zaidan (a.k.a. Abu Abbas) was born in Safed, Israel in 1948. His family fled to Syria that same year. In 1968, he joined the PFLP-GC and he eventually became Ahmed Jibril's representative in Lebanon. He split from the PFLP-GC in 1977 to found the PLF. He was wanted by the U.S. for the murder of Leon Klinghoffer and was sentenced in absentia to five life sentences in Italy. He was captured by U.S. Army Special Forces troops on April 14, 2003 in Baghdad, Iraq. On March 9, 2004, Abu Abbas died of natural causes while being held by American authorities in Baghdad. The U.S. government had yet to decide whether or not to indict him on charges of terrorism or to release him to Italian authorities so that he might begin serving his sentence.

The head of the Damascus-based faction of the PLF is Abu Nidal al-Ashqar.

Organization

The PLF has a couple hundred activists and a presence among the Palestinians based in Lebanon. It has a minor presence in the West Bank and Gaza. The Damascus faction demobilized its 200 fighters in 1993.

Financial Support

The PLF's primary source of support was Iraq. In the past, the PLF received support from Libya as well.

Links to States and Terrorist Organizations

The PLF, under Abu Abbas, is closely aligned with Arafat's Fatah and with Saddam Hussein.

The PLF cooperates with the Arab Liberation Front, a Palestinian faction linked to the Iraqi Ba'athist party. The two Fronts, at Saddam Hussein's behest, have distributed millions of dollars to the families of Palestinian casualties from confrontations with Israel.

Libya helped plan, equip, and transport the 1990 PLF attack on a Tel Aviv beach.

The Syrian government subsidizes the Damascus-based faction.

Areas of Operation

The PLF has operated primarily against Israel, particularly along the Lebanese border. It has shown international reach, as in the *Achille Lauro* attack and in a 1990 plan to attack Israeli tourists in Egypt. The headquarters are in Damascus and there is a substantial presence in Lebanon.

Targets and Tactics

The PLF has focused on attacking Israelis but it also attacks Americans and Jews.

Tactically, the PLF has persistantly sought innovative means to infiltrate Israel – developing a substantial naval and airborne component. PLF terrorists have used high speed watercraft, hang gliders and hot air balloons in their attempts to penetrate Israel's borders.

Chronology of Major Events and Attacks

1977

April – The PLF is founded when Abu Abbas splits from the Popular Front for the Liberation of Palestine – General Command (PFLP-GC).

1978

July – PLF operatives kidnap 51 United Nations peacekeeping troops in Tyre, Lebanon. The Fatah branch of the PLO forced the PLF to release the soldiers several hours later.

August 13 – In an explosion at the PLF headquarters in Beirut almost 200 are killed, the PFLP-GC is suspected.

1979

April – PLF operatives infiltrate northern Israel from Lebanon by sea and attack an apartment building in Nahariya, where they kill a policeman as well as a father and his daughter. PLF head Abu Abbas states that this would be the first of many attacks.

1981

March 9 – Two Lebanon-based PLF terrorists are captured in an attempt to use hang gliders to infiltrate Israel and drop bombs on Haifa.

April 16 – Two PLF terrorists are killed while trying to infiltrate Israel by hot air balloon.

The PLF is first recognized as an independent group when it obtains seats on the Palestine National Council.

1983

The PLF splits during the Fatah rebellion. Abu Abbas heads the largest faction and flees to Tunisia. Abd al-Fatah Ghanim supports Abu

Musa's Syrian-backed rebellion against Arafat and Tal'at Ya'akub tries to steer a neutral course between Syria and the PLO, but ends up in Damascus allied with Syria.

1984

Abu Abbas becomes a member of the PLO Executive Committee.

1985

October 5 – PLF operatives hijack the Italian cruise ship *Achille Lauro*. After holding the passengers hostage for two days and murdering a physically disabled American citizen, Abu Abbas and his squad surrender to Egyptian forces in exchange for a promise of safe passage. They are apprehended at a NATO air base in Sicily after United States aircraft intercept and force down the Egyptian airliner flying the terrorists to a safe haven. Abu Abbas is soon released by the Italian government, but later sentenced *in absentia*. The four PLF operatives responsible for the hijacking are convicted of their crimes and sentenced to prison.

1988

The PLF and PLO Chairman Yasser Arafat feud over the PLO's moderating stance toward Israel and the use of terrorism against Israel.

1990

January 6 – Jenin-based PLF member is convicted in Israel for plotting an attack against Israeli tourists in Egypt.

May 30 – PLF operatives attempt to land on an Israeli beach south of Tel Aviv. The operatives, planning to attack and occupy hotels on the Tel Aviv beachfront, are brought from Libya by a Libyan ship and then use speedboats to reach the beach. One group is intercepted at sea and the second lands where the IDF waits to ambush it. All the operatives are either killed or captured in these incidents.

1991

September 28 – Abu Abbas resigns from the PLO Executive Committee, allowing the United States to negotiate with the PLO.

1992

May 5 – Two PLF operatives attempt to raid the Israeli Red Sea resort town of Eilat. An Israeli security guard is killed before another guard kills one of the operatives and wounds the other. The operatives are believed to have swum from the Jordanian town of Aqaba, located a few kilometers along the coastline opposite Eilat.

1993

The Damascus faction of the PLF demobilizes its 200 fighters.

1996

Abu Abbas enters Israel to attend the PNC summit in Gaza.

1998

Abu Abbas settles in Gaza and claims that he supports peace.

2000

Abu Abbas returns to Iraq.

2001

July – A Ramallah-based PLF cell abducts and murders a Jerusalem teenager.

2003

April 14 – Abu Abbas detained by U.S. forces in Baghdad, Iraq.

2004

May 9 – Abu Abbas has a fatal heart attack while in U.S. custody.

Resources

Strindberg, A., "The Damascus-Based Alliance of Palestinian Forces." *Journal of Palestine Studies* 2000; Vol. 29, No. 3.

Strindberg, A., "Palestinian Nationalist Left Makes a Comeback." *Jane's Intelligence Review* 2002; Vol. 4, No 3.

PLO & its Affiliates

Palestine Liberation Organization and Palestinian National Authority

The Palestine Liberation Organization (PLO) is an umbrella organization, comprised of numerous militant factions as well as other Palestinian associations. But real power is held by Arafat's Fatah organization, which has long controlled the key posts. Fatah is described in its own entry, but its history is intertwined with that of the PLO. Several of the organizations within the PLO are described in greater detail in their respective entries.

The Palestinian Authority (PA) was created by agreements between Israel and the PLO; its leadership is intertwined with the PLO's leadership.

The details of terrorist activities are described in the entries of the individual PLO terrorist organizations.

Ideology and Objectives

As an umbrella organization, the Palestine Liberation Organization (PLO) accommodates a wide variety of ideologies. All member organizations share a commitment to the liberation of Palestine from Israeli control. Much of the PLO's history is defined by ideological disputes over means and ends in the struggle against Israel. The major debates about means have been over the armed struggle and the use of terrorism and of particular terror tactics, such as airline hijackings. In the last decade, the primary debate has been whether or not any recognition of Israel is possible. A related issue has been whether a Palestinian state on part of Gaza and the West Bank is an acceptable end goal, or whether it is just a step towards liberating all of historic Palestine from the Jordan River to the Mediterranean Sea.

While different factions of the PLO advance various Marxist and Arab nationalist ideologies, the dominant ideology has been that of

Yasser Arafat's Fatah movement, which has effectively dominated the PLO since the late 1960s. The Fatah movement's focus has always been on taking action to liberate Palestine. Class struggle, the Arab nationalist movement, and Islamic fundamentalism have always been subordinate to this primary goal.

In signing the Oslo agreement, the Palestinian Authority (PA) committed itself to building a Palestinian state next to Israel within the land that Israel occupied in the 1967 war. However, official statements broadcast in the official PA-controlled media continually refer to Palestinian claims to areas within Israel's pre-1967 war borders.

History
Origins

In late May of 1964, the first Palestinian Conference was held in Jerusalem. In early June, under the sponsorship of Egypt's President Gamal Abdel Nasser, the Palestine Liberation Organization (PLO) was founded. Ahmed Shukairy, a long-time Nasser crony, was elected Chairman of the Executive Committee of the PLO. The conference decided to transform itself into the Palestine National Council (PNC).

The Palestine National Charter, adopted by the PNC defined Palestinians as those Arab citizens who were living in Palestine up to 1947 and every child who was born to a Palestinian Arab father after this date. It considered the British 1947 partition of Palestine and the subsequent establishment of Israel as illegal and opposed the very existence of the state of Israel. The PLO opened offices in the Arab states and established the Palestine Liberation Army with brigades in Syria, Gaza, and Iraq. These brigades were under the control of the nations where they were based.

Rise of Fatah

After the 1967 defeat, the Arab world was demoralized, and Nasser's reputation in particular was deflated. This had a profound impact on the Palestine Liberation Organization.

Founded in 1959 by Yasser Arafat, Fatah began launching commando and terrorist operations against Israel in 1965. These operations had a minimal practical effect. But, in the face of the massive Arab failures in the conflict with Israel, these attacks, magnified by extensive coverage in the Lebanese press (which at the time was the media center of the Arab world) gave Fatah a reputation for redeeming the Arab world's military failures. In particular, Fatah became the leading Palestinian organization in the refugee camps in Lebanon.

In December 1967, Shukairy resigned as Chairman of the PLO and was replaced by Yehya Hammoudeh as acting Chairman. Shortly thereafter, Fatah joined the PLO.

In 1968, Israel attacked Fatah's headquarters at Karameh in Jordan. Regular Jordanian forces joined the battle and repelled the Israeli attack. The Fatah contribution to the battle was minimal. But to the victory-starved Arab world the Battle of Karameh was a triumph and Fatah became the new standard bearer of Arab national pride.

In February 1969, at the fifth Palestine National Council, Fatah leader Yasser Arafat became the Chairman of the Executive Committee of the PLO. In 1971, he became the General Commander of the Palestine Forces and his name became synonymous with the PLO.

After the Battle of Karameh, the PLO acquired important patrons. Arab states began contributing arms and money. To advance its Cold War ambitions in the Middle East, the Soviet Union became a major patron of the PLO – contributing arms, training, money, and diplomatic support. With the Soviet Union's support, the PLO became a central organization to international terror with links throughout the world including the Irish Republican Army (IRA), the Basque separatist group ETA, the Sandinistas of Nicaragua, and the Baader-Meinhof Gang. Innumerable PLO fighters trained in the Warsaw Pact countries. Terrorists from around the world trained in PLO camps in Lebanon, Yemen, and Algeria.

Headquartered in Jordan, the rising prominence and militancy of the PLO was bringing it into conflict with the Jordanian monarchy. Because over half of the people of Jordan were of Palestinian origin, the PLO presented a substantial threat to the Jordanian regime. Also, Jordan's quiet accommodation with Israel and defacto joint administration over the West Bank was at odds with the PLO's uncompromising hostility towards Israel. These tensions boiled over in September 1970.

On September 6, 1970, the Popular Front for the Liberation of Palestine (PFLP), the second major faction of the PLO after Fatah, hijacked three civilian airliners, forcing two of them to land in Jordan. A few days later another airliner was hijacked and forced to Jordan. All of the passengers were held in Amman. The airplanes were blown up on the airfield and the passengers were treated badly. King Hussein of Jordan felt his regime was in danger and attacked the PLO. In two weeks of fighting several thousand Palestinians were killed and the PLO had been expelled from Jordan. At least 100 PLO fighters fled across the Jordan river to surrender to Israeli authorities rather than the Jordanian security forces.

The Palestine Liberation Organization in Lebanon

Relocated to Lebanon, where it already had an extensive network, the Palestine Liberation Organization (PLO) achieved new levels of international legitimacy. PLO factions perpetrated terror throughout the world including the massacre of Israeli athletes at the 1972 Munich Olympics, the 1976 hijacking of an Air France jet to Entebbe, Uganda, innumerable attacks on Israelis around the world, and bloody raids into Israel itself.

In 1974, the PLO adopted the strategy of phases. This permitted the PLO to pursue diplomatic solutions that would permit the establishment of a Palestinian state on any "liberated Palestinian territory" as a first step towards the complete liberation of all of historic Palestine. This willingness to temporarily come to terms with Israel's existence - rather than insist on the absolute primacy of violent struggle – caused some PLO factions to form a Rejection Front opposed to any agreements with Israel.

The strategy of phases received Arab League support at an October 1974 conference where the PLO was recognized as the "sole legitimate representative of the Palestinian people on any liberated Palestinian territory." This recognition brought major financial benefits. Palestinians worked in professional and managerial positions throughout the wealthy Gulf states. Arab League members began collecting a tax on Palestinian salaries that was then distributed to the PLO through the Palestine National Fund.

In February 1974, the PLO was granted full membership in the Organization of Islamic Countries and on November 13, 1974 Yasser Arafat addressed the United Nations General Assembly plenary.

In 1976, the PLO became a full member in the Non-Aligned Movement.

Within Lebanon, the PLO built a terrorist and criminal infrastructure that was beyond the control of the weakened, fractious Lebanese government. PLO forces effectively governed portions of the country, particularly South Lebanon, where they murdered, raped, and tortured Lebanese citizens. The PLO also took control of parts of the Lebanese economy where it engaged in predatory pricing.

Lebanon dissolved into ethnic civil war in 1975, a situation exacerbated by the PLO, which backed the Sunni Muslims against the Maronite Christians. Under Arab League auspices, in June 1976, Syria intervened in Lebanon. Aiding the Maronite Christians, Syria attacked and reduced the power of the PLO and the Sunni Muslims, and established itself as the dominant power in Lebanon. At the 13th Palestine National Council (PNC) in 1977, the PLO and Syria reconciled.

The PLO used southern Lebanon as a base from which to attack Israel and used the people of South Lebanon as human shields against Israeli responses. After a major terror attack in March 1978, Israeli forces occupied Southern Lebanon up to the Litani River, withdrawing two months laterunder United Nations auspices.

In July 1981, Israel and the PLO agreed to a ceasefire. PLO attacks on northern Israel continued and, over the next 11 months, 29 Israelis were killed by PLO attacks from Lebanon. The PLO also continued to launch terror attacks worldwide, killing an Israeli diplomat in Paris (Abu Nidal Organization, a PLO breakaway faction, concurrently grievously wounded Shlomo Argov, Israel's ambassador to London). On June 6, 1982, Israel launched a massive invasion of Southern Lebanon.

Israeli forces quickly defeated PLO and Syrian forces in Lebanon. By mid-June, Israel had surrounded Beirut, where the PLO was headquartered. After two months of siege, the United States brokered a Palestinian withdrawal from Beirut. At the end of August 1982, the PLO began to evacuate from Beirut. Over 14,000 PLO fighters left. The PLO headquarters relocated to Tunisia.

On September 14, 1982, a bomb killed Bashir Gemayal, the Maronite Christian leader and Israeli-backed president of Lebanon. Israeli forces moved into Muslim West Beirut searching for pockets of PLO resistance. Christian Phalange forces entered the Palestinian refugee camps of Sabra and Shatila and, in the course of battle with PLO fightes, killed hundreds of Palestinian men, women, and children.

In May 1983, Arafat reestablished himself in Tripoli in northern Lebanon. Dissatisfaction with his retreat from Beirut led to a mutiny from within his Fatah organization led by Abu Musa and Abu Saleh. They were backed by Syria, which was attempting to take control of the PLO. Syrian forces defeated Arafat's forces and Arafat was again forced to leave Lebanon in late 1983 under French protection with 4,000 fighters.

The Palestine Liberation Organization in Tunisia

Without proximity to Israel, the West Bank, and Gaza, and carefully monitored by the Tunisian government – which was anxious to avoid the fates of Jordan and Lebanon – Palestine Liberation Organization (PLO) activity was severely circumscribed through much of the 1980s.

The PLO engaged in diplomatic efforts to remain the recognized representative of the Palestinian people. This was particularly urgent in the face of growing ties between Israel and Jordan, King Hussein of Jordan's rival claim to Palestinian leadership, and the growing power of Palestinian notables on the West Bank who sought a compromise with Israel.

During this period, the PLO did not refrain from terrorist activity, although their ability to launch attacks was limited. On September 25, 1985, three Israelis were killed by the PLO in Cyprus. In response, on October 1, Israel bombed the PLO headquarters in Tunisia. On October 7, 1985, the Palestine Liberation Front (PLF), a faction of the PLO, hijacked the cruise ship *Achille Lauro* and murdered wheelchair bound Leon Klinghoffer, an elderly American Jew, and dumped his body overboard.

In 1987, the Intifada broke out among Palestinians in the West Bank and Gaza. While generally viewed as a spontaneous uprising, led by newly emergent Islamist factions, PLO factions played a key role in funding, instigating, and coordinating the Intifada. In the five years of the Intifada, over 1,000 Palestinians were killed; Some in clashes with Israeli troops, but many by Palestinian terrorist groups for collaborating with Israel. Collaboration included employment by the Israeli administration or even contact with Jewish Israelis. In 1988, Israeli commandos assassinated Khalil al-Wazir (a.k.a. Abu Jihad), one of Arafat's co-founders of Fatah and the second highest-ranking figure in the PLO after Arafat, in Tunisia. Abu Jihad was playing a central role in coordinating between the PLO and the Islamist groups Hamas and the Palestinian Islamic Jihad (PIJ).

On November 15, 1988, almost a year after the beginning of the Intifada, the 19th session of the Palestine National Council (PNC) in Algiers adopted the Declaration of Independence of Palestine and a political communiqué accepting Security Council Resolution 242 of 1967. Resolution 242 called for Israel to withdraw from territories occupied in the 1967 War. In accepting United Nations Resolution 242, the PLO implied that it recognized Israel's existence. By also renouncing violence, the United States could begin negotiating with the PLO.

During the 1990-91 Gulf War, the PLO broke with most of the Arab world by supporting Iraqi President Saddam Hussein's invasion of Kuwait. On the diplomatic front, the PLO worked to prevent Arab-wide initiatives to isolate and condemn Hussein. In Kuwait, PLO operatives assisted Iraqi forces in controlling Kuwait. When Saddam fired Scud missiles at Israel, Palestinians in the West Bank cheered.

When the war ended in an Iraqi defeat, the PLO was more isolated and weaker than before. Kuwait expelled its Palestinian workers for collaborating with the Iraqi invaders. In part due to its isolation, the PLO redoubled its diplomatic efforts. The PLO's focus dovetailed with Israel's frustration with the ongoing Intifada and with the United States' ambition to foster a political settlement in the Middle East.

The PNC convened its 20th session in Algeria in 1991. The session approved the Palestinian participation in the Madrid Peace Conference based on the principle of land for peace and Security Council resolutions 242 and 338. The Council authorized the Central Council of the PLO to deal with the matter.

In October 1991 at the Madrid Peace Conference, Israeli representatives met with PLO representatives who were present under the auspices of a Palestinian-Jordanian delegation. This set in motion the peace process.

In August 1993, Israeli and PLO representatives secretly negotiating in Oslo, Norway agreed to a Declaration of Principles (DOP). On September 9, 1993, in letters to Israeli Prime Minister Rabin and Norwegian Foreign Minister Holst, PLO Chairman Arafat committed the PLO to cease all violence and terrorism. On September 13, 1993, the Declaration of Principles between the Israelis and Palestinians was signed in Washington, DC.

In Tunisia in October 1993, the PLO Central Council accepted the Declaration of Principles and authorized the PLO Executive Committee to form the Council of the Palestinian National Authority for the transitional period. In response, several PLO factions, led by the Popular Front for the Liberation of Palestine (PFLP) and the Democratic Front for the Liberation of Palestine (DFLP), suspended their participation in the PLO. Led by the head of the PLO Political Bureau, Faruq Qaddoumi, a few PLO figures allied with Arafat remained in Tunisia and refused to travel to the new political entity until all of "Palestine" was liberated.

The Establishment of the Palestinian Authority

In Cairo on May 4, 1994, Israel and the PLO signed the "Agreement on the Gaza Strip and Jericho Area" and on May 13 the Israeli military authorities handed over the administration of the city of Jericho to representatives of the Palestinian Authority (PA). Five days later, Israeli troops pulled out of Gaza City. This established Palestinian self-rule under the auspices of the PA, headed by Yasser Arafat.

On July 1, 1994, PLO Chairman Yasser Arafat entered Gaza. A few days later Arafat traveled to Jericho. Arafat staffed the nascent PA institutions with his longtime supporters from Tunisia and elsewhere in the Arab world. This caused friction with the residents of Gaza and the West Bank. Almost immediately, allegations of corruption and oppression began to surface.

Shortly after it was established in July 1994, the PA effectively shut down *Al Nahar*, a leading independent Jerusalem-based Arabic newspaper. *Al Quds*, the other leading independent Palestinian paper, has since been very careful to hew to the established PA line.

Initially, under Oslo, the PA security forces were limited to 9,000 officers with light weapons. The PA established eight different security services with overlapping mandates, with 40,000 personnel equipped with artillery, rocket launchers, and armored personnel carriers. PA security forces became notorious for their brutality and lack of discipline. These various security forces have violently suppressed any sign of opposition to Arafat's rule. Individual critics of Arafat were arrested and tortured. On November 18, 1994, PA security forces clashed with Hamas and Palestinian Islamic Jihad (PIJ) members, 13 were killed and over 200 were injured.

Almost from the beginning, questions were raised about misallocation of international aid money donated to the nascent PA. Arafat required that donations to Palestinian non-government organizations be funneled through his accounts. An interlocking set of monopolies was set up to control the economy of the West Bank and Gaza. Monopolies were granted to various groups to gain their political support.

Under the Oslo agreements, Arafat was required to fight terrorism by arresting Hamas and PIJ members and abstaining from incitement and hostile propaganda. However, arrests of Hamas and PIJ members were characterized by a revolving door policy in which the arrested were released by or "escaped" from sympathetic guards after a brief incarceration. Anti-Semitic vitriol was published by newspapers linked with Fatah and Arafat and broadcast by television and radio controlled by Arafat. The PA started summer camps in which Palestinian children were given paramilitary training and encouraged to fight for Palestine.

The PA failure to crack down on terrorism and the incitement of anti-Israeli riots has led to frequent Israeli closures of the West Bank and Gaza – preventing Palestinians from traveling to Israel to work and buy or sell goods. This has had severe economic consequences for Palestinians on the West Bank and Gaza.

On January 20, 1996, the first Palestinian general elections were held. Members of the Palestinian Legislative Council were selected, and Arafat won the election to the PA Presidency. On March 7, 1996, the 88 members of the Council took part in the first meeting of the Council held in Gaza City. Ahmad Qurei (a.k.a. Abu Alaa') was elected speaker of the Council.

On April 21, 1996, the PNC met and reportedly changed the Palestinian charter, eliminating the portions calling for the destruction of Israel. A list of the attendees was never publicly realeased, leading to allegations that the meeting did not abide by the PNC's procedures and that consequently the charter had not been changed.

Throughout this period Israel was handing control of cities and towns on the West Bank over to the PA.

Palestinian-Israeli violence continued. On February 25, 1994, Baruch Goldstein fired on Muslim worshippers in the Haram al-Ibrahimi Mosque in Hebron, killing 29. From October 1994 until March 1996, Hamas and the PIJ launched a series of suicide bombings primarily on buses and at bus stops that killed over 120 Israelis. PA security forces detained Hamas and PIJ operatives, but Israel claimed that the operatives were only held temporarily and that the PA was not taking steps against terrorist infrastructure. On April 14, 1995 PA and Hamas representatives met and agreed that Hamas could not launch attacks on Israel from PA-governed territories. No restrictions were placed on Hamas attacks emanating from outside of PA territory. Israel responded by capturing and, in some cases, assassinating terrorist leaders.

On October 4, 1995, an Israeli extremist opposed to the peace process assassinated Israeli Prime Minister Yitzhak Rabin. Shimon Peres succeeded him. In 1996, a rash of suicide bombings struck Israel and Likud candidate Binyamin Netanyahu campaigned against the peace process and won the May 29, 1996 election.

The Peace Process Under Netanyahu

At dawn on September 24, 1996, the Israeli government opened a tunnel under the Temple Mount linking the Via Dolorosa with the Western Wall. The Temple Mount is also the location of the Dome of the Rock and the al-Aqsa Mosque, holy sites for Muslims. The PA propagated rumors that this tunnel was a part of an Israeli plan to destroy the al-Aqsa Mosque. Over the next four days, Palestinian rioters and PA security forces clashed with Israeli forces in Jerusalem, the West Bank, and Gaza. In what became known as the Tunnel War, 85 Palestinians and 16 Israelis were killed, and more than 1,200 Palestinians and 87 Israelis were wounded.

Despite Netanyahu's opposition to the peace process and continuing violence, the Israelis and Palestinians continued negotiating agreements for expanding the areas of Palestinian administration.

On January 15, 1997, under American auspices, the Hebron Protocol was negotiated. The Hebron Protocol required Israel to redeploy forces from 80% of the city of Hebron in the West Bank, established the presence of international observers in Hebron, and outlined three further Israeli deployments from the West Bank to take place from March 1997 to mid-1998.

These redeployments were not implemented because of Israeli concerns that the PA was not fulfilling its agreements regarding the arrest of Hamas and PIJ activists, limiting the size of its security forces, and preventing incitement. On October 1998, another conference, sponsored by President Clinton, was held at the Wye River Plantation in Maryland with Arafat, Netanyahu, and the ailing King Hussein of Jordan. Israel committed to conduct its redeployments and to release Palestinian prisoners held in Israeli jails. The Palestinians committed to carrying out security arrangements, including collecting illegal Palestinian weapons and arresting Palestinian Hamas and PIJ activists. The United States Central Intelligence Agency was to oversee Israeli-Palestinian security cooperation and a joint United States-Israel-PA committee was to monitor incitement to violence on both sides.

In December 1998, the Palestine National Council was assembled in Gaza and, in the presence of President Clinton, again changed the parts of the Palestinian charter that called for Israel's destruction.

Palestinians and outside observers complained that this meeting was invalid because it was not held in accord with established procedures. No list of participating delegates has been published.

The peace process continued to deteriorate. The PA did not collect weapons in the hands of Hamas and the PIJ. The incitement committee could not agree on a workable definition of incitement, and the PA arrest policy remained a revolving door in which prisoners were released shortly after their arrests or escaped with the help of their guards. Israel released criminals rather than "political prisoners" who were incarcerated for violent actions against Israel, leaving the Palestinians dissatisfied.

On May 4, 1999, the five-year interim period established in the Oslo negotiations came to an end. Because key issues had not been resolved, the Palestinian leadership discussed declaring independence unilaterally. Under international pressure, for fear that such a move and the Israeli reaction would lead to a large-scale confrontation in the Middle East, Arafat did not declare a Palestinian state. In the Israeli elections of May 17, 1999, Labor's Ehud Barak, a former IDF Chief of Staff, defeated Netanyahu. While the Israeli elections were primarily focused on internal Israeli issues, Barak campaigned with the stated intention of bringing the peace process to a successful, negotiated resolution in the near future.

Barak, Camp David, and the Breakdown of the Peace Process

At the Sharm El-Sheikh summit on September 4, 1999, Israel and the Palestinian Authority attempted to lay the foundation for a long-term negotiated settlement. Short-term Israeli withdrawals were delayed in lieu of establishing a framework for final status negotiations.

In May 2000, large-scale riots broke out throughout the West Bank and Gaza as Palestinians commemorated al-Nakba (Arabic for catastrophe, which is how the Palestinians refer to Israel's 1948 War of Independence). Over 1,200 Palestinians were wounded and 12 were killed. On May 23-24, Israel withdrew from Southern Lebanon ending an 18-years presence established to protect northern Israel from rocket and artillery attack from Lebanon, first from the PLO and later from Hizbullah. Israelis were frustrated with the ongoing engagement in Lebanon and steady trickle of casualties from the fighting with Hizbullah. Throughout the Arab world, and particularly among the Palestinians, this was viewed as an enormous victory for the few hundred Hizbullah fighters over the "invincible" Israel Defense Forces.

In July 2000, Israeli and Palestinian negotiators led by Prime Minister Barak and Arafat, met at Camp David in Maryland, where President Clinton attempted to broker a final settlement. The negotiations were unsuccessful. In Israel, Barak was criticized for offering the Palestinians too much. Refusing to accept less than a complete Israeli withdrawal to the 1967 borders (including all of East Jerusalem and the Old City) and the complete right of return for Palestinian refugees, Arafat was lauded by Palestinians for resisting American and Israeli pressure. Later that month in an interview with Israeli TV, President Clinton praised Barak for his willingness to compromise.

Disappointed that the most generous Israeli offer did not approach their demands, and inspired by the example of Lebanon, Palestinians began preparing for a violent confrontation with Israel. While the Palestinian leadership continued to discuss the next stage of negotiations, the PA-controlled media instructed Palestinians to prepare for a renewed Intifada.

Al-Aqsa Intifada

On September 28, 2000, Ariel Sharon, the leader of the Likud party visited the Temple Mount. The next day, the eve of the Jewish New Year, Palestinian riots erupted at the Temple Mount and spread throughout the West Bank and Gaza. The Palestinians hold Sharon responsible for the 1982 Phalange Christian killings of Palestinians in the Sabra and Shatila refugee camps in Beirut. Sharon's visit to the Temple Mount was widely viewed as the provocation that set off the riots, although in the months after the outbreak of violence, some Palestinian leaders, including the Fatah Secretary-General of the West Bank Marwan Barghouti, stated that Sharon's visit provided a convenient pretext to launch the Intifada. Because it was sparked by events at the Temple Mount (the location of the al-Aqsa Mosque) and rumors of Israeli plots against it, the Intifada became known as the al-Aqsa Intifada.

The Palestinians used several tactics in the al-Aqsa Intifada. The PA and its security forces were officially neutral. Palestinian leaders insisted that the riots were popular and rooted in the anger of the Palestinian people. Many members of the PA security forces were also members of various Palestinian terrorist organizations, including Fatah Tanzim, Palestinian Islamic Jihad (PIJ), and Hamas. PA security forces also provided support for violent activities, particularly Force 17. All of the Palestinian terrorist organizations cooperated. Central to these activities was Fatah, which is headed by Yasser Arafat. At the same time, the failure of the PA security forces to openly confront Israel led to popular Palestinian dissatisfaction with them.

The initial rioting involved young people, teenagers and children attacking Israeli positions with stones. In the midst of these crowds, gunmen fired at Israeli soldiers, using the children as human shields. The Tanzim coordinated these protests and PA buses were used to bring children to the demonstrations. While these tactics resulted in the death of a number of Palestinian children, they did not gain the Palestinians international sympathy or result in international intervention on their behalf.

In October 2000, Palestinian terrorist groups began attacking Israelis driving on the roads of the West Bank and Gaza. These attacks were coordinated between the terrorist groups and PA Security, particularly Arafat's personal security unit, Force 17. The Israel Defense Forces (IDF) responded by cutting down trees and destroying buildings near these roads in order to ensure freedom of movement for Israelis in the West Bank. The IDF also expanded its system of checkpoints and other controls on Palestinian movement.

By the end of October, over 120 Palestinians had been killed and nearly 6,000 wounded.

The PA released over 80 Hamas and PIJ operatives, who began plotting suicide attacks against Israeli civilians. As the violence escalated, Israel began assassinating the operational leaders of Hamas, the PIJ, and Fatah Tanzim. Israel also began launching airstrikes against PA security installations. In these attacks, the IDF usually warned the PA, allowing them time to evacuate the targeted facility.

In November 2000, Israel restricted the flow of nonessential goods into the West Bank and Gaza, and blocked Palestinians from entering Israel to work.

In December 2000, the Barak government fell and elections were called. In a last-ditch effort to end the violence, Israeli and Palestinian negotiators met at Taba, Egypt in January 2001. While the head of the Israeli negotiating team claimed that the two sides had never been closer to an agreement, the head of the Palestinian delegation claimed that the gaps between Israel and the PLO had never been clearer.

On February 6, 2001, Ariel Sharon was elected Prime Minister of

Israel with 65% of the vote. He campaigned on a promise of bringing security to Israelis.

At the end of January 2001, the Palestinians introduced a new tactic, firing mortars into an Israeli settlement in Gaza. A few weeks later they fired mortars into Israel proper. The IDF responded with major incursions into PA territory in order to clear areas used to stage mortar attacks.

On May 18, 2001, a suicide bombing in a Netanya mall killed five Israelis and wounded over 100. On June 1, 2001, a suicide bomber struck a discotheque in Tel Aviv, killing 21 — mostly teenagers — and wounding 120. Arafat publicly condemned this attack under international pressure, but sent a note of congratulations to the attacker's family. International attempts to negotiate a cease-fire were attempted and failed as violence continued. A public condemnation by Arafat and a failed international attempt to negotiate a cease-fire became the pattern, as the frequency of suicide bombings increased. In addition to bombings, there were mass shootings, for example, on January 17, 2002, a gunman affiliated with the Fatah Tanzim entered a banquet hall in Hadera and shot and killed six people at a bat mitzvah reception. The primary perpetrators of these suicide attacks have been Hamas, PIJ, and cells aligned with the Fatah movement.

In response to the escalation Israeli response expanded to larger scale and longer-term incursions into PA-administered territory. On August 10, 2001, after the August 9 suicide bombing of a Jerusalem restaurant in which 15 were killed, the Israeli government closed the Orient House which was the de facto PA office in East Jerusalem and the PA governor's compound in Abu Dis, Jerusalem. Under the Oslo agreements, the PA was not permitted to open offices in Jerusalem. More than 100,000 documents were seized by Israel from Orient House. These documents showed Arafat authorizing payment to Fatah terrorists and terrorists being added to the employment rolls of PA security forces for carrying out successful operations.

On October 17, 2001, Popular Front for the Liberation of Palestine (PFLP) operatives killed Israeli Tourism Minister Rehavam Ze'evi. The murder was to avenge the IDF killing of PFLP leader Abu Ali Mustafa in August. This was the first time a terrorist organization had killed a such high-ranking Israeli official.

In December 2001, after a series of terror attacks in which 37 Israelis died, Arafat gave a speech on December 16, 2001 calling for an end to

Palestinian terror attacks. However, within a few days he again praised suicide bombers. The PA also did not crack down on terrorist organizations. United States special envoy retired Marine Corps General Anthony Zinni presented Arafat with a list of 36 wanted terrorists. After the December 16 speech five of the 36, along with 180 lower level operatives were detained – primarily under a minimally supervised house arrest.

On January 3, 2002, the Israeli Navy captured the *Karine-A*, which was smuggling heavy weapons to Gaza. The weapons came from Iran, and Hizbullah coordinated the shipment. As part of the payment, Iran was allowed to open a hospital in Gaza. This was the third ship smuggling weapons that the IDF had captured. All of the ships had received assistance from the PA Coast Guard. The heavy weapons on these ships included sophisticated anti-aircraft systems, anti-tank weapons, and artillery – including 122 mm Katyusha rockets, which if launched from the West Bank could hit all of Israel's population centers. These items were forbidden under the Oslo Accord. Arafat denied any knowledge of the arms shipment and fired his top financial officer, Fuad Shubaki for his role in arranging the smuggling of arms.

Operation Defensive Shield

The next few months brought a string of suicide bombings in which dozens of Israelis were killed. On March 27, 2002, 28 people were killed and 140 injured in a suicide bombing in the Park Hotel in Netanya in the midst of a Passover seder with 250 guests. Hamas claimed responsibility for the attack. Israel had previously submitted the bomber's name to PA security forces and requested his arrest.

Israel responded by launching Operation Defensive Shield. Over the next three weeks, the IDF entered PA territory in the West Bank and arrested dozens of terrorists with all of the active Palestinian factions. The IDF entered major Palestinian cities and refugee camps and engaged in fierce house-to-house fighting. The most difficult fighting was in the town of Jenin where there were active, well-armed cells from all of the Palestinian factions. In Jenin, houses were booby-trapped and Palestinian terrorists used human shields in their firefights with the IDF. On April 9, in an ambush, 13 IDF soldiers were killed and seven were injured. Overall in the fighting in Jenin, 23 IDF soldiers were killed and over 50 Palestinian terrorists were killed.

The IDF also surrounded Arafat's compound (Mukata) in Ramallah for one month, preventing Arafat from leaving until he agreed to hand the leaders of the PFLP, who had plotted Ze'evi's murder, over to the IDF. On May 1, Israel agreed to end the siege when the PA sent the prisoners to a PA facility under international supervision. Arafat left the compound on May 2. While besieging Arafat, the IDF entered portions of the Mukata and captured documents as well as large quantities of weapons, including rocket-propelled grenade launchers (RPGs), which the PA was forbidden to possess under the Oslo accords. The documents included memos from Arafat authorizing the transfer of PA money to Tanzim and al-Aqsa Martyrs Brigades leaders to underwrite their terrorist activities.

According to captured documents, Fuad Shubaki, Arafat's chief financial officer who was supposedly fired after the *Karine-A* affair, played a central role in disbursing money to terrorist cells, for establishing weapons factories and for organizing weapons shipments to the PA. According to the captured documents, Shubaki, whose office is close to Arafat's, continued these activities after his involvement in the *Karine-A* affair was disclosed. As part of the deal made to end the siege on the Mukata, Shubaki was also placed in a PA jail in Jericho under international supervision. The PA High Court released him in December 2002.

IDF forces also surrounded the Preventive Security Service headquarters in Betunia on March 30, 2002. The Preventive Security Service was providing refuge to terrorists wanted by Israel.

Operation Defensive Shield severely damaged Palestinian terror operations – resulting in the arrest of terrorists, seizure of documents, and destruction of weapons production facilities. Nevertheless suicide bombings continued. After a series of devastating bombings in June 2002, the IDF began operations to reoccupy Palestinian cities in the West Bank. Since then the IDF has made numerous incursions into PA-administered territory in the West Bank and Gaza. Hundreds of terrorists have been arrested and several terrorist leaders have been killed.

Calls for PA Reform

As the depth of Arafat's and the PA's active involvement in terrorism became explicit in the wake of Operation Defensive Shield, attention began focusing on the need for an alternative Palestinian leadership. In May 2002, Israeli Prime Minister Ariel Sharon stated that a new Palestinian leadership would be necessary for real peace. On June 24, 2002, United States President George W. Bush called for a new

Palestinian leadership and for the reform of PA institutions. Two days later Arafat announced that the PA would hold elections in 2003.

Initially reform focused on the PA security apparatus. In June 2002 Arafat appointed veteran PLO functionary Abd al-Razak Yechia as Minister of Interior with oversight over the security services. In July 2002, Jibril Rajoub was forced out of his position as head of the Preventive Security Service in the West Bank. District Governor of Jenin, Zuhair Mansara, replaced him. Mohammed Dahlan, head of the Preventive Security Service in Gaza resigned to become Arafat's National Security Advisor. Rashid Abu Shubak replaced Dahlan as head of the Gaza Preventive Security Service, although Israel objected to his appointment, claiming he had been involved in terrorism.

Palestinian leaders, including Abd al-Razak Yechia, Mohammed Dahlan, and PLO Executive Committee Secretary Mahmoud Abbas began to criticize the violent turn the Intifada had taken. Arafat also became the subject of criticism by Palestinian leaders. On September 11, 2002, the PLC forced Arafat's cabinet to resign. Yechia resigned as Minister of Interior, claiming he was frustrated by Arafat's refusal to reform the security apparatus.

After a suicide bombing in Tel Aviv on September 19, 2002 that killed six, the IDF again surrounded the Mukata and demanded the handover of several PA security officials who had been involved with terrorism. The most wanted figures were West Bank General Intelligence Chief Tawfik Tirawi, who also ran Fatah cells, and several Force 17 officers. The siege ended inconclusively after 10 days.

After the siege ended, Arafat emerged with renewed popularity. He named a new cabinet, including senior Fatah official Hani al-Hassan as Interior Minister. In October, Dahlan resigned from his position as National Security Advisor and in fall 2002 the PA began having severe problems continuing to manage civil administration, particularly in the West Bank. The IDF began assuming those responsibilities.

In October 2002, the PA, in conjunction with Fatah, became embroiled in a feud with Hamas. PA Colonel Rajah Abu Lehiya was kidnapped and killed in Gaza. Colonel Lehiya had led the crackdown on the October 2001 Hamas uprising in which three people were killed. Colonel Lehiya's death sparked another round of Fatah-Hamas fighting in which five were killed. A massive show of PA/Fatah force forestalled further fighting, but Hamas' popularity was increasing at Fatah's expense. This rise in Hamas' popularity was due, in great part, to PA corruption. Hamas and Fatah began negotiations in Cairo under Egyptian auspices. The negotiations were designed to maintain national unity and determine the best strategy for continuing the Intifada.

In December 2002, Arafat postponed Palestinian elections indefinitely.

Leadership
Yasser Arafat

Yasser Arafat (a.k.a. Abu Ammar) was born in Cairo, Egypt in 1929 to Palestinian parents. He lived in Jerusalem for short periods during his childhood. He attended King Fouad I (now Cairo) University where he studied engineering and briefly fought with the Egyptian army in Israel's War of Independence in 1948. At the University, he became involved with the Muslim Brotherhood and the Palestine Students Association. In 1952, he was elected its Chairman. It was during this period that Arafat came into contact with the young Palestinian activists that would later form the core of the Fatah movement.

In 1954, Egyptian authorities imprisoned Arafat for his connections to the Muslim Brotherhood. Arafat, like many young Palestinians, moved to Kuwait because of its employment opportunities and worked for the Department of Public Works. While in Kuwait he stayed in contact with a group of Kuwait-based Palestinians. In 1959, he founded Fatah and, in 1964, he left his job in Kuwait to devote himself full-time to political activities.

Because of Fatah's terror attacks against Israel, Arafat gained increasing prominence among the Palestinian people. Arafat and Fatah's survival of the 1968 Battle of Karameh made him the leading Palestinian figure in the Arab world. In 1969, he was named Chairman of the Palestine Liberation Organization (PLO) Executive Committee, a position he has held since. In that role, he has traveled continuously throughout the world, meeting world leaders and speaking about the Palestinian cause.

In 1994, Arafat shared the Nobel Prize with then-Israeli Prime Minister Yitzhak Rabin and then-Israeli Foreign Minister Shimon Peres. He was elected President of the Palestinian Authority in 1996 with 87% of the vote. Arafat exercises control of the PLO-PA-Fatah apparatus by holding over 30 positions within these organizations. The most important of these positions is Chairman of the PLO Executive Committee, President of the PA, and member of the Fatah Central Committee.

Arafat's *nom de guerre* is Abu Ammar. It refers to Ammar Abu Yasser, a companion of Mohammed and a commander of Mohammed's army.

Mahmoud Abbas

Mahmoud Abbas (a.k.a. Abu Mazen) was born in Safed, Israel in 1935. He became the Secretary of the Palestine Liberation Organization (PLO) Executive Committee is 1996 and has been a member of the committee since 1981. He is also a member of the Fatah Central Committee and joined Fatah shortly after its founding in 1959. Since 1980, Abbas has been the head of the PLO Department for International Relations and has handled relations with Russia since the collapse of the Soviet Union. In March 2003, bowing to international pressure, Yasser Arafat appointed him Prime Minister of the Palestinian Authority. He resigned from the post less than six months later.

Described as a PLO moderate, Abbas has carefully studied Israel. His Ph.D. thesis from Moscow University addressed how a state of peace would increase the polarization of Israeli society. He was a central figure in the negotiations with Israel and a drafter of the Oslo Accords.

Since relocating to the Palestinian Authority, Abbas has constructed vast residences in Gaza and Ramallah, leading to accusations of corruption.

Ahmad Qurei

Ahmad Qurei (a.k.a. Abu Alaa') was born in Abu Dis in 1937. He rose to the position of Speaker of the Palestinian Legislative Council and became Prime Minister of the Palestinian Authority after Abu Mazen's resignation. He is also technically Arafat's successor as President of the Palestinian Authority (PA) in the event of Arafat's death. Qurei has also been a member of the Fatah Central Committee since 1989 and was the head of the Palestine Liberation Organization Economic Department and was previously PA Minister of Economy. He was also a central figure in the negotiations with Israel and a drafter of the Oslo Accords.

Faruq Qaddoumi

Faruq Qaddoumi (a.k.a. Abu Lutf) was born near Nablus in 1931. He has been the head of the Palestine Liberation Organization's (PLO) Foreign Minister and has been head of the PLO political department since 1973 and has often acted in the role of the organization's foreign minister. A founding member of Fatah, Qaddoumi studied political science and economics at American University in Cairo and worked at the Kuwaiti

Ministry of Health. In the early 1960s, he managed Fatah's relations with Egypt. He joined the PLO Executive Committee in 1969 and managed the PLO's relations with the Soviet bloc and the Third World.

An outspoken opponent of the Oslo process, Qaddoumi has refused to travel to the Palestinian Authority and remains in Tunis. His authority has been in decline over the last decade. Now his primary responsibility is PLO-Syrian relations.

Nabil Sha'ath

Nabil Sha'ath was born in Safed, Israel. He is the Palestinian Authority Foreign minister. He was a drafter of the Oslo Agreements, was head of the Palestine Liberation Organization Political Planning Bureau, and is on the Fatah Central Committee. Until very recently he served as the Palestinian Authority's minister of Planning and International Cooperation-effectively the foreign minister of the PA and he has played a central role in administering international aid. In August 1998, the Palestinian Legislative Council demanded he be removed from his post for embezzling public funds and engaging in non-competitive business practices.

Organization

Structure

Both the Palestine Liberation Organization (PLO) and the Palestinian Authority (PA) are officially democratic. In both cases, real power is in the hands of Arafat's Fatah movement. In particular, Fatah keeps a tight grip on the PLO political department, which oversees PLO international relations and the PLO department of national affairs (equivalent to the department of interior). Both include a range of political, administrative, financial, diplomatic, and military units with parallel and sometimes overlapping authority. Overall, the breakdown in responsibility is that the PA is responsible for the West Bank and Gaza, while the PLO handles Palestinian affairs outside of the PA, particularly in Lebanon. Throughout the organization, and particularly at the top levels, individuals simultaneously hold key positions in the PA, the PLO, and Fatah. Arafat himself is Chairman of the PLO, leader of Fatah, and President of the PA

Palestine Liberation Organization

The Palestine Liberation Organization (PLO), in theory is governed by the Palestine National Council (PNC), which has representatives from a range of Palestinian organizations. Real power is in the hands of the PLO Executive Committee, which is headed by Arafat. The PLO Executive Committee has 18 members, with five (including Arafat) representing Fatah and six "independents" who are closely linked to Fatah.

The PLO includes a number of public organizations including Palestinian professional unions and student organizations throughout the world. Through these organizations the PLO recruited activists and maintained its dominant position in Palestinian politics.

Besides the dominant Fatah (which is described in its own entry), there are several other terrorist organizations, which have belonged to the PLO. The most prominent, the Popular Front for the Liberation of Palestine (PFLP), Democratic Front for the Liberation of Palestine (DFLP), and the Palestine Liberation Front (PLF) are detailed in their own entries. Other, minor factions include:

<u>Arab Liberation Front (ALF)</u>   The Arab Liberation Front was established in 1968 by Abd al-Rahim Ahmed and is allied with the Iraqi Ba'athists. In cooperation with the Palestine Liberation Front, it has, since the beginning of the al-Aqsa Intifada, distributed over $15 million of Iraqi funds to the families of people killed in fighting with Israel. First priority in distributing funds is given to the families of suicide bombers. The families of unmarried men receive $10,000; the families of married men receive $25,000. In October 2002, Israel arrested the West Bank head of the ALF, Rachud Salam in Ramallah in the West Bank. The ALF has about 400 members.

<u>Popular Struggle Front</u> The Popular Struggle Front was established on July 15, 1967 and was united with Fatah for a short period. It split into two factions, one allied with Arafat, headed by Dr. Samir Ghoseh, and the other, based in Damascus and opposing Oslo. In the 1970s and 1980s, it carried out terrorist raids against Israel. The faction's 700 Lebanon-based fighters have been demobilized for several years.

<u>Palestinian Democratic Union (FIDA)</u> The Palestinian Democratic Union split from the Democratic Front for the Liberation of Palestine in March 1990. Palestinian Authority Minister of Information Yasser Abd Rabbo leads it.

The PLO has a number of institutions that provide services to the Palestinian people. The Palestine National Fund (PNF) collects "taxes" from Palestinians working throughout the Middle East and raises funds throughout the world. The Palestine Red Crescent Society provides medical and health care to the Palestinian people. Palestinian Martyrs

Works Society and the Sons of Martyrs provide social and economic services to Palestinians. In addition, the PLO effectively controls the UN Relief and Works Agency, which provides services to Palestinians in refugee camps, although it does not contribute to the organization financially. The PLO also maintained an army, but it was primarily controlled by the states in which its units were based. Since the PA's founding, the PLO's military wing has been subsumed by the PA security forces.

The Palestinian Authority

The Palestinian Authority (PA), like the Palestine Liberation Organization (PLO), is nominally democratic and ultimately under the leadership of a legislative body, the Palestine Legislative Council (PLC). Real power is, again, in the hands of Yasser Arafat. The PLC's efforts to assert its authority have been stymied by Arafat, who has refused to sign crucial legislation or submit the PA's budget for review. The PA is responsible for the civil administration of almost all of the Palestinians living in the West Bank and Gaza Strip. It provides education, health, and infrastructure services through over 21 ministries. Efforts by these ministries to provide services have been hampered by massive corruption as well as Arafat's need to personally controlling even the smallest cash disbursements.

The PA security services were defined under the 1994 Gaza-Jericho agreement and the Oslo II agreement. These agreements delineated the role, size, and armament of these PA security forces. The Gaza-Jericho agreement only referred to the Palestinian Police and limited their numbers to 9,000, as well as restricting the numbers of firearms and possession of heavy weapons. The Oslo II agreement expanded the Palestinian police to 30,000. Despite the restrictions, PA security forces grew beyond the Oslo limits in number and in armaments.

The Gaza-Jericho agreement also established the structure of Palestinian security forces, placing all of them under the General Security Service (GSS), and giving each unit a separate command for Gaza and the West Bank. The PA established several security services that were not described in the Oslo agreement, and others that were outside of the GSS rubric and answered directly to Arafat.

The current head of the GSS is Hani al-Hassan, a senior Fatah official and longtime Arafat loyalist. Following is a brief description of the Palestinian security forces that are within the GSS command structure.

<u>National Security Force (NSF)</u> The National Security Force is the largest Palestinian security service, with 20,000 officers. Its role, as outlined in the Gaza-Jericho agreement is patrolling the Palestinian borders, including conducting joint patrols with the IDF. It is the nucleus of a regular army, with nine infantry battalions and heavy weapons, armored vehicles and anti-tank systems – all of which were forbidden under the Oslo agreements, Consisting primarily of officers from the Palestine Liberation Army, it has not, so far, played a substantial role in the al-Aqsa Intifada, Most of the NSF's heavy equipment, artillery and armored personnel carters were destroyed by the CDR during the al-Aqsa Intifada Saeb Ajez, a longtime Arafat loyalist, commands the NSF.

<u>Civil Police</u> The Civil Police also known as the Blue Police, was formed under the Gaza-Jericho agreement to undertake standard law enforcement duties under the PA. It has 10,000 officers including a special 700-man rapid deployment force for riots and special operations. Many unit commanders of this rapid deployment force received advanced Soviet training and provide training for officers throughout the PA security apparatus. Arafat loyalist Ghazi al-Jibali commands the Blue Police.

<u>Preventive Security Force (PSF)</u> The Preventive Security Force is the largest Palestinian intelligence service, with over 5,000 men. Under Oslo II, the PSF was charged with counter-terrorism and collecting intelligence on Palestinian opposition to the PA. Because it was a plainclothes service it was difficult for Israel to keep track of its personnel – consequently it grew quickly, allowing the PA to evade Oslo's restrictions. The PSF became known for abducting Palestinians, torturing detainees, involvement with criminal activities, and human rights violations. Several detainees died under PSF torture. The head of the PSF in Gaza is Rashid Abu Shubak and the PSF chief in the West Bank is Zuhair Mansara. The former heads of the PSF, Mohammed Dahlan in Gaza and Jibril Rajoub in the West Bank, are both veterans of the first Intifada against Israel and were imprisoned several times by Israel. Dahlan and Rajoub are often identified as possible successors to Arafat. The PSF received counter-terrorism training from Israeli security services and the CIA, and at times cooperated with Israel in preventing terrorist attacks.

<u>General Intelligence Service (GIS)</u> The General Intelligence Service is the official PA intelligence agency under the Gaza-Jericho agreement and has about 3,000 men. It conducts internal and external espionage,

counter-espionage, and builds relations with foreign intelligence agencies. It is headed by Amin al-Hindi, an Arafat loyalist. The head of the West Bank branch, Tawfik Tirawi is wanted by Israel for his involvement in terrorist activities. He ran Fatah cells that included GIS personnel and were responsible for numerous attacks including the November 2001 suicide bombing in Afula.

Military Intelligence Military Intelligence gathers intelligence on and investigates illegal actions by PA security. It includes a Military Police unit and has several hundred men. Yasser Arafat's cousin Moussa Arafat heads it and it is not described in any agreement with Israel.

Coast Guard The PA's Coast Guard is based in Gaza, has about 1,000 men and maintains five machine gun-armed motorboats. Its personnel came from Fatah's naval unit. Several members of the Coast Guard have had special commando training. Under Oslo it was charged with patrolling and countering smuggling off the Gaza coast. However, it has been involved in smuggling arms into the PA. The captain of the *Karine-A*, Omar Akkawi, was an officer in the PA Coast Guard. The Coast Guard was complicit in other Palestinian attempts to smuggle heavy weapons into Gaza by sea.

Aerial Police The PA's Aerial Police was based on Force 14, Fatah's aerial unit. It maintains the PA's five helicopters, which are primarily used to transport Arafat and are not described in any agreement with Israel. According to records captured during Operation Defensive Shield, these helicopters were also used to smuggle weapons. The IDF has destroyed the helicopters.

Civil Defense Civil Defense operates fire and rescue services and is described under the Gaza-Jericho agreement.

County Guard The County Guard is a small police force that provides security for PA officials. It is not described under the agreements with Israel.

In addition, Arafat established two security services that are not within the GSS framework and report directly to him. Neither force is permitted under the agreements with Israel. The Presidential Security Force, or Force 17, was designated by Israel as a terrorist organization for its direct involvement with attacks on Israeli civilians and is detailed under its own entry. The Special Security Force, headed by Arafat loyalist Yusuf al-Wahidi, was established in January 1995 to gather intelligence on the other PA security services. It is has a few hundred officers.

Financial Support
Lack of Transparency

It is not possible to make definite statements about Palestine Liberation Organization (PLO)/Palestinian Authority (PA) finances. PLO budgets were never made public and PA budgets were submitted late and were extremely vague. Donations to the PLO or PA are often placed directly in personal accounts controlled by Arafat or other PLO/PA figures, and even small disbursements are controlled directly by Arafat.

Palestine Liberation Organization Finances

Since 1974 a mainstay of the Palestine Liberation Organization's funding was the taxes levied by Arab countries on resident Palestinian workers. The taxes are approximately 5% to 7% of their salaries and are deducted at the source and transferred to the organization's accounts in Switzerland and Spain. The Palestine National Fund administers the program, which takes in several hundred million dollars annually.

In the past, this income was supplemented by financial support from Arab governments, particularly Saudi Arabia, and donations from around the world.

The PLO also runs commercial enterprises. In 1970, the PLO formed a conglomerate called Samed that had over 10,000 employees and dominated Lebanon's economy. The PLO owns businesses throughout the world, particularly in Europe. Samed made numerous airport-related investments, owning duty free shops at airports throughout Africa. Parallel to this, the PLO engaged in illegal operations, participating in Lebanon's lucrative drug trade, arms deals, and extorting corporations using threats of terrorism. In the mid-1980s, it was estimated that the PLO's annual budget was about $1 billion.

It is believed that the PLO controls at least $10 billion in assets worldwide and high-ranking PLO officials acquired a reputation for lavish living in Beirut and also in Europe.

Because of the PLO's support for Iraq in the Gulf War, Palestinian workers in Kuwait were thrown out of work, and the PLO was denied hundreds of millions of dollars. At the same time, the Gulf States ceased donating money to the PLO, and the Soviet Union collapsed. This collapse of the PLO's finances was one of the reasons it entered into negotiations with Israel.

Palestinian Authority Finances

The Palestinian Authority (PA) has benefited from international largess. The annual PA budget in the late 1990s was about $1.7 billion, with one-third to one-half coming from foreign aid. The PA has been the largest beneficiary of European Union (EU) foreign aid receiving almost 1.5 billion Euros from the EU from 1994-2001. EU member states donated another billion Euros. The World Bank, the Holst Fund, and the United States Agency for International Development (USAID) have also been major donors, although much of this money is officially intended for private sector development. In 1993, at the Conference to Support the Middle East Peace Process, the United States government committed to providing $500 million over a 5-year period to the PA. This money is comprised of $375 million from USAID and the rest from the Overseas Private Investment Corporation (OPIC). In 1995, America committed an additional $500 million to the PA.

Reports of corruption have plagued the PA since its inception. The Palestinian Legislative Council launched several investigations, finding massive misappropriation of funds. The investigations found that PA money had been embezzled by PA leaders; companies owned by people close to PA leaders were not taxed; and PA agencies were excessively staffed with far more Deputy Director-Generals than necessary. An independent audit of the 1997 budget could not account for $323 million. The primary expense of the PA was salaries, particularly those of the security services, which have a budget of almost $500 million. The documents captured by the Israel Defense Forces in Operation Defensive Shield showed how the PA redirected funds intended for general operations to supporting terror cells.

The PA also profited by establishing a series of monopolies, under the control of Arafat's economic advisor Mohammed Rashid. Arafat's wife, Suha, was the primary beneficiary from a monopoly on importing cement. Jibril Rajoub and Mohammed Dahlan were beneficiaries from a monopoly on oil imports. PA officials and PA security personnel have also engaged in criminal activity such as extortion and counterfeiting. They have cooperated with Israeli criminals, particularly in auto theft. Thousands of Israeli cars have been stolen and transferred to the PA.

During the al-Aqsa Intifada, Israel suspended payment of taxes it collected on the PA's behalf. The EU has provided approximately 10% (10 million euros per month) of the PA's monthly budget. The Arab states, led by Saudi Arabia, have provided about half of the PA's budget.

Links to States and Terrorist Organizations

The Palestine Liberation Organization (PLO)/Palestinian Authority (PA) is granted the status of a nation by many governments and international organizations. It is a member of the Arab League, has ambassadors to the United Nations and the European Union, and has embassies and missions throughout the world.

Arab States

While the Arab world always pays lip service to the importance of the Palestinian cause, relations between the PLO and specific Arab states defined by a complex calculus of interest.

The Ba'athist Syrian regime is committed to building greater Syria, which includes Israel, the West Bank, Gaza Strip, Jordan, Syria, Lebanon, and part of Turkey. Consequently, Syria supports several Palestinian terror groups in order to influence the Palestinian movement and advance its own position.

Jordan has a complicated relationship with the PLO due to its own claims to the West Bank and its majority Palestinian population. Jordan supports a Palestinian state in order to end claims that declare Jordan to be the Palestinian state. But Jordan also seeks to ensure that a Palestinian state on the West Bank will not try to take control of Jordan.

Egypt was the initial sponsor of the PLO and is supportive in diplomatic circles. Egypt has also permitted massive smuggling of arms to the Palestinians in Gaza through tunnels passing under the Israeli-controlled zone separating Egypt and Gaza.

Libya has been a strong supporter of the PLO, paying for arms and providing logistical support for operations, as well as training camps.

In the 1980s the PLO became closer to Iraq, supporting it in its war against Iran and in the Gulf War. Palestinians cheered when Iraqi missiles struck Israel and the PLO has played a leading role in ending Iraqi isolation in Arab circles and advocates on Iraq's behalf in Arab League meetings. Iraq supports Palestinian martyrs, offering $10,000 to $25,000 to the families of Palestinians who die in fighting with Israel.

Other States

Fatah and the Palestine Liberation Organization (PLO) had been receiving some Soviet support since the mid-1960s. In 1971, the PLO became a key ally of the Soviet Union, receiving massive arms shipments and diplomatic support from the Soviet Bloc. PLO operatives trained in China, Vietnam, and North Korea. Besides direct support from the Soviet Union, the PLO was given assistance with running disinformation campaigns from Romania's Nicolae Ceaucescu and received logistical support for terror operations from East Germany. That support dissipated as the Soviet Union collapsed.

The PLO also had relationships with revolutionary movements worldwide. Since the mid-1960s, the PLO and Fatah operatives trained in Cuba. The Sandinista regime in Nicaragua gave the PLO ambassadorial status and the PLO also provided bodyguards for the former Ugandan dictator Idi Amin.

The PLO opened relations with the Islamic regime in Iran shortly after its 1979 revolution. Abu Mazen was the liaison between the Soviet Union and the Islamic republic. Iranian revolutionaries had trained at PLO camps in Lebanon before the revolution. Iran and the PLO may have collaborated on terrorist attacks, and Fatah helped found Hizbullah. Hizbullah's chief of operations, Imad Mughniyah, had been a member of Force 17.

PLO-Iranian relations declined when the PLO supported Iraq in its war with Iran. But as PLO-Hizbullah cooperation has deepened, relations have improved. For example, the *Karine-A* arms shipment originated in Iran. In return for the arms shipment, the PA permitted Iran to build a hospital in Gaza.

Terrorist Organizations

The Palestine Liberation Organization (PLO) operated camps for training terrorists throughout the world; over 3,000 terrorists trained at these camps. There were particularly close links between the PLO and the Irish Republican Army, the Basque separatist group ETA, and other radical European groups, such as the German Baader-Meinhof Gang and the Italian Red Brigades.

The IRA links may still be effective. On examining the booby traps in Jenin, a British explosives expert stated that the bombs he examined were identical to IRA-constructed bombs. He also noted that the Palestinians used similar tactics in Jenin to tactics he had observed in

Northern Ireland. Israeli intelligence also believed that an IRA sniper might have been responsible for a March 2002 attack in which a single sniper killed seven Israeli soldiers at a checkpoint near Ofra. When the sniper fled, he left his weapon – a trademark IRA practice.

For more information on PLO terrorist activities, see entries of the following member organizations: Fatah, Force 17, Popular Front for the Liberation of Palestine (PFLP), Popular Front for the Liberation of Palestine-General Command (PFLP-GC), Democratic Front for the Liberation of Palestine (DFLP), and the Palestine Liberation Front (PLF).

Chronology of Major Events and Attacks

1959

October – Led by Yasser Arafat, a group of Palestinians working in Kuwait establish Fatah. A month later they publish the first issue of *Filastinuna* (*Our Palestine*).

1964

June 2 – The PLO is founded by Egyptian President Nasser, with Ahmed Shukairy as the Chairman of its Executive Committee. The Palestinian National Covenant, which calls for the destruction of Israel, is drafted and accepted.

1965

January 1 – Fatah operatives carry out their first armed operation against Israel, bombing Israel's National Water Carrier. This is the first of a series of raids on Israel.

1967

June 5 – The Six-Day War begins. Israel defeats Syria, Egypt, and Jordan and becomes responsible for the administration of the Arab population of the West Bank and Gaza.

November 22 – The UN Security Council passes Resolution 242, which calls for a negotiated settlement between the Arabs and Israel, for the Arab states to recognize Israel's right to exist, and for Israel to withdraw from an unspecified amount of the territories it occupied in accordance with negotiations.

December – The Popular Front for the Liberation of Palestine (PFLP) is founded. Ahmed Shukairy resigns as PLO Chairman and is replaced by Yehya Hammoudeh. Fatah joins the PLO.

1968

March 21 – Battle of Karameh. The Jordanian army repels an Israeli attack on Fatah headquarters in the Jordanian town of Karameh. Fatah takes heavy casualties, but in surviving the Israeli attack its status in the Arab world increases dramatically.

July 23 – PFLP operatives hijack an El Al plane from Rome and divert it to Algeria. Passengers are held for three weeks, until Israel releases 12 Palestinian terrorists.

October – Ahmed Jibril breaks with the PFLP and founds the PFLP-GC.

1969

February – Yasser Arafat becomes chairman of the Executive Committee of the PLO.

February – Nayef Hawatmeh's faction splits off from the PFLP to form a new organization, which becomes the DFLP.

1970

September 6 – PFLP operatives hijack two airliners and force them to land outside of Amman, Jordan. A concurrent attempt at hijacking an El Al plane is foiled, but a fourth plane is hijacked and diverted to Cairo. Six days later, another plane is hijacked and diverted to Jordan. All of the planes are blown up after their passengers are evacuated. The international attention given the hijackings and the growing PLO threat to the stability of the Jordanian regime triggers the events of Black September. Jordanian security forces attack the PLO and expel it from Jordan. The PLO relocates to Lebanon.

1973

October 6 – The October or Yom Kippur War takes place.

October 22 – The United Nations Security Council passes Resolution 338, which echoes Resolution 242.

1974

February 19 – The PNC adopts the Strategy of Phases, which authorizes the PLO to establish a Palestinian state on any part of the land evacuated by Israel as an initial stage to destroying Israel. The Rejectionist Front is formed to oppose the Plan of Stages because it entails recognition of Israel.

October 28 – The United Nations General Assembly and Arab League recognize the PLO as the sole legitimate representative of the Palestinians.

November 13 – Arafat addresses the United Nations for the first time.

1975

April – The Lebanese Civil War begins. The PLO fights Maronite Christian militias.

November 10 – United Nations General Assembly Resolution 3379, which states that Zionism is a form of racism, is adopted.

1976

April 12 – The first West Bank municipal elections take place.

June – Syria enters the Lebanese Civil War and attacks the PLO. A three-way fight between Fatah and its allies, Syrian-backed factions, and Iraqi-backed factions ensues.

September – The PLO is accepted as a member of the Arab League.

1978

March 11 – Fatah terrorists hijack a bus in Nahariya in Israel and kill 36 Israelis and wound 80. Israel launches Operation Litani, an invasion of Southern Lebanon up to the Litani River.

September 17 – Presidents Carter and Sadat of the United States and

Egypt, and Israel's Prime Minister Begin of Israel sign the Camp David Accords, which propose a settlement to the Middle East conflict.

November 29 – The first International Day of Solidarity with the Palestinian People is declared by the United Nations.

1982

June 4 – Israel invades Lebanon, driving the PLO headquarters out of Lebanon.

August 21 – PLO begins evacuating Lebanon, the headquarters are relocated in Tunisia.

September 16-18 – Lebanese Christian militiamen allied with Israel enter the Sabra and Shatila refugee camps near Beirut and massacre 700-800 people, primarily Palestinians.

1983

November – Abu Musa, a senior Fatah officer, leads a Syrian-backed revolt against Arafat. Arafat is forced to abandon his base in Tripoli, Lebanon and move to Tunisia.

1985

June – Israel withdraws from most of Lebanon occasioning the PLO's return.

October 1 – Israel bombs the Tunisian headquarters of the PLO in retaliation for the September 25 murder of three Israelis in Cyprus.

1987

December 9 – The first Intifada begins after four Palestinians are killed when a truck driven by an Israeli collides with two vans carrying Palestinians in Gaza. It continues until 1992 and is characterized by large-scale riots, and grenade, stone, and Molotov cocktail attacks.

Over 1,000 Palestinians are killed, many by Palestinian terrorists for collaborating with Israel. PLO factions play a central role in organizing and funding the Intifada.

1988

November – At the 19th PNC in Algiers, UN Resolution 242 is accepted, and the PNC issues its declaration of an independent Palestinian state.

December – The United States announces its intention to open a dialogue with the PLO.

1990

June – The United States suspends contacts with the PLO after the PLF attempts a terrorist attack on an Israeli beach and the PLO refuses to expel the PLF.

1991

January 15 – Salah Khalaf (a.k.a. Abu Iyad), number two in the PLO after Arafat, is assassinated in Tunis by the ANO.

January 17 – The Gulf War begins, for two days Iraq fires missiles at Israel.

October 30 – The Madrid Middle East Peace Conference begins with delegations from Israel, Egypt, Syria, Lebanon, and the joint Palestinian-Jordanian delegation.

November 6 – PFLP suspends its membership in the PLO.

1992

February 19 – Yitzhak Rabin is elected head of the Labor party in Israeli elections.

1993

September 13 – The Israeli-Palestinian Declaration of Principles is signed at a White House ceremony by Israeli Foreign Minister Peres and PLO official Mahmoud Abbas (a.k.a. Abu Mazen).

October 25 – Israel releases 660 Palestinian prisoners.

1994

February 25 – Twenty-nine Palestinians are killed by Jewish extremist Baruch Goldstein who opens fire on Muslim worshippers at the Haram al-Ibrahimi Mosque in Hebron.

May 4 – The Palestinian Authority is established when Israeli Prime Minister Yitzhak Rabin and PLO Chairman Yasser Arafat sign the Gaza-Jericho Self-Rule Accord which establishes the PA.

July 1 – Arafat enters PA.

August 29 – Israel and the Palestinian Authority sign the Early Empowerment Agreement on the transfer of five civilian authorities (education, health, social affairs, tourism, and taxation).

November 18 – Clash between Hamas and PIJ supporters and Palestinian police leave 13 dead and 200 injured in Gaza.

1995

September 28 – In Washington, Israel and the PLO sign the Oslo II Agreement on the second stage of Palestinian autonomy.

October – Israeli forces begin redeploying from towns in the West Bank to be handed over to PA control.

November 4 – Yitzhak Rabin is assassinated by law student Yigal Amin at a peace rally in Tel Aviv.

1996

January 20 – The PA holds elections; Arafat is elected Chairman of the PA. Hamas and several other factions boycott the elections.

March 7 – The Palestinian Legislative Council (PLC) holds its first official session.

May 29 – Binyamin Netanyahu is elected Israeli Prime Minister.

September 24 – The Israeli government opens a tunnel under the Temple Mount. Palestinians respond with rioting and Israeli and Palestinian security forces clash. After several days of fighting, 62 Palestinians and 16 Israelis are dead and over 1,200 Palestinians and 87 Israelis are injured.

1997

January 15 – The Hebron Protocol is signed. Under this agreement, Israel agrees to withdraw from 80% of Hebron; a team of international observers is established in Hebron; and Israel agrees to three further redeployments from the West Bank between March 1997 and mid-1998.

1998

October – The Wye River Memorandum is negotiated after Israel does not carry out promised redeployments because of Palestinian failures to arrest PIJ and Hamas members. Under the Wye River Memorandum the CIA oversees PA-Israeli security cooperation.

1999

May 17 – Ehud Barak is elected Prime Minister, defeating Binyamin Netanyahu.

September 4 – Sharm El-Sheikh Agreement is signed to lay the groundwork for final-status negotiations.

2000

July – Israeli and Palestinian negotiators, including Arafat and Barak meet at Camp David under the auspices of United States President Bill Clinton. Although Barak makes unprecedented concessions, no agreement is reached.

September 28 – Ariel Sharon, leader of the opposition Likud Party visits the Temple Mount. The next day riots erupt at the Temple Mount, and throughout the West Bank and Gaza. This is the beginning of the al-Aqsa Intifada.

2001

January – Palestinians begin firing mortars at Israeli settlements in the West Bank and Gaza. Israeli forces respond with incursions into Palestinian territory.

February 6 – Ariel Sharon is elected Prime Minister of Israel, defeating Ehud Barak.

August 27 – PFLP Secretary-General Mustafa Zibri is killed in his office by rockets fired by Israeli helicopters. This is the first time Israel assassinates the leader of a Palestinian faction.

October 17 – PFLP operatives kill Israel's outgoing Tourism Minister, Rehavam Ze'evi outside his hotel room at the Jerusalem Hyatt. Ze'evi is the highest level Israeli official killed by a Palestinian faction.

2002

January 3 – Israeli commandos capture the *Karine-A*, a ship commanded by an officer in the PA Coast Guard that was loaded with weapons from Iran intended for Gaza.

March 2002 – In response to a series of Palestinian suicide bombings, including the March 27 Passover Massacre, which killed 27, Israel launches Operation Defensive Shield – a large-scale invasion into PA-controlled territory intended to break up terrorist networks. The IDF lays siege to Arafat's Mukata, and unearths documentation of PA-terrorist collusion.

June 24 – United States President George W. Bush states that Israeli-Palestinian peace is only possible if a new Palestinian leadership is elected.

September 11 – The PLC forces Arafat's cabinet to resign.
September 19 – The IDF again lays siege to Arafat's Mukata in response to a suicide bombing.

October – PA Colonel is kidnapped and killed by Hamas operatives in Gaza, followed by Hamas-Fatah clashes.

December – Arafat postpones Palestinian elections indefinitely.

Resources

Becker, J., *The PLO*. New York: St. Martin's Press, 1984.

Ehrenfeld, R., *Where Does the Money Go? A Study of the Palestinian Authority*. New York: American Center for Democracy, 2002 – available at public-integrity.org.

Haetzni, N., "In Arafat's Kingdom." *Commentary* October 1996; Vol. 102, No. 4.

Legain, J., " The Successions of Yasir Arafat." *Journal of Palestine Studies* 1999; Vol. 28, No. 4.

Luft, G., "The Palestinian Security Services: Between Army and Police." *Middle East Review of International Affairs Journal* June 1999; Vol. 3, No. 2 -available at meria.idc.ac.il/journal/previouslj.html./

Luft, G., "Who is Winning the Intifada?" *Commentary* July/August 2001; Vol. 112, No. 1.

Palestine Liberation Organization Negotiation Affairs Department website www.nad-plo.org .

Palestinian Academic Society for the Study of International Affairs website www.passia.org.

Palestinian Authority Information Ministry website www.minfo.gov.ps.

Palestinian Permanent Representative to the UN website www.palestine-un.org.

Pipes, D., "How Important is the PLO?" *Commentary* May 1983; Vol. 75, No. 4.

Rubin, B., *Revolution Until Victory?: The Politics and History of the PLO*. Cambridge: Harvard University Press, 1994.

Rubinstein, D., *The Mystery of Arafat*. Leon, D. (Translator). S. Royalton, Vermont: Steerforth Press, 1995.

Schenker, D., *Palestinian Democracy & Governance: An Appraisal of the Legislative Council*. Washington, D.C.: The Washington Institute for Near East Policy, 2000.

PLO & its Affiliates
Popular Front
for the
Liberation of Palestine

The Popular Front for the Liberation of Palestine (PFLP) is known in Arabic as al-Jabha al-Sha'biyah li-Tahrir Filastin. Since 1991 the PFLP has suspended its membership in the Palestine Liberation Organization (PLO).

Ideology and Objectives

The PFLP is a Marxist-Leninist Arab nationalist organization focused on the liberation of all of Palestine through armed struggle. While its first priority is the foundation of a secular Marxist Palestinian state, the PFLP remains loyal to its roots in the Arab nationalist movement. The struggle for Palestine is only the first stage in the pan-Arab social revolution and ultimately the worldwide socialist revolution. The PFLP officially opposes the "reactionary" regimes of the Arab world, particularly monarchies, and views the United States as the fount of global imperialism. The PFLP makes common cause with Marxist revolutionaries worldwide.

History
Origins and the Rivalry with Fatah

The PFLP grew from the Movement of Arab Nationalists (MAN). The MAN was a pan-Arab organization founded in 1949 at the American University in Beirut that placed a high priority on the liberation of Palestine. Its first Secretary-General was George Habash, a Palestinian Christian medical doctor. Until the 1967 war, Egyptian President Gamal Abdul Nasser heavily supported MAN, which acted on Nasser's behalf.

After the 1967 Arab defeat in the Six-Day War, Nasser's pan-Arabism was discredited. Fatah, which focused specifically on the

Palestine issue, was gaining stature in the Arab world for its attacks on Israel. Backed by Nasser, the PFLP was founded in December 1967 as an Arab Nationalist counterweight within the Palestinian movement to Arafat's Fatah, which was backed by Syria. Three organizations came together to form the PFLP: the Young Avengers, the Palestinian military wing of MAN, set up in 1964; the Heroes of the Return, a Lebanon-based group of MAN activists and PLO dissidents set up in 1966; and the Palestine Liberation Front organized in 1959 by Ahmed Jibril, a Palestinian officer in the Syrian army. Dr. Habash, a charismatic figure in pan-Arab circles, was elected Secretary-General.

The PFLP quickly became the leading rival to the Fatah within the PLO. However, two factions broke off from the PFLP. In 1968, Ahmed Jibril left the PFLP and founded the Popular Front for the Liberation of Palestine-General Command (PFLP-GC). In February 1969, Nayef Hawatmeh split from the PFLP and set up the Popular Democratic Front for the Liberation of Palestine (PDFLP). Several years later, under threat of violence from the PFLP, Hawatmeh renamed the organization the Democratic Front for the Liberation of Palestine (DFLP). While differences in ideology, strategy and tactics were a factor in these splits, Habash's autocratic leadership style was also a major factor.

Pioneers of International Terror

On July 23, 1968, the PFLP inaugurated the era of mass terror by hijacking an El Al plane and forcing it to land in Algeria. The passengers were held hostage for three weeks and Israel was forced to release a dozen Palestinian terrorists. This was the beginning of an international war of terror against Israel and the West, masterminded by Habash's deputy, Dr. Wadi' Haddad.

The PFLP continued its campaign of airline hijackings, culminating in September 1970. On September 6, the PFLP simultaneously hijacked three airliners landing two in Amman, Jordan and blowing up the third in Cairo. A fourth plane was hijacked on September 9 to Jordan. On September 12, the hijackers released 255 hostages, holding 56. Unsatisfied with the pace of the negotiations, they blew up the airliners. These hijackings and the PFLP and PLO behavior that followed threatened the Jordanian regime. Jordanian security forces attacked the PLO and its factions, headquartered at the time in Jordan, and expelled them from the country. In two weeks of intense fighting several thousand Palestinians were killed. The PLO, including the

PFLP, relocated to Lebanon, where it continued to carry out terrorist attacks throughout the world, masterminded by Dr. Haddad.

During this period, the PFLP achieved international renown and some of its operatives became international celebrities. Leila Khaled, who helped carry out a 1969 hijacking of a TWA flight, achieved fame as the "girl terrorist" and the "deadly beauty." She took part in an attempted fifth airline hijacking in September 1970. The passengers and crew of the El Al flight fought back and the attempt was unsuccessful. The plane landed at London's Heathrow Airport where Khaled was taken into custody and held for 28 days. She was released in exchange for the remaining hostages held by the PFLP. She remained involved in the PFLP, becoming the head of its women's division and a member of the Palestinian National Council.

In May 1972 in Tel Aviv, Israeli commandos stormed a plane hijacked by the PFLP and rescued the passengers. The PFLP responded a few weeks later by organizing an attack by its allies in the Japanese Red Army. In the May 30 attack, 27 people, mostly Christian pilgrims from Puerto Rico, were killed at the Tel Aviv airport. Israel began assassinating PFLP leaders, sending the letter bomb that killed PFLP official and poet Ghassan Kanafani in July 1972.

In the early 1970s, the PLO leadership debated whether any political solution was possible and whether international terror (terror against non-Israeli targets) – particularly airline hijackings – was an acceptable tactic. The PFLP was a leader in the Rejectionist Front, which opposed any political solution. While as early as 1972 PFLP leaders agreed that airline hijackings were not effective, it is unclear when the PFLP ceased conducting international terror operations. Reportedly, Wadi' Haddad carried out hijackings and the 1975 attack on OPEC headquarters without Habash's approval. But Haddad's official expulsion from the PFLP was announced in November 1977, after a Lufthansa plane was hijacked to Mogadishu, Somalia. The announcement, however, stated that the expulsion took place in 1976. Haddad died, probably from cancer, in 1978. The exact relationship between Haddad and the PFLP in the mid-70s is unclear. However, after that point, the PFLP primarily focused on Israeli targets.

The PFLP in the War in Lebanon and the Peace Process

Along with the rest of the PLO, the PFLP was expelled from Lebanon in the 1982 war with Israel. Relocating to Damascus, it rebuilt some of its Lebanese infrastructure. As the Soviet Union began to collapse in the late 1980s, its support for the PFLP dwindled. Lacking a direct border with Israel and with diminished resources, for a time the PFLP became less active in conducting terror attacks. The PFLP had begun organizing in the West Bank and Gaza during the mid-1970s and played a major role in the first Intifada, organizing over 100 attacks in 1991 alone. In September 1992, Israeli security forces launched a massive crackdown on the PFLP, arresting 463 PFLP operatives. Under Syrian sponsorship, the PFLP assassinated moderate Palestinian leaders in the West Bank.

After the war in Lebanon, Fatah moved closer to negotiations with Israel. In 1984, the PFLP took the lead in founding the Palestinian National Salvation Front with the other PLO factions that opposed any compromise with Israel. In response to the Oslo process, the PFLP led PLO factions, plus Hamas and Palestinian Islamic Jihad, in founding the Damascus-based Alliance of Palestinian Forces (APF). While the PFLP suspended its membership in the PLO in 1991, it never left the PLO and maintained contacts with the Palestinian Authority (PA). In 1997, after being condemned by the APF for its continued contacts with the PA and Arafat, the PFLP left the APF.

In September 1999, PFLP Deputy Secretary-General Mustafa Zibri, a.k.a. Abu Ali Mustafa, with permission from the PA and Israel, moved the PFLP headquarters to Ramallah in the West Bank. Ill with cancer, longtime PFLP Secretary-General George Habash resigned in May 2000. Mustafa Zibri became Secretary-General of the PFLP.

While once the second major faction of the PLO, the PFLP is now a second-tier Palestinian faction. Polls of Gaza and West Bank Palestinians usually show the PFLP as having single-digit support. Hamas, by comparison, usually has 15-20 percent popular support.

The al-Aqsa Intifada and the Assassination of an Israeli Cabinet Minister

The PFLP has played an active role in the al-Aqsa Intifada, launching a number of bombings. In response, on August 27, 2001, PFLP Secretary-General Mustafa Zibri was killed in his office by rockets fired by Israeli helicopters. In October 2001, the PFLP Central Committee elected Ahmed Sa'dat Secretary-General and on October 17, 2001, PFLP gunmen killed Israel's outgoing Tourism Minister, Rehavam Ze'evi, outside his hotel room at the Jerusalem Hyatt.

Mustafa Zibri's assassination was the first time Israel assassinated the head of a major Palestinian faction and Ze'evi's assassination was the first time an Israeli cabinet minister was assassinated by a Palestinian faction. Israel made the PA's handover of Ze'evi's assassins, including Secretary-General Sa'dat, a central Israeli condition for restarting negotiations. The PA has been unwilling to hand the leader of a Palestinian faction over to Israel.

The PFLP continued to launch terror attacks against Israel, including a foiled May 2002 plan to place truck bombs in the Azrieli Towers, Israel's tallest buildings. In the May 2002 battle in Jenin and in other operations, the PFLP fought in tandem with other Palestinian factions. The PFLP also carried out several suicide attacks.

In May 2002, as part of the arrangement to end the siege on Arafat's compound, Ahmed Sa'dat and Ze'evi's assassins were placed in a prison in Jericho under international supervision. Israel has complained that Sa'dat is directing PFLP activity from prison.

Israel has targeted the PFLP leadership. Faction leaders in the major towns of the West Bank have been killed and in June 2002, Israeli security forces arrested de facto PFLP leader Abd al-Rahman Malah. In August 2002, Mohammad Sa'dat, brother of the PFLP Secretary-General, was killed when Israeli forces attempted to arrest him. Reportedly, the PFLP infrastructure in the West Bank has been reduced substantially, although the less extensive network in Gaza remains intact.

Leadership
Ahmed Sa'dat
Ahmed Sa'dat (a.k.a. Abu Ghassan), the PFLP's Secretary-General, was born in 1953 in al-Bireh near Ranallah in the West Bank. In 1975, he earned a degree in Mathematics from the Teachers' College in Ramallah and in 1967 joined the Union of High School Students, which was part of the National Liberation Movement. He joined the PFLP in 1969. Sa'dat was imprisoned eight times between 1967 and 1992 and was elected to the PFLP Central Committee in 1981 and elected to the PFLP Politburo in 1993. He has been in charge of the PFLP's West Bank branch since 1994. Since 1993, he has been listed as "wanted" by the Israeli army and Israeli authorities arrested him three times in 1995 and 1996. On October 3, 2001, after the assassination of Mustafa Zibri, Sa'dat was elected Secretary-General of the PFLP.

Abdil Rahim Mallouh, PFLP Deputy Secretary-General

Abdil Rahim Mallouh (a.k.a. Abu Sharif), the PFLP's Deputy Secretary-General, was born in Jaffa in 1945 and left with his family in 1948. He attended the Jiflik UNRWA School and went to work in Kuwait in 1963. He was in the Palestinian Liberation Army in Baghdad in 1965 and while there, completed his studies and took advanced military courses. Mallouh was involved with the founding of the Popular Front for the Liberation of Palestine in 1967 and was injured twice fighting Israeli forces, including at the Karameh battle in 1968. In 1971, he was injured fighting the Jordanian Army. From 1977-1978, Mallouh was detained in Jordan. During the war in Lebanon he commanded PFLP forces in Beirut and he took in military courses in the former Soviet Union. Mallouh was elected to the Politburo of the PFLP in 1973 and to the Executive Committee of the PLO in 1991. In 2000, he was elected head of the political department of the PFLP and was elected Deputy Secretary-General of the PFLP in October 2001.

Organization

The PFLP is believed to have about 800 active members and several thousand supporters. The strongest support is in Ramallah and Bethlehem. The armed wing is now known as the Battalions of the Martyr Abu Ali Mustafa, after the Secretary-General who was killed by Israel in August 2001. Previously its operatives in the West Bank and Gaza Strip were known as the Red Eagles. The PFLP Youth Group is known as the Volunteers. To combat Israeli infiltration efforts, the military and political wings are isolated from each other and the leaders of the military wing are closely guarded, secret to all but a few of the political leadership. The PFLP also has a presence in the refugee camps in Lebanon and Syria.

Financial Support

The PFLP primarily relies on state support, particularly from Syria and Libya. Before it collapsed, the Soviet Union provided extensive support to the PFLP. But the Marxist PFLP has also operated commercial enterprises and investments. In Lebanon, the PFLP owned the Modern Mechanical Establishment, a metal works in Sidon just south of Beirut. In the 1970s by importing inexpensive raw materials from East Bloc countries and using predatory pricing, the PFLP dominated the Southern Lebanon market for metal products. The

PFLP also conducted criminal activity, particularly forgery, worldwide. A PFLP cell in the U.S., based in Florida, operated a food coupon redemption fraud ring that raised millions for the organization.

Links to States and Terrorist Organizations
Relations with States

Currently, the PFLP's primary benefactor is Syria, which hosts several Palestinian organizations as part of its ongoing efforts to take control of the PLO. It has received support from Libya and in the past, the PFLP received substantial support from the Soviet Union and in the 1960s, Nasser supported the organization. The Arab nationalist regime that dominated Yemen in the 1960s and 1970s allowed the PFLP to establish training facilities there.

Relations with International Terrorist Organizations

As part of the international far-left terror network, in its heyday, the PFLP had relationships with terror organizations throughout the world. The PFLP has a long-standing relationship with the Irish Republican Army (IRA) and the Basque Homeland and Freedom (ETA). Starting in the 1960s and continuing through the 1970s, IRA terrorists trained at PFLP camps and the PFLP helped the IRA acquire weapons. Thomas McMahon, who was convicted for the murder of Lord Mountbatten and his family in 1979, trained in a PFLP camp.

The PFLP had relationships with the Japanese Red Army as well as far-left German terrorist groups, including the Red Army Faction (RAF – a.k.a the Baader- Meinhof Gang), and the Movement of the 2nd of June. Beyond logistical support, the PFLP launched joint operations with the RAF and the Japanese Red Army (most famously the 1972 attack at Israel's Lod Airport).

Relations with Palestinian Terrorist Organizations

In the al-Aqsa Intifada, the PFLP has cooperated with all of the other Palestinian organizations. In the past, PFLP supporters in the West Bank and Gaza have clashed with Hamas supporters. But more recently, the secular PFLP has cooperated with Islamist terror groups, including Hamas, Palestinian Islamic Jihad (PIJ), and Hizbullah. Initially, their shared sponsor, Syria, brokered this cooperation. Despite the split between the DFLP and PFLP, the two organizations have cordial relations and cooperate politically.

While the PFLP is a long-standing rival of Arafat's Fatah for control of the PLO, it has also cooperated with Fatah in carrying out operations. At first, the PFLP refused to recognize the PA. However, when the opportunity arose, the PFLP relocated to the PA-controlled West Bank and Gaza Strip.

Areas of Operation

Since September 1999, the PFLP's headquarters has been in the West Bank. The organization still has offices in Damascus and operates a training camp in Lebanon.

In the past, PFLP attacks took place throughout Europe, the Middle East, and Africa. Currently, PFLP activity has been focused in Israel, the West Bank, and Gaza.

Targets and Tactics

The PFLP has a long history of high profile targets. In 1968, the PFLP initiated the age of mass terror with the first politically motivated airplane hijacking. The PFLP has also assassinated Palestinian moderates, particularly West Bank mayors and has not shied away from attacking political leadership, such as the 1975 seizure of OPEC headquarters in Vienna or the assassination of Israeli cabinet minister Rehavam Ze'evi. In the al-Aqsa Intifada, the PFLP began suicide bombings. Echoing the 9/11 attacks, in May 2002 the PFLP planned to attack the Azrieli Towers, the tallest office buildings in Israel.

Chronology of Major Events and Attacks

1967

December – The Popular Front for the Liberation of Palestine (PFLP) is founded as an Arab Nationalist counterweight to Arafat's Fatah. Dr. George Habash, a Palestinian Christian physician, is the Secretary-General.

1968

Rival factions of the PFLP split, forming the Popular Democratic Front for the Liberation of Palestine (later the Democratic Front for the Liberation of Palestine – DFLP) and the Popular Front for the Liberation of Palestine – General Command (PFLP-GC).

July 23 – PFLP operatives hijack an El Al plane from Rome and divert it to Algeria. The passengers are held for three weeks, until Israel releases 12 Palestinian terrorists.

December 26 – PFLP operatives attack an El Al plane in Athens with guns and hand grenades. One passenger is killed and two stewardesses are wounded.

1969

February – PFLP operatives kill one and wound five aboard an El Al plane during an attempted hijacking Zurich at Kloten Airport in Switzerland. One PFLP operative dies and three operatives are wounded by Israeli security.

August 29 – PFLP operatives hijack a TWA flight from Rome to Athens and divert it to Damascus, where the 113 passengers are released.

1970

September 6-12 – The PFLP simultaneously hijacked three airliners landing two in Amman, Jordan and blowing up the third in Cairo. A fourth plane was hijacked on September 9 to Jordan. On September 12, the hijackers released 255 hostages, holding 56. Unsatisfied with the pace of the negotiations, they blew up the three airliners. The last 56 hostages were released a few weeks later after the U.K. released Leila Khaled and Germany and Switzerland released six other Palestinian terrrorists.

1972

May 8 – Four PFLP operatives hijack a Sabena (Belgian) airliner bound for Tel Aviv. At Tel Aviv airport the hijackers demanded the release of 317 Palestinians held by Israel. Israeli commandos storm the plane, kill two hijackers and wound two, and accidentally kill one passenger.

May 30 – Under PFLP guidance, three Japanese Red Army operatives attack Israel's Ben Gurion International Airport. Twenty-seven people are killed, most of them Christian pilgrims from Puerto Rico. Two of the operatives are killed and the other is captured. The attack is in retaliation for Israel's successful attack on the May 8, 1972 hijackers.

July 8 – Ghassan Kanafani, PFLP spokesman and member of the Political Bureau and editor of the PFLP publication *al-Hadaf* was killed by a letter bomb sent by Israel. A few days later another PFLP leader, Bassam Abu Sherif is severely wounded by a letter bomb sent by Israel.

1973

July 24 – PFLP operatives hijack a Japanese airliner en route to Tokyo from Paris and force it to land in Benghazi, Libya. The passengers are released and the operatives are arrested by Libyan police but later released.

1975

December 21 – PFLP operatives attack OPEC headquarters in Vienna in tandem with the Baader-Meinhof Gang. Taking 90 hostages including "Oil Ministers," the infamous Venezuelan Communist terrorist, Ilyich Ramirez Sanchez, best known as "Carlos the Jackal", leads the raid.

1976

June 27 – *Entebbe Hostage Crisis*: Members of the Baader-Meinhof Group and the PFLP seize an Air France airliner bound for Tel Aviv and its 258 passengers. They force the plane to land in Uganda, where, on July 3, in a world famous operation, Israeli commandos successfully rescue the passengers.

1977

October – Four PFLP operatives hijack a Lufthansa airliner to Mogadishu, Somalia, with the help of German terrorists. German police storm the plane, killing three operatives and capturing the fourth.

1984

March – PFLP operatives kill three passengers on a bus in Ashdod, Israel.

April – PFLP operatives kill one passenger and wound eight others in a bus hijacking in Ashkelon, Israel.

1986

March – PFLP operatives assassinate Nablus mayor Zafir al-Masri in order to block any potential agreement with Israel.

1990

August – A prominent Nablus attorney is killed by the PFLP, for alleged collaboration with Israel.

November – Five IDF soldiers and two PFLP operatives are killed in a clash in Southern Lebanon.

1991

October – The PFLP claims responsibility for an attack on a bus carrying Israelis from Nablus to Ramallah. Two Israelis are killed and five injured.

November 6 — The PFLP suspends its membership in the PLO.

1992

September — The IDF arrests 463 PFLP activists.

1993

April 18 — PFLP operatives axe to death an Israeli who served as advisor to the European Community in Gaza.

October 9 — PFLP operatives kill two Israelis hiking in Wadi Kelt in the Judean Desert. The PFLP and the Islamic Jihad 'al-Aqsa Squads' each publicly claim responsibility.

December 31 - Two Israelis are found murdered in a Ramle apartment. Identification cards of two Gaza residents are found in the apartment, along with a leaflet of the PFLP 'Red Eagle' group claiming responsibility for the murder.

1996

June 9 — Gunmen believed to be affiliated with the PFLP open fire on a car near Zekharya, killing a dual United States/Israeli citizen and an Israeli.

December 11 — A woman and her son are killed by gunfire from PFLP operatives while driving in the West Bank.

1999

September — The PFLP relocates from Damascus to the Palestinian Authority-controlled West Bank.

2000

July — Ill with terminal cancer, George Habash steps down as Secretary-General of the PFLP. His longtime deputy, Mustafa Zibri (a.k.a. Mustafa Abu Ali) succeeds him.

2001

February 8 – Five civilians are lightly wounded in a car bombing on the Beit Israel road in Jerusalem.

July 2 – Two PFLP car bombs explode in Yehud, a suburb of Tel Aviv, wounding 11 civilians.

August 27 – PFLP Secretary-General Mustafa Zibri is killed in his office by rockets fired by Israeli helicopters.

September 3 – Nine civilians are injured when a car bomb and three remote control bombs planted by the PFLP explode in Jerusalem.

October 3 – The PFLP Central Committee elects Ahmed Sa'dat Secretary-General.

October 17 – PFLP operatives kill Israel's outgoing Tourism Minister, Rehavam Ze'evi outside his hotel room at the Jerusalem Hyatt.

2002

February 16 – A PFLP suicide bomber in Jerusalem kills two and wounds 30 people.

May 19 – A PFLP suicide bomber in Netanya kills three and injures 60 people.

June 20 – Two PFLP operatives infiltrate the West Bank settlement of Itamar, killing five (including a mother and her three children) and wounding eight civilians.

Resources

Karmon, E., "Fatah and the Popular Front for the Liberation of Palestine: International Terrorism Strategies (1968-1990)." The International Policy Institute for Counter-Terrorism, Nov. 25, 2000 – available at www.ict.org.il.

Khalil, A., "George Habash and the Movement of Arab Nationalists." *Journal of Palestine Studies* 1999; Vol. 27, No. 4.

Popular Front for the Liberation of Palestine (PFLP) website: www.pflp-pal.org/main.html.

Strindberg, A., "The Damascus-Based Alliance of Palestinian Forces." *Journal of Palestine Studies* 2000; Vol. 29, No. 3.

Strindberg, A., "Palestinian Nationalist Left Makes a Comeback." *Jane's Intelligence Review* 2002; Vol. 4, No 3.

PLO & its Affiliates

Popular Front for the Liberation of Palestine–General Command

In Arabic the Popular Front for the Liberation of Palestine – General Command (PFLP-GC) is Jabhat al-Sha'biyah li-Tahrir Filastin al-Qiyadat al-Ama. The PFLP-GC is a member, but not an active participant in the Palestinian Liberation Organization (PLO).

Ideology and Objectives

The PFLP-GC emphasizes the centrality of armed struggle, advocating the complete destruction of Israel, and rejecting any possible political settlement with Israel. The PFLP-GC rejects the 1974 PLO Strategy of Phases, in which a Palestinian state could be established on part of historic Palestine as a step toward establishing a state on all of Palestine. The PFLP-GC's argument against the Strategy of Phases is that it could lead to Palestinian moderation and acceptance of the existence of Israel.

This viewpoint is underpinned by the PFLP-GC's pan-Arab ideology, which views the violent confrontation with Israel as essential for unifying the Arab people. Beyond this principle the PFLP-GC has been marked by ideological flexibility. It does not have a comprehensive vision for a Palestinian state. The PFLP-GC employs Marxist and Ba'athist rhetoric, referring to Israel as a neocolonialist and imperialist state. As its relationship with Iran has deepened, the PFLP-GC has also adopted Islamist rhetoric.

The PFLP-GC has been Syria's primary proxy in Palestinian affairs and its actions reflect Syrian attempts to dominate Palestinian organizations and conduct Palestinian affairs, including the conflict with Israel, according to its own interests.

History

Origins and Early History

In 1959, Ahmed Jibril, a Syrian army officer, formed the Palestine Liberation Front (PLF), which carried out its first attack against Israel in 1965. In 1967, the PLF joined the Popular Front for the Liberation of Palestine (PFLP) and, in 1968, Jibril and his faction left the PFLP and started the PFLP-GC. The split occurred in the context of a falling out between PFLP leader George Habash and the Syrian regime. Jibril felt the PFLP was too focused on political issues and insufficiently focused on violent opposition to Israel.

At first, the PFLP-GC was active in international terrorism, bombing a Swissair jet headed for Israel in February 1970 – an attack in which 47 people were killed. In April 1974, the PFLP-GC claimed to have carried out the first suicide bombing when 3 terrorists strapped with explosives killed themselves and 18 hostages near Kiryat Shmona in Israel.

But in the mid-1970s, the PLO called for a moratorium on international terror and the PFLP-GC officially complied, focusing its efforts on infiltrating Israel. The PFLP-GC led the rejection front, which opposed the 1974 resolution calling for the Strategy of Phases.

In 1977, the PFLP-GC split over Syria's intervention in the Lebanese Civil War. Jibril supported Syria's intervention in the war and its attacks on the Arafat-controlled PLO. Mohammed Zaidan (Abu Abbas) left the PFLP-GC and formed the Palestine Liberation Front (PLF), which supported Iraq as the dominant sponsor of the PLO. On August 13, 1978 the PFLP-GC blew up the PLF's headquarters, 200 people, including several of the PLF's top commanders, were killed.

The Israeli War in Lebanon

After Israel's 1982 war in Lebanon, the PFLP-GC, along with the other Palestinian organizations, evacuated Beirut. In the war's aftermath, the PFLP-GC attacked United States Marines participating in the international peacekeeping force.

During the 1982 war, the PFLP-GC captured three Israeli soldiers. In 1985, Jibril negotiated a prisoner exchange with Israel in which over 1,000 Palestinian terrorists held in Israeli jails were released. Jibril negotiated the release of activists from a broad range of Palestinian groups – raising his prestige throughout Palestinian militant circles. One of the prisoners released was Hamas leader Sheikh Ahmed Yassin.

In 1983, Jibril supported a Syrian-backed rebellion against Arafat led by Fatah officer Abu Musa. The following year, the PFLP-GC was expelled from the PLO and in 1985 it joined with Abu Musa's Fatah Intifada organization to form the Palestine National Salvation Front devoted to opposing any peace overtures toward Israel.

Return to International Terror

In the aftermath of the 1982 war, Jibril announced that the PFLP-GC would again carry out terror activities in the international arena. In the mid-1980s the PFLP-GC cooperated with the Abu Nidal Organization (ANO) and the Popular Struggle Front in Syrian attacks on Jordan. In 1987, due to financial constraints and international pressure, Syria reduced its support for terrorist organizations. The PFLP-GC relocated to Libya where PFLP-GC pilots fought on Libya's behalf in Chad. In 1989, Libya, under international pressure to reduce its support for terrorism, forced the PFLP-GC to leave – the group returned to Damascus.

The PFLP-GC also built a network in Germany, making use of the large Palestinian community there. The cell grew to 34 members and was in contact with the Popular Struggle Front cell in Sweden, which had carried out attacks on Israeli and American targets in Scandinavia and the Netherlands. On October 26, 1988, German authorities arrested the cell members. Hafez Dalkamani, the cell leader, admitted to bombing American military trains on August 31, 1987 and April 26, 1988.

Despite being a secular group, the PFLP-GC became the first Palestinian organization to receive support from the Islamic Republic of Iran. In December 1987, Jibril, seeking new sources of support, met with Iran's Foreign Minister. They discussed creating an Islamist organization to liberate Palestine. In 1988, the PFLP-GC began cooperating with Hizbullah in Lebanon.

The organization and Iran may have collaborated in other terrorist attacks. While the December 1988 bombing of Pan Am flight 103 has generally been blamed on Libya, the PFLP-GC was initially the primary suspect. There is evidence, particularly the reports of PFLP-GC defectors and the similarity of the devices used in the Pan Am bombing to devices captured with the PFLP-GC German cell, to suggest that the PFLP-GC was involved in the Pan Am bombing.

The PFLP-GC may have been paid by Iran to destroy an American airliner to avenge the July 3, 1988 accidental downing of an Iranian airliner by an American warship. However, in the Gulf War, the

United States needed Syrian support and was unwilling to pursue the PFLP-GC link to the Pan Am bombing because it would have required a confrontation with Syria.

A device similar to the Pan Am bomb was used to destroy a French airliner flying over Niger in September 1989 – leading to speculation that this attack was also committed by the PFLP-GC on Iran's behalf.

In the Two Intifadas and under Oslo

The PFLP-GC has a minimal presence in the West Bank and Gaza, its major role in both the first and second Intifadas has been indirect. In 1988, the PFLP-GC set up *al-Quds* radio station, which broadcasts propaganda to Israel and the West Bank from the Syrian-controlled Golan Heights. There were some attempts to infiltrate Israel but they were of limited success. The PFLP-GC also participated in launching Katyusha rockets from Lebanon at Israel.

Opposing the Oslo process, the PFLP-GC played a leading role in the Damascus-based group of Palestinian organizations opposing any peaceful settlement with Israel. Jibril threatened to assassinate Arafat for his dealings with Israel.

The PFLP-GC helped build relations between different terrorist organizations and provided training for other terrorist organizations. In December 1992, Israel deported several hundred Hamas and Palestinian Islamic Jihad (PIJ) leaders to Lebanon. The PFLP-GC brought these organizations into contact with the Damascus-based group of Palestinian organizations, Hizbullah, Syria and Iran. In 1996, and later in 1998 Jordanian intelligence arrested dozens of PFLP-GC and Fatah-Uprising operatives plotting terror attacks in Jordan. Both in training terrorists and in conducting its own terror attacks, the PFLP-GC was furthering Syrian ambitions in Jordan, Lebanon, Israel, and among the Palestinians.

The PFLP-GC remained staunchly opposed to any compromise with Israel and consistently called the Oslo process a betrayal of the Palestinian people and reportedly even attempted to assassinate Arafat. Unlike the PFLP and the Democratic Front for the Liberation of Palestine (DFLP), the PFLP-GC did not change its positions enough to be permitted to operate in the Palestinian Authority.

When Israel withdrew from Southern Lebanon in May 2000, Hizbullah's utility as a proxy against Israel was constrained because it had been fighting under the auspices of liberating Lebanese territory.

Syria began preparing the PFLP-GC to continue the proxy war with Israel, increasing PFLP-GC forces based in Syrian-controlled Lebanon and equipping them with T-55 tanks. On May 20, 2000, the Israeli Air Force bombed the Syrian-PFLP-GC Dir al-Raza base in Lebanon destroying 10 tanks and discouraging further PFLP-GC attacks.

With the outbreak of the al-Aqsa Intifada in September 2000, the PFLP-GC joined the National and Islamic Front along with other major Palestinian groups in order to direct the Intifada. The PFLP-GC had been smuggling weapons to the West Bank and Gaza since at least spring 1996, but expanded this activity when the Intifada started. On May 7, 2001 off the Gaza shore, the Israeli Navy captured the *Santorini*, a Lebanese smuggling boat, carrying over 40 tons of Iranian weapons intended for Hamas, PIJ, and Fatah in Gaza. The weapons included SA-7 surface to air missiles and Katyusha rockets. Under interrogation, the crew revealed that they were smuggling weapons on behalf of the PFLP-GC and that this had been their fourth smuggling run to Gaza. In a statement, Jibril vowed that he would continue to ship weapons to the West Bank and Gaza.

The PFLP-GC also began attempting to attack Israel directly. PFLP-GC operatives began attempting to infiltrate Israel from Lebanon. In April 2002, the organization began firing Katyusha rockets into northern Israel and later that month, Lebanese authorities arrested PFLP-GC operatives planning further Katyusha attacks.

On May 21, 2002 in Beirut, Jihad Jibril, PFLP-GC's chief of operations and the son of PFLP-GC Secretary-General Ahmed Jibril, was killed by a bomb in his car. The previously unknown "Movement for Lebanese Nationalists" claimed credit for the bombing. Israel was a suspect. In an interview on *al-Jazeera*, Jibril claimed that his son might have been assassinated by Jordanian intelligence. Jihad Jibril was directing PFLP-GC operations in Lebanon and was believed to be the liaison between Iran and the PFLP-GC.

In December 2003 the PFLP-GC formally asked to be readmitted to the PLO.

Leadership

The PFLP-GC Secretary-General is Ahmed Jibril; he was born in 1932 near Abasiya (Yehud) in what is now Israel. After Israel's War of Independence, he and his family moved to Syria where he joined the Syrian army, attended military college, and rose to the rank of captain in the engineering corps where he was an expert in explosives. He founded the PLF, the precursor to the PFLP-GC, while serving in the Syrian army. The PFLP-GC Deputy Secretary-General is Talal Naji and the head of the Political Bureau is Fadl Shururu.

Organization

The PFLP-GC political leadership is organized into a General Secretariat, a Political Bureau, and a Central Committee. The PFLP-GC is primarily a military organization and has between 500 and 1,000 armed fighters based in Syria and Lebanon. The PFLP-GC has very little popular following in Gaza or the West Bank, but in 1988 started *Saut al-Quds* (Voice of Jerusalem) a Damascus-based radio station that broadcasts to the West Bank.

Financial Support

The PFLP-GC's main sponsor is Syria, which provides bases, funding, training and logistical support. The PFLP-GC received weapons and financing from Libya from 1986 until 1989 when Qadafi ostensibly renounced terrorism. Shortly thereafter, the PFLP-GC approached Iran and began receiving its support. The PFLP-GC has carried out operations on behalf of all of these governments – fighting for Libya in Chad, helping Iran and Libya assassinate opposition leaders abroad, and advancing Syrian interests within Palestinian circles. In the 1970s and 1980s, the PFLP-GC received arms from Communist-Bloc countries.

Links to States and Terrorist Organizations
Syria and Syrian-backed Palestinian Organizations

The Syrian Ba'athist regime seeks to create a greater Syria, which includes Lebanon, Jordan, all of Israel, the West Bank, and Gaza. As part of this ambition, Syria has long sought to control the PLO and dominate the Palestinian movement. Syrian support for the PFLP-GC, which has been described as an arm of Syrian military intelligence, is the cornerstone of this Syrian policy. Because of this close relationship with the Ba'athist Syrian regime, the PFLP-GC is the only Palestinian terrorist organization that Syria has given tanks or permitted to operate bases in Lebanon outside of refugee camps.

The PFLP-GC works closely with several other Palestinian terrorist organizations backed by Syria.

Popular Struggle Front The Popular Struggle Front was founded in 1967 and is closely aligned with the Arab Nationalist Ba'ath party that rules Syria. With the beginning of the Oslo process, the PSF split into two opposing factions. The pro-Arafat faction is led by one of the organization's founders, Sami Ghoseh. The Damascus-based faction is headed by Khalid 'Abd al-Majid and maintains a few hundred fighters in Lebanon and is absolutely committed to the armed struggle. In the late 1980s, PSF cells in Sweden cooperated with the PFLP-GC's cell in West Germany.

Fatah-Intifada Fatah-Intifada was founded in 1983 by Fatah colonels Abu Musa and Abu Saleh. In the wake of the PLO collapse after the 1982 war with Israel, these Fatah officers, with Syrian backing, tried to wrest control of Fatah from Arafat. Ideologically, the organization claims to be the real Fatah, and accuses Arafat of betraying Fatah's values. In the early 1980s, Fatah-Intifada had a close relationship with the ANO. Fatah-Intifada supports 1,000 to 1,500 militants in Syria and Lebanon.

Sa'iqa (The Thunderbolt) Sa'iqa is the armed wing of the Palestinian branch of the Syrian Ba'ath party. Founded in 1967, it was used as Syria's proxy in its initial incursions into Lebanon and against Fatah in the 1975 Lebanese Civil War. In 1976, Sa'iqa forces massacred over 500 Lebanese Christians in the town of Damour. In the 1970s, due to massive Syrian support, it was the second largest PLO faction after Fatah. In 1979, its Secretary-General, Zuhair Mohsen, was assassinated by the ANO (working for Iraq) and the organization stagnated. Sa'iqa is very closely aligned with Syria and has about 1,000 fighters in camps in Syria and Lebanon.

Iran

Despite being officially secular, the PFLP-GC has a close relationship with Iran. When Syrian support began to decline in the mid-1980s, the PFLP-GC was the first secular terrorist organization to turn to Iran for support. The 1988 destruction of Pan Am flight 103 over Lockerbie, Scotland may have been an early product of this collaboration. As its relationship with Iran has grown, the PFLP-GC has adopted more religious rhetoric.

Other Terrorist Organizations

The PFLP-GC has played a central role in facilitating contacts between different terrorist groups. PFLP-GC has been cooperating with Hizbullah in Lebanon since 1988. In 1992, when Israel expelled 400 Hamas and PIJ members to Lebanon, the PFLP-GC helped bring them into contact with Hizbullah, the Syrian government, the Damascus-based group of Palestinian organizations, and Iran.

The PFLP-GC has been willing to cooperate with groups across the secular-religious spectrum, so long as they are committed to violent confrontation with Israel. Since the outbreak of the al-Aqsa Intifada, the PFLP-GC has ignored past disputes and supported all of the Palestinian terrorist organizations involved with fighting Israel. The PFLP-GC trains Hamas terrorists at its bases in Lebanon.

But the PFLP-GC opposes organizations that are willing to compromise with Israel on any level. In August 1999, the PFLP-GC participated in an attack on the DFLP's offices in Syria and Lebanon because of the DFLP's moves towards accepting the peace process.

In the past, the PFLP-GC has had links and helped to train international terrorist organizations including the Japanese Red Army and the Provisional Irish Republican Army.

Areas of Operation

In the past, the PFLP-GC has operated throughout Europe and northern Africa, as well as in Syria, Lebanon, and Israel. Currently, Syria is limiting PFLP-GC's international operations, and the PFLP-GC is primarily trying to infiltrate Israel's borders and smuggle weapons to the West Bank and Gaza. The two main PFLP-GC camps are near Damascus in the Yarmouk refugee camp and there are several bases in the Syrian-controlled Bekaa Valley of Lebanon. There is also a major PFLP-GC presence in the Bourj and al-Baddawi refugee camps in Lebanon. The organization's headquarters is in Damascus.

Targets and Tactics

The PFLP-GC has been an innovator of terror tactics such as the suicide bombing (1974) and the 1987 infiltration of Israel by motorized hang glider (which were supplied by Libya). The PFLP-GC also has substantial expertise in preparing sophisticated explosives – such as those found with the PFLP-GC cell in Germany in the late 1980s.

The PFLP-GC has built a substantial conventional capability, including SA-7 anti-aircraft missiles, heavy artillery, and T-55 tanks allotted them by Syria.

In recent years the PFLP-GC has primarily targeted Israel by infiltration and the launching of Katyusha rockets from Lebanon. In the past, in addition to its anti-Israel activity, the PFLP-GC has committed terror for hire, blowing up airliners, and assassinatingLibyan and Iranian dissidents. At the behest of its sponsors, the PFLP-GC has targeted Americans, Europeans, Jordanians and rival Palestinians.

Chronology of Major Events and Attacks

1968

October – Ahmed Jibril breaks off from the PFLP shortly after its formation and forms the PFLP-GC.

1970

February 21 – PFLP-GC operatives bomb a Swiss airliner, killing 47.

May 22 – PFLP-GC attacks an Israeli school bus, killing eight children and four adults, and wounding 20.

1972

August 16 – A bomb smuggled onto an El Al plane by PFLP-GC operatives explodes, injuring four.

1974

April – PFLP-GC operatives attack the northern Israeli town of Kiryat Shmona and take hostages. Twelve children and six adults are killed when three operatives detonate explosives strapped to themselves.

1977

April – Abu Abbas, second-in-command of the PFLP-GC, leaves to form the Palestine Liberation Front (PLF).

1978

August 13 – The PFLP-GC bombs the headquarters of the PLF, killing over 200 people.

1982

June – The PFLP-GC fights Israel in Lebanon War, capturing three

Israeli soldiers. When the PLO evacuates Beirut in September, the PFLP-GC decamps to Damascus.

1983

The PFLP-GC supports Abu Musa's Syria-backed rebellion against the PLO.

1984

The PFLP-GC is expelled from the PLO for supporting rebellion against Arafat.

1985

The PFLP-GC forms the National Salvation Front with other Damascus-based Palestinian groups to oppose negotiations with Israel.

The PFLP-GC secures the release of 1,000 Palestinian terrorists held by Israel, including Hamas leader Sheikh Yassin, in exchange for three Israeli soldiers captured in 1982 in Lebanon.

1987

August 31 – The German PFLP-GC cell bombs a United States military train; there are no injuries.

November – Using a motorized hang glider to cross the Israeli border from Lebanon landing just outside an IDF base, a PFLP-GC operative kills six Israeli soldiers and wounds seven others before being killed.

1988

The PFLP-GC begins cooperating with Hizbullah in Lebanon.

April 26 – The German PFLP-GC cell bombs a US military train; there are no injuries.

October 26 – Hafez Dalkamani, leader of the German PFLP-GC cell, is arrested. German and Swedish police break up cells with dozens of arrests.

December 21 – Pan Am flight 103 explodes over Lockerbie, Scotland. Two hundred fifty-nine passengers and crew are killed, and 11 people on the ground are killed. The PFLP-GC's involvement is suspected.

1989

Libya forces the PFLP-GC to leave as a result of international pressure to reduce its support for terrorism. The PFLP-GC returns to Damascus.

1990

December – PFLP-GC operatives detonate a bomb in Bethlehem, killing one Israeli soldier and wounding two others.

1991

June – German courts convict PFLP-GC leader Hafez Dalkamani for bombing United States Army trains in Europe.

1993

July 8 – The PFLP-GC claims responsibility for an attack, in which two Israeli soldiers are killed and three others are wounded near the village of Ayshiyya, on the northern border of Israel's security zone in Southern Lebanon.

1998

May – Jordanian intelligence uncovers a PFLP-GC and Fatah-Intifada plot to assassinate Jordan's Prince Hassan and the Jordanian Prime Minister.

1999

August – The PFLP-GC participates in an attack on the DFLP's offices in Syria and Lebanon because of the DFLP's moves toward a peace process with Israel.

2000

May 20 – The Israeli Air Force raids a PFLP-GC base in Lebanon and destroys 10 PFLP-GC tanks.

2001

May 7 – The Israeli Navy captures the *Santorini*, a cargo ship carrying 40 tons of PFLP-GC weapons to Palestinian terrorist groups in Gaza.

2002

January 26 – Heavily-armed PFLP-GC operatives attempt to enter Israeli territory. Two are killed and the third is wounded and captured by Lebanese security.

April 4 & 8 – The PFLP-GC fires Katyusha rockets into Israel. Later that month, Lebanese authorities arrest PFLP-GC operatives as they are planning to launch Katyusha rockets against Israel.

May 21 – Jihad Jibril, the PFLP-GC's chief of operations and son of PFLP-GC founder Ahmed Jibril, is killed by a car bomb in Beirut.

Resources

Gambrill, G., "Sponsoring Terrorism: Syria and the PFLP-GC." *Middle East Intelligence Bulletin* September 2002; Vol. 4, No. 9 – available at www.meib.org.

Levitt, M., Waldoks, E., "The Return of Palestinian Nationalist Terrorism." *Peacewatch* May 3, 2002; No. 379 – available at www.washingtoninstitute.org.

Middle East Intelligence Bulletin, website www.meib.org, provides several articles on the PFLP-GC's possible involvement with the Lockerbie bombing.

Strindberg, A., "The Damascus-Based Alliance of Palestinian Forces." *Journal of Palestine Studies* 2000; Vol. 29, No. 3.

Strindberg, A., "Palestinian Nationalist Left Makes a Comeback." *Jane's Intelligence Review* 2002; Vol. 4, No. 3.

Tal, D., "The International Dimension of PFLP-GC Activity." *INTER – International Terrorism*, JCSS Project on Low Intensity Warfare & *The Jerusalem Post*: The Jaffe Center for Strategic Studies, 1989, pp. 61-77 – available at www.ict.org.il.

Selected Bibliography

Writing this book entailed reading thousands of articles from a range of scholarly publications, newspapers, and popular magazines as well as perusing dozens of books. The following is not intended to be a comprehensive bibliography, but rather a guide to particularly useful and accessible resources.

Websites

ESSENTIAL RESOURCES

The International Policy Institute for Counter-Terrorism (ICT)
www.ict.org.il
ICT is the world's leading online resource on terrorism. It includes background information on terrorist organizations, a database of terrorist attacks, articles by its affiliated scholars and others, and links to background information.

The U.S. Department of State's Counterterrorism Office
www.state.gov
The State Department's Counterterrorism Office is a crucial source of information on terrorism and U.S. counter-terrorism policy. The website includes the State Department's annual report on world terrorism – Patterns of Global Terrorism, official U.S. statements and policies on terrorism, lists of designated terrorist organizations, and links to other U.S. government websites that deal with terrorism.

Terrorism: Questions and Answers
www.terrorismanswers.com
This site, which is a project of the Council on Foreign Relations (CFR – www.cfr.org), is in a very accessible Q&A format and stays current on terrorist activity worldwide.

National Memorial Institute for the Prevention of Terrorism
www.mipt.org.
his site, includes RAND Institute database of terrorist incidents and numerous articles

MIDDLE EAST RESEARCH CENTERS
Global Research in International Affairs (GLORIA)

gloria.idc.ac.il

Global Research in International Affairs publishes the Middle East Review of International Affairs (MERIA), a fine online journal that publishes in-depth articles on issues and events in the Middle East. GLORIA also publishes monographs and guides to other Middle East resources.

Jewish Institute for National Security Affairs (JINSA)

www.jinsa.org

The Jewish Institute for National Security Affairs has a number of publications about terrorism available on its website.

Middle East Forum

www.meforum.org

The Middle East Forum publishes two journals of Middle East affairs: Middle East Quarterly and Middle East Intelligence Bulletin (MEIB – available at www.meib.org). Middle East Quarterly has a bound edition, but back issues are available online. The Middle East Forum website also has other articles published by Middle East Forum scholars.

Middle East Media Research Institute (MEMRI)

www.memri.org

The Middle East Media Research Institute monitors, translates, and analyzes the media of the Middle East. Its website contains numerous translations of speeches, interviews, and articles by terrorist leaders.

The Washington Institute for Near East Policy (WINEP)

www.washingtoninstitute.org

The Washington Institute for Near East Policy publishes issue briefs that are disseminated by fax and e-mail, many of which deal with terrorism. WINEP also publishes monographs and in-depth reports.

ASIA
South Asia Terrorism Portal (SATP)

www.satp.org

The South Asia Terrorism Portal is a comprehensive site detailing terrorist organizations on the Indian sub-continent. The website has analysis papers, background information on terrorist organizations, and chronologies of terror attacks.

Partial Bibliography of Books and Monographs

Adams, J. *The Financing of Terror: Behind the PLO, IRA, Red Brigades and M19 Stand the Paymasters.* New York: Simon and Schuster, 1986.

Alexander, Y. *Middle Eastern Terrorism: Selected Group Profiles.* Washington, D.C.: Jewish Institute for National Security Affairs, 1994.

Baer, R. *No Evil: The True Story of a Ground Soldier in the CIA's War on Terrorism.* New York: Crown Publishers, 2002.

Becker, J. *The PLO.* New York: St. Martin's Press, 1984.

Bergen, P.L. *Holy War, Inc.: Inside the Secret World of Osama bin Laden.* New York: Touchstone, 2002.

Ehrenfeld, R. *Where Does the Money Go? A Study of the Palestinian Authority.* New York: American Center for Democracy, 2002 – available at public-integrity.org.

Emerson, S. *American Jihad: The Terrorists Living Among Us.* New York: The Free Press, 2002.

Friedman, T.L. *From Beirut to Jerusalem.* New York: Doubleday, 1989.

Goren, R. *The Soviet Union and Terrorism.* Becker, J. (Editor) London: George Allen & Unwin, 1984.

Gunaratna, R. *Inside al-Qaeda: Global Network of Terror.* New York: Columbia University Press, 2002.

Lesser, I.O., Hoffman, B., Arquilla, J., Ronfeldt, D., and Zanini, M. *Countering the New Terrorism.* Santa Monica, CA: RAND, 1999.

Levitt, M. *Targeting Terror: U.S. Policy Toward Middle Eastern State Sponsors and Terrorist Organization, Post-September 11.* Washington, D.C.: The Washington Institute for Near East Policy, 2002.

Netanyahu, B. *Fighting Terrorism: How Democracies Can Defeat the International Terrorist Network.* New York: Farrar, Straus, and Giroux, 2001.

Netanyahu, B. (Editor). *International Terrorism: Challenge and Response*. New Brunswick (U.S.A.): Transaction Publishers, 1989.

Pipes, D. *Greater Syria: The History of an Ambition*. New York: Oxford University Press, 1990.

Pipes, D. *The Long Shadow: Culture and Politics in the Middle East*. New Brunswick (U.S.A.): Transaction Publishers, 1989.

Pohly, M. *Political Extremist Organizations: The Islamist Network*. Washington, D.C.: Jewish Institute for National Security Affairs, 1996.

Ranstorp, M. *Hizb'allah in Lebanon: The Politics of the Western Hostage Crisis*. New York: St. Martin's Press, 1997.

Rashid, A. *Taliban*. New Haven: Yale University Press, 2001.

Raviv, D., and Melman, Y. *Every Spy a Prince: the Complete History of Israel's Intelligence Community*. Boston: Houghton Mifflin, 1990.

Reich, W. (Editor). *Origins of Terrorism: Psychologies, Ideologies, Theologies, States of Mind*. Washington, D.C.: Woodrow Wilson Center Press, 1990.

Rubin, B., and Rubin, J.C. *Anti-American Terrorism and the Middle East: Understanding the Violence*. New York: Oxford University Press, 2002.

Rubin, B. Revolution *Until Victory?: The Politics and History of the PLO*. Cambridge: Harvard University Press, 1994.

Rubinstein, D. *The Mystery of Arafat*. Leon, D. (Translator). S. Royalton, Vermont: Steerforth Press, 1995.

Schenker, D. *Palestinian Democracy & Governance: An Appraisal of the Legislative Council*. Washington, D.C.: The Washington Institute for Near East Policy, 2000.

Sterling, C. *The Terror Network: The Secret War of International Terrorism*. New York: Holt, Rinehart and Winston, 1981.

Index

About the Author

Aaron Mannes is a widely published author and expert on the Middle East, U.S. national security and terrorism. He served as the Director of Research for the Middle East Media Research Institute (MEMRI) from 1998 through 2001. Currently living in the Washington, D.C. area, Mr. Mannes travels nationwide to speak about and provide detailed briefings on issues ranging from political culture to emerging threats.